Playing them

Bob Dixon has also written:

Catching Them Young
vol 1: Sex, Race and Class in Children's Fiction
vol 2: Political Ideas in Children's Fiction
Pluto Press 1977

Now Read On
Recommended fiction for young people
Pluto Press 1982

Agitpoems
Artery Publications 1985

Playing them false

A Study of Children's Toys, Games and Puzzles

Bob Dixon

tb

Trentham Books

First published in 1990 by Trentham Books

Reprinted 1992

Trentham Books Limited
Westview House
734 London Road
Oakhill
Stoke-on-Trent
Staffordshire
England ST4 5NP

© 1990 Bob Dixon

British Library Cataloguing in Publication Data
Dixon, Bob
    Playing them false: a study of children's toys, games and puzzles.
    1. Toys
    I. Title
    688.7'2
    ISBN 0-948080-31-0

Cover photos by Blod Churcher

Typeset and designed by Trentham Print Design, Chester
and printed in Great Britain by BPCC Wheatons Ltd, Exeter.

*this book is dedicated
to
Dan Garrett
and Sue Yates
with deepest thanks
for their
kindness
and help*

Contents

List of Illustrations

ACKNOWLEDGEMENTS

No book is ever the work of one person alone and this book provides ample evidence of that fact. I'm very grateful to the following friends and helpers who have contributed in so many ways.

For giving information and practical help, lending materials or providing contacts and sources for research, I'd like to thank: Terry Foley, Anna Paczuska, John Pearce, Pete Negri, Dennis Newson, Margaret White of the Woodcraft Folk and Jim Riordan who also helped with translations from Russian. Here, I wish to thank, as well, Angela Auset, Sara Hinton, Ron Huzzard, Dick Dear who also helped with translations from German, Friedegund Pautzke who translated German material, Mara Chrystie, Claude Delmas who also checked material in Swedish for me, Pete and Val Rance, Carol Carnall, Mike Hayes, John Green, Carol Fox, Warrill Grindrod and Jane Sprague. Also, Jane King, David Pritchard, Frankie Rickford, Richard Allen, Martyn Jenkins, Tim Rowett, Kay Ekevall, Michal Boñcza, Basil Davidson, Elvena Brumant, Jane Lane, Margot Brown and Thames Television. And I'd especially like to thank John Haylett, deputy editor of the *Morning Star*, whose help was invaluable. Here, I remember, but with sadness, Brad Chambers, of the Council on Interracial Books for Children, and Miloš Zavadil who both helped me during the preparation of this book but died before it was finished.

I also wish to thank those whose academic or campaigning work has been of help to me: Nic Nilsson, President, International Association for the Child's Right to Play; Bernhard Kroner of the University of Bielefeld in West Germany and Mark Hannam of Christian Aid. I've had useful material, as well, from the campaigning organizations, Österreichische Kinderfreunde (Austrian Friends of Children) and Terre des Hommes (World of Mankind).

Mainly in connection with the historical background to this study, I've received help from: Richard de Peyer of the City of Birmingham Museum; Alan Garlick of the Abbey House Folk Museum at Leeds; the staff at the Museum of Childhood in London; and from Linda Hannas who showed me her collection of early jigsaws. My thanks to them.

I've been glad to have the help of a number of people who work more or less directly with children in various ways — teachers, librarians, playgroup and toy library workers and others — who have given me the benefit of their experience or provided me with facilities, or both. Here, I'm grateful to: Dave Reynolds, Stephen Howard and Gloria Findlay; the playgroup helpers at St Swithin's Church Hall, and at the Cricket Club, and the committee and helpers at the Toy Library for handicapped children (all in Bromley, Kent) for their courtesy during my visits and for the information they supplied. Here, too, I should like to thank Judy Denziloe, formerly of Play Matters, and Ruth Fabricant who also read and commented on part of the manuscript.

For reading and commenting on parts of my work, I'm grateful to Pat Dixon, Annie Garrett and Mick King.

Several children and young people and their parents have tried out toys and played games for me and with me and have also provided information. My grateful thanks to: Dan, Leoni, Tessa and Reuben Garrett, Derek Finch (junior), Daniel Guedalla, and Brian, Paul and Ruth Smith.

In the toys and games industry, there have been some honourable exceptions — those responsible enough or kind enough to co-operate in various ways (apart from in the matter of illustrations). In this connection, I'd like to record my thanks to: Ricki Chavez-Muñoz, Gibsons' Games, C S T McCollum of Hammant and Morgan, the firm of Artur Fischer, Trevor King of Kingsway Educational Supplies, L D Vargerson of Earlyplay, Clive Bailey and Peter Darvill-Evans of Games Workshop, Kompan, Mike Halward, Ian Smith of the firm of E J Arnold, Richard Boulton of Mirrorsoft, Mel Croucher formerly of Automata and Christian Penfold of that firm, Jo Parry of Lego, and TSR.

With regard to the illustrations, I wish to thank the following companies who gave permission for copyright material to be reproduced or who themselves provided photos — page numbers of the relevant illustrations follow the names: Tri-ang Toys 32,49; Milton Bradley 46 (top); Johann Gg. Schopper 46 (bottom); Earlyplay 53; Pedigree 78, 99; Mattel — Barbie © 1989 Mattel Inc. All Rights Reserved and He-Man © 1989 Filmation Inc. All Right Reserved 73, 135; Hasbro 80, 266; Spearhead Toys 91; Lego 108; Thomas Salter 113; Rainbow Toys 138; Lambeth Toys and Unity Learning Foundation 173; Family Pastimes 178; Waddingtons 195; Tactical Studies Rules (TSR) 210; and Personal Software Services (PSS) 250. I'm very grateful to Dan Garrett for the illustrations on pp. 29, 39, 73, 109, 135, 173, 195, 250 and to Peter and Ben Fox for those on pp. 123, 124, 156, 178, and I wish to add a very special word of thanks here to Blod Churcher who took the cover photos. I'm especially grateful to Dan Garrett for composing the diagram on p.156.

For permission to reproduce material in the text, my thanks go to Godhawari, Rakhal and Rupa Sarkar and also to Eleanor Ferguson, though I didn't manage to trace her.

Thanks to my publisher, John Eggleston of Trentham Books. I hope he'll feel it was worth it.

Lastly, my especial, but hopelessly inadequate thanks to two people: Sue Yates who generously and efficiently took upon herself the labour of typing the greater part of the book, and Dan Garrett who helped in all sorts of ways, most of all by undertaking the arduous task of reading and commenting, in detail, on the whole manuscript.

Preface

My purpose in this book is to show what ideas, views and attitudes are presented to children through toys, games and puzzles; and how, and by what means, they are presented.

During my studies on the subject, I soon came to realize that the effect toys and, to a lesser extent, games have — overwhelmingly and above all else — is to divide children along sex lines and according to supposed sex roles, that is, according to the imagined abilities, preferences and even duties of either sex. This is so much the case that most playthings are thought of as being either for boys or for girls, but not for both, and part one of my book reflects this. Such a division is promoted by other aspects of children's culture also, and by the whole of society, in fact, but toys and games are particularly important in laying the foundations.

When children are dragooned into roles thought to be proper to their sex — when boys are told they mustn't play with dolls and girls are denied train sets, for example — then the potential of all children is limited. That isn't the worst of it, however. Many toys and games such as those which promote the masculine gender role of fighter, are simply unsuitable for human beings of either sex, and my study has centred on playthings of this kind.

I shall also show that, within a basic gender division, other main ideological areas, such as those to do with race and class, are reflected in playthings; and, lastly, I'll give an overview of the whole, pointing to the social implications.

In many ways, this book is a continuation of the work in my first book, *Catching Them Young*. There, I was concerned with the opinions, values and beliefs put forward in fiction for children, especially fiction of the more popular kinds. Here, in this book, I deal with another large area of the popular culture that surrounds children and analyse the way of looking at life it presents them with.

Toys and other playthings make up a large part of a child's world from a very early age and they must be very important in shaping a child's attitudes and ideas. After all, children play with toys and games during some of the most impressionable

1

years of their lives, starting, in the case of toys, from before they can read and even before they can understand spoken language. In spite of this, and except for a few scattered articles, there's been little attempt in English to analyse the ideas embodied in playthings. I felt this needed to be done urgently, mainly because of the question of aggression and especially in the light of the growing power of the toy and game industry, its increasingly international character and its irresponsibility.

When I was working on children's fiction, I thought that publishers were irresponsible enough but now I realize how polite, refined and socially answerable the world of children's publishing is compared with the toy and game industry. And this industry will certainly protect itself and won't lightly allow anybody to get in the way of its single-minded pursuit of profit. At one end of the scale is the individual firm which, all too often, treats enquirers as if they were industrial spies and, at the other, is the International Committee of Toy Industries, a body which watches over such things as trade barriers, restrictions on television advertising and publicity about war toys. An odd fact, in this connection, is that most toys and many games are anonymous. We don't know the inventors, the people who must bear responsibility in the first place. Add to this the fact that most of the products of this industry are never reviewed, as books are, and the fact that they are usually sold packaged in such a way that they can scarcely be seen, or cannot be seen at all, let alone examined; and perhaps it isn't surprising that there's been so little work done in such an important field. I found ways of dealing with the problems, though it's been difficult and has taken a long time. This all means that there's a great need for this industry to be opened up to public gaze.

This book is meant for everybody involved in the welfare and upbringing of children, whether as parents or through their work or both. It's meant for anyone who realizes the urgent need for change in society and believes in starting at the beginning. I've not only tried to give an insight into what toys and games do, but have also tried to provide the beginnings of a defence against the advertising of playthings. Parents should be on their guard against high-pressure sales offensives, and mothers — in particular — should beware, as many such campaigns are targeted specifically at them, especially where the advertising of toys for small children is concerned. For too long, parents have felt helpless at the hands of the advertisers and I don't see why they should put up with it. Teachers and others responsible in their work for helping children to develop in positive ways shouldn't have to spend so much of their time and energy in trying to undo the harmful and negative effects of most toys and games. I hope this book will help such people, even if only by defining the problem and showing where to start. For those who aren't directly involved with children but who would like to see a different and better society, I hope I've provided food for thought at least. It's never failed to astonish me that so many people, sincerely concerned about the overall, future development of society, actually ignore the powerful influences brought to bear upon the minds of children. They turn a blind eye while the damage is done and then try to undo it when the children have grown up.

The subject of this study is commercially-produced playthings, of the most popular and typical kinds, for children of all ages. Where toys are concerned, I've gone as far as to include playground equipment as this is a very important part of a small child's world of play. I've also had something to say about vehicles for children as this helps complete the picture. As regards games, I've focused on those played on boards and on tables but I've excluded card games as children don't go in for these very much. On the other hand, I have dealt with microprocessor games and also with puzzles. Sports and outdoor games fall outside the scope of this book and I haven't included party games or any jumping-about sort of games. Altogether, in the vast field of play, it was difficult to know where to draw the line, but if I say that the overall stress is on *products,* of a non-traditional kind, then I think the picture will become clearer. The study also takes in packaging, promotion, advertising and marketing, but not physical safety (to any great extent).

I've dealt, basically, with toys and games available in Britain and also throughout most of the capitalist world, during the period 1979-89 (which is just when I happened to be able to work on this project). However, I've included historical background where I felt it would be helpful in bringing about a better understanding of the situation. Although I'm focusing on a particular period, I'm describing and analysing a *process* rather than the particular products that happened to be around during the period under study. Commercial playthings change continually, and have to, in the never-ending search for greater profits. Therefore, it's important to see beyond particular toys and games, which are forever changing, to the values that they embody, which don't change fundamentally. Some toys and games I've referred to will no longer be on sale by the time this book is published. In fact, some of them are no longer available — at least in Britain — as I write. The attitudes and ideas represented by such toys and games, however, are unlikely to have disappeared but will merely have taken on different forms in other toys and games.

So much for the scope of the book. I now have to sort out some difficulties peculiar to this study; first, those arising from the nature of the toys and games industry.

There are difficulties over dating. Toys don't generally have dates on them, not all manufacturers' catalogues are dated and not all firms have new catalogues every year, though they bring out new toys. I've adopted a simple approach to cope with this situation. When I've given a date for a toy, it refers to the year when the catalogue in which it appears was current or, simply, I've known that the toy was on sale in the year in question. Of course, it could also have been on sale both before and after but I haven't been able to go into the history of each toy. In practice, I think these matters will be clear enough. Where games are concerned, I've sometimes given a copyright date when I had no other but I've always made it clear that I've done this. The trouble here is that a copyright date cannot always be taken as the date when a product was first marketed.

Trying to determine in which country firms have their headquarters is more difficult than it might seem. I hope I've sorted it out sufficiently to give a reasonably accurate picture, though it's one that's changing all the time. My practice, with foreign firms, has been to name the relevant country at the first mention but not thereafter, unless for some special reason. If you want to remind yourself of the national base of a firm you should look up the first reference to it in the index. A firm not so identified should be taken as British, at least at the date indicated or at

3

the time of writing. However, I've sometimes mentioned firms as being British to make particular points.

As regards quotations from trade materials — faced with all kinds of lettering, as well as a whimsical attitude towards capitals, apostrophes and so on, I've tried to bring some consistency into the matter without misrepresenting it and without being tiresome in the use of 'sic'. Manufacturers also have a carefree way with facts and figures and I've dealt with this as best I could, trying never to mislead.

Sometimes words used in the trade can be confusing; for instance, when there are different terms for the same things. I've used the word 'trundler' for the vehicle that small children sit astride and propel by pushing against the ground with their feet. These are known also as ride-a-strides, ride-'ems, ride-ons, sit 'n' rides, coasters, ride-on toys and trundle toys. In the same way, I've used 'playclothes' instead of playsuits, playwear or dressing-up clothes for the clothes children wear in order to take on various roles in the adult world. Other difficulties of this sort I've dealt with as they've occurred.

Another language problem is to do with gender and sex and the difference between the two. I use the word 'masculine' when referring to a role thought to be appropriate for males in our society and the word 'feminine' for a role thought to be appropriate for females. These are gender roles. Since people often don't fit these roles very well, or prefer roles other than the ones allotted to them by society, it follows that women can take on masculine roles and men feminine roles. The words, as I use them, have nothing to do with sex in a biological sense. These words, therefore, refer to social or gender differences, while the words 'female' and 'male' refer to biological or sex differences.

Since there's so much confusion over the use of the word 'black' in reference to people, I should explain that, when I don't wish to be more specific, I use it to refer to those who originated in central and southern Africa. By 'white', I mean people of European origin. I hope other terms I've used in connection with race will be clear.

Lastly, I want to say something about the way this book is organized. In a child's life, toys come before puzzles and puzzles come before games, though there are overlaps. Broadly speaking, the book reflects this.

As regards the various themes I've followed in the book, that of gender roles is paramount and forms the overall framework. Within this, however, I've tried to keep questions of race and class to the fore and I've also touched on other questions such as environmental issues. In short, I've tried to present an overall, ideological analysis of playthings.

My approach in part one has been to arrange most of the material under the four main gender roles, as it was clear that most toys, and all the main ones, could be grouped in this way. I've therefore gathered together my evidence from wherever necessary. In part two, after the introduction and chapter eight, in which I've again drawn together material from various sources, my approach has been to deal with games in categories, as it seemed to me that almost all games fell into three of these. Accordingly, in chapter nine, I've dealt with games which are political in quite specific ways, even though this may not be obvious at first sight. (I believe that almost all playthings are political, in the broadest sense.) In chapter 10, I've examined fantasy role-playing games, and in chapter 11, I've focused on war games. Lastly, in part three, I've given an overview of the whole and have pointed to some matters that need urgent attention. Throughout the book, I've looked at toys, games and puzzles in a wide cultural context.

August 1989

PART ONE
TOYS

CHAPTER 1

INTRODUCTION

All children need toys, or playthings of some kind, to help them develop both physically and mentally. In this chapter, I want to raise some general questions about toys which I'll enlarge on later. Here, also, I want to broach the main issue I'll be dealing with throughout the book — how a particular kind of society passes on specific cultural messages through the medium of playthings and, in this way, as well as in other ways, reproduces itself. All societies do this, more or less automatically, but I'll be concentrating on economically developed capitalist societies.

Differences between toys, games and puzzles

I think it'll be helpful to bear a few distinctions in mind at the outset. Toys, in varying degrees, involve the use of the imagination (though there's little scope for it in the case of many present-day toys). Games, of the kind I'll be analysing in this book, tend to involve more in the way of knowledge and memory. Toys call for physical co-ordination and deftness: games, when they don't depend entirely on luck, require mental skills. There are few hard and fast distinctions between toys and games but one is of overall importance: playing with toys doesn't involve rules whereas games always have rules. This is linked to the fact that games usually involve more than one player while children usually play by themselves with toys. This, again, is connected with a major distinction. With games, there's an end in view: they are resolved in some way, usually when someone wins. With toys, there's no such structure nor any structure, in fact, unless children invent one or unless manufacturers impose one through the nature of the toys themselves. (More of this later).

Puzzles, and in this connection I'll be dealing especially with pre-reading materials and jigsaws, are close to games in several ways. Games are resolved: puzzles are solved. Puzzles, however, normally involve a solitary player, though someone else, somewhere, who might even be thought of as an opponent, has built in the challenge. In this light, video games, for instance, might be thought of as puzzles except that normally the player never solves them and never wins but just goes on moving from one level of difficulty to the next.

Some toys are, in part, like puzzles. For example, putting together a model car from a kit is rather like solving a puzzle, but you get instructions on how to do it — it's not really a finding-out situation. Similarly, construction sets also have a puzzle-solving aspect.

Toys don't normally involve any competitive element whereas games usually do. By playing with toys, children, especially in their early years, learn about their bodies and faculties and learn basic facts about the outside world — those to do with weight, texture, shape and size for instance. As they grow older, children will, more and more, be presented with ideas about their society and their expected roles in it, through the medium of toys. This process is assisted by the fact that toys usually represent, on a smaller scale, something in the adult world.

I think that's enough, in the way of generalization, to be going on with. All these distinctions get blurred at the edges and I'll not bother with all the exceptions to the foregoing statements. These will come out later and I'll just leave my comments as they stand to prompt or provoke thought.

Toys, education and profits

Now, I'll begin to open up some of the arguments and debates that have traditionally surrounded toys.

The issue of educational and non-educational toys is, to my mind, a non-debate and I don't think it's useful to make distinctions of this sort. Children can learn from all toys as all toys carry messages and embody ideas. Of course, toys can teach particular skills, such as how to count, or general ideas, such as might is right; but I think it's better to consider toys as a whole and to ask what they stimulate in children or convey to them, and by what means, rather than to dismiss toys that might be called non-educational as harmless.

For instance, we might ask whether toys give rise to imaginative play. Children make up stories and dramas about their toys as they play with them but the toys themselves can set limits on such creativity. Some toy cars, for example, are specifically made for crashing while fashion dolls, in their narrow but well-stocked little worlds, offer small scope for imaginative and varied role play.

To take another instance, anybody might think that articles such as the various makes of plasticine and modelling clay would give the greatest scope to the imagination. However, even here there's been a closing of doors as the endless search for novelty, and therefore further profits for the manufacturers, has usually worked against creativity. Up to a point, the tools and moulds that are sometimes supplied with these products are all right but when you get to gadgets such as the 'extruder' toys, which the US firm of Palitoy was including in its Play-Doh sets for a number of years, then the doors are beginning to shut on imagination. Such a toy, by means of which Play-Doh is forced through holes of various shapes, features in the grotesque Barber Shop Set. In this case, the holes were in the heads of figures and the Play-Doh became 'hair' which you then groomed.

Similarly, colours for painting, by themselves, might be expected to give free rein to the imagination. The system of painting by numbers, however, which has been around for a long time now, puts a stop to anything of that sort. All children have to do is copy, and in the most narrow, circumscribed way. As in the wide range, both for oil and water colours, which the US firm of Milton Bradley (MB) were marketing in 1980, the pictures are usually trite, sentimental and, as you might expect, dead. This firm also had a tapestry-by-numbers range while, at the same time, Allan Industries were marketing their Feather Felt Kits. With these you could make pictures of exotic birds by sticking ready cut felt 'feathers' onto positions numbered for colour within the outline shapes of the birds.

Even making paper aeroplanes, long a part of the traditional sub-culture of the classroom handed down from generation to generation, has come in for the same kind of treatment. John Adams Toys, in 1982, had a Paper Aeroplane Pad of 'brightly-coloured paper, lined and numbered for easy folding'. (In fairness, I should add that this was not typical of the firm which, at that same time, had many very good craft and art products.) These examples, all from the field of arts and crafts, show how commercial pressures work against creativity and imagination. After all, children seem to have a natural interest in such activities and it's wrong to stifle this or direct it in stultifying ways. Children only need to be guided and helped.

In this connection, I think we should ask whether there's any real need for many kinds of commercially-produced toys anyway. Parents often give children toys instead of affection and time but this isn't satisfying a real need.

Lots of materials are more or less ready to hand for art and craftwork — things about the house, such as: covers, lids and caps from jars and bottles (for making patterns on plasticine or cutting it, for example); boxes of various sorts, especially cardboard egg boxes; bobbins; rubber bands; the insides of old clocks and watches; clothes pegs of the traditional kind; and half walnut shells (for making little mice). Outside, acorns and acorn cups and beechnuts and beechnut shells may be available, and all sorts of leaves for printing and making rubbings. Beautiful spore prints can be made from fungi (but only older children, those aware of the possible dangers, should be allowed to do this). Perhaps natural clay can be found, which has the advantage, for children anyway, of being mucky.

These are only a few of the things children can use in their play — and, of course, normal care has to be taken. Small children shouldn't be given things they might swallow. Also, certain plastics can be dangerous. For example, some people are allergic to certain forms of expanded polystyrene, the familar, white, moulded, packing material and, in addition, it burns down to a hot liquid giving off fumes.

I don't agree with the common practice in schools of using dough, rice, lentils, split peas, barley or any other foods for art and craft work as I think children should be taught not to waste food. Small pebbles, shells, and buttons, or melon seeds, can be used instead of edible seeds and, if those aren't available, the educational suppliers Invicta have all sorts of coloured counters, beads and the like which should do just as well. For the same reason, I don't agree with the use of potatoes for printing: corks can be used instead. (Also, commercial products may be made from foodstuffs — Play-Doh is, for example.)

This all goes to show how ideological considerations enter into all aspects of play. As far as the school situation is concerned, we should also ask what influences children bring into school from society outside — in this case the influences of commercial playthings — and how far these work against what the most aware teachers are trying to do.

Growing concern over the influence of toys

A general recognition that toys (and games) are important in shaping the ideological outlook of children has, very slowly, begun to emerge in recent years. In this section, I'll outline some of the developments that have taken place up to now, first of all in several countries and then internationally.

In Britain, the Toy Libraries Association was founded in 1972 to cater for the needs of handicapped children. Although it still maintains this special concern, the association has, over the years, widened its scope to deal with the play needs of all children. Over the years, as well — and very interestingly — there's been a growing awareness, in the association, that toys and games give rise to ideological questions. This was not noticeable in 1979 when, in a letter in answer to a query of mine, the toy development officer of the association stated: 'generally speaking we do not have a policy with regard to war toys, racism and sexism, as we consider toys from a functional and structural view point'. From that time, however, the changing emphasis could be seen in the introductory remarks to *The Good Toy Guide,* the association's annual publication. In 1981, for instance, it was stated that toys were not classified in the guide according to whether they were 'for boys' or 'for girls' and, furthermore, it was pointed out to toy manufacturers that Britain was a multi-ethnic society. In the following year, these statements on gender and race were enlarged upon and the fact that many children were growing up 'in other than a two parent family' was also mentioned. In 1983, the guide had a new section on dolls in which the importance of providing opportunities for both boys and girls to play with dolls was stressed. It was also stated that the association had 'looked closely for dolls with clearly defined racial features' and ones which did not 'impose traditional sex stereotyping'. Nevertheless, in spite of this, the fashion dolls Sindy and Barbie were brought into the list of recommended playthings to join Action Man who had been there in previous years.

The broadening of approach, to take ideological considerations into account, continued in 1984 when the organization extended its name to: Play Matters/The National Toy Libraries Association. However, I have to record a setback in this quarter. In the autumn of 1986, the *Good Toy Guide* was replaced by a very badly produced, glossy, colour magazine, *What Toy* (sic). It's true that, in this first issue, there was a mention, although very much in passing, of toys in a multicultural society. But there was no other indication of any particular concern over the attitudes and values embodied in playthings, and in the 1987 issue of the magazine (still badly produced) there was no trace of any ideological concern whatsoever. Furthermore, the illustrations showed children in stereotyped gender roles. Such matters, together with the ever more obtrusive advertisements and, above all, the institution of a What Toy award in 1987 — at the Hilton Hotel in London — seem to suggest that glamour and commercialization have won the day. Nevertheless, the association has assured me (April 1988) that they are still concerned about gender and race.

It's important to note that Play Matters/The National Toy Libraries Association has never shown any awareness of a class issue in playthings, nor has there ever been any concern with aggression.

As regards the latter, it seems almost as if the organization called Play for Life has stepped in to fill the gap. It was started in early 1984, with encouragement and help from the Quakers, and is mainly concerned with aggression, violence and competition in playthings while seeking positive alternatives. The group's publication, *A First Guide to Playthings for Life 1984-1985* is a list of such alternatives, with commentaries, basically for the age range five to 12. It's very interesting to note — especially considering the path taken by Play Matters/The National Toy Libraries Association — that, by 1986, Play for Life had also widened its scope to take in the issues of gender and race.

Now, to look at toys from a more obviously political viewpoint, we move on to West Germany. Heiko Kauffmann, in his booklet *Die Militarisierung des Kindes* (The Militarization of Children) tells of how the West German market, at Christmas 1977, was flooded with plastic figures of Hitler, Göring and other fascist leaders, represented giving the nazi salute and marked 'made in Austria'. Kauffmann also mentions that there was a boom in sales of such items as model planes, tanks, ships and dioramas, all showing swastikas and, in this connection, he mentions the firms, Airfix and Matchbox, the US firm, Revell and the Japanese firm, Tamiya, as being the main culprits. He adds that the German edition of the Matchbox kits catalogue showed a battlefield diorama with shattered buildings and the nazi eagle and swastika.

In the same booklet, Kauffmann gives an interesting insight into some of the legal implications of toys in West Germany. He tells of how the federal government had repeatedly indicated its displeasure over toys showing nazi emblems and stated that it would be pleased to support prosecutions, but that the bodies who had to prosecute were the regional governments, or Länder. It seems that these did nothing, as it was left to the Humanistic Union to take out a private case against those who dealt in and imported model kits showing swastikas. This case was rejected. The Berlin public prosecutors, giving their reasons, stated that the swastika was not only a symbol of the nazi party 'but at the same time the great symbol of a state'. This rejection constituted a double scandal, as the same two prosecutors had, five years before in 1973, taken up a case against the newspaper, *Berliner Extra-Dienst* which had published caricatures showing swastikas but with deliberate intent to criticize nazis. The newspaper was charged with 'the propagation of national-socialist symbols'. This charge was, apparently, also dropped, but a toy distributor *was* fined in West Germany in 1979 for supplying tanks and planes in packaging displaying nazi emblems.

By far the biggest and most important debates that have surrounded toys have been about war toys and, although my purpose in this book is to make an overall, ideological analysis of toys and games, the issue of war and aggression will, inevitably, emerge as the most important theme.

In Sweden, war toys have been banned except for those representing weapons and armaments in use before 1914. This seems one good way of meeting the arguments of those who, faced with the idea of a ban and inclined to be against it, want to argue about definitions and ask what's to be done about toy swords, bows and arrows, catapults, pea-shooters and suchlike. This legal step was taken in Sweden within the context of a national debate on violence as it affects children. Toys covered by the ban were not to be supplied to shops after 1 January 1979. Here, I should perhaps add that banning war toys isn't straightforward and wouldn't, in itself — of course — provide a solution to the problem of war. I'll be returning to this subject towards the end of the book.

At international level also, there's been concern over war toys. This led to the adoption, by the European Parliament, of a resolution on the matter in which it was, first of all, pointed out that:

> in the upbringing of children, and particularly in school and pre-school syllabuses and texts, emphasis should be given to the virtues of peace and to its achievements ... whilst pointing out the ruinous consequences of war and violence.[1]

The resolution also called on the governments of member states 'to take steps to ban the visual and verbal advertising of war toys' and recommended that 'the production or sale of war toys should be progressively reduced and replaced by toys which are constructive and develop creativity'. Amongst other considerations put forward in the resolution, it was noted that, in West Germany, the major toy producer in the European Economic Community, opinion polls showed that 83 per cent of the population were in favour of banning war toys.

This resolution was adopted on 13 September 1982 but it was little more than an expression of disquiet. Because (not surprisingly) the EEC treaty makes a ban on the manufacture and sale of war toys illegal, the resolution could only make recommendations and urge reforms on member countries. In fact, it seems that even if one member state wanted to ban war toys by prohibiting their manufacture, it still could not prevent the importing of such toys without breaking the EEC treaty.

On a world-wide scale, the work of the United Nations Organization should be taken into account here. Although the following instances aren't specifically concerned with toys, they are concerned with education and peace and therefore can be seen as attempts to counteract the culture of violence which war toys do so much to foster.

The first United Nations Special Session on Disarmament in 1978, in clause 106 of the statement it put out, urged governments and international, non-governmental organizations to 'develop programmes of education for disarmament and peace studies at all levels'. Further, in clause 107, it urged the United Nations Educational, Scientific and Cultural Organization (which the USA has now left, followed by Britain) to step up its programme on disarmament education as a distinct field of study through the preparation, amongst other things, of teachers' guides, textbooks, readers and audio-visual materials. Although Britain was a signatory to this statement, it has never made any positive steps towards implementing the suggested policy. The present Conservative government, in fact, has consistently attacked the idea of peace education.

Alongside UNESCO, another body, the United Nations International Children's Emergency Fund (UNICEF) has produced a teachers' kit on peace education with the aim, amongst others, of deglorifying violence on the individual, national and international levels.

We should keep this background — national and international — in mind in any discussion about war toys. (Strangely, there's been no similar concern shown about war games.)

Before leaving (for now) the subject of war toys, and peace, it's important to note two further points. Firstly, concern on this question has also come from some unexpected quarters. The allied armies of occupation in Germany after the second world war banned all modern militarism and toy-makers were restricted to such themes — racist, however — as cowboys and 'indians'.

Secondly — and to take up a different viewpoint — with war toys all that matters is what they stand for, and there's no dispute about this. A toy tank, for instance, is held to be harmful simply because it's a tank. There's little or no need to go into questions of how, exactly, it conveys its warlike message. On the other hand, the way in which toys, not necessarily held to be harmful in themselves, are mediated or presented to children by adults is a different matter but it obviously has a bearing on how children regard such toys. Most mediation goes on in the area of gender roles. Boys and girls are directed away from, or not given, toys which adults think are inappropriate to their sex. So, generally speaking, dolls are given to girls but not to boys. I can illustrate this process, and at the same time put things into a wider historical perspective, by reference to the work of the Soviet educationist, E A Flyorina. Round about the early 1940s and in the context of pre-school education, she wrote about how parents presented children with traditional gender roles through the medium of toys:

> It's very well known that, even today, in the bourgeois family, toys for boys and for girls are sharply differentiated. While a boy enjoys a rich variety of technical, military and other toys, a girl is given a doll and household furniture and set up with a huge number of beautifully made domestic articles. The underlining of the difference in the upbringing of boys and girls and the limiting of girls' interests to issues concerning the family and motherhood are bound to have their effect in children's play.[2]

Later, Flyorina mentions the 'reproach' made to boys who played with dolls: ' "A boy, and you play with dolls" '. This is the earliest example I've come across of an ideological approach to children's playthings.

Toys and the messages they carry

After toys held to be harmful in themselves just because of what they are, such as model tanks, and toys not necessarily held to be harmful in themselves but only harmful in the way they are mediated or presented to children, such as baby dolls, we now have to broach the more difficult question of *how* toys embody or carry ideas, attitudes and values — ways of looking at the world.

First of all, the whole approach to the making of playthings determines, and often limits, the way they are played with. Most playground equipment, such as slides and climbing frames, is for individual play and, even when several children can use the same piece of equipment at the same time, they don't have to co-operate in order to do so. A comment such as Terry Orlick's in *The Cooperative Sports and Games Book* can prompt some timely thoughts about the assumptions held by designers of playground equipment. He writes:

> We desperately need play materials that make it easy for little people to cooperate and likely for them to succeed. We should design at least some playground and playroom equipment that functions well only when two or more children play together to make it work (e.g., tricycles built for two, swings built for three, rocking horses built for four ... and slides built for five or six, and so on).[3]

Once Orlick has pointed it out, it isn't hard to see that the way the play equipment in question is usually constructed not only sets limits to play but carries an important and fundamental idea about life, and in this case the message is individualism.

Playground equipment obviously involves movement and takes up a good deal of space. These factors, however, can relate also to toys meant for indoor play. We need to ask: do toys encourage movement? do they take up space? Those thought of as being for boys often do. There are a lot of vehicles, for instance. 'Girls' toys' — dolls' houses, for example — tend to be static and to confine children to a particular spot.

Many aspects of toys as well as the way they are constructed and what they represent, can carry coded messages to children and convey values and ways of thinking. The sounds some toys make, and in the case of certain dolls even the way they smell, can be important. The messages are often, and in the first place, to do with gender roles, and some of the most explicit ones can be found in toy figures: those marketed for girls, such as the fashion dolls Sindy and Barbie, and those marketed for boys, such as the Masters of the Universe figures. The former, for the most part, are simply meant to *be,* to exist, not to do anything much: you can pose them and make them look decorative. The latter are meant to *do,* to be active in the world: though the only thing they do is fight. The colour and the shape or form of such figures, together with the expressions on their faces; as well as the materials they are made of, the way in which they are articulated and the kind of postures they can be made to adopt — all these things can be important in conveying to children the gender roles thought to be appropriate to their sex. Figures for boys, for instance, are mostly in strong, definite colours and fashion dolls don't, as a rule, have visibly jointed knees, which would spoil their appearance. Often, all such factors work together to one end, which is gender role stereotyping in the examples given. (Of course, in the present case, I don't mean to imply that it's simply a matter of getting boys to play with fashion dolls and girls to play with He-Man and the like. We don't have to suppose that such figures are suitable for children at all.) I'll be returning to the various ways in which messages can be encoded in toys and dealing with them in more detail in the following chapters.

The codes have to be broken, so that we can read the messages and become more aware of the issues. As we move, more firmly now, onto the question of race, the golliwog provides a good illustration of the process. Here, the colour of the doll, the exaggerated and stylized features and expression, and the clothes carry the message, yet awareness of the golliwog as a racist caricature has only come about in Britain since the early 1970s or thereabouts. Before then, nobody had broken the code, although it seems an easy one.

The wider question, of dolls which are racially non-European, hasn't been properly dealt with at all, though there have been many complaints about the lack of good ones. This lack, it should be said, in itself shows an attitude just as, in British fiction for children, the general scarcity of non-Europeans, especially in major, positive roles, also shows an attitude. The dearth of such dolls and such fictional characters suggests that they're less important, or don't matter. Most of the black dolls produced up to now have been made in the same moulds as the manufacturers' white dolls and just given a different colour. In other words, they are white dolls in blackface. The differences in physical features, apart from the hair perhaps, have been ignored. The colour of such dolls is token and the message is that racial identity doesn't matter. Try imagining a realistic black doll in whiteface.

The packaging that toys come in also carries messages. Here, colour and illustrations play an obvious part but lettering is important, as well — apart from what the words actually say — and especially when contained in logos. In the toy industry, a logo usually consists of one or more letters, words or symbols specially designed to be used as a trade mark. The shape and colour of logos and their components can be very revealing. Compare the letters of the word 'masters' in the Masters of the Universe logo with the letters of the Sindy logo, for instance. In the first, the letters are solid and bold and even the letter 's' is made as angular as possible, while in the second, soft, rounded shapes are emphasized and the heart for the dot of the 'i' suggests the love and romance to be associated with Sindy. Then, although both sets of letters have depth, those in 'masters' are more dominating and confront us directly whereas the letters of 'Sindy' are slanted away. (Also, the former has strong colours while the latter is in paler, warmer colours.) Look at the capital letters of 'masters', seemingly made out of metal, and compare with the small letters and the more personal, handwritten effect of 'Sindy'. All these points add up to a hard, masculine signal in the case of Masters of the Universe and a gentle, feminine signal in the case of Sindy. The Action Man and Barbie logos show similar features.

Messages about gender are also carried in advertisements for toys, sometimes in not so obvious ways, as Patricia Marks Greenfield has reported in the case of television: 'Commercials for girls' toys contain more fades, dissolves, and back-ground music; those for boys' toys contain more toy action, frequent cuts, sound effects, and loud music'.[4]

Toys in children's cultural surroundings

Toys don't exist in a vacuum and here I want to point to some close links with other aspects of the world of commercial culture handed down to children. These links take place through the process known as character merchandising whereby firms holding registered trade marks for their commodities can license other firms to use the same trade marks or any other distinctive features of the original products. In writing, copyright works in a similar way. Character merchandising — an express-ion which stretches the meaning of the word 'character' — has grown enormously during the period covered by this book and toys have played a big part in this growth. Many agencies have been set up to handle all kinds of marketable properties — and people — ranging from Snoopy and Barbie, to the Dungeons and Dragons game system, to the *The A-Team, Star Wars* and all other popular television series and films, to sports stars, the RSPCA and the London Symphony Orchestra.

With children's playthings, however, it's usually some kind of toy figure that's in question and all sorts of interchanges go on amongst the toy industry, television, radio, films and fiction including comics. The golliwog, for instance, began as a doll and then became very popular as a character in a series of picture books. After that, and until recent times, the golliwog continued to be very popular both as a doll and in fiction. Winnie-the-Pooh and the other characters best known from the stories by A A Milne started as soft toys and, through their popularity in fiction, became soft toys again. On the other hand, Paddington Bear and Thomas, the Tank Engine, began in fiction.

To-ing and fro-ing such as this has gone on for a long time. What's new is the extent of such links and the growth of marketing by means of character merchandise. Never have children been more surrounded by an ideology, by the same messages before their eyes or dinning in their ears. In 1979, one firm, Model Toys, was producing the following using characters from the *Mr Men* series of picture books: badges, name-plates, light-switch plates, coat hooks, bag-tags, wall safes, tooth-brush holders, toy watches, salt and pepper sets, money banks (of two kinds), pencil holders, Christmas tree decorations and a springy toy.

Other toys key children in — at a very early age — to the world of commercial youth culture. Model Toys in the same year, for example, had two 'fun guitars' for young children, one of them in a Mickey Mouse design, and also four guitars for older children. Two of these had the name Chartbuster and the other two were called Top Twenty guitars. Also in 1979, Mettoy was marketing its Frisco Disco DJ unit which, according to the catalogue, enabled the child to 'run his [sic] own disco show'. At a more serious level, fashion dolls have usually had a foot, or two, in the world of pop music. So, Sindy got her Pop Star Set in 1983 and a new Disco Set in 1986. At the same time, Barbie acquired several Rock Star outfits. The advent of Jem, though, in the same year was of another order altogether. Here was a fashion doll — or, rather, a whole group of fashion dolls — together with plenty of outfits and other equipment, all built into a strong story line set entirely in the pop world.

This must serve, for now, to give some inkling of the cultural network which surrounds children in their everyday lives. I'll be making more links — between different kinds of playthings — in the next chapter while, throughout the book, I'll be trying to place toys, games and puzzles in a wide cultural and ideological context. In the conclusion, I'll be returning to the matter of links and connections to show the broader significance.

References
1   Official Journal of the European Communities, Luxembourg, vol.25 no. C267, 11 October 1982, p.15.
2   E A Flyorina, *Igra i Igrushka* (Games and Toys), Moscow, Prosvyeshchenie 1973, p.53.
3   Terry Orlick, *The Cooperative Sports and Games Book:* Challenge Without Competition, London, Writers and Readers Publishing Cooperative 1979, p.61.
4   Patricia Marks Greenfield, *Mind and Media:* The Effects of Television, Computers and Video Games, London, Fontana 1984, p.34.

CHAPTER 2

TOYS FOR VERY YOUNG CHILDREN

The influences brought to bear on very small children lay the foundations for more specific indoctrination later on. Here, I'll be pointing out some of the messages that are bound up in what these children are offered for their play.

It's important to call to mind at the outset, however, that these messages are underlined in other ways. Furthermore, they fall into three main categories — those of gender, race and class. From birth, children will have been spoken to, and about, and handled and treated differently, according to their sex. Babies are beginning to be able to distinguish between male and female adults, in pictures shown to them, at about the age of one. At around the age of eighteen months, they begin to be aware of their own sex. That is, they can associate themselves with one or other of the adult groups. Language starts to develop at about the same time, so the messages can be reinforced in more conscious ways, as well. Children become aware of race, and their own racial identity, from about the age of three. This means, of course, that in a racist society they pick up racist messages. A conscious knowledge of class will come later still, if it comes at all. As regards class, however, I'll be showing how children get quite a lot of nudges which they can't be conscious of.

In this chapter, I want to touch on a large variety of playthings. These range from baby toys and soft toys to model vehicles, play figures and playsets, and take in an example of a consciously 'educational' toy on the way. Then, I'll move on to the kind of playthings which more obviously invite children to take on roles: vehicles for them to ride in or on and playclothes and playhouses. These also involve more space and more moving about. Then, we'll range further afield to playground equipment and festival or fairground amusements while calling at one or two shops on the way.

The main idea is to note the underlying similarities between the attitudes and values built into some very different examples. Apart from overall notions about gender, race and class, these playthings carry assumptions to do with militarism, patriotism and royalty, and law and order from an establishment point of view. Many promote competition and aggression. Some of the playthings dealt with here also signal a destructive attitude towards the environment, so I'll be keeping ecological questions to the fore as well.

Baby toys, soft toys and gentlemice

Baby toys, for children up to the age of about two, are for making and hearing sounds, creating movement, recognizing shapes, colours and reflections, learning through touch and manipulation, or any combination of any of these.

A lot of these toys are about as neutral as you can get, as far as attitudes and ideas are concerned but it's here, amongst the rattles and mobiles, the push-along and pull-along toys, that the story begins. Amidst the flowers and animals of early toys, vehicles soon begin to appear and these will become more and more important in play. The best ones, at this stage, don't represent any specific vehicles. Instead, they are simple and bright like the red and black, wooden crawler car from the West German firm of Artur Fischer. A very small child could get a good grip on this and, push it while crawling around. The toys in this firm's Fischerform range, mostly meant for children up to about two or three years old, are carefully worked out to correspond with the various stages of child development.

The well-known US firm of Fisher-Price concentrates mainly on pre-school toys. They have a nursery in New York where children play with toys and are watched by researchers through a one-way mirror. The children's reactions are passed on to academic specialists who act as Fisher-Price consultants. So the worlds of commerce and learning meet and mingle. For testing baby toys, the firm has a system whereby a mother and one child are watched by a researcher, who's normally a woman, it seems. In fact, no fathers, or any men, appear to be involved in this system at all, so there are certain built-in assumptions. However, Fisher-Price does have some sense of responsibility, unlike most toy manufacturers.

Other assumptions on the part of manufacturers can be easily seen in their catalogues and advertisements and in the packaging of their toys. Generally all of these show white children in stereotyped gender roles. I'll have more to say, from time to time, about how toys are presented.

Probably the most powerful assumptions are built into the toys themselves. There's no reason why the popular stacking and nesting toys shouldn't simply be plain and brightly-coloured like the plastic beakers from the educational suppliers, E J Arnold. There are 12 of these and they can be nested one inside another or built up into a stack — and then knocked down, of course. Pedigree have stacking rings but also stacking 'castles' with battlements and a 'king' holding a flag to go on top and they also have another stacking toy which shows a rabbit on one side but a guardsman on the other. With such as these, ideas begin to enter on the scene. Pedigree fire another shot with Billy Cannon. His red nose acts as the trigger for firing two male figures! All these examples are small (but typical) and none of them is very realistic in appearance. They only have meaning within the general context of militarism and the presentation of establishment values in children's playthings. I don't argue that there should be no representational element in these toys. It's what they say that matters. The Matryoshka, the traditional and well-known, Russian nesting toy, for instance, says something about motherhood in a very simple yet symbolic way.

Abbatt and Escor and the Swedish firm of Brio all make simple, brightly-coloured wooden toys but some aspects need to be noted here, if only because they'll form an important part of the picture later on. Amidst the vehicles, many of them lorries, engines, wagons and tractors from the ordinary workaday world, we begin to see racing cars, from Brio and Escor, thus introducing children to the world of competition and speed which will loom so large in toys for later years. The little peg-people, that go with many of these toys, increase the range of things that toymakers can say to children. Escor, with its figures, says to them that it's an all-white, mainly male world where guardsmen make up a sizable part of the population. A more active arm of the establishment, the police, can be seen mingling with the peg-people.

Another common kind of toy for small children consists of a little bench with holes in it through which you hammer pegs. Slap Sticks, however, made by Ambi of Holland and marketed here by Galt, add another dimension. Here, there are six little men which you hammer down by beating them on the head. This seems a rather different matter, to me. Edward M Swartz, in his book, *Toys That Don't Care* (which is, however, mainly about the physical safety of toys), shows us this same attitude taken a step further, by Milton Bradley in their toy Bash!, where the object is, in the words of the firm, to 'Hammer the BODY pieces from under the HEAD'. The box shows a picture of a man holding his head which is covered with lumps and on which a hammer is descending. He's a cartoon man, so it must be fun.

There'll be a lot to say, before I've finished, about the fostering of attitudes towards other living things, as well as people, and about ecology — the relationships of living things to their surroundings. Here, I'd just like to mention Fisher-Price's Bob-Along Bear, a circus bear in a bow tie with front paws that twirl around as it's pulled along. In view of all that's been said about performing animals in recent years, it's surprising to note that this toy was recommended in *The Good Toy Guide*, from 1981-3. I've given a fairly typical sample here, so it's pleasant to end this section with a mention for the cheerful and popular, pull-along Clatterpillar which certainly doesn't invite aggression, or suggest degradation

Soft toys, which make up a very large group, give rise to a lot of questions but they also include some of the most attractive of playthings. Dakin, which is the European subsidiary of a US firm, and which works from Belgium and has its products distributed in Britain by Newfeld who trade under the name of Bendy Toys (the toy industry *is* rather like that) has a lot of ranges of soft toys and bean-bag toys and also glove and mitt puppets. They're almost all animals, and are colourful and distinctive. This firm's zip-pouch animal rugs (though not of real skins) did raise an ecological question but these now seem to be discontinued, I'm glad to say.

You wouldn't think much could be done with teddy bears, apart from making them attractive and cuddly. The drive for ever-increasing profits, however, has led to all sorts of gimmicks. There's the Drink and Wet Teddy from Pedigree, complete with bottle and nappy, and Superted, who had his own television cartoon series, from Diane Jones Soft Toys. You unzip his skin to reveal the Superman outfit. Then, there's Moonbear (Pacton Craft) who arrived in 1980 in a lunar suit and plastic

23

moonboots. Six books of his adventures were planned. Pedigree's Space Teddy is dressed in a silver space suit with a Union Jack on the front and he has a helmet and several accessories. The weirdest of all, though, is Sleepy Bear from the USA (Rock-A-Bye-Baby Inc.) which contains what is described as 'an integrated circuit on which [the firm has] synthesized actual sounds from inside an expectant mother's womb'. The firm claims that this is 'the ultimate *natural* [my emphasis] baby pacifier' and that it 'quiets and calms most newborns to sleep quickly and naturally'. You just turn the knob and watch. On second thoughts, the teddy bear from Rexard is, perhaps, even more gruesome, though in a very different way. This is dressed as a policeman with a helmet and plastic badge. The card on it says it's called Sweet Dreams and has a picture of a little girl in bed cuddling up to her policeman teddy bear. I saw this in a very exclusive and expensive toy shop, Hummel's, in Burlington Arcade in London.

Policeman and guardsman dolls are quite common in Britain, for instance, in Newfeld's Little Bendy range.

Now, we come to the golliwog, along with the teddy bear the best known of the soft toys and notorious as a racist caricature. Although it began as a doll in the United States, it wasn't until after its appearance in literature, in 1895, that it became the popular toy of recent times. In literature, golliwogs have often been presented in frightening roles, and it's interesting to note that this association — of fear or alarm with blackness — goes back further in history, where toys are concerned. For instance, the original illustrations, by Richard Doyle and John Leech, to Dickens's *The Cricket on the Hearth,* show Jacks-in-boxes which look rather like golliwogs. The book was first published in 1845.

We should note the symbolic role of golliwogs, as well, even though this may be largely unconscious. The sign outside the Museum of Childhood in Edinburgh shows, amongst eight playthings, a golliwog and a guardsman with a cannon. Together, these seem an apt enough commentary on Britain's imperial past. The trouble about the past though — and we'll see this again and again in toys — is that it won't go away. This is shown clearly by the account an ex-paratrooper gave, of his service in Aden, in the *Socialist Worker* of 12 June 1982. He describes how each platoon would pin up a golliwog (from the labels on Robertsons' preserves) for every Arab killed. The platoon with the most golliwogs got a free crate of beer.

The Times of 20th August 1981 reported that the production of toy golliwogs had dropped in the face of what it chose to call 'sniping' by such groups as the National Committee on Racism in Children's Books, backed by the Commission for Racial Equality. The article stated that only 2,500 a year were being sold, as against 200,000 in post-war years and that, whereas there had been up to a dozen soft toy manufacturers producing golliwogs, there was only one left. This was Dean's Childsplay (incorrectly referred to as 'Dean's Gwentoy') and they were reducing their range to one model. Perhaps it shows how the political climate has changed again (although I think, also, that the article was inaccurate) but in 1983 Lefray Toys had golliwogs in three sizes, Bendy Toys had one and Dean's Child-splay were still making them. Bambola, as well as marketing the — on the whole — good range of dolls of various ethnic origins (to be described in the next chapter) were also producing a golliwog. In August of the same year, I noticed that Heal's, the large London department store, were selling golliwogs with paper labels stuck to them saying, 'Approved by the British Toymakers' Guild'. At the same time, Hamleys, the large London toyshop, were selling five different golliwogs. There was the one from Dean's Childsplay, one from Nisbet (presumably, the one made since 1978 on licence from Robertsons) one from Merrythought and two orphans, with no makers' names on them. I noticed another amongst Telitoy's products in 1984. And, of course, it didn't stop there. From Fantasia, there were balloons with golliwogs printed on them. It seemed a further sign of the times that, in May 1984, there were enormous posters of golliwogs around the streets of London (and, no doubt, elsewhere) advertising Robertsons' products. As we shall see, increasingly, toys cannot be considered in isolation. They are part of a whole society which they reflect, and help to reproduce. All the manufacturers mentioned in this connection are British. In fact, the golliwog, in recent times, has seemed peculiarly British.

The question of class arises in various ways as regards toys. Sometimes, it's just a matter of how much they cost but then, expensive toys are usually found in expensive shops. Also, such toys are often hand-made or are simply large and showy. At Christmas, 1982, Harrods were offering a Merrythought teddy bear, of mohair stuffed with fibre, for £99. It was big, but the one from Real Soft Toys made of mixed fibres with nylon, and labelled a 'Prestige Product', was enormous, far bigger than most children, and cost £93. Hamleys, catering for a larger section of the social spectrum, had 38 different bears in their 1981 catalogue, ranging from £4.25 to £86. Their soft, and expensive, toy animals on display in August 1983 ranged from £25 up to Paddington Bear at £145. The two biggest ones hadn't prices on. For sheer vulgarity, however, we have to go back to Hummel's who, at this same time, were offering mink teddy bears, about 25cm tall, for £90 each. Apart from the question of class, let's spare a thought for the minks who were so senselessly sacrificed. And, apart from anything else, I think there must be doubt about whether these toys would meet with the relevant safety standards. The assistant was very vague about who made these things and where they were made, but she said the shop sold quite a few.

The hand-made 'mouse characters' from Diane Freeman Designs are usually found in the more expensive shops but they give rise to other considerations as well. I first came across them through a reference, in the British Toy and Hobby Manufacturers' Directory for 1983, to '6" high boy and girl mice dressed in over 45 styles of Victorian costumes'. I knew at once that this was something I couldn't afford to miss! so, the following morning, I went along to the stand indicated at the Earls Court Toy and Hobby Fair. (The Directory is published for the yearly fair and is, in effect, a guide to it.) Curiously, they were adult mice, not children, but this was by the way. I realized, immediately, that I was in the presence of a better class of mouse altogether than the ones I'd been used to. These mice were ladies and gentlemen, apart from about eight and these eight included servants and a soldier, a sailor and a policeman. The vast majority of the population of Victorian Britain weren't represented. They wouldn't have had 45 different styles of costume anyway.

There was also a very curious matter, to do with gender, which gradually dawned on me as I looked at this fantastic collection. The little black noses of the men pointed straight out, into the world, or were even tilted above the horizontal. The women's noses were pointing modestly downward towards the ground. There was some variation, naturally, but I'd say that the average difference in the angle between female and male noses would be about 90°. I wrote to the company and asked whether this amazing consistency happened by accident, since they were all hand-made, or whether there were some overall guide-lines, but I received no reply. That the males stood up straight on their hind legs almost goes without saying. The females, I can reveal, had no legs at all. They had a hard, cone-shaped, seemingly plastic core which made do for the body and legs and this was covered by an under skirt or petticoat which was attached to a cardboard disc which formed the base. Over this, there was a long dress, or a dress was attached directly to the disc.

A miniature world

We can note model vehicles and aircraft in passing here, as they usually form part of the toy collection of little children, especially boys, but further details will be added about this group of toys in chapters five and six.

Small boys are likely to have the Dinky, Corgi and Matchbox die-cast models, that is, ones made by the ordinary method of casting metals in moulds. The corner newsagent is likely to sell these. Amongst them (and to make links with points that have been made earlier or will be made later) there's likely to be a very strong police presence and quite a lot of military vehicles and aircraft, usually British, US and German. Alongside these and the fantastic superheroes and space models, however, it makes a nice change to see the odd road sweeper or refuse wagon here and there. Vehicles from popular television programmes, usually police serials, are very well represented. The Corgi catalogue of 1979 features the Kojak and Starsky and Hutch cars, for instance. As we'll see, these have given way to others but it's only the names that change, really. A new range, the Convoy, was added to the Matchbox models for 1982. This range consisted of eight enormous US road transport lorries. There may be political debate in Britain about the weight of lorries to be allowed onto the roads, and this has to do with both economic and ecological matters. Such considerations wouldn't be likely to occur to young children playing with these toys but, it seems to me, their attitudes would be influenced for the future. Appealing to the emotions, and by-passing reason, otherwise known as indoctrination, is supposed to be a bad thing to do. It happens with toys all the time. The catalogue tells us to 'play King of the Road with these brand new miniature models of giant longhaul trucks'. The additional points raised here, about masculinity and aggression, will be expanded on in later chapters. Another point to note in a political context, is the extent of commercial advertising on many of these models. Although it could be argued that this is necessary if the models are to be realistic, a lot of advertising goes on which can't be excused on these grounds.

An important aspect of the toy industry is what has come to be known in the trade as 'collectability'. As many parents will know, to their cost, the main point about these models is that you're meant to collect them. The Matchbox catalogue I've referred to, in fact, is called a 'Collectors' catalogue'. The illustrations have reference letters and numbers and also a little box. 'Tick the boxes as you collect them', we're told cheerfully.

Playmats have arrived on the scene in fairly recent years but they've become quite popular, especially in playgroups and nursery schools. The mats have scenes or plans printed on the upper surface, while the underside is of some non-slip material. They are big enough for three or four children to play on them and around them at once, usually with small vehicles and figures.

The Recticel Sutcliffe playmats, which are probably the best known, have a coloured design on a carpet surface, and a honeycombed rubber base. Their Battleground and Wild West playmats, which were available in 1979, are now discontinued, I'm glad to say. The first used to be supplied with two packs of Airfix soldiers. Their Super Roadway Playmat (there's a smaller version) shows a village roadway layout, with pictures of buildings, a river, and fields round about. The basic idea is good — to help children learn about traffic regulations, road signs and markings, and road safety — and this mat has been available since at least 1976, to my knowledge, which means it must have sold well. I doubt, though, whether many children, and even most country children, could identify with this very prosperous-looking, middle class village with its nine large detached houses and what might be one small terrace of houses. (It isn't very clear.) This type of plaything, therefore, gives rise to the same sort of questions that have been so often asked in recent years about the illustrations in children's books.

Similar products from other manufacturers, such as Waddingtons' Giant Country Roadway and Giant Town Roadway, give the same general well-off impression.

Quartec produce the Motormaster kit (and I can only suppose they haven't realized the implications of the name, as it can't be in their interests to imply that girls are excluded). The kit itself looks rather interesting, as it consists only of roadway which is printed on 28 pieces of laminated card which fit together like jigsaw pieces, so that various layouts can be made. Sample layouts are included, together with a booklet on road safety.

Now, we move on to consider play figures and playsets. Hans Beck, in West Germany, devised the system known as Playmobil. Until about 1981, it was known in Britain as Playpeople, and by 1983 the firm had established a British subsidiary. Like the Danish construction system, Lego, for instance, it presents almost a complete world of its own, or way of looking at the world, and therefore it's very important to ask just what values, attitudes and ideas are being presented to children by these means.

The simplified plastic figures in the Playmobil system, which are about 6½cm tall (adults), have arms, legs and heads that move. All are basically the same but you can tell females from males by the way they are dressed and by the hair style. Males have a kind of short, cut-away jacket and females have a short dress. Children are smaller versions of the adults. All are smiling. Different occupations are shown by differently-coloured uniforms, by accessories and, especially, by head-gear.

27

Basically, the system presents a comfortable, conventional western European way of life with all that implies from the point of view of gender roles, occupation and interests. You can get small units like a boy with a handcart or a girl with a doll and pram. These illustrate, very neatly, gender roles in Playmobil as a whole. Then there are small, medium and large sets differing in the number of figures, buildings and accessories involved. Vehicles, aircraft and boats, and also buildings can be bought separately. The system is planned so that you can go on and on buying more and more items to add to your collection.

Certain main themes — law and order, firefighting, building and construction work, and a hospital theme can be followed throughout. You can build up a very large collection just by keeping to a 'western' theme — with stereotyped cowboys and 'indians', a large US cavalry presence and all the conventional paraphernalia. As always, the components will fix the limits of imagination and play. All children can do here, for instance, is to enact racist rituals, in the manner of 'western' films. There's also a zoo theme, with some rather contented-looking captive animals, and a space theme.

There's the odd figure in blackface here and there and a smallish proportion of females. Given the themes, it might be argued, as with other, similar toys or toy systems, that they are male-dominated or, to put it another way, that men have more varied and interesting jobs. On the other hand, it's necessary to break out of the vicious circle. And, certainly, it's difficult to see how Playmobil's claim, in their 1984 press release, that 'all Playmobil sets are designed to appeal equally to boys and girls' can be justified.

I should add, to give credit where it's due, that there's no modern military theme in the Playmobil range of products. There's fighting, as with the cowboys and 'indians' and with the pirates and medieval knights, but this is, at least, always distanced in time. The 1983 Playmobil catalogue claims that 'over 400,000,000 Playmobil figures are being played with by boys and girls in over 40 countries of the world'.

Fisher-Price produce three main types of small figures. Their Play Family, which consists of very simple, peg-top figures, is meant for children from the age of about two. Whereas the Playmobil figures all have the same bland look, the Play Family (much fewer in number) have more varied expressions on their faces. One looks very grumpy, another looks gleeful. The female figures are all white but a few of the male ones are, simply, coloured brown. However, none of them is meant to be very realistic. These figures go with the kind of playsets that might be expected: a garage, a fire station, a school and a circus train, amongst others. The Play Family house and, more still, the Play Family car and camper set point to a fairly well-off life style. In 1983, Fisher-Price claimed that there were over 500 million Play Family figures around the world.

The figures that go with this firm's 'Trucks' range, meant for slightly older children, have movable limbs and are all white and male. Moreover, they're described as 'husky' (a basically US term meaning stocky and muscular, or burly). In this range, there's a strong bias towards building and construction work but

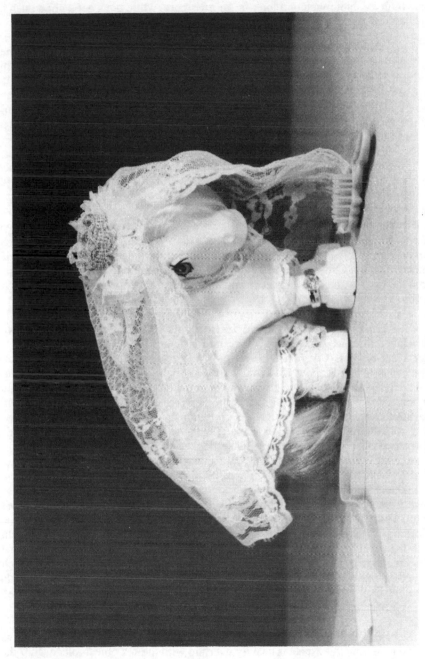

1: My Little Pony — Wedding Bells set with Confetti Pony

there's also a 'husky' farmer (with a 'husky' bull) and two 'husky' policemen, with their vehicles. Not much of a look-in for girls here, while boys get a good push in the direction of the macho image.

Fisher-Price's Adventure People, also known as Action Figures, and the sets that go with them, are meant to take in slightly older children. These figures with movable limbs are all white, nearly all men and a bit difficult to stand up. They go exploring the ocean or space, or they race dragsters or motorbikes. Although here there's a stronger prompting towards the world of speed and daring, the range isn't military at all (1983) and, it should be mentioned, the Alpha Probe set has a woman astronaut.

Similar types of figures on sale give much the same impression as those described here while toy soldiers and other military and aggressive figures will be dealt with in chapter six.

To keep the ecological theme in mind, it's interesting to note the Magic Clown Circus Train in Pedigree's 1983 catalogue with its broadly smiling lion in a cage and two performing seals. In the same year, during the week ending on 2 April, the Greater London Council voted to ban circuses which included performing animals from their parks and open spaces. Apparently, this has happened in other places as well.

Finally, in this section, something 'for little girls'! The US firm of Knickerbocker introduced their My Little Pony range into Britain in 1983 aiming at the four to eight-year-old range. At first, there were six 'collectable', pastel-coloured, cartoon-type ponies standing about 15 cm high. They had large, soulful eyes and long manes and tails, and the idea was to groom and plait the hair. Each came with a comb and ribbon and it was also possible to buy the My Little Pony Grooming Parlour with its various accessories. The range was a popular success and so, following a typical pattern in the industry, it was expanded for the following year, by which time the US firm of Hasbro had bought up Knickerbocker. In 1984, girls could collect ponies in three different poses: sitting, standing and with head 'turned coyly to the side', as it says in the press handout. Then, there was a Pony Show Stable, a Pony Gymkhana Set, each with various accessories, and even a Pony Jewellery Box. Also, there were pony outfits: a raincoat and hat, a nightdress and bonnet and, weirdest of all, a party outfit complete with tiara. By 1986, My Little Pony had become an enormously popular concept and had followed the familiar pattern of development, with many outfits and playsets and a fictional line to hang them on. At this time, Hasbro claimed that, in Britain, 82 per cent of all girls aged four to nine years old owned at least one pony. Some of the creations are really grotesque, like the Wedding Bells set in which the Confetti Pony is decked out with a wedding dress and veil, a garter and a ring (see illustration, p. 29).

It's easy to see how this concept draws upon the caring, 'mother' role but we should note how this aspect is heavily overlaid with the sex object role, even if this is transferred onto ponies, in this case. And it all latches onto the pony fixation so widespread in popular fiction for girls. The My Little Pony range may be an odd mixture, but the ingredients are very familiar. Also, they'll turn up again and again in playthings for older girls.

An 'educational' toy

We've seen how so many of the baby toys had a conscious educational aim. This is carried on in many toys for older children.

The Alphabet Teacher, brought out by Hestair Kiddicraft in late 1982, is a plastic toy consisting of a keyboard with 50 hinged keys. You press the lower part of a key and a flap, on a hinge, springs up thus revealing two more surfaces, the underside of the flap and the base which has been uncovered. There are three sets of keys. One set, of 30, shows the letters of the alphabet and the four basic digraphs: ch, ph, sh, and th. Then, there's a set of 10 coloured keys and a set of 10 keys showing pictures. These three sets correspond as follows. If you press a colour key, you reveal a picture on the base and the name of the colour on the underside of the flap. The pink colour key, for example, reveals a picture of a pink baby (message — babies are pink) and the word 'pink' in pink letters. If you press the picture key showing the same pink baby you get, on the underside of the raised flap, the figure 1 and the word 'one', in pink letters. On the base, you see, on a pink background, the words 'one pink baby'. If you press 'b', you turn up the same pink baby. So, the point is driven home three times over — babies are pink. There are no other babies referred to in this toy. If you press brown, you get a rabbit and, more arbitrarily, if you press yellow, you get a tractor and you can go up to 'ten orange oranges'. But babies are pink.

Playthings for taking on roles

Children are pushed further into their allotted social roles once they get their own vehicles to ride in, or on.

Anybody might think that, when it comes to this kind of toy, there'd be little reason for making any kind of distinction between the sexes. It's even more difficult to understand why profit-hungry manufacturers should restrict their markets to 50 per cent of the relevant age group when it could be 100 per cent. I really think it can't occur to them to question stereotyped gender roles.

Admittedly, the Lil' Lady trundler, from Milton Bradley (under its Playskool trade mark) is one of a range of items (under the Lil' Lady logo) which includes a party set and a dolly chair, and all have characteristics in common which girls have been socially conditioned to respond to: bright, but not strong colours, curved and rounded shapes and flower decorations. The trundler has flower-shaped hubs on the wheels. Also, the dot of the 'i' in the Lil' Lady logo is a flower. Boys would know the trundler was not for them. On the other hand, the angular Star Rider which is mainly in shades of grey and slate blue and which represents the driving seat and control panel, complete with light and sound effects, of a space ship, would key in to boys' conditioning:

Under attack from enemy ships? [the Playskool 1981 catalogue asks]. Press the emergency button to warn the squadron with exciting sounds. Then fire lasers at the enemy. Trace their path on the electronic screen and when the explosion hits, blast their ship out of space!

Although the catalogue mentions 'girl or boy' (but, nevertheless, shows a boy in the photo) girls would know it wasn't for them. I don't think it's suitable for anybody, really.

In this area also, the establishment gets a boost. Raleigh have a trundler with the word 'police' on the side and a panda car with sergeants' stripes on the front. This is 'for the "Teeney Sweeny" set'. Sharna Tri-ang have a trundler police car, two police pedal or powered cars and two police pedal motor bikes. Rolly, the Italian firm, have a police tricycle trundler and a police tricycle with helmet and goggles. Superjouet of France also have similar police vehicles for tiny tots.

How very different are the beautifully-made, strong, simple trundlers in plain wood from Community Playthings. In this case, stultifying attitudes aren't foisted on the children, there's plenty of room for imagination and, from what I've seen of them, I'd say they'd take a lot of hard wear and tear.

We now move up the age range, and up the social scale. Hamleys were offering, in 1981, a plastic, pedal-driven Formula 1 racing car for £67.50; the Team 7 Busta, a chain-driven pedal car for £129.50; and the Sizzler Fun Kart with four stroke engine, disc brake and automatic clutch for £450. They also had a Rolls Royce pedal car for a mere £138.95. I think this must have been the one from Sharna. At any rate, in 1983 Sharna had two models, one pedal-driven and one battery-driven, of

2: *Rolls Royce*

the Rolls-Royce Corniche. The battery-driven one first came onto the market in that year. These cars were meant to be scale replicas and were of an overall length of about 120cm (see illustration p. 32). Both had electric accessories. In their 1984 press handout, Sharna, or Sharna Tri-ang as they had by then become, reported that orders for the battery model had 'flooded in' 'from all corners of the globe' (but mainly, it seemed, from the USA). This toy would 'provide hours of untold fun and prestige' for the child, it was claimed, and all for about £275. However, this is nothing really. Hamleys also had on offer in 1981 a child-sized version of the Volkswagen Beetle for £2,500. I should think this was the same as the one Harrods had on display the following Christmas, costing £2,950. This toy was manufactured by J P Products and had a fibre-glass body; steel chassis; 5hp engine; automatic clutch; an electric system for the starter, lights, CB radio and horn; and an uphol-stered and carpeted interior. Its overall length was 220cm and the top speed could be preset to anywhere between five and 20 mph.

The same firm in 1983 were marketing several other petrol-fuelled miniature cars, some hand-built, with similar specifications, including an Old English Racing car. In fact, during the period covered by this study, there have always been several of these expensive cars around.

But it would be more discreet, perhaps, to spend your spare money on something like rocking horses. The range from Pegasus in 1983 went up to a fairly modest £169.95 (Or, you could buy their almost life-size lion, not a very soft one, for £239.85 and then, no doubt, wonder what to do with it.) As soon as the Earls Court Toy and Hobby Fair opened in 1983, someone who, according to *Fair News* of 30 January, 'sells rocking horses at agricultural shows round the country', placed an order for 50 from Haddon Rockers. Prices — presumably trade prices in this context — ranged from £182-£400. Maybe it was one from this range that Harrods had for sale the previous Christmas for £625.

But, especially with vehicles in mind, there are different ways of looking at the world, and at children's toys. The wholly original Moon Rover, manufactured by the Danish firm, Kompan, is powered by means of a pedal axle which drives the front left-hand wheel. There's no chain. You steer with two handles which turn the back wheels. The vehicle is made of tubular steel with a bonded plywood seat and pneumatic wheels. A tipper or scoop can be fitted to the front. This vehicle is designed for children's play, not to initiate them into aggression or competition nor to hook them into upper-class notions of prestige. I enjoyed my ride on it. A model for older children and, interestingly, one for mentally-handicapped adults are being developed.

In this section, I wish to deal with playclothes and associated gear, such as dress accessories and weapons. These are for children to wear in order to take on specific roles in play.

In general, the playthings on sale in this category don't leave much to the imagination, and only prompt children into rituals to do with power, race and gender.

33

This is a pity, as children like dressing up and this kind of play could be imaginative and could help them to grow in all sorts of ways.

So, what roles are presented to children in this very specific way? Wells Kelo in 1980 had a very large range of playclothes in three sizes: small, for children from two to four years old; medium, for five to seven years; and large, for eight to ten years. These included the usual uniforms linked with gender roles, race, the establishment and war. (There are overlaps, of course — waging war is a masculine gender role.) Consider the list of the available playclothes: nurses' uniforms (for girls); policeman and guardsman uniforms; cowboy and 'indian' suits; and various military uniforms such as British Army Commando and Jungle Fighter. These give rise to several points. Girls aren't offered much beyond the caring role which can be thought as an extension of the 'mother' role, though they could choose to be a cowgirl or a squaw. This would enable them to join in the race ritual which goes under the name of cowboys and 'indians'. Needless to say, no attention is paid to the fact that there was a large number of native American nations and there were many different cultures. These playclothes, typically, simply draw upon a galli-maufry of exotic items and it's worth pointing out that, in the case of 'indian' dress, children don't assume a role in the usual, occupational sense — such as nurse or even cowboy — but, instead, take up a racial stereotype. Regarding the military playclothes, we might ask, for example, what jungle a British boy might assume he had the right to be fighting in. Interestingly, also, amongst these military uniforms, is one called Colditz and one called Afrika Korps. Each is described as a ' German Officer's' uniform. Here, as with all toys and playthings and also comics and other fiction, where the second world war is in question, there's no indication that it was, basically, about fascism.

From Cheryl, in the same year, 1980, there were similar playclothes, in different sizes to fit children from two to nine years old. We should note, as being also typical, the (US) spaceman suit and the Batman costume with hooded headgear and cape. Capes seem to be very suggestive to small boys. In one playgroup I visited, there were capes which the boys made for as soon as they arrived. They then wore them for most of the session.

Dekker is another firm which, over the years, has gone in strongly for playclothes and other gear. Besides the superheroes outfits, which are quite usual — Superman, Batman and Spiderman — we find here, also, and less usually, a Wonder Woman costume. Cheryl have Superwoman.

More usual are Dekker's other products for girls such as the Bride Outfit with accessories, advertised as being for girls from four years old. This firm certainly believes in encouraging girls to grow up quickly. Their 'Silver Lady' Accessory Set, which includes shoes, a purse with chain, an imitation watch, a medallion on a chain, ear-rings, bangles and rings, is aimed at girls from three years old. 'Every little girl can join the "Jet-Set" with this exciting and fashionable dressing-up outfit', the 1982 catalogue says. The Girl About Town umbrella, bag and accessories set, though, was intended for sophisticated girls of six and upwards. In 1983, the Golden Glitter Girl Set appeared, described as 'party accessories' and consisting of gold brocade sandals with matching draw-string bag and belt. This was meant for girls of three and upwards while the Golden Glamour set, consisting of bits and pieces similar to the ones already mentioned, was advertised as being for girls of six years and above.

Downmarket, as they'd say in the trade, we can get such things as the Little Bride set with white plastic adornments and the Beauty Set, with plastic comb, brush and mirror. I found these carded sets on sale in W H Smith's in April 1983. The only information on the cards was, 'not suitable for children under 3 years' and 'made in Hong Kong'. These cheaper, anonymous versions of articles which appear in manufacturers' catalogues illustrate a common pattern in the toy trade.

The most insulting items on offer to girls, I think, are those imported by Acamas 'direct from the U.S.A.' and now going under the general name of Cheerleader. In 1982, there were 'Genuine American majorette twirling batons', claimed to be for girls of five and upwards, and pompoms. By 1984, 'thumbshakers' had appeared, as well. These, perhaps I should explain, are the articles wielded by the women who parade up and down on the field at football and other matches in the USA. 'Support your team', the girls are told: reduce yourself to a mere decoration would be another way of putting it.

The boys, meanwhile, have been getting more of the action, though I don't mean to imply that being a mindless killer is better than being a decoration. Military playclothes, which are in plentiful supply, have already been mentioned. Now, we turn to focus more on the equipment which is usually meant to go with such playclothes. I'll pick out typical sets or kits and also try to show the way things are going. In 1979, J and L Randall, who conduct their business under the Merit trade name, had two commando kits in their catalogue, one of which was sold out. They included such items as a helmet, a water bottle, a compass, a knife and camouflage instructions and identity discs. No bangles or rings here! The Commando Helmet and the Commando knife — 'safe', 'harmless' — with its retractable blade, could also be bought separately.

This is all fairly typical. It wasn't until rather later, it's my impression, that the toy industry swung firmly behind the Special Air Services, although these had come to public notice several years before at the siege of the Iranian embassy. Hamleys' 1981 catalogue had shown an SAS outfit consisting of a khaki uniform complete with beret and SAS emblem. There was a choice of sizes for ages three to five for £13.00. For Christmas 1982, but maybe not in a very seasonal spirit, Harrods had Bell's SAS Rescue Kit on sale. The rescuing involved a knife, handcuffs and a machine gun, amongst other things, and it was all 'developed with the assistance of the 22nd SAS Regiment'. Cheryl had SAS and also paratrooper playclothes on display at the Earls Court Toy and Hobby Fair in 1983. There'll be more to say about these regiments later.

Language, as we'll see more and more, is a very important factor in the naming and presentation of all playthings. In the area I'm now considering, the word 'assault' has grown to be very important. So Thomas Salter brought out their Commando Assault Kit in 1983, with 'everything the young Commando wants'. This included a 'unique break-down sub-machine Gun'. The box shows soldiers with the usual frenzied expressions, amidst shell-bursts. At the same time, Salters' Paras' Assault Kit was on sale. This, it said on the box, was 'designed with the co-operation of the Parachute Regiment Headquarters, Aldershot'. There was a gun, a grenade, binoculars, a helmet, a walkie-talkie, a water bottle and another item I couldn't identify.

'Adventure' is another key word in the toy industry. It generally means 'violence'. In 1984, Salters were offering a much expanded range of what they called Adventure Kits. Although a leaflet stated that these were for five- to 12-year-olds, some of the boxes had 'age 3 and up' on the front. The leaflet claimed that the kits would 'make little men out of little boys'. It's a curious idea — that growing up, for males, must involve aggression — and we'll be coming across it again.

These kits contain not clothing but various items of gear appropriate to various aggressive roles, which may originate from television, from other toys or from life, as some people live it. Several of the kits have involved the purchasing of rights from other toy manufacturers or from film or television companies. This is very characteristic of the way the toy industry works. Some of the kits are like those already mentioned. There's now a Paras Patrol Kit, for instance, alongside the Assault Kit. There are three Action Force kits: the Tank Commander Set, the Combat Kit and the Communication and Code Kit. (There'll be a lot more to say about Action Force in chapter 6. Suffice it to say here that they all contain the usual military weapons and gear.) Spiderman, who tends to rely rather more on muscle, has two kits which appear peaceful by comparison. His Adventure Kit, for instance, includes mask and working camera, torch and binoculars. The Masters of the Universe kits (again, more on this toy concept in chapter 6) carry on the fantasy theme. The He-Man Weapons were new in 1983. Now Skeletor Weapons are added. A lot of men don't grow out of this kind of thing. It only take different forms, often more realistic ones, as many males get larger. Sometimes, nothing appears to change. I saw several grown 'cowboys' riding along a Surrey country road one Sunday morning. One of them, to his credit, did look rather self-conscious. Then, on 19 January 1984, I looked in on 'Watch It' in the children's programmes on commercial television. It was about men who dress up and play cowboys (though one said he preferred the name 'westerners') at a kind of film set township which they call Frontier City. For six months every year, they put on shows for the public.

Despite all this, some progress was made. In 1981, a toy project was launched in Lambeth as a result of concern about the lack of relevant playthings for multicultural inner city areas. A co-operative was set up and, with help from the Greater London Council, Lambeth Toys was soon distributing its products by mail and through Nottingham Educational Supplies.

One of the first concerns of this group of Asian and Afro-Caribbean women was playclothes. At first, they made Nigerian, Punjabi, Hindu and Chinese costumes for girls and boys, which were meant to fit over the children's own clothes. Authentic materials with traditional designs were used and the outfits came with information on their history and on how to wear them. Later, eight more costumes were added including Gujarati, Japanese, a Ukrainian costume for a boy and a Russian girl's dress.

In what seemed to be a natural development, Lambeth Toys went on to produce their Afro-Caribbean Face lacing toys. There were two large faces, one a full face and one a profile, made of 6mm thick plywood with holes in the scalp areas for taking the 'hair' and beads provided. An Afro comb and lacing guide were included and many kinds of lacing and plaiting could be practised. At first sight, this might seem not very different from other doll hair-do sets but the intention here was quite different. In this case, the idea was to foster black consciousness and self-respect, not to create sex objects and mindless consumerism.

But Lambeth Toys, like so much else that's positive and creative in education and culture, couldn't survive in present-day Britain and the co-operative was bought up by the Unity Learning Foundation in the autumn of 1987. However, the lines developed by Lambeth Toys were to be kept on in some form or other.

Playhouses, tents, furniture and similar articles for children are obviously closely connected with the playclothes and other accessories just dealt with. They're all part of the same kind of play. Also, as we might expect, the assumptions and attitudes of the manufacturers — who are mostly not the same ones as were mentioned in the last section — are basically similar.

The Log Cabin and Fort from Abbatt Toys are clearly meant to prompt the kind of racist rituals, involving cowboys, 'indians' and cavalry, that have already been mentioned. Furthermore, and in spite of the mention of 'cowgirls' in the catalogue, it seems very likely that boys, given their early conditioning, would appropriate these. On the other hand, most children, I'd say, would think of the Wendy House, so much a part of infant classrooms, as being mainly for girls. I don't think it's a very good name for a playhouse.

The French firm of Mundia, which specialises in tents and playhouses, seems almost to be running a campaign to promote the racist mythology of the 'wild west' amongst children. Their 1981 catalogue contained no fewer than 10 'indian' tents, as well as a Wells Fargo tent, a covered wagon tent and a saloon and general store tent. They also had time to promote the interests of a multi-national oil firm, with their tent representing an Esso garage, and they threw in a camouflaged commando tent for good measure. Mundia were encamped, I noticed, at the 1983 Earls Court Toy and Hobby Fair. In the same year, the Tepee from Community Playthings (a company to be dealt with in more detail shortly) hadn't the usual dreadful designs on it, at least, but the photos in the catalogue and in their booklet 'Criteria for Selecting Play Equipment' showed the usual confused masquerade known as 'playing indians'. As part of their education, children need to learn about the history and culture of various native American nations just as much as about those of any other nations. In fact, they need it more, as there are so many wrong ideas and attitudes to be sorted out.

Regarding furniture for children, it's interesting to note — though there's certainly nothing unusual about it — how often manufacturers, in the way they present their products, seem bent on restricting children's play rather than giving it free rein. There's nothing wrong with producing small desks for children but a Junior Executive Desk, such as we have from both Baveystock and Britwood, seems less an object for play than a means of placing children at a particular point in a particular political spectrum. Pegasus produce a Stafford Executive Desk.

Even in children's furniture, the obsession with guardsmen goes on. 'Two Guardsmen carry a blackboard at the slope — so much more fun' the Tiger Toys 1978-9 catalogue tells us. Then, they have a desk and chair and also a clock with guards' bandsmen designs and, of course, the guards carry the bookcase as well. Children like to measure their height so what better than to measure it against a guardsman (R F Development) or a Beefeater (Abbatt Toys)? On the other hand, if you don't want to involve your children in dreary establishment rituals, you can get a very nice-looking height measure from Invicta which also measures clearances from the floor.

Sometimes, toys in themselves say little about gender stereotyping. However, the manufacturer will often present them as being decisively for boys, or for girls, if not on the packaging, then by means of the catalogue. This will give a line to retailers who, through their presentation, perhaps by having areas of their shops labelled 'for girls' or 'for boys' or through other means, will signal to the buyer. The buyer usually knows, anyway, from other sources.

So, although Mayco's toy barrow is called Bizzy Lizzy, the catalogue says it's a 'barrow just like Dad's'. The toy lawn mower is a 'realistic version of Dad's mower' while a picnic basket is described as the 'ideal toy for all girls'. However, I should add that the Mayco toy work bench, for very small children, is described as 'for boys and girls'. Also, girls are shown at work benches in A J Lain's catalogue.

A large, colour photo in the Arnold 'Offspring' catalogue of 1982 sums this whole matter up very neatly. We see a boy with a wheelbarrow and are told that it's 'just the toy for the boy who likes to help Dad in the garden'. Alongside him is a girl with a 'baby buggy' and we read that 'this ... toy ... makes the owner feel just like Mum when taking her family for a walk'. That isn't all. In the barrow are what appear to be wooden blocks while in the pushchair there's a doll. The girl is standing, looking at the boy who seems just about to set off for somewhere.

But the world can be otherwise. The library service of the London Borough of Tower Hamlets has various playhouses — West Indian, Somali, Maltese and others — which they lend out to schools. These were made by local community groups and contain the appropriate household articles, furnishings and cooking utensils. To go with the houses, there are playclothes representing the traditional wear of the countries or regions in question. The contents of the houses, as well as the clothes, were also either made or provided by the local community groups. These play materials, I understand, are very popular and I certainly found them very attractive. Playhouses like these, representative of various lands and cultures, had appeared in several London boroughs by the spring of 1983 when I saw the ones from Tower Hamlets.

Playthings in the world outside

As we range further and further from the cradle, moving not only out of doors but to the public world outside, we come to consider playground equipment.

Anybody might think that swings, slides, rockers, climbing frames and the like would be about as neutral as you could get. I thought so, anyway, until a few years ago when, walking past a small recreation ground, I saw a metal climbing frame in the outline shape of a tank (see illustration). This gruesome object seemed to me such a gross abuse of small children that I felt I had to look into the matter.

It was made by SMP(Staines Metal Products) and supplied by them to the London Borough of Bromley. There are two, that I know of, in this borough. The tank, which is in tubular steel, has a very prominent gun and you can climb into the turret and pretend to fire it. There's not much else you can do, as it's very limited as a climbing frame. However, SMP claimed, in the 'Surveyor Supplement' pamphlet, dated 10 September 1981, which came with their catalogue, that this tank was so popular that a rival firm had copied it and they instanced this as 'perhaps another sign of the moral decline of the nation'. SMP were also producing a Fighter Jet climbing frame and two very simple climbing frames called Sentry and Policeman, though these two were not really recognizable as such. In April 1984, I heard that SMP had decided not to manufacture, in future, their Tank and Fighter Jet climbing frames. This seemed to me surprising, especially in view of the stated popularity of the Tank. I therefore wrote to the firm, explained what I was doing (preparing this book!), said I was glad to hear the news and asked for confirmation and, if it was true, the

3: Tank climbing frame

reason or reasons for the decision. I was thankful to receive a reply, as that's such an unusual event where the toy industry is concerned. The managing director informed me that the SMP Tank climbing frame had been copied by 'other manufacturers both in the UK and overseas'. He confirmed that the Tank had been dropped from the new catalogue, putting this down, simply, to 'progress', but added that it would be supplied on request. 'Progress' had also affected the Fighter Jet, which had been renamed Jet Plane.

Although I think there may be more to the story than that, we should give credit where it's due. The new developments do amount to progress and, while SMP must take responsibility for developing the Tank, as they claim, their rivals who've copied it cannot be excused.

I don't know whether Hunt International, another major supplier of playground equipment, is one of these but there's a tank in the price list sent with their catalogue in April1984. The tank wasn't illustrated. They have, as well, a Commando Bridge, a Commando Slide and Assault Poles and Bridge. An Assault Pole can also be supplied separately or it can be combined with the bridge and the slide. (This system, whereby the manufacturer makes elements which can be combined, is common with this kind of equipment and is in itself a good idea.) With this particular combination, you can climb up the Assault Pole by means of the vertical ladder attachments, then go across the Bridge, which is a horizontal ladder, and so onto the raised platform and finally down the slide.

I think I should say here that, apart from the tanks and a few other things, children wouldn't necessarily think of such equipment, just from the look of it, as having anything to do with military matters. However, if they'd seen army recruitment material or military propaganda documentaries, such as *The Paras* shown on BBC1 in early spring 1983, they'd be able to make the connections. A lot of this equipment is clearly based on the sort used in military training (although calling a slide 'Commando' seems quite unwarranted). Again, a lot depends on how playthings are mediated to children. In supervised playgrounds, children would presumably hear adults refer to this equipment by the names the manufacturer had given it.

Wicksteed have a Junior Commando Bridge, this time a semi-circular ladder, like half the outer rim of a large wheel, and a Senior Commando Bridge which is similar but less than half of a much larger circle. They also have a Racing Car climbing frame for little children and, amongst a lot of other equipment, the interesting-looking crane and lorry climbing frames.

Large mesh nets of rope or plastic-covered chain are common amongst playground equipment and they can be arranged in various ways for climbing. TP Activity Toys have a Giant Scrambler which they refer to as a 'commando frame' in the catalogue, while they describe the Commando Net as 'the beginning of a children's assault course'.

Such examples reveal the attitude of mind in which these manufacturers develop their products. It's worth remarking on, as well, that the military aspects noted here, apart from other considerations, suggest that the equipment in question is thought of as being mainly for boys.

A religious group, the Hutterian Society of Brothers, or Brüderhof Community, began in Germany after the first world war. It was later closed down and its members dispersed or imprisoned by the Gestapo. As the already mentioned Community Playthings company, they make a large range of strong, simple toys in plain wood, from large blocks, and the trundlers referred to above, to child-sized kitchen furnishings. There's also wooden, folding, playground equipment for children of nursery and infant age range. Recently, equipment with aluminium and stainless steel framework has been developed for older children. None of these products presents any of the kinds of problems mentioned in connection with similar playthings from other manufacturers. The group believes in communal living, the giving up of property and self-interest and, naturally, they're opposed to private enterprise. Few people, perhaps, could agree with their religious outlook, which seems to me particularly narrow and puritanical. Furthermore, it includes a sexist bias (the name of the society gives a clue to this) which is quite unacceptable. It's their other social views, however, which have found their way into the playthings they make and I mention these products here to indicate how toys and playthings are the result of attitudes and beliefs.

This is shown even more in the case of the Kompan firm which specializes in playground equipment and which opened up a British subsidiary in 1983. The aim of the firm is stated in their 1982 catalogue:

> Children must be given the opportunity to develop social skills through playing in groups. They need places to meet other children and to learn how to relate to others of their own age.

Although it's far from being the most important point about the tank climbing frame, I think it's worth mentioning, in connection with this question of relating to others socially, that only one person can fire the gun, and no doubt the strongest will claim the honour. Similar points can be made about the various helicopter and plane climbing frames that are about. They don't encourage playing in groups: they encourage competition.

Instead of the usual tubular steel, Kompan believe very strongly in wood for their equipment. It's a natural material, it doesn't hurt so much as concrete or metal if you fall on it and it doesn't get too hot or too cold. This well-thought-out approach is characteristic of the firm down to the smallest details. For instance, a special covering has been developed for the nuts and bolts in their equipment so that children cannot scratch themselves and vandals can't dismantle it. Great attention is paid to the surface of the wood and most large surfaces are in bright, warm colours.

This firm's originality of approach has already been noted in the case of the Moon Rover vehicle. It can be seen in their other equipment also and is most noticeable in the use of very heavy, strong springs to support rocking and bouncing, but fixed, mounts such as Crazy Hen, Crazy Beetle and Crazy Horse. There's an adult-sized Crazy Hen made specially, I think, for exhibitions such as that of the British

Educational Equipment Association, at which I enjoyed a ride on it. There's also a Spring Seesaw and a Multi-Seesaw on springs which has room for two or three children per side and which brings to mind Orlick's call for playground equipment to involve children in co-operation (see p. 16). These avoid the dangers of ordinary seesaws and a safety clamp ensures that fingers or toes can't be nipped in the springs. Amongst a lot of other things, there's a Steam Engine and a Railway Carriage, with wagons, for playing in and climbing on and also dens, houses and huts and climbing structures like Bridge Town. Kompan don't do any military playthings.

HAGS is a Swedish firm which specialises in playground equipment and which has Marleyplay as its British distributor. In outlook, there are similarities to Kompan, as the introduction to HAGS's 1982 catalogue makes clear:

> the products ... were constructed in order to stimulate activities beneficial to development, to encourage co-operation and, last but not least, for enjoyment. ... By means of good play equipment we want to contribute to a more human [sic] society — but also to create a relaxing environment which encourages togetherness between parents and children.

At that time HAGS were selling their equipment in twelve countries in Europe and Asia. Again, the structures are mainly of wood and there's a good amount of variation. For example, the Small Land play equipment system consists of ropes, tyres and large nets as well as platforms, railings, supports and slides.

In general, they seem to take in a slightly higher age range than Kompan, say from about five to nine years old. It goes without saying, I think, that HAGS don't make any military playthings, either. The 'commando nets' of the British firms are simply 'climbing nets' — a much better description — in the Kompan and HAGS catalogues (though HAGS do use 'assault course', in inverted commas, to describe a kind of ladder). My impression is that HAGS don't pay such great attention to detail as Kompan. Nuts and bolts are sometimes left exposed, on their Climbing Mast, for example, and these could possibly cause injury or, more likely perhaps, they could be unscrewed by vandals. I don't want to make too much of this. Bolts are countersunk on HAGS's equipment, when they're more likely to be in the way.

Those local authorities who cannot be touched by human compassion might be moved when considering the following price comparisons: SMP tank, fully painted (1981) — £1,147.00; HAGS sailing ship (1982) — £1,141.00 and Kompan car ferry (1982) — £1,040.00.

Now, we just have time to do a little shopping before going off to the fair!

The firm of R G Mitchell makes a range of Kiddie Ride machines. These are the ones you see, usually just inside the entrance to department stores and supermarkets. You put money in to give the children a ride and it either takes some of the pressure off parents doing the shopping or adds extra demands. I'm not sure which. What is clear is that children get little relief from the ideological barrage which seems to follow them everywhere they go.

Several of the machines represent animals, in more or less traditional fairground style and then, of course, there's the Mini Fire Engine. So far, so good. A little fantasizing by means of the Space Scout and Sky Rider can't do much harm, either, so long as you can get your feet on the ground when necessary. The racing cars, Lotus Ford, Red Flash and Hot Rod signal different messages, however, especially when they have engine sound effects. These are for racing and competing and are generally thought to be more in a boy's line. There's also a Scrambler motor bike with sound effects, and the Submarine has visual effects as well. Submarines are used in war.

It may seem obvious, but I think it's very important to note how many of these vehicles and spacecraft reflect other kinds of playthings, especially die-cast toys.

Lastly, we come to festival or fairground amusements, taking some examples from the May Day Festival for Peace in Victoria Park, Hackney in 1983. No fair is complete, these days, without inflatables and they're great fun. Children enjoy bouncing on them, seemingly for hours. Here, there was one of Wicksteed's. They do several, and the three standard designs are each produced in four basic sizes, the smallest of which is 6.4m by 6.4m. The Castle of Fun is one of these standard designs. It's a platform, reached in two steps, with walls on three sides and towers, on which are enormous guardsmen, at the corners. Fort Playtime is a similar construction, this time with cowboy and 'indian' stereotypes on the towers. Happy Dome, again similar, presents us with bears in dresses juggling balls. All very familiar, tired old images.

On the same day, I chanced to notice a roundabout which did have a few of the traditional animals but these were dominated by a fire engine, a police vehicle and two tanks. At the Festival for Peace! Not that I blame the organizers. I wouldn't expect them to anticipate things like this. Probably, even if they did, they would find that, if you had roundabouts, you probably had to have tanks, or something just as obnoxious.

There were also lucky dips in Victoria Park, in separate barrels for girls and boys.

Later in the same month I went to the Tower Hamlets play day for the under fives. This, like the Festival, was excellent and provided enjoyment and opportunities for gaining awareness in pleasant ways. I congratulate the organizers of both events.

Next time, however, I suggest they might keep a closer watch, if possible, on what fairground people are up to. At the Tower Hamlets play day, one roundabout had a Prince Charles railway engine and a Lady Di ship on it; another had, alongside two 'fire trucks', two Knight Rider cars and two police cars; and a third roundabout included two armoured cars with guns.

I hope that this brief survey of a vast field will help to show how certain attitudes and assumptions, which I pointed to at the outset, can persist and take many different forms in many different, but typical and representative, toys and playthings. I've ranged far and wide because I wanted to show how children are surrounded by an ideology which, in my opinion, can only be harmful to them in the world of today. Of course, I'm quite aware that many people will disagree with me and won't see anything wrong with some or perhaps most of the attitudes and assumptions I've detected in the examples I've used. However that may be, I trust that nobody will be able to deny that such attitudes and assumptions — those to do with gender, race and class, the establishment and the environment — are actually there, embodied in the kinds of toys and playthings I've been dealing with.

CHAPTER 3

THE HOUSEWIFE AND MOTHER

Playthings can help to influence children in many ways but, overwhelmingly, they divide boys and girls along sex lines. We've already seen this happening amongst toys and playthings for very young children. Now, for boys and girls, the paths divide and seldom merge.

First, we follow, for two chapters, the path along which girls are led, or pushed. On the way, we'll keep in touch with the other attitudes and values already pointed out — to do with race and class, for instance — but, mainly, we're now concerned with the question of gender roles. Perhaps I'd better remind readers that I'll use the word 'sex' when referring to biological differences, to females and males, to boys and girls, and the word 'gender' when referring to the roles, usually called 'feminine' and 'masculine', that society has traditionally allotted to the two sexes. As far as anyone has been able to discover, there's no biological or psychological basis for these roles but, as I'll show eventually, there's a political one.

The housewife role and the mother role (here I use the word, 'mother' in a social, not a biological sense) obviously overlap, not only because they both involve caring for or looking after others but also because activities like shopping and cooking cannot be looked on as separate from cither.

Running the home

You can get toy shopper trolleys, for instance from Santos. Their leaflet, in German, French, Spanish and English, shows a photo of a girl with one. The firm of Peter Pan Playthings produce a Supermarket Set which has on it 'learn to shop like mummy' while Pedigree's All Action Fridge is described in the catalogue as 'just right for the young mum'. Superjouet produce items for the kitchen such as a cooker and a sink unit. On the boxes, the French is translated into English, not very happily, as My First Stove and My First Sink. These are intended for ages four to eight and both the catalogue illustrations and pictures on the boxes show girls. This firm also produces blenders, mixers, coffee grinders and percolators either separately or in sets as well as various pastry-making sets. Berwick's Kitchen Set, consisting of pots, pans and cooking utensils, shows a girl on the box. So does their 'Mother's Little Helper' Pastry Set, only this time the box shows mother as well and tells us 'It's fun to help mum'. Press and promotional photos carry the same messages, as with the Lil' Lady Hob from Milton Bradley (see illustration, p. 46).

4: Lil' Lady Hob

5: Model Kitchen

Such toys are all quite typical and are produced in great numbers and variety by many firms in the western world. The West German firm of Schopper, for instance, produces kitchen units (see illustration) in 13 different designs. These are for children to play with themselves or via dolls of about 30cm tall. Schopper also have many sets of kitchen utensils. Girls are shown on the boxes and one smaller kitchen set comes with a model — a male chef.

The same firm has 22 tea or coffee sets. (Now that the shopping and cooking have been done, the meals have to be served!) Again, the catalogues and packaging show, and tell us, that these are meant for girls. It would be tiresome and unnecessary to give every example of this general practice so you can take it that this applies to almost all the toys mentioned in this chapter.

Instead let's note some other points. There are links with film, television and fiction — for instance, in Combex's Donald Duck, Mickey Mouse, Sooty and Noddy tea sets. These are meant for younger children and the designs, on the boxes and on the crockery, show these characters and others associated with them.

Amongst Superjouet's 38 dinner, coffee, tea and other services, there are also some for small children, but the one in 'décor Louis XV' with its silver-looking serving dish and two candelabra and some other similar sets would seem to be pointing more in the direction of class. So would Berwick's Lady Jane tea sets, first brought out in 1983. The box of one set shows Lady Jane carrying a trug with roses in it. She has a cat at her feet. Another box shows her with a pair of dogs and a third shows her in riding dress with a horse. Other buttons are being pressed here, as well. (Girls love flowers and care for animals.)

Then, there's house cleaning and the washing to be dealt with. A woman's work is never done! However, I was interested to see what Gary, a boy of about seven or eight at a London junior school, had to say:

> When I was young I wanted a toy hoover but my mum said no and I asked why and she said its for girls. i was crying and I went to bed and she was angry with me.

I was luckier than Gary, when I was no more than about three or four, as I had a toy carpet sweeper which I remember being very fond of. Perhaps it needs to be said that there's nothing wrong with these kinds of toys, as such, and it's quite natural for children to want to mimic the adult world. What is wrong is that these toys are marketed, and usually thought of, as being exclusively for girls. So, human potential is narrowed down, not widened.

As with other kinds of housework, there's almost nothing from the adult world that doesn't have a toy counterpart. Galts have a clothes airer and an ironing board, as well as a dustpan with, interestingly, a Cinderella design on it. Sharna Tri-ang's

Clean-up Trolly has many accessories including a bucket (decorated with flower transfers), sponge, dustpan and brush (see illustration).

Berwick, in their housework sets, make another kind of link — a commercial one — with the adult world. They tend to link these sets with branded goods. So, there's the Persil Washday Set showing mother and daughter on the box which announces "washday fun with Persil and mum".

Sometimes, a whole collection of toys is given a gender label, as with Wells Kelo's Mini Mum range. The logo carrying this name showed a girl's face and hands until 1982. For 1983, it was changed and showed a girl and boy, holding hands. Ever hopeful, I asked a sales representative whether this meant a move in the direction of sex equality on the part of the company, but he told me it was just a refurbishing. Of course, the name of the range — mainly of Hoovers (another commercial link), cleaning sets and shoppers — stayed the same anyway, as did the promotional language.

Abroad, the general picture is the same. The West German firm of Klein had 22 house-cleaning sets in their 1981 catalogue. These included such items as brushes, dustpans, feather dusters, carpet sweepers and mops, in various permutations. Several of these were being marketed under the firm's logo of the rosy-cheeked Miss Caroline in her apron and mob-cap. There were eight Miss Caroline broom sets available in Britain in 1983 and also 12 washing and cleaning sets, as well as odd brooms, carpet sweepers, vacuum cleaners and the like, most of them presented under the same logo. Superjouet have similar sets, interestingly under the Victoria Plum name (I'll be dealing with her later in the chapter) and with a Victoria Plum design.

Dekker, for their cleaning sets, use the name and character of Roger Hargreaves's Little Miss Helpful from his series of early story books. Again, we need to notice such links which help to ensure that children are surrounded by an environment of consistent attitudes and values. And of course — as if to underline the gender role — there are housework sets for dolls, also: that is, there are doll-sized toys as well as child-sized ones.

Now, it's on to making and mending. There's no time to sit down! Toy sewing machines have been popular for a long time, at least from the end of the nineteenth century, and a German one, the 'Westfalia' dating from about 1910, can be seen in the Edinburgh Museum of Childhood. There are usually several on the market at any one time, some of them, like Berwick's Sew Easy, having special safety features as they're intended for very young girls. There are five in the Petite range (1983) from Byron International (for which Mettoy are the sales agents). One of these is in the Sewing Activity Centre which includes various other accessories and also a booklet 'A Complete Guide to Sewing' which shows a (real or pretend) mother and daughter picture on the front cover. Another model, for very young children, sews paper without the use of needles.

6:   Clean-up Trolly

Knitting and sewing sets and also all kinds of handicraft sets are available and are almost invariably thought of in the toy trade as being for girls. Spears produce a lot of these sets and, even if we didn't have the usual information and illustrations making it clear they're intended for girls, the names of some of the sets act as further signals. The tapestry sets, for example, all go under the name of Penelope while, apart from anything else, it's unlikely that boys would take a second look at sets called My Pet Hankies and Knitting Nancy. Berwick and Dekker are other firms which produce a lot of handicraft sets. On the one hand, it's a pity that so many of these push girls in rather trivial and uncreative directions — making 'charms', 'jewelry' and paper flowers, for instance, or mechanically following instructions, as with Dekker's Paint a Plaque sets. On the other hand, it's a pity that boys will feel excluded from the more creative and useful pursuits, such as weaving, knitting and other kinds of woolcraft.

Girls are 'busy'. The kind of sets I've been talking about come under the general title, on all the boxes, of 'Busy Hands' and fall within a section of that name in Berwick's 1983 catalogue. Their Dolly Bobbin Set is advertised as being 'for busy little girls' and they say that 'little girls can be kept busy' with their Super Woolcraft Set.

It's instructive to note where the lines are drawn. Berwick's Potters' Workshop set is advertised as being 'for both boys and girls' while a boy and a girl are both pictured on the box of the Colour Pegs Picture Set advertised as providing 'creative and educational fun for both boys and girls'. Fortunately, there are exceptions to the general rule. The six Cottage Craft Bags and three First Craft Bags from Anne Wilkinson Designs are presented as being for both girls and boys. The First Craft Bags say so and each shows a boy and girl.

Baby dolls

There are no hard and fast categories, of course, but dolls can be thought of as being in three main groups: baby and small child or toddler dolls which are meant to be looked after and cared for; then, the ones I'll refer to as companion dolls, that is, dolls that a child can relate to more as a friend than as a 'mother'; and, lastly, teenage or fashion dolls. (It's worth noting that there are very few dolls of older people.) I'll be especially concerned with the first of these groups in this chapter as baby and toddler dolls obviously relate to the mother role. However, I'll also have something to say here about companion dolls, so as to make links with fashion dolls in the next chapter and also to show that certain themes, values and ideas continue through all the groups.

The group of baby and small child dolls is, I would say, easily the largest. Competition amongst manufacturers for the vast market has led to all sorts of gimmicks and an ever-increasing realism (which usually involves ever-decreasing scope for the imagination).

We can see this process at work, even in the very early stages of commercial production. Dolls with moving eyes, for instance, appeared in England in about 1825. By the middle of the nineteenth century, the poorer class of dolls had painted eyes and hair while upper class dolls had glass eyes and attached hair. At this time, toy-making was still a cottage industry — that is, certain families were toy makers and worked in their homes. Mass production of toys, and all that it entailed, didn't really begin until this century. In recent years, there have been some strange developments, though Baby Pattaburps, from the US firm of Mattel, was around in 1966. The advertisements said that she drank her milk and then burped after being patted tenderly on the back. Matchbox's Little Baby Burps was on the go in 1979 but had disappeared by 1983. The scene nowadays is varied, to say the least. Fairly typical is Blossom's Baby Cry, a 'crying, drinking and wetting doll'. Their Baby Laugh and Cry has a battery operated voice box. If you lay the baby down and take the dummy out of her mouth, she cries. When you pick her up, she laughs until you put the dummy back.

The Spanish firm of Famosa have a baby doll which dribbles and blows bubbles as well as drinking and wetting. This is one of the damper sorts of doll. Another Spanish firm, Berjusa, produce Minene, a life-sized baby doll which sucks a dummy and, rather weirdly, moves its head without making a sound. The same firm produces the Dulce Marra dolls, one white and one in blackface. These are dolls with dolls. You put the smaller doll into the arms of the larger one which then walks and sings a lullaby. (Past the baby stage, walking and talking dolls are quite common.) The Berjusa firm had 17 foreign representatives in 1983 so these dolls, and all that they suggest, must have got around a bit. Yet another Spanish firm, Vicma, has gone in for realism in a very determined sort of way. Their doll, Dany, drinks from a feeding bottle, wets herself and then gets a nappy rash which can be made to disappear by the application of some cream. The straighforwardly-named Pis-Pipí wets himself and moves his head when you press his body. Apparently, these two are no longer manufactured, and Naricitas, who had a runny nose and Besucón, who belched, seem also to have disappeared. A representative of the firm told me they used to have a doll that did 'big jobs' (i.e. shat) but this was just another gimmick that, in time, gave way to others. Now, there's a doll which makes mouth movements and moves its head as it sucks, and boy and girl dolls that cry and stop when you tell them to. There's a device in the ear. The one I tried always started crying again as soon as I put it down and I couldn't stop it. Very realistic. Then, Vicma have twin dolls which cry when separated and stop when put together. If one drinks from its bottle, the other cries until given a bottle as well. These examples give some idea of the range of gimmicks, usual and not so usual, that have been tried.

The West German firm of Zapf make a great many dolls, including a lot of baby dolls. Some of these have genitals or, as it's sometimes expressed, are 'sexed'. This, with regard to realism, would seem to be an important question, yet not many dolls have genitals. Even the wetting dolls generally just have a hole at the bottom end somewhere. It seems to me that most baby and toddler dolls, especially if they're meant to be dressed and undressed, should be realistic in this way even if only because the absence of genitals seems to suggest there's something wrong about such parts of the body. Fashion dolls and dolls representing older people never have genitals, of course, but with these I think the case is different as the genitals of adults are private in a way that those of babies and very small children are not. Nevertheless, it's a fairly open question.

Realism, as thought of in the doll trade, gives rise to other questions, as well. Many baby dolls come with a dummy. When you remove it, they start crying and stop when you put it back. But the use of a dummy merely as a device for shutting up the baby can be questioned. Pedigree have a variant. If you remove the dummy from Baby Fuss a Lot's mouth she'll 'writhe' until it's put back.

The matter of race brings in another kind of realism. How realistic is it if almost all dolls are white? And how realistic is it if most of the others are identical with the white dolls, apart from the colour and perhaps the hair? What sort of a picture of the world does this convey? Fortunately, several firms have made responsible attempts to face up to the situation and I'll concentrate on these.

Vicma, the firm already mentioned, have made a serious attempt with black dolls. They worked from 60 photos to get the facial features right. Then, from 18 of these, they got an 'average' by the use of something called a pantograph. Three black dolls were made, the same apart from size and, in two of the sizes, there were male and female pairs distinguished by dress. Gino and Gina, Eva and Liza and Jon all look good and they cost the same as their white counterparts. The black dolls from Zapf — there was one, curiously named Little Cloud, in 1982 and a second was added the following year — also look good, and have features and hair different from those of the white dolls. Again, Angelo Negro, a black doll from the Cicciobello range of the Italian firm, Sebino, isn't simply a white doll in blackface but one with different features and hair. For some unknown reason, the name is translated into English as Little Angel, instead of Black Angel which would have been much more meaningful. You can get either a laughing or a crying version, they're about 45cm tall and are of about toddler age. In the catalogue, pleasantly, a white girl is shown feeding Black Angel. Sebino also produce a nice-looking Chinese doll.

However, perhaps the most all-round attempt at ethnically correct dolls has been made by Dandolls, the toy division of the Danish firm DVP (Dansk Vacuum Plastic). They've produced a group of toddler dolls, all 42cm tall and made of vinyl. The group, called Children of the World, consists of pairs of girl and boy dolls from South America, Europe, India and China and there's also a black and a native American pair (see illustration). Earlyplay market these dolls in Britain. In all of them, a good attempt has been made to create racially accurate features and hair. Skin colour is very good overall, though not so successful, I think, in the case of the Chinese pair which are an orangey-yellow shade. The female dolls, in most cases, have eyelashes and red lips. In mid-1986, the Children of the World were produced in 'anatomical' versions, as they say in the trade. Dandolls also make some white ones and another black pair, Joseph and Josephine, with genitals. These two also have sleeping eyes and, as Andy and Mandy, are supplied, undressed, as the Children of the World usually are, to schools. Most recently, Dandolls have produced an excellent set of Nigerian dolls and, all in all, this collection shows a serious effort on the part of the manufacturer to meet the challenge of a very important kind of realism.

It's rather odd that, in this context of race, it's been Spanish, West German, Italian and Danish firms who've been making the running and there isn't a very sizeable

7:   Children of the World

non-white presence in any of the countries concerned. DVP's biggest foreign market for their Children of the World group of dolls is the USA.

Now, we should note certain commercial developments in connection with baby and toddler dolls. Some have expanded into large ranges with outfits and accessories of all kinds. So, consumerism is promoted and a link made with other dolls, notably fashion dolls.

In 1965, Tiny Tears was born to the firm of Palitoy. She measured about 40cm. As a drinking, crying and wetting doll which blew bubbles, she must, at that time, have been just about the dampest doll ever. Her little sister, Teeny Tiny Tears, was born not long afterwards but appears to have died at an early age. Deluxe Tiny Tears, with a realistic sucking action, came along in 1982. At that time, you could get a Care Set, a carry-cot which could be converted into a feeding chair or nappy changing tray and a Merry-Go-Pushchair (in which *two* seated dolls could revolve, to the tune of a built-in music box, as they were pushed along). Then, there were 10 ordinary outfits, four of them new that year, and three 'de luxe' outfits which came with accessories for feeding time, bath time and the beach. There were two assortments, one of clothing and one including items such as a bath and a 'potty'. Finally, there were packs of bottles and 'soothers'. In 1983, Tiny Tears got a remoulded face and became vanilla-scented. She also got 14 new outfits and two nursery assortments. A Tiny Tears club was started.

First Love, from Pedigree, is a similar kind of project. She was brought out in 1976 (or 77, some say) as the firm wanted a baby doll with the consumer possibilities of their fashion doll, Sindy — that is, with lots of accessories and outfits. First Love measured 40cm. In 1982, there were two versions: First Love Feeding, Crying and Wetting and Poseable First Love. She had a large array of outfits (which would also fit other baby dolls of the same size) as well as a Bath Time Set, a Change Set, a Dropside Cot and a high chair which converted into a swing. In addition, she had a push-chair, a pram and a high chair of matching design and with floral decorations. New in 1982 were a Babycare Set, with all sorts of accessories, and a Babycare Centre, also with accessories. This was meant to promote 'collector possibilities'. Accessories of this kind are not only added to each year but are changed as well. So, the high chair/swing of 1982 replaced the Multi-Purpose Chair of 1979, which had converted to a high chair, a low chair, a chair and table or a car seat with safety harness. First Love's Rocking Cot of 1979 was replaced by a cot on four legs. And so it goes on. It's interesting that, in 1983, First Love got an entirely new face. (Tiny Tears' remoulded face, in the same year, didn't amount to much of a change, however.) As usual, in 1984, outfits and accessories were added to in the by now well-established pattern. In fact, First Love, like Tiny Tears, is less of a doll and more of a range. This is even more obviously the case when you consider that there were, in 1984, five First Love dolls on the scene: Crying and Wetting First Love, Cuddly Baby, Baby Precious, Baby Posey and the new arrival, the 'completely waterproof' Bath-time Baby First Love.

Other firms produce baby doll accessory sets and items, presumably, or mainly, for dolls which don't have their own. Bambola, for instance, have 'potty' sets, dolls' baths and feeding sets while Casdon have a Baby Bathtime set with 'potty and bath

54

styled for the '80s', a Doll's Changing Set and even a dolls' Hospital Bed. Superjouet have several Baby Nurse sets, in portable cases, with the usual accessories for baby care. Bell have their Miss Merry's Diaper Bag Set and Wash 'N' Change Set and Klein have 11 Miss Caroline dolls' care sets.

Then, of course, there are all the prams and push-chairs which are sold as separate items. The Italian firm of Bieffe have a very large range of these as well as cots, beds and ironing boards for dolls. As with other items, girls can have their own, child-sized ironing boards, in imitation of (mother's) full-sized one, then their dolls can have ironing boards and presumably their dolls' dolls could also have ironing boards. It's like a hall of mirrors or, perhaps, a jail. Wesba had 20 prams, seven carry-cots and a push-chair in their 1981 leaflet, together with some accessories. There were 16 new models of prams in that year. Some prams from RF Development are said to be for children of as little as fourteen months old, which brings to mind again that succession of mirrors, with the reflections getting ever smaller.

After all this, it may seem surprising to learn that dolls representing babies, rather than older children or adults, haven't been around for very long. The historical evidence I've seen is rather conflicting but it does seem that baby dolls developed, gradually, in the nineteenth century. Certainly, in the large collection at the Bethnal Green Museum of Childhood, most are companion rather than baby dolls and there's a sprinkling of adults.

There can be no innate desire on the part of children, either girls or boys, to play with baby dolls. I don't see anything wrong in it, especially if it encourages children to care for others. What we've seen here, however, has more to do with the creation of unnecessary wants in the search for ever-bigger profits than with any genuine concern for children.

And let's not forget that these dolls are directed exclusively towards girls. Children soon get the message. Here's Ben, aged five, talking with his teacher, Mara Chrystie, at a London infants' school in 1982. Polly is his sister, then aged eight, and another child, Vareina, adds a comment towards the end:

Mara: And which toys don't you like here?

Ben: The darts and the pram and the dollies.

Mara: Why don't you like them?

Ben: Because I haven't got a baby at home to put them in my pram.

Mara: Would you like to have one at home?

Ben: No, I like playing my football best of all with my dad.

Mara: Have you got any dolls or prams at home?

Ben: No, they're all Polly's ha ha ha ha!

55

Mara: What does Polly do?

Ben: She's made a — my dad's made a cot for Polly's baby, my mum's knitted a cover for Polly's baby, my granny's bought a cover for the baby and my mum's bought a cushion for the baby for its cot.

Mara: Is it a real baby or a doll?

Ben: A doll.

Mara: Would you like to play with it sometimes?

Ben: Yes — no, I don't.

Mara: You don't?

Ben: No, I don't because I'm the dad. I must only hold her when she's crying and mummy — Polly — isn't here.

Mara: But when Polly's here don't you hold her?

Ben: No, Polly has to hold her then.

Vareina: You said you're a dad.

Mara: If you're a dad why don't you look after the baby too?

Ben: Because Polly has to look after her. Polly has to get her dressed, she has to put her in her nightie, she has to put her to bed, but Polly and me have to stay up later than Polly's doll which she's made, which she's got.

It's interesting that, in answer to the question 'Would you like to play with it sometimes?' Ben, for a moment, forgets his role.

Companion dolls and dolls' houses

The second main group of dolls — a very varied one — is companion dolls. These overlap considerably with the first group of dolls and can represent ages ranging from toddlers to, say, 10- or 11-year-olds. The younger ones share some of the characteristics of baby dolls — they're meant to be cared for and looked after — while the older ones point towards the teenage dolls. I want to single out, however, the ones that children can regard as friends and through which they can act out stories. In fact, this fictional element is, perhaps, the main thing that distinguishes this group from baby dolls. Psychologically, companion dolls seem to fulfil some of the needs that, for instance, teddy bears or children's imaginary friends do.

Victoria Plum is typical of certain dolls in this group and also gives a good illustration of how commercial interests are interwoven. She's a woodland fairy in a floral dress and with a Hedge Bindweed flower for a hat, and she started as a greeting card character in 1978. In 1981, several firms began to market Victoria Plum products under licence and, to coincide with these developments and promote the products, Purnell published four picture books featuring Victoria Plum, each with an initial print run of 50,000 copies. Angela Rippon, the former television news reader, had been asked to write the stories for these. There were also Victoria Plum clothes, lampshades, toiletries and stationery and, by 1983, Combex had a tricycle, a pram and a push-chair with Victoria Plum designs. H Schelhorn, under their Telitoy trade name, make the rather attractive dolls in four different sizes, along with other Victoria Plum products including the Play Scene with Victoria Plum's tree house and garden.

Palitoy's Strawberry Shortcake also originated in the greeting card world and illustrates, in addition, how a cult is developed. The magazine, *Toys International and the Retailer* reported as follows in January 1981:

> Strawberry Shortcake is currently the new cult in the States. With new mini dolls, the Purple Pieman, a range of new outfits, three rag dolls, figurines, card games and the Strawberry Musical Carousel all launched this year and supported by two national television campaigns, comic campaigns, full point-of-sale support and an active in-store promotion, the World of Strawberry Shortcake is destined to be a success in the UK too.

Other firms were joining in with Strawberry Shortcake merchandise such as scented gift tags, paper plates, stationery, books, jewelry and ice cream. All were aimed at the three- to six-year-old group and were claimed to have 'obvious cult-building effects for the concept'.

Strawberry Shortcake is a cartoon-type, little girl doll with a strawberry theme in the design of her dress. Her many 'friends' include Huckleberry Pie, Lemon Meringue, Raspberry Tart and Orange Blossom, who is the one token black doll. Their dress also matches their names in colour, decoration and so on. In 1982, they each got a pet. Strawberry Shortcake's was Custard, a cat, while Raspberry Tart got a monkey called Rhubarb. The mini dolls, of smaller size, are scented and smell like the fruits in their names. Accessories, all in the same fantastic vein, are, for instance, the Snail Cart 'pulled by Escargot the super snail' and Flitter-bit, the Strawberry Shortcake Butterfly. Two of the mini dolls can ride on it.

The whole vast system shows the trend towards themes which is a typical development of recent years. It seems to me that there are two characteristics of the theme approach. One is that it's meant to encourage collecting — fairly obviously — and the other is a fictional element. Palitoy, for instance, refer to 'the strong linked story line ... behind the whole world of Strawberry Shortcake'. Here, as I'll show, this goes beyond the simple theme of food — so dear to children's hearts, or stomachs, especially when it's sweet food like fruit cakes and pies.

With regard to collecting, dolls are produced in various sizes in the overall Strawberry Shortcake range. As well as the mini dolls, for instance, there are also miniature dolls. 'Lots of fun to collect' the 1982 catalogue says and 24 more of these 'collectable' dolls were added in 1983, making 36 in all. Then, in 1983, the

Strawberry Shortcake Baby Doll was introduced, along with Baby Apricot and Baby Lemon Meringue. Each blew a scented 'kiss' when squeezed. In the same year, a new line on mini dolls was started, the idea being, so it seemed, to develop some kind of national theme. So, we got the Spanish Café Olé and Burrito the donkey and the French Crêpe Suzette with her poodle Eclair.

The fictional aspect is promoted by having, in the range, Strawberry Shortcake's 'friendly foe', the Peculiar Purple Pieman of Porcupine Peak, who has a rather evil-looking little bird as his pet. He was joined in 1983 by a woman, Sour Grapes, with her pet, Dregs, the snake. So, there's a basis for conflict, the essential ingredient of all stories. The story element is also furthered by sets such as the Gazebo Garden House and the Berry Bake Shoppe which are obviously meant to be places where stories can happen. It was not surprising, in view of this kind of development, to see that a Strawberry Shortcake comic was to be brought out in 1983 and given away free to buyers. It told the story of Strawberry Shortcake in Big Apple City.

The worlds of toys and fiction have always been close and there's always been a to-ing and fro-ing between them. I think that play, as a whole, can be seen as fictions acted out — either directly, as with playclothes, or indirectly, through the medium of toys. As far as dolls are concerned, the fictions that are possible range from dramatic role play closely modelled on real life, as with baby dolls, to the fantasies prompted by Victoria Plum and, even more, by Strawberry Shortcake. This question of fiction is something that I'll be returning to later.

A Swiss woman, Sasha Morgenthaler, designed the Sasha dolls having in mind, it's said, 'a vision of how a child would look and move in the age of innocence', whatever that means. The Sasha dolls and their brother Gregor all have the same wistful look, the boys and girls being differentiated mainly by hair style and dress, though six of the outfits that could be bought in 1982 were for either boys or girls, which is a very welcome development. There are a few dolls in blackface but an attempt has been made to make their hair realistic. I'd say the Sasha dolls are typical of the companion group and the range, made by Trendon Toys, is refreshingly free from the outlandish kind of business manoeuvres I've been describing in connection with other dolls. Undoubtedly, the main emphasis is on outfits, and smart and stylish ones at that. However, the do-it-yourself clothes kits, to cut out and sew, are a move in the right direction and, as there are very few accessories and no playsets, these dolls — unlike Strawberry Shortcake and friends — leave a lot to the imagination. This certainly makes a welcome change.

In some of the companion dolls, we can see some familiar attitudes and values being continued or developed. Even in the case of baby dolls, we could see a determined effort, on the part of manufacturers, to preoccupy girls with clothes and fashion, with having different outfits for different occasions. This is carried on in the companion dolls as well.

Pedigree's Belinda Jane wears a 'fine flower print dress with tucks and lace trim on bodice, sleeves and hem ... under a broderie anglaise pinafore also trimmed in white lace'. Others in the 1979 catalogue have similar detailed descriptions. The Miss Pedigree range, in the same catalogue, has dolls in garden party, cocktail, evening and Ascot dresses. 'A touch of class' the catalogue so rightly says. The cocktail dress is a 'full length backless gown .... made of glittering pink lurex. The transparent toned poncho has a feather boa edging.' Dolls such as this also take us virtually into the teenage fashion doll area but her the class element seems to me much more important. The Amanda Jane range, produced by the firm of that name (which became Pemmay Designs in 1985), shows very well how links are made with dolls for younger and also older children. Amanda Jane herself is clearly a companion doll and represents a child of about five years old. She's intended for girls of about three to eight years old. The idea of many different outfits for different occasions is pushed and, along with this, comes 'a touch of class' and establishment values. Amanda Jane has Brownie, Riding and Ballet outfits and a Bridesmaid's Dress. She has other accessories, as well, including the very necessary wardrobe. The 'older' doll, Miss Amanda Jane, almost take us into the fashion doll world. In fact, it seems that an attempt is being made to bridge two worlds here. Miss Amanda Jane still looks a child, though she has a 'range of more sophisticated outfits' including a Weekend Set and a Dinner Gown and Stole. Amanda Jane Baby takes us back to the baby doll world. She, again, has various outfits and accessories. There are blackface versions of Amanda Jane and Amanda Jane Baby.

At this stage, dolls' houses come to the fore and we pick up the earlier theme of housekeeping, though dolls' houses carry other notions as well, the most important being to do with class.

In fact, dolls' houses have upper-class origins and, as we'll see, the associations of this historical background still live on. The earliest examples in England date from around the beginning of the eighteenth century and were made by the carpenters (the 'lower' classes did the work, of course) on the large country estates. They also made miniature furniture to go in the houses, in addition to carriages and farm wagons. There's some doubt about how far these houses were toys and how far novelties, items for display. They'd originated, in Germany and Holland, as display cabinets or small rooms, in which valuable miniature objects, often of silver, could be shown off. By about the middle of the nineteenth century, as the following extract from *The Cricket on the Hearth* shows, there had been considerable developments. Dickens is describing the workroom of Caleb Plummer and his blind daughter Bertha, the toymakers. The whole passage is worth quoting:

There were houses in it [the workroom], finished and unfinished, for Dolls of all stations in life. Suburban tenements for Dolls of moderate means; kitchens and single apartments for Dolls of the lower classes; capital town residences for Dolls of high estate. Some of these establishments were already furnished according to estimate, with a view to the convenience of Dolls of limited income; others could be fitted on the most expensive scale, at a moment's notice, from whole shelves of chairs and tables, sofas, bedsteads, and upholstery. The nobility and gentry and public in general, for whose accommodation these tenements were designed, lay, here and there, in baskets, staring straight up at the ceiling; but in denoting their degrees in society, and confining them to their respective stations (which experience shows to be lamentably difficult in real life), the makers of these Dolls had far improved on Nature, who is often froward and perverse; for they, not resting on such arbitrary marks as satin, cotton-print, and bits of rag, had superadded striking personal differences which allowed of no mistake. Thus, the Doll-lady of Distinction had wax limbs of perfect symmetry; but only she and her compeers; the next grade in the social scale being made of leather; and the next of coarse linen stuff. As to the common people, they had just so many matches out of tinder-boxes for their arms and legs, and there they were — established in their sphere at once, beyond the possibility of getting out of it.[1]

As we'll see, things haven't changed in any very fundamental ways.

In 1979, Tiger Toys had a Queen Anne Dolls' Mansion as well as the 'thatched' and 'timbered' Gingerbread Cottage, described as 'a " get away from it all" weekend cottage for dolls who are fed up with town life'. Lovell Toys produce a Georgian Manor House and a Tudor Hall with furniture to match, all in one twelfth scale. The firm stresses 'quality' and the fact that the dolls' houses are 'hand built'. Better known, however, is the Caroline's House range from Barton Toys. They've been producing dolls' house furniture for about 34 years, were exporting to more that 20 countries in 1980, and also stress the 'quality' of their products. The Caroline's Home Dolls' House is obviously a luxury one. But then, there's also a Super De Luxe version and a Chalet. The vast array of boxed sets contains furnishings and fittings for the various rooms of the houses. For instance, you can get a Regency Dining Set and three different lounges — the Windsor, Sandringham and Buckingham. With these, the manufacturer is obviously playing on the mainly royal associations of the names. Many items can be bought separately. For example, 18 different dolls' house lamps are available. (The houses have electrical circuits.) Certain accessories point up the class element further: Old Master Paintings, a Silver Tea Set, a Champagne for Two Set and a set containing two crystal wall lamps and a gilt-edged mirror. Here, however, we move down the social ladder, from royalty to the merely upper class. The Hound and Pups Set also has a point to make. The whole range is expensive, as anybody might expect, but was selling quite well at Harrods in December 1982, judging by a half-empty display stand. The dolls' houses and furnishings from the Swedish firm of Lundby are also aimed at small social climbers. You can get a Manor House, a Luxury Villa (and a garage extension with stable, if desired). There's a Lounge Elegance IV, a Dining Room Classic with a 'period' set of furniture, though it doesn't say which period, and a Lounge Symphony. Brass table lamps and chandeliers are also available. You can get doll house families to go with both Caroline's Home and the Lundby system. These are white and consist, naturally, of mother, father, boy and girl. In the Lundby system, grandfather and grandmother can be added.

The overall point to be made here is that these examples of dolls' houses and furnishings have a great deal to do with the indoctrination of particular social attitudes and not very much to do with children's play, as such. In particular, the amount of detail in these products must set severe limits on the imagination. Some other dolls' houses and sets of furniture on the market, fortunately show a very different approach.

The Abbatts' Roundabout dolls' house, for example, is meant to be slotted together to form a roofed but open-sided, four-roomed house on a circular base of about 45cm in diameter. This can be moved round on a pivot, thus giving good access for play. The Openside Dolls' House designed by R Limbrick and marketed by Galt is also meant to be assembled and has eight intercommunicating rooms, thus allowing several children to play together. It has a detachable roof in two sections but no outer walls. Galt's Simple Dolls' House lives up to its name as it consists of two pieces of wood which form the inner walls of the rooms and which have cut-out doors and windows. These pieces slot into one another at right angles to form four open rooms. There's neither roof nor outer walls but different ground plans are possible depending on how the pieces are slotted together. The Susan Wynter dolls' house, available to educational institutions from Arnold, is another open-sided, eight-roomed house. Dolls' houses such as these all encourage real play and imagination, instead of social rituals, and they also make it easier for children to play together and relate to one another.

Several sets of furniture in solid wood, some painted, some plain, are available to go with these houses. These vary in the amount of detail, though there's never much and, of course, there's none of the tiresome fussiness of the Caroline's Home furniture. Instead, the designers of this furniture have tried to get past the detail and down to simple, basic shapes. The most simplified and attractive I've come across are the Susan Wynter First Furniture Set and the Arnold dolls' house furniture. The Galt sets are slightly more detailed.

As we would expect, this whole area of play, to do with housekeeping or homemaking, is thought of, at least by most manufacturers, as being exclusively for girls.

Jobs for girls

The range of work presented to girls through playthings is very narrow and most of the jobs can be seen as extensions of the housewife and mother roles — that is, they are ones that involve caring, providing and servicing.

Nursing is a job which, typically, involves caring for and looking after others. It can, therefore, be seen as an extension of the mother role. The various nurses' uniforms and accessories have already been mentioned.

Almost anything connected with food is thought proper for little girls. So, for instance, we have the Supermarket Check-out Till from Eisenmann, which is illustrated in the section of their catalogue headed 'Little Girl's World'. From Crescent, there's Electrocash 2000, a battery-driven cash register with a girl shown prominently on the box, playing with it. The Petite range of toys is described on a leaflet in French, German and English, as being 'a range of quality products for girls from pre-school age to their early teens'. A very simple cash register was on offer in 1979 and an electronic one in 1983.

However, the Petite typewriters are better known. (Girls become secretaries.) There are five in the 1983 range, including two, with dials instead of keys, for very young children and one Talking Typewriter which is meant to help with spelling. There's also an office Activity Centre (portable like the Petite Sewing Activity Centre mentioned earlier in the chapter). This contains one of the simple typewriters and also a toy telephone, clock, and switchboard and radio, together with various items of stationery. I should perhaps record that, on the front of the 1983 Petite leaflet, a boy is shown using the phone of this set. He's obviously very much in the boss's role, however, and a girl is hovering beside a typewriter, as if waiting for his instructions.

Again, it seems strange that a manufacturer will cut potential sales by 50 per cent while, of course, suggesting to boys that the highly useful skill of typing is not for them.

Being an air hostess is bound to remain a fantasy for most girls but the toy world seldom leaves a fantasy unexploited. So Combex have the British Airways Hostess Case with 'passport', 'ticket and baggage check' and imitation money, but also with various cosmetic items.

In the way of jobs, there's not much else suggested to girls through toys. Overwhelmingly, as far as toys are concerned, the stress is on the traditional domestic role of women and even the jobs deemed suitable for them can be seen as extensions of this.

Dolls promoting establishment values

Lastly, I want to deal with what is, maybe, an unusual corner — though it's a significant one — of the doll market. This is the Nisbet range of dolls. They exist mainly to be collected, though, as far as ideas and attitudes are concerned, they'll serve very well to tie up some of the points about the establishment and about class, which have been made, here and there, in this chapter.

In general, the Nisbet dolls constitute a song of praise to the establishment, mainly British, though it did include the Shah and Empress of Iran in 1979 and possibly later. The Shah, according to the catalogue, carried out 'great reforms' including 'the emancipation of women'. Amongst the 'Historical Portrait and Costume Dolls', there are a great many royal figures. For instance, 1983 brought us 'royal Baby models of The Princess of Wales carrying Prince William and the Prince of Wales'. (This was not the feat of strength that seems to be suggested.) The third 'Limited Signature Edition' in the 'Royal Family limited edition sets', and following Royal Wedding and Royal Baby, was entitled Royal Visit and was, in fact, a kind of royal round-up. These royals are British, of course. Nisbet also have, in a range of nine American Presidents and Historical Characters, two of Ronald Reagan, one of them dressed, appropriately enough, as a cowboy, and one of Nancy Reagan.

In the Leadership Series, there are, for example, Winston Churchill and President Anwar Sadat, together with the Archbishop of Canterbury, Pope John Paul II and Margaret Thatcher. The card that comes with this last doll says, on the front, 'Commemorating Restoration of Liberty in the Falkland Islands'. Inside, it says:

In April of 1982 the free world was stunned to learn of the invasion and capture of the Falkland Islands by the armed forces of Argentina.

Her Majesty's Government under the resolute leadership of the Prime Minister Mrs Margaret Thatcher, lost no time in seeking a resolution of the United Nations requiring the Argentinians to cease hostilities and withdraw. But it took a mighty task force to sail 8,000 miles to the South Atlantic to restore liberty in the Falkland Islands.

The Prime Minister gave her Country strong leadership in its hour of crisis in 1982.

This is a 'Special Collector's Signature Edition' and Nisbets certify that the model 'is limited to production undertaken in 1983' — which is something to be thankful for, at least. Then, there's a space on the card for the signature of Alison Nisbet, the daughter of Peggy Nisbet, the founder of this firm which has been going for more than 30 years.

As Peggy Nisbet makes clear in an account of her 1977 US tour — which appeared in the Peggy Nisbet Limited Doll Collectors' Club International Newsletter, volume 1 number 6, of January 1978 — it's mothers and grandmothers who initiate young girls into the dreary world of Nisbet.

This is, maybe, the most obvious way in which girls are turned towards establishment values. These make up a conservative complex which, of course, includes the idea of women as being largely restricted to domestic roles.

Reference
1   Charles Dickens, *The Cricket on the Hearth,* London, Dent 1963, pp.139-40.

CHAPTER 4

THE SEX OBJECT

We now turn to the other main role presented to girls through toys and playthings — the sex object — and we'll be considering fashion or teenage dolls, and make-up and hairdressing sets and products. The fashion dolls in particular, however, have strong overtones of the class and political bias we saw coming out in companion and even baby dolls.

A brief glimpse at the historical background of fashion dolls will give us a context and some important ideological clues, before we go on to see what Barbie and Sindy and some of their rivals have been up to lately. Then, with make-up and hairdressing, we'll see more particularly how girls are taught to package themselves for the marriage market while enriching the toy manufacturers at the same time.

Fashion dolls, past and present

In the Bethnal Green Museum of Childhood, there's a doll, which dates from about 1760, dressed in Spitalfields silk made in the east end of London. There's also a richly-dressed English doll dated 1757. Fashion dolls, in fact, often richly dressed in contemporary fashions, go back to, at least, the mid eighteenth century. The date is interesting because, at about the same time, the first books and board games meant specifically for children were being marketed. At about this time, also, the beginnings of large-scale capitalism could be seen and the industrial revolution was looming.

The kind of fashion dolls mentioned here were obviously not meant for working-class children who, if they had dolls at all at this time, had home-made ones or cheap ones bought from pedlars.

Not all fashion dolls were for children, however. From approximately the end of the seventeenth century to the late eighteenth century, before fashion magazines existed, French fashion dolls, called Pandoras, were used as manikins to show off dress fashions. These seem to have mostly been rather big and we would probably call them models now. In the latter part of the nineteenth century, the French 'lady-dolls' or 'Parisiennes' had all sorts of dresses and accessories, rather like the fashion dolls of today. They were popular amongst the upper classes, though less for play, it seems, than for the competitive display of wealth.

Although it's easier to see present-day fashion dolls against this background, it's important to note, also, that fashions aren't restricted to teenage dolls. Manufacturers, abetted by the larger retailers especially, have made considerable efforts to hook children onto the idea of fashion as early as possible. So, for example, Hamleys' 1981 catalogue advertises 'a completely new range of rather superior French Haute Couture Clothes' for baby dolls, with comments from a 'leading Fleet Street Fashion Editor'. Amongst many other outfits, there are lemon satin dungarees with matching shoulder purse and a 'fleecy-lined' ski suit with matching mittens. The firm of Knickerbocker were also reaching down the age range when they introduced their Dolly Pops into Britain in 1982. The *Toy Trader,* in its January issue that year, described these as 'pre-school fashion dolls based on an eight inch fashion doll with colourful pop-on accessories'. These were plastic.

It can't be denied that, in recent decades, children — and perhaps girls especially — have been 'growing up' earlier, in the sense of reaching puberty. It has been claimed that the development of fashion dolls in recent times is related to this. Another way of looking at it, however, suggests that manufacturers, in their never-ending drive for profits, are robbing children of their childhood.

The fashion dolls of today are usually about 28-30cm tall, possibly with related dolls of other sizes; they represent older teenage girls and boys or young adults; they are 'poseable', that is, their limbs and bodies are articulated in various ways; and they normally have large arrays of outfits and accessories. According to 'The Fashion Doll Review' produced by Mattel's British subsidiary in January 1983, the most likely owner of a fashion doll is a girl between the ages of four and 12 and such dolls reach the peak of their popularity with girls aged between six and eight.

The two main fashion dolls on the market during the years covered by this study have been Barbie, from Mattel and Sindy, from Pedigree (later from Hasbro). Before going on to the history of these two, and the way of life they present to children, a detailed description and comparison of the actual dolls will bring some interesting facts to light.

First of all, Barbie, at about 30cm on tiptoe (of which, more later) is some 2cm taller than Sindy, also on tiptoe. The torsos of the dolls are made of hard plastic and the heads and limbs of what seems to be a rubbery kind of plastic, the limbs being harder in Barbie's case. The heads are hollow except for where the neck piece is fitted in. Sindy has a much bigger head: Barbie has a much bigger bosom. A report in the magazine, *Which?* in November 1969 scaled up their bust, waist and hip measurements which, respectively, brought Sindy out at 32, 24 and 35 inches (81, 61 and 89cm) and Barbie at 42, 22 and 36 inches (107, 56 and 91 cm). This may partly account for the fact that Barbie looks older, though Sindy's large head gives her a more babyish appearance. Her head is, in fact, about twice the size of Barbie's. The appearance of the dolls has obviously been carefully planned, down to the smallest of details. Sindy has a high, bulging forehead, large blue eyes set widely apart and a short, snub nose. These features contribute towards the babyish appearance and are less well pronounced in Barbie, though Barbie's eyes are relatively large, as well. In both dolls, the eyes are of particular importance and, in Barbie's case, the eye colour and eye make-up vary according to the outfit she's sold in. Great

Shape Barbie, for example, who has a green outfit, actually has green eyes and green and blue eye make-up. Sindy's eyes don't seem to change from one doll to another, but they are more elaborate. She has upper eyelashes made of some kind of short, dark fibre which is densely packed and gives the effect of mascara. Four long eyelashes are painted on at the outer corner of each eye. Barbie has no fibre eyelashes but also has ones that are painted on. The eyes of both dolls are highlighted, each eye having a white dot on or near the pupil. Barbie's face has changed over the years, though now she always seems to have a glittering smile: the typical Sindy's face never changed (but see below) and she doesn't smile, though her lips are slightly parted. She's usually described as having an 'innocent' look, though I think she looks gormless. Barbie is usually thought to be more ' sophisti-cated'. The hair varies from doll to doll, with both Barbie and Sindy, though, obviously, a great deal of care and attention is always lavished on this very special aspect. (I'll have more to say about hair later.) Other bodily parts of the dolls tell us more about their role in life. Sindy's hands are open and almost flat, with the fingers slightly apart. Barbie's are similar but the fingers are joined. In neither doll can the hands grip, so that an accessory meant to be carried, such as a handbag, has to be slung over the arm. Objects meant to be held, such as a hand-mirror, are often made with slots so that they can be passed over the fingers. These hands aren't for doing anything very much and they don't have to be like this, as we'll see when we come to examine dolls for boys. The feet also tell us things about the kind of life led by Barbie and Sindy. Both dolls have very tiny feet but more important is the fact that these are made for high-heeled footwear. This, and the size of the feet, means that the dolls cannot actually stand on their own, with or without footwear. There's no problem, over standing, as far as manufacturing is concerned. Dolls of this size, which stand, can be made, but a decision has obviously been taken against having these ones stand in order to promote the fashion and sex object aspects. (Some fashion dolls are provided with figure stands which help to counteract this very serious handicap.)Barbie and Sindy can sit or lie, in certain restricted ways, or they can be propped against things, and that's all. Further pointers to what the manufac-turers are aiming for with Barbie and Sindy (and how, in the process, they restrict the creative possibilities of play) can be seen in the ways the dolls are articulated; which means, in the number and type of joints they have. In this respect it should be said that it's possible to make joints for such dolls so as to simulate practically any bodily movement. Basically, two types of joints are used: swivel joints, which allow for movement in one plane only, and ball and socket joints. The most obvious way in which the notion of the fashion doll (which is part of the sex object complex) has involved setting a limit on imaginative play can be seen in the construction of the knees. These have no visible joints — which would, no doubt, be considered unsightly. Instead, the legs have internal armatures that allow them to be bent, beneath the knees, only into four or five positions including, in the case of both dolls, an unrealistic forward position. So, here again we see that the postures the dolls can be made to adopt are very limited and, in this case, don't even include any kind of kneeling ones. Furthermore, the wrists, elbows and ankles allow for no effective movement in either doll. Otherwise Sindy and Barbie can swivel at the waist, but not bend, and can only move their arms directly forward or back because the joints at the shoulders are of the swivel type. Barbie's hip joints are also of this type but Sindy has ball and socket joints at the hips and this allows for more realistic movement. Overall, movement is very much less than it could be (see pp. 122-24 and compare the Action Man doll) and this is clearly because of the allotted function of these dolls.

Bearing these matters in mind, we can now go on to examine the history, development and way of life of Barbie and Sindy and also certain factors to do with marketing. We start with Barbie, the first of the modern fashion dolls to appear.

Barbie

In 1958, the doll manufacturer, Maar, of Bavaria in West Germany, produced Lilli, a doll with sex appeal. Her creators had been inspired by the cartoon character and sex symbol of the same name from the newspaper, *Bildzeitung*. Mattel bought up the prototype, renamed her Barbie and began to market her in the USA in 1959. She was strongly promoted, and became a business success. Barbie was not, as claimed by Mattel, the 'first-ever fashion doll'. More likely, as stated in the US reference book *Everybody's Business* (©1980) she (or Lilli) was 'the first doll with developed breasts'. At any rate, deliberate sex appeal does seem to be the only new aspect and this is the main thing that concerns me in this chapter.

Something else new, at least in scale, was the style of marketing applied to Barbie and, afterwards, to the other fashion dolls which followed. They became less dolls than whole ranges, or 'concepts' (to use a favourite trade term) which presented a way of life.

When Barbie arrived in Britain, at around the beginning of 1964, she had, according to *Toys International* dated March-April of that year, 53 outfits, a series of 'glamorous' wigs, a 'dream house' and a 'miniature fashion shop'. Her younger sister, Skipper, arrived not too long afterwards, along with a very full wardrobe, and boy friend Ken was soon on the scene and has not been far from her side since. He and Barbie have many interests in common, as we'll see, but their main interest seems to be in clothes. Over the years, other friends and relatives have come and gone such as Barbie's girlfriend Midge who had a boy friend called Allan and the twins Tutti and Todd and *their* friend Chris. These appear to date from the late sixties and the *Which?* report already referred to gives us the picture at the end of 1969. Then, Barbie had an 'English' girl friend, Stacey, as well as Skipper and Ken. Her cousin, Francie, who was also available in a 'Coloured' version, was then being withdrawn. Barbie and Stacey were available in talking versions and said such things as: 'I think mini-skirts are smashing'; 'I love being a fashion model'; and 'Stacey and I are having a tea' (sic).

Mattel's promotion kept pace with all this. In 1966 or 7, they had bought up the British firm of Rosebud, in order to begin their European offensive. By 1968, Rosebud Mattel was the biggest toy advertiser in Britain, spending £230,566 on television and press advertisements.

Another 'English' angle was tried in 1981 when a new 'starter pack' was brought out, called My First Barbie. According to the January issue, of that year, of *Toys International and the Retailer,* this doll was 'more like a little English girl' and only available on the British market.

Animals, especially horses, play an important part in the fashion doll world. Barbie's 'new poseable horse', Dallas, taking its name from the television series, arrived in the same year. Her Afghan Hound, Beauty, has been on the go for several years while Fluff, the kitten, arrived in 1983. I noted from a boxed set I saw at Christmas of that year that, by then, Beauty had acquired two pups, a collar, three leashes, a crown, a dog dish, a hat, three ribbons, a comb and brush combined and also — to be cut out from the box — bones, a newspaper and so on. (The 'pedigree papers' mentioned in Mattel's 1982 catalogue didn't seem to be there, however.) As another boxed set revealed, Fluff already had a carrying case, a scratching post, a bed and mattress, a collar, cat food and a dish, and came along with a 'How to Care' booklet. Fluff's cat litter wasn't on offer in this playset.

I hope this has given some general idea of the way this particular system is worked. To give a more precise idea, I'm now going to focus closely on developments over a period of two or three years.

The Barbie range of 1982 gives a very good idea of the various kinds of product on the market and we can see the pattern of development. There were 12 new outfits called Barbie Best Buys at 'a pocket money price', according to the catalogue, while the 12 Fashion Collectibles were 'at a mid price point'. The doll, Pink 'n' Pretty Barbie, was a prominent feature and came with six costume pieces which could be assembled into 'over 10 absolutely dreamy looks'. Pink seems to be Barbie's favourite colour.

The way in which manufacturers use language in order to manipulate, needs special attention. For instance, there are a lot of dreams for sale. Then, they're fond of talking about what they call 'play value'. This usually means ringing the changes on some trivial theme. Pretty Changes Barbie, for example, is said to have 'play value' as you can change her hair colour, her hats and her outfits. Western Barbie, new in 1982, is said to be 'fully jointed and poseable for maximum play value', giving a slight twist, so to speak, to the idea of changes. Magic curl Barbie has 'hair which can be curled and straightened and curled again!' She thus forms part of the hair and horses complex that fashion doll manufacturers seem to have. This doll arrives with a supply of 'magic mist solution', which makes her hair straight, and with other hairdressing accessories. 'Magic' is another word to be on the look-out for.

Indian Barbie — actually meant to be an east Indian — was something of a surprise in 1982, but she didn't stay around very long. Usually, the dolls are white, and typically they're blonde and blue-eyed. However, I'm certainly not saying that all Barbie needs is a change of colour.

There are nearly always wedding dresses around, such as Bridal Barbie's in 1982. A second wedding dress, 'especially made for Barbie's "Big Day" ' was available at the same time. You could also get a bridesmaid's outfit to go with it and a navy pin-stripe suit for Ken to complete the scene. These give an important clue as to what the whole business is about. The wedding is the reward for conforming to the

69

role of sex object. This message might be more explicit in a lot of cheap fiction aimed at girls but I feel it's there, as well, implicit and encoded, in fashion dolls.

Play packs and accessories, added each year, carry on the saga and give us some important clues about Barbie's life-style. New in 1982 were the 'western' and water sports play packs, the first including 'cowboy'-style accessories and the second, accessories for various water sports. 'Camping' and 'beach' packs were already available. A note of well-off and self-indulgent leisure is struck.

The Beauty Bath gives a good idea of accessories. It's a sumptuous bath in pink with a pump for making soap bubbles. There's also a seat and 'vanity bar', a shower attachment and other bits and pieces. This is 'for Barbie to relax in'.

As we press on, further, into Barbie's world, a review of the new items (only) for 1983 should give a good overall grasp of marketing strategy and aims. We can also piece together the kind of life presented to girls as an ideal.

The usual system is for the manufacturers to add about five or six new dolls every year. Each is a basic Barbie doll, often with some gimmick, and dressed in an outfit which isn't available separately. Then, there will be perhaps fifty or so outfits, as well as packets of accessories such as shoes, hair pieces and coat hangers. New play packs and play sets will be introduced, as well as additions to previous ones.

In 1983, then, Twirly Curls Barbie appeared, along with 'a magical mechanical device' for styling Barbie's hair, a 'hairdressing chair' and other accessories to do with hairdressing. I found the 'twirly curler' difficult to use but, if you can get the knack of it, you can twist strands of Barbie's hair separately and then twist them together. This doll carries on the hair theme (or fixation) from Magic Curl Barbie. Angel Face Barbie also has 'hair-play accessories' but the main thing about her is that she comes with make-up and 'applicators', in a pink 'cameo' case. The 'ultra-glamorous' Dream Date Barbie, with her jewelry and hairdressing accessories, joined the throng, along with the trio, Superdance Barbie, Supersport Ken and Superdance Skipper. The first of these has, amongst other things, pink woollen leg warmers. (Fashion doll manufacturers don't miss tricks like this — leg warmers were very popular at the time.) Supersport Ken has a purple and lavender T-shirt 'with muscleman motif'.

There were six new outfits, by this time often simply called 'fashions', for My First Barbie. These, 'with the younger child in mind', were designed for easy dressing. Barbie herself got 44 new outfits in categories such as Fashion Fun, Fashion Fantasy, Fashion Classics, Designer Collection and Haute Couture Collection, the last of these 'exclusively created by top European fashion designers'. Ken got eight new outfits, though two of them looked very similar, and Skipper also got eight. Wedding of the Year was made up of (another) Bridal Costume for Barbie, a Groom Ensemble for Ken, a Flower Girl Outfit for Skipper, and there was also a Bridesmaid Outfit. These were available separately, though it would be difficult to know what you could do with a bride or groom separately.

A new play pack was based on a country picnic while several new assortments of accessories, such as Hats along with Glasses, and Shoes together with Purses, were added to back up the outfits.

Fluff, the well-provided-for kitten, and new this year, has already been mentioned in another context.

The new McDonald's Restaurant play set with working features and accessories galore, makes an interesting commercial link and takes in a certain area of contemporary youth culture. In this connection, we can note that Angel Face, the name of one of the new Barbies, is a registered trade mark of the US firm Chesebrough-Pond's Inc., and was used with their permission. These examples give us a glimpse into the way children are commercially and ideologically surrounded.

Although Barbie is frantically occupied in keeping up with the very latest trends in popular youth culture, she does seem to have a hankering for the life-style of the idle upper class of the nineteenth century, as shown by the Dream Carriage and Horse Set with its mock convertible roof and 'gold finish lamps'. This is clearly just to indulge in a romantic dream, however, and of course she has a jeep as well. What she never does is look to the future or think of how different, and how much better, the world might be.

Amongst the larger sets, is the Dream Store de luxe with its three departments — the Make-up one available in 1983 and Dress-up Jewellery and Hats and Purses to be added later. Altogether, the Dream Store would contain over 70 items 'for fabulous shopping fun'. There are even little, pink, plastic carrier bags, in two sizes, with 'Barbie Dream Store' printed on them. The overall colour scheme of the Dream Store is in pink and lilac with some white trimmings. Then, there's the Electronic Light-up Vanity Unit with a mirror that lights up and a working hair dryer. Pool Party is a new 'low price' swimming pool set. There's lots of new 'dream furniture' for bedroom, living room and dining room, together with lots of accessories; 68 for the dining room, for example. This stuff could be used in Barbie's new 'cosy retreat', the Dream Cottage or, no doubt, she could use it to refurnish her older properties, the Dream House and the Town House. Lastly, amongst Barbie's new acquisitions in 1983, is the pink and white four-poster bed (another touch of nostalgia) with its foam mattress and heart-shaped pillow.

So, the juggernaut rolled on into 1984 and brought us a whole new set of Barbies: Playtime, Pretty Party, Fabulous Fur, Ballerina and Horse Lovin' Barbie. There was also Crystal Barbie in a shiny 'rainbow ballgown' and Crystal Ken in his white tuxedo and sparkling waistcoat and, much promoted, Loving You Barbie in a gown with 'velvety red hearts' who came with a heart-shaped, child-sized stationery set for the occasional 'love note'. There was the usual array of new outfits for Barbie, in the usual kind of ranges, and also more new outfits for Ken and Skipper. (None of her other friends or relations had survived.) There was a Wedding of the Year playset which included a cake, a punchbowl and gifts and invitations; a Bubbling Spa for the dolls to play in; and a Beauty Salon, with lots of accessories, as well as a Bath and Beauty Centre with three furniture pieces and, according to the catalogue, 28 accessories. This year, the Dream Cottage could be bought furnished; and Barbie got another car; also, a van for going camping (she already had the Star Traveller Motor Home, complete with Vanity Area); a motor bike; and Prancer, a Dream Horse. It may be, that she earned the money for all these things in her Dream Store. It seemed to be doing well, anyway, as in 1984 the Hats and Purses Boutique and the Jewellery Boutique, advertised in 1983, were finally added.

So it goes on, year in, year out, each year bringing more of the same sort of thing. The token black doll, Dee Dee, which appeared in 1986 as a member of the Barbie Rock Stars group, certainly didn't improve matters. She's not exactly in blackface but isn't racially accurate either and has a rather vacant expression.

As regards Barbie's way of life, there's not a lot to add. I'm afraid it may be all too clear, in fact. However, a publicity leaflet from Mattel's British subsidiary in 1983, sums it all up (see illustration). She has 'the most glamorous lifestyle of any doll', it says, and is the only fashion doll in Britain to have a boy friend and little sister. Her interests are:

> Dancing, horse riding and driving; entertaining in her dream home; driving fast cars; camping holidays in her own motorhome; swimming in her dream pool; playing the piano; eating at McDonalds with her boyfriend and sister; styling her hair, trying out new make-up ideas and wearing fashionable clothes.

You might think this is a narrow life of idle pleasure, a life turned in upon itself, self-absorbed and self-indulgent. You might wonder why she obviously isn't interested in work, for example, or even interested in other people, to any extent, least of all in their hopes, or sorrows or sufferings. How could she be? She hasn't got the outfits or equipment for that sort of thing.

Here, I'd like to make a link with the last chapter, where I spoke of the fictional and narrative elements built into some ranges of toys and dolls, for instance Strawberry Shortcake. It's easy to see that many of the Barbie accessories — most obviously the play sets, such as the camping and Wedding of the Year ones — are meant to prompt stories, or (perhaps a better description) miniature dramas. There's no end of stage props provided. In this connection, though, it's important to note that play can also be limited by what's provided and that, in this case, there's scarcely any room for creative imagination. Fantasy, day-dreams and rituals are catered for, but nothing more constructive, nothing that engages with real life, as most people know it. The Barbie products set the agenda for a ceaseless round of triviality and self-indulgence. There's no room for anything else.

As so often happens with toys, especially dolls, there's an overlap with actual fiction. There's a Barbie annual, and a Barbie comic strip was running in *The Mail on Sunday* in the summer of 1983. The first episode of 'Tunnel to Danger', for example, appeared in the paper on 14 August. It contained many of the trappings so drearily familiar from the stories of Enid Blyton: a 'secret panel', a tunnel, an

Barbie vital statistics

Born:	1959, USA
Parents:	MATTEL Inc., the world's No. 1 name in toys
Status:	Top-selling fashion doll in the world
Personal details:	Blonde; blue eyes; 11½" tall
Personality:	Glamorous, exciting, popular with little girls, guaranteed to be the life and soul of the store
Career so far:	★ 150 million sold worldwide ★ conquered USA, Canada, Australia, Italy, France, Germany – dominates worldwide doll sales ★ appeared in UK TV commercials worth over £½ million in 1982 ★ has been making more and more personal appearances in stores throughout Britain
Vital statistics:	★ the largest range of costumes and accessories of any fashion doll in the UK ★ the largest purchaser of ladies fabrics in the world ★ has the most glamorous lifestyle of any doll ★ the only fashion doll in the UK to have a boyfriend, Ken, and little sister, Skipper
Future appearances:	★ Barbie will star in a £650,000 advertising campaign in 1983 ★ Barbie will appear on TV, in the cinema and be featured in comics ★ Barbie plans to double the number of stores she is stocked in during 1983
Interests:	Dancing, horse riding and driving; entertaining in her dream home; driving fast cars; camping holidays in her own motorhome; swimming in her dream pool; playing the piano; eating at McDonalds with her boyfriend and sister; styling her hair, trying out new make-up ideas and wearing fashionable clothes
Ambition:	To become the top-selling fashion doll in the UK.

the world's no. 1 name in toys.
Mattel UK. Limited,
Derby Road, Loughborough,
Leics. LE11 0BQ.
Tel:(0509) 268101

8: *Barbie, Pink 'n' Pretty*

obvious villain, talk of 'spies', a clever animal, a girl in danger (Barbie) and (I suspect) it was leading to an impending rescue by a boy (Ken).

With the possible exception of wordless comic strips, fiction generally doesn't exist without language. It's time now to draw together some of the points I've been making about language because, in a very important way, most toys don't exist without language either. Along the way, in this chapter, we've seen how manufacturers have used certain words again and again, as if they were pressing buttons. 'Dream', 'fashion', 'vanity' and 'beauty' are obvious favourites, while 'magic', 'glamorous' and 'fabulous' turn up frequently. 'Haute couture' and 'de luxe' add an exotic touch, as do 'patio' and 'barbecue', if to a lesser degree. These words occur in the names of the items, in the catalogue descriptions (where they signal what the manufacturers are aiming for) and on packaging. Also, and very importantly, they're used in advertising.

I think the word 'fun' is in a different category. There's less of the grown-up in it and more of the child; it has less to do with the role of sex object and more to do with play; it's what fashion doll manufacturers want to pretend their products provide for children. How else could they attempt to justify their activities?

So, I just want us to have a look at the use of the word 'fun' before moving on. 'Funtime fashions' we've already seen, in connection with outfits, and 'fashion fun' is only a variation. It seems the meaning of the word is being stretched here as, whatever little girls get out of changing dolls' outfits, it could scarcely be described as 'fun'. The Dream House, 'built for years of fun' does offer a bit more scope but, as it's 'packed with deluxe working features and furniture', leaving little to the imagination, it seems that children would soon end up with rituals of high life. Regarding the Dream Pool, we're told, 'Barbie's pool and patio has [sic] all the luxuries for hours of fun', so, again, the connection is made between luxury and 'fun'. 'Play fun', in connection with the horse, Dallas, seems to consist of grooming its tail and mane and posing it. 'Fun' was linked with the Barbie Perfume Maker which came out in 1980 and the word is normally used in connection with make-up. The Barbie Play Make-up, for instance, which is for children, is presented as 'fun'. With the word 'play' here, as well, we can see the manufacturer reaching out to the child though, on the other hand, we're told that, with the Play Make-up Case, 'girls can spend hours in a grown up dream of glamour'.

Mattel's Play Make-up for children, introduced under the Barbie brand name in 1982, seemed an obvious development. There had already been make-up for Barbie: now the girls were to be invited to take the easy step of trying it on themselves. A vast array of items could be bought in various combinations. There was the already mentioned Play Make-up Case, a Cameo Cosmetics Case and two Beauty Sets, as well as smaller sets and single items. The range included: four shades of lipstick; four shades of nail polish; two shades of cheek blusher; and nine shades of eye shadow. Some of the lipsticks were flavoured and here the manufacturer reaches out for the child in the girl. Some of the names of the colours seem to have been chosen to appeal especially to children — for instance 'hot pink' for one of the lipsticks and (more obviously) 'cherry pie' for one of the nail polishes. Otherwise, the names —'pastel pink', 'satin rose' and 'powder blue' — seem to point more towards cosmetics for adults. There'll be more to say about make-up later in the chapter.

Finally, as regards Barbie, we turn to look at her from a different angle, from the point of view of promotion, sales and, in a small way, economics — Barbie as business, in fact.

Figures are very unreliable in the toy industry but I think we can get a general idea from them. The following refer to sales, throughout the world, of Barbie dolls. The magazine, *Toys International,* in October 1974 gave the figure of 80 million; Mattel claimed, in a press release of 1980, more than 110 million; the US reference book, *Everybody's Business* (©1980) said more than 112 million; the magazine, *British Toys and Hobbies,* in January 1981 reported that over 120 million Barbies had been sold; a Mattel leaflet of 1983 gave a figure of 150 million; in the Thames Television programme, *Sindy and Barbie with Love,* which went out in April 1985, a figure of 200 million was quoted; and by the beginning of 1988, Mattel were claiming that well over 450 million had been sold. No doubt, all the figures came from Mattel, but at different times and places, and the general outline seems clear. It's staggering to think of the influence this one doll must have over much of the world.

Since 1980, at least, Mattel have been claiming that, with Barbie over 20 years old, the first generation of Barbie owners have become mothers themselves and buy Barbie dolls for their daughters.

But Mattel don't leave it to chance. We've seen how they reach down to younger children with My First Barbie. This doll comes with a handbook of Barbie puzzles and games and an application form to join the Barbie Friends' Club. On the other side of this is a letter from Barbie in which she tells children, 'Now you can join me in my glamorous world of fashion and excitement by becoming a member of my very own club'. On sending £1.00 to join, children would get, amongst other things, a membership certificate, a badge, an 'autographed' photo and regular newsletter. The club's newsletter number two, of Christmas 1981, gave the results of a competition to design outfits, and put forward some party ideas (such as 'Find Barbie' and 'Guess the Missing Barbie Items'). In a letter on the back page, Barbie confides that she's been to Paris for a week-end and 'took enough clothes to last [her] a month!'.

There are other ways of promoting Barbie. In 1983, it was intended to hold Barbie Fashion Shows at which live models would show off full-size versions of Barbie's outfits for that year.

In another kind of development, the Italian firm of Vivi, for 1984, produced a range of Barbie bikes, on license from Mattel. These carry the graphics and logo from the Barbie range and are meant to attract girls aged five to 12.

Most of the firm's expenditure and effort, however, seem to go on the usual kind of advertising. Early in 1983, Mattel reported that the cost of Barbie advertising in 1982 had been £737,479. They estimated they would be spending £618,000 in 1983, though elsewhere they put this figure at £650,000. In 1987, up to the end of November, they claimed to have spent £956,000. In spite of her many alleged attractions, Barbie seems to need a lot of help.

Sindy

Sindy was designed by Dennis Arkinstall for the firm of Pedigree, and first appeared on the market in 1963. Barbie arrived in Britain shortly afterwards and soon fashion dolls, in their modern form, were beginning to make an impact here. *Toys International,* in their March/April issue of the following year, referred to the '*latest* [my emphasis] craze for teenage dolls with large wardrobes'. Sindy and Barbie were mentioned as the 'two main dolls' in this category, and Sindy's most popular outfits were said to be Country Walk and Lunch Date.

In the early years, Sindy had friends. Paul, her boy friend, arrived on the scene in 1965 or 6, complete with outfits: Seaside, Casuals, Motorway Man, London Look and Time Off. He soon got washable, rooted hair, instead of moulded hair but, in spite of this added attraction, he disappeared in the early 1970s. The full story is shrouded in mystery but it's a fact that Sindy didn't get another boy friend until 1986. Another strange fact is that, in 1966, Sindy had a little sister, Patch — at least, that's not so strange in itself. The strange thing is that Patch disappeared at about the same time as Paul, which must give rise to speculation.

But let's return to Sindy. She seems to have had a normal sort of life, for a fashion doll. In 1965, she had, amongst her outfits, Happy Traveller, Centre Court and Air Hostess. The following year, she got a horse and plenty of gear for it but this was, perhaps, only to be expected as she already had a Pony Club outfit. Rather astonishingly, Sindy got an outfit called Housework, with accessories as well, in 1967. However, at the same time, Sindy had an evening gown, Come Dancing. She also had the usual kind of things — a dressing-table with beauty accessory kit, for example, and a bedside table (with a framed photo of Paul).

Soon after that, Mitzi and Betsy arrived, in time for Christmas 1967. Mitzi was Sindy's continental girl friend and Betsy was Patch's friend from the USA. About two years later, at the time of the *Which?* report already referred to, Sindy had an English girl friend, Vicki, and her little sister, Patch, had a friend called Poppet. These have all gone now.

Over the years, Sindy went on in much the same way as Barbie, accumulating more and more clothes and accessories, though it's worth remarking that she was going in for beauty contests round about 1968 as she had a Miss World outfit then.

In 1975, Active Sindy arrived, in a ballet outfit and with a figure stand. She had extra joints and also improved ones but her knees were still inadequate. According to the 1984 catalogue, Active Sindy was 'still the ultimate in poseability', a claim that couldn't possibly be supported.

Now, I'm leaving the (rather chequered) earlier career of Sindy to focus on recent years, as I did with Barbie. There are overall similarities between the two dolls and it should be enough to give examples of these, without going into too much detail. There are also differences, but they aren't very important in an overall, ideological sense.

Funtime Sindy and Keep Fit Sindy, from Pedigree's 1979 catalogue, seem familiar enough, and very much in Barbie's style. Sindy had a home by then — which had just been 'completely redecorated to reflect Sindy's lifestyle'. It consisted simply of walls crossing at right angles to form four open-access rooms (in the manner referred to in the last chapter).

In 1980, however, Sindy got a new home, described in Pedigree's January press release of that year as 'in 3-storey town style, robustly constructed with a lift to all floors and a spiral staircase to the roof patio'. Sindy's battery-operated Magic Cooker arrived at the same time. It made various cooking noises and had an 'infra red glow' amongst other things. Barbie seems to have lagged behind a little in the matter of kitchens and kitchen furniture and accessories. Her Dream House, which she acquired in 1982, did have the necessary equipment but she didn't seem to bother much with it. She's caught up quite a lot, in this respect, but it almost seems as though she's been pushed into it by Sindy.

We move on to 1982, noting that Sindy's outfits of that year were almost entirely different from her 1979 ones, even when they were for similar occasions such as a wedding, being out in the rain or spending an evening out.

The general heading, in the catalogue, of Sindy's Fashion Parade, has within it a 'funfashion range' including Beachgirl and Disco Glitter outfits and a range of Super-fashions. This includes Sindy's wedding dress and an evening dress. Sindy's Boutique range contains, so they say, 'outfits for work or play, sleeping, riding or just dreaming', though it's hard to see where the work comes in. With the Quick-change set, you get colour sticks to change the colour of Sindy's hair and also a spare head and shoulders to practice on.

Having focused on what Barbie got in 1983, I'll now do the same for Sindy, so that a comparison can be made. First of all, it's interesting to note that the pattern is the same: a few new, ready-dressed dolls, a lot of outfits and then various accessories, play packs and so on.

The new dolls were Party Girl; Holiday Girl, dressed for the beach and with a radio to disturb other people; Pop Singer, complete with guitar and 'electronic' organ; and Hair Stylist, with shoulder cape, two crimpers, six hair rollers, a brush, setting lotion and a 'puffer spray'. Fashion Faces, another new doll, came with a beauty case containing about ten items, including hair colouring pencils, so that the child could play at making up the doll.

There were 28 new outfits in ranges such as Casuals, Boutique and Classics. Outfits such as Cocktail Party and Disco Date seem to show an attempt to bridge two worlds but, overall, the emphasis is very much upper class as the Alpine Sports and Dressage outfits show. Beautiful Bride, in the 'Classic' range, was a new wedding dress for Sindy.

There were 'pocket money accessory assortments' also, some, such as the shoes and fashions assortments, for adding to the outfits, and others, like the vacuum cleaner and mixer blender, for adding to the house. The simple, open-access dolls' house didn't appear in the 1983 catalogue. The three-storey house, however, had been redesigned and redecorated and became Super Home, and you could now build on extensions such as another bedroom and a stable and garage combined. Sindy also got a new bath 'with 3-piece splashback and mirror' while there was a new colour scheme for the rest of the bathroom fittings. The newly-designed kitchen had a new cooker and a new washing machine unit. This last was battery-driven, had a soap tray and could wash, rinse and spin clothes. At the Earls Court Toy and Hobby Fair there was someone who seemed to have the special job of giving demonstrations of this. As items like the washing machine unit show, Sindy does have a homely side, which can scarcely be said of Barbie. However, even with Sindy, this is very much overshadowed by the sex object role. Whatever Sindy's job might be, it must pay very well as she was also able to afford a new Range Rover in 1983.

A few of the 47 new items for 1984 deserve mention and will help to fill in the picture for Sindy. There were the usual new dolls including Funtime Sindy and Beach Party Sindy and 28 new outfits, or 'fashions', in ranges such as Boutique, Designer and Classic, the four outfits in this last range being described as 'Haute

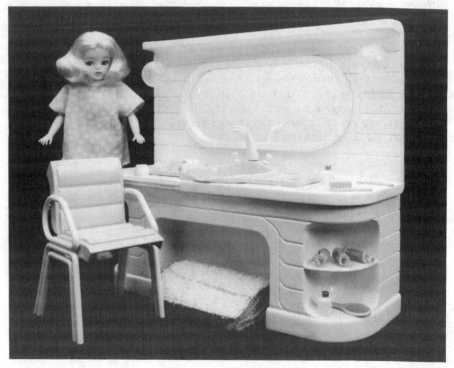

9: Sindy — Beauty Salon

Couture outfits'. One of these was a new wedding dress for Sindy — Wedding Bells. A new variation on the hairdressing theme was introduced with Cut 'n' Style Sindy. You can insert a cartridge of hair into her back so that it can 'grow' again after you've cut it. The set contains spare hair, a 'vanity' mirror, a stool and a beauty case with various accessories. Sindy also got a battery-operated, bedside coffee and tea maker (as well as a new bed and bedroom furniture); a Keeping Fit set consisting of an exercise bike, a 'waist trimmer' and a battery-operated sun bed, together with various accessories; and a Beauty Salon which had in it a hand-operated pump for the extendible shower head (for hair washing) and a battery-operated hair dryer, along with other accessories (see illustration). (Barbie got a Beauty Salon at the same time.) Sindy also acquired a fridge, crammed with food accessories. (Barbie, at the same time, got a refrigerator and freezer combined, and also very well stocked.) Another homely touch was added, with the Spring Clean Set, but Sindy also acquired a new horse, with head and neck that move up and down, and a foal as well. (By a strange coincidence, Barbie also got a new horse and foal in 1984. What's more, each horse had a mane and tail that could be groomed.)

And so it continued until 1986 when another, cheaper Sindy doll came onto the market to take the place of the old one. The head of the new version was smaller and the faintest of smiles appeared on her face. She came with eye shadow ready applied but had no fibre eyelashes and (mysteriously) only had three painted eyelashes instead of four. The general effect is to make her look older than the original Sindy and less babyish and vacant in expression. Her torso is more shaped, with pointed breasts, a navel and the suggestion of a groin. Compared with the original Sindy, the possibilities of movement are even further reduced as there's no joint at the waist, only swivel joints at the hips, and no joints, of any kind, at the knees. The legs are straight and made of hard plastic. She can, with difficulty, be made to stand up, though only in an ungainly posture and not upright — in other words, it's just a balancing act. However, in spite of her drawbacks, this Sindy is not without friends. She has a girl friend, Marie, and (in response to consumer demand, so they say) a boy friend, Mark. Moreover, Sindy and Mark are provided with Getting Married outfits.

This Sindy had a short life, however. By September of the same year, Hasbro had bought her up and, after another overhaul, they 'relaunched' her in 1987.

In spite of what the promotion says, this 'new look' Sindy isn't all that new. The body is very similar — in the matter of joints, also — to that of the first Sindy, but the breasts are more shaped. Like the second Sindy, she has a smaller head, and she has a more pleasant face than either of the others. The eyes have received a lot of attention, as usual. They ordinarily have no eye shadow but (very mysteriously) the right eye has six eyelashes on the upper lid while the left has seven. Each eye has three eyelashes on the lower lid. A surprising feature of this Sindy is that she can stand up, properly — at least, she can in the flat shoes that come as part of the City Girl outfit, which are built up inside. Rather strangely, there hasn't been any mention of this new accomplishment of Sindy's in the publicity, but maybe it's just accidental that she can stand up. Otherwise, Sindy's life continues much as before — except that Paul, now somewhat altered in appearance, has come back, after all these years. There's a White Wedding outfit!

10: Pearly Princess Sindy and Pearly Prince Paul (1989)

Sindy was entirely remodelled for 1989 and Mattel started legal proceedings, claiming that she looked too much like Barbie (see illustration).

In piecing together Sindy's way of life, let's take the firm's point of view first. In the *Toy Fayre and Herald Daily* of 31 January 1982, Allan Ayers, the Sindy brand-manager, was quoted as saying:

> Sindy becomes all the things a girl wants to be in later life and the range of accessories turns the playroom into an exciting world of fun and adventure. She can go horse riding, camping, caravanning, spend her time at home, tidying and arranging her house for dinner parties, or dressing up in her ballgown for a night at the Opera.

What's surprising here is that this is thought of as being not only an 'exciting' way of life but also, so it seems, a varied one. We find the same thing in a booklet, 'Sindy — the Story so Far ...', produced by Pedigree in 1983. They say, 'Sindy has a wide range of interests' and mention horse riding and being in 'evening dress at a candlelit dinner party' to illustrate this range! What seems striking to me is the narrowness of Sindy's life. And, in spite of links with the everyday world of most people, what comes over very clearly is a rather wealthy life-style in which self-indulgence and possessions matter most.

Her clothes and house, and possessions in general, point to such a life-style, even in details. The Vanity Unit, for instance, has a 'period style bureau', though they never say which period. The 'luxurious four-poster bed' and the gig and horse point in the same direction.

These, along with the motor bike and the dog and pram are referred to as 'scenesetters' and are obviously meant as items around which a child could build some small drama. (The use of the word 'scene' is interesting in this connection.) However, what's important is that items such as this and, in fact, everything else in the Sindy range limit play as much as promote it.

In other words, you can only play out fictions suggested by the items themselves. As a rule, children are very good at adapting but these playthings are so detailed that it would be very difficult to put them to any uses other than the obvious ones.

This brings me to the very important question of what *isn't* in Sindy's world and this will also throw light on her life-style. There's no fork-lift truck 'scenesetter', for example, to play at working on the shop floor. There's not even a supermarket trolley. It's true that Active Sindy is a ballerina and Sindy used to have an air hostess outfit but such work, for most girls, is only in the realm of dreams. Sindy has no fashionable overalls she might wear at the supermarket check-out and neither is there any Firefighter outfit. Most of her outfits would look a bit out of place on a picket line in winter. I don't know what she'd wear to go on a demonstration and she doesn't seem to have an outfit for, let's say, spending a few days at Greenham Common. In any case, even if she did turn up there, her smart, new Camping

Adventure set would look very much out of place beside the benders of the peace women. You simply can't, with what's available, base play on any such scenes.

We can look at life-style from a different angle. Is Sindy happy? we might ask. Is Sindy fulfilled? Is there a secret sorrow in the Secret Diary in the 'period style bureau'? Why is her 'best friend' a red setter? Especially during Paul's disappearance, apart from attending to her horses' needs, her life was almost entirely focused upon herself.

This section began with Pedigree's point of view. It ends with some further comments from this manufacturer. A term used in the trade at the moment to describe play with fashion dolls is 'aspirational' and, clearly, it's dreams that are meant. In a section about 'play value' in 'Sindy — the Story so Far ...', there are some revealing comments:

> Sindy play can be aspirational — every girl dreams of being a ballerina, a horserider or of owning a home with a swimming pool, and Sindy enables the child to act out these aspirational roles.

Other kinds of play are mentioned, as well:

> Imitative and experimental play is also important. Sindy is used either to enhance or extend the current interests and activities of little girls or she can be used to rehearse the future, perhaps acting out some of the adult roles the girl sees herself fulfilling one day.

'Dreams' and 'roles' seem to be the key words in these passages. These 'dreams' and 'roles' amount to a narrow and inward-turned way of life and this is what you buy, along with Sindy.

Sindy, like Barbie, also has an existence in fiction. By early 1966, there had already been several paperback 'storybooks' featuring Sindy, published by Young World Publications. However, I'll concentrate mainly on an annual and on magazines.

The *Sindy Annual 1983* (which, I believe, came out in 1982) was published by IPC Magazines. They also publish about half the comics that appear in Britain. Although I've used the word 'fiction', the annual, for the most part, is really a long series of advertisements thinly disguised as fiction. The comic strip, 'Sindy's Disaster Day', for example, has a farcical story but we do see Sindy in seven of her outfits. (We're told, incidentally, that Sindy ran a 'boutique shop' and that she also did modelling.) The text of 'Dining in Style' is little more than a caption to a large picture but it shows how the slenderest thread of narrative links the advertisements:

> Sindy's luxurious dining room with its elegant table and chairs is the perfect setting for a candlelit meal for four. When the guests arrive, she is ready in one of her beautiful gowns to greet them with a tray of ice-cold drinks. Of

course, having an up-to-the-minute cooker with an automatic oven timer leaves her free to relax and chat to her guests.

And so on. The picture shows Sindy carrying in a tray. 'The Great Outdoors' and 'A Look for all Occasions' follow the same pattern. We see, and hear about, Sindy's outfits and paraphernalia. 'A Dream Come True' is along the same lines but it shows us what the Sindy saga is all about:

> A once-in-a-lifetime day calls for a once-in-a-lifetime dress to wear. Sindy's fairly-tale dream of a wedding dress in snowy white lace, complete with lucky horse shoe and bouquet will make quite sure that she remembers the special day for ever and ever.

The comic strip, 'Sindy's Little Monster' is centred on the Miss Junior World competition and the following 'world fashion tour' during which an attempt to hijack a plane and force it to fly to Cuba is foiled. The paper and cloth collages of 'some of our famous kings and queens' also gives the more obvious kind of political alignment. Certain well-worn fictional themes appear in the annual and these would no doubt have the effect of making the readers feel at home. The 'Ghost Ballerina' comic strip, for instance, gives us a ballerina in a wheelchair, one of the variations on the ailing ballerina syndrome so familiar from comics. Then, it's not surprising, perhaps, to find a racist strip featuring a kind of female Tarzan. Apart from three names on art work, one seemingly a pen-name, the annual is quite anonymous.

Here — and bearing in mind the 'scenesetters' in particular — it's worth remarking on another kind of way in which a deliberate attempt is made to prompt children into restricted and conventional fictions. The advertisements for Sindy on television in late 1983 were presented in fictional form. The one I saw on 14 November, for instance, showed Sindy getting ready for a beauty competition and having problems because somebody had, apparently, stolen her outfit. The advertisement ended with the words, 'don't miss the next glossy adventure' — so, as might be expected, the advertisement the following week began with 'the story so far'. The week after, the voice told us they were continuing the 'Saga of Sindy in "Doll House"' and, at the end, we were told not to miss the next instalment.

The *Sindy* magazine first came out in early 1984. It was large, glossy, mostly in colour and cost 75p. According to a press handout at Earls Court Toy and Hobby Fair, it had a starting print run of a quarter of a million copies. Like the annual, the magazine is basically a vehicle for advertising the Sindy system. The comic strips, which are all about Sindy and in which she appears in many of her new outfits, include one in which she becomes a ballet star; one in which she's a very successful fashion designer; a horse story in which she foils some nasty-looking horse thieves; and another in which she turns out to be just the right girl for the star part in a film. The puzzles and stories in the magazine all focus on Sindy and her possessions, while the sections which openly advertise Sindy are closely linked to the comic strips. For instance, the 28 new outfits for 1984 are all shown, in colour photos, on four pages in the course of the fashion designer strip.

Another Sindy magazine was issued in 1985 but this and the one from the previous year were just odd publications and were probably put out to test the market. A comic-strip Sindy magazine began in the spring of 1986 but its future, like that of the doll itself, was in doubt towards the end of the year. The similar Barbie magazine, however, which was first published in the autumn of 1985, was still going strong. The fictional material in these, like the fiction I've just dealt with, follows the trite themes found in girls' comics. Also, a Sindy club was started in early 1986.

As in the case of Barbie, the Sindy range has led, by an easy step, to the development of cosmetics for girls. The Sindy Vanity Case, with an assortment of items for make-up, was new in 1981, though a different one had been available the year before. The Sindy Beauty Care range was new in 1982, like the Barbie Play Make-up. The usual items —lipstick, nail colour, blusher and eye shadow — were available in various combinations. There were four beauty sets, two of them 'de luxe'. The boxes announce 'The gentle introduction to make-up', these words being enclosed in the heart symbol often used on Sindy products. Overall, and again like the Barbie Play Make-up, the colour scheme for the range is basically various shades of pink. Again, language is important and shows an attempt to bridge the world of the child and the adult world. The lipsticks, for instance, are called Poppy, Peach Pink, Nice 'n' Spicy and Peekaboo Pink. Moreover, each lipstick has 'a distinctive fruit or mint flavour'. There'll be more to say about cosmetics later in this chapter.

We can move on to some particular points about language while remaining, for the moment, with make-up. As usual in the toy world, make-up is presented to girls as a normal part of life. The 'Sindy beauty care first Make-up book' announces, in its first sentence, 'Playing with make-up is a natural part of growing up'. Here is one of the more obvious distortions in the language of toy manufacturers. Whatever else might be said about cosmetics, they simply can't be called 'natural' so playing with them can't be natural either. The next sentence in the booklet begins, 'It is fun' and the word 'fun' is repeated twice more, in a determined sort of way, in the next few lines. (This word was dealt with, in some detail, in the context of language in the Barbie range.) Obviously, the word 'vanity' is also very important in the fashion doll world. As the main meanings are to do with futility and a rather overblown personal pride, this might not seem far wrong. Such self-regard, however, is presented as a good thing and the use of the word is extended in rather ridiculous ways. A 'vanity case', such as Sindy's in her Hair Styling Set, shows the word used in a long-standing sense. However, to call 'a period full length mirror and wash-stand' a Vanity Unit is stretching the meaning a bit far, and when the wardrobe is described as having a 'vanity mirror' and the Star Traveller Motor Home as containing 'vanity drawers' we might well think that all is vanity.

Manufacturers of fashion dolls keep on and on about how 'poseable' the dolls are and this is obviously important. We should note, however, that the word implies manipulation and that it points up the decorative and passive aspects of these dolls. This all fits in well with the role of sex object.

Before leaving Sindy, and to take the comparison with Barbie further, I should add some points about promotion, sales, and economics. Some familiar developments could be seen at an early stage. In 1966, for instance, Pedigree were marketing playclothes for girls based on Sindy's outfits. Other moves at about that time, however, were more unusual. The ICI paints division marketed a wallpaper showing Sindy, Paul and Patch in many different outfits. Then, in 1967, Sindy was used to promote a new Ford car. She was to get an outfit with the same name as the car. Illustrating a more common kind of development, whereby products are made for the girls themselves, rather than for the dolls, there's the Sindy 'carrycase' and wrist watch which were around in 1982. The first simply has the Sindy logo on it, as well as a lot of luggage labels showing the names of large towns across the world (including Johannesburg in South Africa). The wrist watch has the Sindy logo and a large, pink heart in the centre, and shows Active Sindy in a ballet pose.

It's interesting to see, from an account of the development of the Dunbee-Combex-Marx company, that Sindy and Barbie were both involved in that company in 1972 (as it owned Rovex which made Pedigree Dolls and had taken over Mattel's British interests under licence). This account, which seems to date from late 1973 or early 74, states that the company's products were 'finding their way into children's hands in countries throughout Europe, Asia, North and South America, Australasia and Africa'. Sindy and Barbie were both doing well at the time, though Sindy was just starting her foreign conquests.

Modern fashion dolls have always depended heavily on advertising. Pedigree announced they would be spending 1.3 million, overall, on advertising and promotion in 1983. Much of this would be on Sindy products, as they form such a large part of the firm's output. The Sindy expenditure ranged from television and the usual press advertising (notably in women's magazines) to 'Talking Sindy'. This is a boxed display scene, for use by retailers, in which Sindy appears to talk — about her many wonderful possessions, of course. It was redesigned with a new scene for 1983 and could be rented from Pedigree at a charge of £100 or £150 per three-week period, depending on the time of year.

Sindy's success abroad has important cultural implications, so we should have some idea of what's going on. An army of Sindys invaded five European countries in 1973. Ten years later, she had reached 12 countries in Europe. (Also, 1983 sales were more than 100% up on 1982.) In 1975, Sindy won the Brunte toy award in Sweden and, in late 1976 and early 77, sales of the Sindy doll were higher per head of population in Belgium than in any other European country. Colette Mansell, in *The Collector's Guide to British Dolls Since 1920*, which was published in 1983, states that Sindy is 'currently supplied to seventy-five export markets'.

Mattel's 'Fashion Doll Review', dated November 1983, is a survey of fashion dolls carried out in the summer of 1983 in Britain, France, Italy and West Germany. It will help to fill in the picture. A main conclusion of the review is that 'the fashion doll market has not yet realised its full potential in Britain'. Some idea of the scope of the fashion doll offensive can be gauged by the fact that Mattel claim they invest £17 million per year in research and development programmes for the fashion doll market, which in their case means, at present, the Barbie range. The figure, I think, must be taken as referring to the British subsidiary company as they produced the review. No doubt the parent company in the USA spends much more. Other interesting points come to light in this review. There are, it's stated, more fashion dolls per child in France, Italy and West Germany than in Britain and, in the USA, children have about twice as many dolls as British children have. In their 'Fashion Doll Review' of January 1983, the British subsidiary of Mattel claim that their research shows that, in the USA, most girls who own fashion dolls have up to as many as six by the time they're eight years old. (We now return to 'The Fashion Doll Review' of November.) In Britain, Sindy is better known than Barbie but Sindy isn't well known, they say, in the other three countries, where Barbie holds sway. In spite of Sindy's European conquests, this seems to be true. My general impression is that Barbie is much more of a globetrotter. In any case, it wasn't until 1983 that Sindy reached France and West Germany and she hadn't got to Italy at all by that time. The fashion doll sector is growing and amounts to about half of total doll sales — in the countries in question, of course. Italy has the lowest income per head of the four countries and yet spends the most on fashion dolls and, whereas in Britain the average age at which a child first receives a fashion doll is four and a half, in Italy it's three and a half. In Britain, each child with a fashion doll, or dolls, has, on average, 14 outfits, which is considerably fewer than in Italy or West Germany. According to Mattel's review, mothers buy 70% of all fashion dolls. Certainly, the manufacturers pay a lot of attention to mothers in their advertising. The review estimated that £1½ million would be spent on Sindy and Barbie advertising in 1983. This is double the amount spent in 1981. It's not only the scale of the operation that's important but also its speed.

As far as Britain is concerned, Pedigree were claiming, in early 1984, that Sindy had 80% of the fashion doll market and represented 5% of all toy sales. So much for 'variety' and 'choice' — apart from any other considerations.

Now, having some idea of where the goods are sold, we might ask where the wealth is actually made. Nearly all Mattel's fashion dolls and outfits are made in Hong Kong, Taiwan and the Philippines or by independent suppliers in Hong Kong and 'Korea' (I presume South Korea is meant). This is where the cheap labour is, and it gives an idea of the general pattern, not only for fashion dolls, but for other toys as well. Around 1979, the bodies and limbs of 3,500 Sindy dolls were turned out per day at Pedigree's factory in Canterbury. The heads, and many of the outfits, were made in Hong Kong. I had a borrowed Sindy doll of a later date, with 'Made in Hong Kong' stamped on the body, so perhaps by then more of the production had been shifted there.

Where do the profits go? The wholesale or trade price of all the 69 Barbie items in Mattel's 1983 catalogue was £513.25. The trade price for the 98 Sindy items available in the same year was £388.09. A 'retail price guide' was given for each of these Sindy items and the amounts, added together, totalled £667.78. Therefore, the retail profit was 72.06% or £279.69. (This is about an average retail profit on toys and games.) Although details are hard to come by, I think we can assume that the manufacturers will get the lion's share. Details from the Companies Registration Office show that Pedigree's 1983 turnover, for the manufacture and distribution of dolls and toys, was £21,085,000. Profits for that year were £2,983,000. No separate details were available for the Sindy range but it does form a big part of their output, taking up, for instance, 32 pages out of 68 in the 1983 catalogue. Although it's supposed to be a legal requirement, Mattel hadn't bothered to provide any information since 1981.

Other fashion dolls, with their bits and pieces and wedding dresses, have come and gone over the years. Sometimes, particular aspects — such as fashion, in a context of upper class self-indulgence — have been stressed. Daisy doll, for example, first marketed by Flair Toys (or Model Toys — sources differ) in about 1972 or 3, had outfits by Mary Quant, the fashion designer. Ginny Fashion and Charm, a new doll from Lesney in 1980, would, according to a press release, 'wear only the best of "Haute Couture" ' while the Glamour Girls, which Palitoy first brought out in 1981, also had their eyes on the top of the social ladder. The magazine, *Toy Trader*, in January 1982 said, presumably quoting the manufacturers, that these dolls were meant to 'represent the world of fantasy high-life glamour, fashion and sophistication to girls aged four and above'. Ginny, at about 38cm, was an attempt at a taller-than-average fashion doll whereas the Glamour Girls, at just over 11cm, were quite small. These two lines both came ready dressed. The Glamour Girls, aimed at children as young as four, let's remember, give rise to another issue. With these, you could get three Datelines, each consisting of a boy doll and, according to the 1982 catalogue, 'a range of scene-setting accessories for [either] "Dinner", the "Beach" or a ride on a "Scooter" '. This range, again, shows how pressures from toy manufacturers have the effect of depriving children of the possibility of growing up in a calm, unhurried and unharried way. Instead, they're hooked into consumerism and drawn into narrow and senseless gender roles. Little girls, unmolested by toy manufacturers, would have no interest in such things as Datelines.

In fact, children can't play in any meaningful sense with fashion dolls. They can only go through rituals and, although these may well provide a certain amount of the security children need, it doesn't have to be provided in this form. Moving from one to another playset within a fashion doll concept is like moving from one to another of Enid Blyton's stories: there's enough, each time, in the way of surface variations or gimmickry to prevent boredom for a while but, underneath, roughly the same measure of dope is constantly being provided.

Make-up and hairdressing sets

We've already seen manufacturers move, in the case of the Barbie and Sindy cosmetics, from products for dolls to products for the children themselves. It's now time to look more closely at such products which, after all, play a much more direct part in encouraging girls to look upon themselves as sex objects. As well as the various make-up and hairdressing sets, I'll include here such things as the model heads, and faces, for girls to practise on. There are many overlaps, however. Some products fall into various categories, or straddle them, and there's a strong link between some of the items discussed here and the sets of gear (bracelets, imitation jewelry, purses, shoes and so on) already dealt with (see pp.34-35). The accessories with the hairdressing sets and model heads — I don't want to give a list each time — are, for make-up, such as those I've already mentioned and, in fact, such as can be found for adults, or similar ones adapted for children's use. For hairdressing, there are such things as combs and brushes, hair curlers, hairgrips and hair rollers, hair colouring sticks, possibly shampoos and perhaps ribbons — in various numbers and combinations.

The Model Girl range, from Model Toys, gives us a good start even though the Hair Styling Set is rather unusual. It consists of model head, a wig and various hairdressing accessories. After preparing the wig on the model, the girl can wear it herself. The Model Girl Beauty Centre is claimed to be 'every little girl's dream for her dressing table'. As well as the usual make-up accessories — eye-shadow, blusher and lipstick in various shades — there's perfume and shampoo, a brush, mirror and comb and also four cards giving 'hints' on make-up and hairdressing. The Dressing Up Set in the same range also includes make-up items.

The Hollywood Make-up Set from Bell Toys consists of a plastic face with removable eyelashes and various make-up accessories. The title gives us a clue to the particular twist in this case and, on the box, it says 'make her up for different roles with real cosmetics'. Four examples of 'roles' are shown on the box: 'glamour', 'exotic', 'sweet' and, interestingly, 'career girl'. What a strange, and restricted, view of women is implied here! By 1982, Hollywood Make Up Set No.2 had appeared which was the same but with the addition of two interchangeable 'hair pieces'.

In Dekker's range of Learn About Beauty Sets there's a Bath Set, two make-up sets and sets for 'nail care', and 'hair care'. 'Learn from fun' is the general motto of this range, though the boxes show girls preening themselves in a rather serious and dedicated way. However, this is unusual. Generally, the packaging of products like these shows girls gleefully brandishing the various items and having great 'fun'. The make-up set 'with real cosmetics' was advertised as for girls 'from 7 years' in the 1982 catalogue whereas the following year the lower age limit had dropped to six for a basically similar set. This just goes to show how girls are growing up more quickly all the time. Dekker's Make Up to Music set was a new gimmick in 1983. It comes with a cassette tape which gives 'full instructions for applying cosmetics properly', according to the press release. Moreover, these instructions are 'set to relaxing music'. Although Dekker describe this as 'the revolutionary new idea for girls', I wonder what the description would convey to girls in, say, Nicaragua or Cuba. I found the cassette quite desperately boring. If girls weren't indoctrinated from an early age, I suggest they'd feel the same way.

Pedigree's Young Girl range, consisting (1980) of five 'beauty care' sets and one set for perfume making, shows the process taking place. 'Each pack', the catalogue says, 'is comprehensively designed for the younger child to fully appreciate the need of beauty care at an early age'. They don't say how early.

In recent years, modelling heads have been on the market in large numbers. These are female heads, nearly always white, life-size or smaller, and with the neck, the inner part of the shoulders and upper part of the chest forming a stand. The whole is something like one of the model heads used in shop windows for displaying hats or hair styles. Alternatively, the head can be set in a plastic stand which, in turn, can form a tray, and so on. They all have hair and are meant for hairdressing and usually for making-up as well.

The best known in Britain is Palitoy's Girl's World. (What an insult, to call this a 'world'!) However, this, according to the magazine, *Toys International and the Retailer* in January 1981, at that time led 'the market for modelling heads with a share of about 75 per cent at market value'. Girl's World has 'hair that grows' and both hairdressing and make-up accessories. In 1981, there was also Super Girl's World, featuring 'eyes that change colour by tilting the head'. You had to 'choose an eye colour then style the head accordingly', the catalogue said. At the same time, you could get Girl's World Glittering Make-up which had stars, sequins and unusual colours. (This seems much more like fun!) The following year, it was claimed that Girl's World was 'more sophisticated than ever' with a new range of cosmetics 'in the very latest fashion shades'. New that year (and following a familiar tactic) was My First Girl's World which had 'easy to use' accessories 'with the younger girl in mind'.

We can discount the usual extravagant claims of the manufacturers (although we shouldn't ignore the messages they convey). What is, in a way, more disturbing is to find Girl's World 'Highly Recommended' in several sections of *The Good Toy Guide* for the years 1981-3. Astonishingly, it was described as 'good for encouraging conversation' in the *Guide* for 1981. How can it do that? The 1983 *Guide,* in a comment which could have come straight from the manufacturer, says, 'Provides hours of fun in creating hairdo's and practising with makeup'. If this is guidance, then truly we're lost.

According to *Toy Trader* in November 1981, there were 6,000 entrants in the Miss Girl's World competition of that year. The idea was to create a 'look for the Eighties' using Super Girl's World. The winner was to get a day out in London and £50 to spend — on Palitoy products.

At the same time, the French firm of Berchet (a member of the large Superjouet group) were running their competition, 'Miss Happy Hair 1981' for parents who bought Coiffeuse. This is a trolley with two trays and a mirror mounted on top and with nearly 20 hairdressing and make-up accessories. It could be used for looking after dolls' hair, as well. Each parent entering the competition had to create a hairstyle for her, or his, daughter and then send a photo of it to the firm, granting permission for it to be used in any Berchet publicity. The winner was to get a free trip to Paris for herself and family and even the third prize — a cheque for £75 — made Palitoy look mean by comparison.

In the issue of *Toy Trader* just referred to, Coiffeuse was described as 'already a best seller in France'. Nevertheless, in spite of all this, Coiffeuse was not in the 1983 catalogue. It was replaced by Coiffeuse-case, a folding-up case containing the usual hairdressing and make-up accessories. A little booklet of advice came with it and you could also get a stand to put it on and a model head for practising.

This brings us back to heads again. New in the 1983 Superjouet catalogue (in English and German as well as French) was the Bella range which included three different model heads, each with accessories for hairdressing and making-up. With two of them, you could get a shower tray and shower.

Pedigree had two model heads, blonde and brunette, in their beauty salon range in 1980. A 'de luxe' version, extra accessories and a battery operated hair drier were also available. Pedigree (surely tongue-in-cheek) claimed that this would provide 'still further learning and creative play for the child'.

Then, there was the World of Beauty model head from Blossom, claimed to be 'one of the best selling products in Great Britain during 1979' with real make-up the girl could use on herself. A blackface version, called Coloured World of Beauty, was also to be had with 'appropriate lipstick, eyeshadow and blusher shades'.

From West Germany, there was a model head called Miss Betsy, manufactured by Zapf, with 40 accessories and a hairdressing booklet, in five languages, giving information on how to create 20 hair styles and, in Spain, Berjusa produced Milaydi while Vicina produced Ficrela — and all these came in their versions and variations and often with quite bewildering numbers of accessories.

We return to sets, and it should be sufficient if I try to complete a general picture of this area of the toy market — if, in fact, 'toy' is the right word here — in order to give an idea of its extent and also to pick out any of the less usual features.

Superjouet have six hairdressing sets in their Miss Beauté range, one with 21 items, including an electric hair drier. Two of these sets have electric blow-dry brushes. There are the usual make-up sets and also mock jewelry sets as well. It's interesting that the word 'vanity' (not vanité) is now used in French for a case of make-up.

Klein, in 1981, were marketing 24 hairdressing sets in boxes and cases, two in the form of trolleys and one hairdressing table. Thirteen of these were on offer in Britain. By 1983, Klein were manufacturing a boxed cosmetics set and also several cases of cosmetics. Six, including one which had hairdressing items as well, were on the market in Britain. Overall, about half of these products were under the firm's Miss Caroline logo used, you may remember, for a lot of their housework sets.

The gimmick in Action GT's Fresh 'n Fancy (sic) 'cosmetic kit' is that the girl makes up the cosmetics herself from the ingredients provided (in a sizable pink tray). The front of the box shows a large photo of a girl's face alight with wonder as she applies lipstick.

In their Tomorrow's Girl range, Harbutt's have a make-up and hairdressing set combined, a make-up set and a Pin-on Jewellery set. The presentation of these gives me a chance to draw together some of the points I've been making about language. Firstly, there's the title of the range, which looks excitedly to the future while with the jewelry, described as 'trendy', the emphasis is on being in with the swing of things. Secondly, here again we come across the view, or assertion, that what's going on is a natural part of life. The claim is made, on the box of the cosmetics set, that make-up 'is a part of growing up'. This seems to be in contradiction with claims

11: Girl's World — 1989 version

made elsewhere. If it's all natural, why is there an 'instruction booklet' with the set and why have the contents been 'specially formulated' and 'designed to introduce young girls to the art of make-up application and hair styling'? Surely, all this effort isn't necessary to promote something that comes naturally? Lastly, there's the usual emphasis on 'fun'.

Firms based in the USA play an especially large part in the sector of the toy market described in this chapter. It's appropriate, therefore, to end with two of them. The examples are taken from products available in 1983.

Firstly, we have the many 'beauty products for girls', which come from the firm of Tom Fields and are sold under the brand name of Tinkerbell. The lip glosses and lipsticks come in six different flavours, four of them fruit, together with peppermint and bubble gum, and there are also fruit scented skin creams. These aspects, as well as the packaging of the items, show that the aim is to attract very young girls. The Soap Animals and the Crazy Cream Machine also point in the same direction.

Hasbro, in taking over Knickerbocker, became responsible for the large range of Crayon Girl cosmetics. These are also aimed at very young girls and most, if not all of the carded items are — so it says on the cards — 'recommended for ages 4 and over'. The dodge with the larger items is to play upon the love children have for things secret and hidden. So, the Secret Beauty Case, for example has 'two secret drawers, activated by concealed catches'. The Disco vanity set looks like a small record player but its 'hidden storage compartment' contains a mirror, nail polish and blusher, and there's also 'a hidden radio that enables the child to tune in to her favourite D. J. whilst making up'. Truly, things are not what they seem. This battery-powered radio, a representative of the firm told me, would get local stations. By such gimmicks, as well as by the fruit-scented items and the names of the products, children are drawn into this whole wearisome business.

In a leaflet advertising their toys for the spring and summer of 1983, however, Knickerbocker revealed that it wasn't all left to gimmicks. Referring to their television advertising, they said, 'When Knickerbocker introduced Crayon Girl Play Make-Up in 1982 [into Britain], it instantly became a brand leader — and with an aggressive campaign in 1983, we mean to keep it there'.

Playthings to do with make-up and hairdressing come and go, over the years, but there always seem to be plenty of them about. Girl's World itself disappeared for a few years but then came back, refurbished, in 1989 (see illustration, p.91).

Barbie, Sindy and the others are systems of planned obsolescence, designed to keep girls on the hook as endlessly unsatisfied consumers. At the same time, and amongst other things, they promote the idea of women as sex objects. The hairdressing and make-up sets do this more directly, though not necessarily with greater effect. It seems to me that those who exploit the minds of children in such ways have a lot to answer for.

CHAPTER 5

THE HANDYMAN AND BREADWINNER

This chapter deals with mainly peaceful roles generally thought appropriate for males and as presented to boys through their playthings. There will, however, be an overlap with the next chapter which is specifically concerned with war and killing. Certain parts of this chapter will move us into that area while, as regards the model vehicles and other craft described here, we'll find that, although these are not military in themselves, they heavily emphasize the aggression that's thought to be appropriate for males and which underlies the whole of chapter six.

There's been very little written about masculine gender roles and the way in which they are laid down. In some quarters, it's just been taken for granted that men come off best in any comparison of gender roles, and although this is bound to be true in everyday life in a male-dominated society in peacetime, a lot more needs to be said on this subject.

The roles of handyman and breadwinner can be seen as corresponding to the roles of housewife and mother. All point to the home and the family but only one of the four, the breadwinner, is normally based outside the home, in the workplace. The two masculine gender roles often overlap. A part of both, for instance, is that boys are thought to be more 'mechanically minded' and to have more of a bent towards science. Another way of looking at this, however, is to take the view that they are turned away from most of their emotions, or at least from expressing them. Only emotions associated with competition and aggression, such as anger, are generally left open to boys.

The kinds of toys and playthings to be dealt with here — model vehicles and other craft, construction sets, tool kits and science sets — have traditionally been given to boys. A lot of these toys have something in common — putting things together — and in the better examples this means making sense of the world and increasing an awareness of space.

Language and names, as usual, are very important in this chapter and I want, now, to bring this aspect to the forefront. Several words, usually only applied to males, point to failure in work roles. 'Layabout, 'loafer' and 'idler' are obvious ones, as are 'shirker' and 'skiver'. Other words, such as 'lubber', 'bumpkin' and 'clodhopper' have wider meanings but they all include the sense of physical awkwardness or clumsiness which would be ill-suited to labour. The last two have agricultural associations, in particular. Other expressions, although more general, still point to masculine roles: 'to be a man', 'to make a man out of someone', 'to separate the men from the boys', 'to be a man's man' (compare a 'ladies' man') and 'to take it like a man'. In these ways, language carries assumptions about what men should be, and do. As we move on to model toys we'll see how language continually reinforces traditional masculine roles.

Model toys

With this kind of toy, power and aggression are emphasized, overwhelmingly, and speed, stunts and crashes, or sheer size, are very much to the fore.

The Buddy 'L' range of steel model vehicles from the USA, which has been marketed by various companies in Britain, is typical, with its various Brute 'series' including Super Brutes, Big Brutes and even Lil Brutes. A new model in 1983 was Brute Force. Both strength and lack of human sympathy are emphasized in the word 'brute', while the many models of enormous transport vehicles add notions of power. The Mack Big Rig, for instance, is called 'the Convoy King'.

The four ranges marketed by Matchbox, all of which seem to originate in the USA (although, at about this time — 1982-3 — Matchbox passed under the control of a company based in Hong Kong) take us further into this strange territory. First, the Burnin' Key Cars, which are quite small and meant to be collected, are worked by keys which are inserted into the back. 'Speed' and 'power' are emphasized on these carded items and stunt sets with ramps can also be bought. Racing motor-bikes were included in this range in 1983 to add, according to the catalogue, 'a new collectible dimension to the hottest vehicles made'. Next, the wind-up vehicles in the Stunt Riders range do 'wheelies', amongst other things. This is when the cars move along on two wheels, a side wheelie being on the wheels of either side and a back wheelie being on the two back wheels. Thirdly, from Matchbox, we have the range of motor-bikes called Power Blasters, in which speed and loud engine noise are emphasized. In this assortment, there's also a Turbo Team for 'high speed racing and daring stunt riding', and a Fall Guy bike with rider which 'allows kids to re-enact the thrills seen on television'. Quotations are from the 1983 Matchbox catalogue. Fourthly, there's the Rough Riders series which continues the stunt and crash obsession. There are trucks, cars, jeeps and pick-ups — and all do side wheelies. Then, there's the Rough Riders 'Hot Shoe' racing motor-bike (or 'dirt bike') assortment which do back wheelies as well as other feats understandable only to the initiated.

It seems quite to be expected that actual racing should enter in here. The various Powertrack sets from Matchbox contain sections of electrified track along which two children can race their model cars, regulating the speed by hand-held controls. The sets differ in length of track and in various refinements and accessories. This system, known as slot-racing, has developed into a hobby and there are clubs whose members meet to race their cars. A local club seemed to be all-male with members of various ages down to about 10. There are also radio-controlled model cars for racing.

Mattel's Hot Wheels range of die-cast metal vehicles was first introduced into Britain from the USA in 1969. They seem to have been re-introduced in 1980 when 60 models were available. By 1984, there were 98 models, all small 'collectables' at 'real pocket money price', according to the catalogue of that year. The heat and speed association is carried on in the Hot Wheels logo which is based on the idea of a flame. It's true, and fair to say, that the range does include work vehicles and a construction site set but, overall, it's very easy to see what attitudes are being encouraged, and interests cultivated, with sets such as: Speedblaster, Flying Fire-bird, Jumpmasters, the Loop and Chute Stunt Set and the Dash and Crash Racing Set. There are three Zap 'n' Go Action Sets: the Barrel Blaster, the Pretzel Bend and the Mount Twister. They all involve portions of track with loops, or gaps over which the cars leap. The stress is on risks and danger, as well as speed, stunts and crashes, as usual. New for 1984 was the Crack-Ups Bash 'n' Smash Set for which there's a range of eight cars which can be smashed and then repaired. The idea is for two boys to send their cars along the track to crash at the cross-roads. 'Crash 'em! Fix 'em! Bash 'em again!' it says cheerfully in the catalogue. At least with the figure-of-eight Criss Cross Crash Set, which was available in 1982, it was possible to avoid a crash. With this later set, the actual object is to crash the cars.

The Stompers range, also originating in the USA, is described as consisting of '4-wheel drive, battery-powered, hill-climbing vehicles'. Again, the rough-and-tough name carries its own message. I only mention them to give an idea of the overall pattern and to add one or two details. Action GT introduced the range into Britain in early 1984 claiming that, since they were first launched in the USA in 1981, over 33 million had been sold throughout the world. Although it seems that about 20 million of these were sold in their home country, according to the January 1984 issue of the magazine *Toys 'n' Playthings,* that still leaves a lot to make a considerable cultural impact elsewhere. The ideas and values promoted by these toys are similar to those noted in connection with other ranges, with the addition of a more overt kind of aggression in the Stomper Mobile Military Force.

Some other points can be noted from Mettoy's large Corgi range. This includes a group of 'All Weather Trekkers' which are 'tough action vehicles' that 'traverse rough terrains'. 'Weather' and 'terrain' are often brought in like this to emphasize an all-round ruggedness.

The Corgi range, in addition, gives a good example of the links between toys and comics, films and television, and reminds us that toys can seldom be seen in isolation. So, from the world of the superheroes who began in comics, Mettoy have a Spiderbike, a Batbike and a Batmobile. These three are available in a smaller size, also, along with Supermobile, the Superman Van and the Hulkcycle, a Batman Set and a Superheroes Set. From the novels by Ian Fleming via films, there are three James Bond cars, in each of two ranges, and also the 'Octopussy' Gift Set. Making the link with television, there's a Starsky and Hutch car.

This brings us to the whole question of the connections between television and toys. It's a question that we'll meet again in the next chapter. Here, I just want to point out that, in Britain, there's an almost constant supply of television serials from the USA, which deal with some aspect of 'law and order' and which feature, usually, special kinds of vehicles that are soon produced as toys. The main characters are usually men who spend a lot of time chasing one another about in various vehicles and other craft, shooting at one another with assorted guns, or throwing or launching various kinds of missiles. For a change, there are fist fights. The stories are just pegs on which to hang the violence.

According to a study carried out in the USA by the National Coalition on Television Violence and Pennsylvania University, there was an average of 23 violent acts per hour in the serial *The Dukes of Hazzard.* This seems to be good for business. The *Daily News,* a special publication for the Earls Court Toy and Hobby Fair, reported on 1st February 1983 that $250 million worth of licensed merchandise had been sold, arising from this serial. Part of this sum had no doubt been paid by Knickerbocker to enable them to produce their General Lee 'crash' and 'stunt' cars. Ertl, yet another US firm, which tends to specialize in lines licensed from popular US television serials, was in on this as well and received a special award in Britain from the National Association of Toy Retailers for its range of *Dukes of Hazzard* die-cast cars. Ertl did very well with these, especially the General Lee car. This is the one with the Confederate flag design on the roof, that is, the flag of the reactionary and racist southern states of the USA in the civil war. Geraldine L Wilson, in an extremely perceptive article on toys, in which she noted how the confederate flag had proliferated in 1981, calls it, 'the symbol of the South's oppression for Black people'.[1]

Ertl also have in their output, vehicles from *Hardcastle and McCormick, The A-Team, The Fall Guy* and *Knight Rider,* all US television serials. This last, according to the study on television violence mentioned earlier, has an average of 18 violent acts per hour. In this serial, Knight clears up crime with the aid of a talking (computer) car which does various stunts such as spectacular leaps. In early 1984, I noted, without trying to make a thorough check, that at least five companies were marketing toy *Knight Rider* vehicles. (We last met this car on a merry-go-round at a play day for the under fives.) A fast, special car is also prominent in the *Hardcastle and McCormick* serial which follows a common formula of car chases, car crashes and shooting, all hung on a slender thread of narrative.

It's difficult to believe how such a constant fare of violence could fail to de-sensitize children, at the very least. However, there's evidence to suggest that it does much more.

It may seem that we've now moved some distance away from the basic handy-man and breadwinner idea. However, the model cars and motor-bikes in question are still — at least technically — peaceful toys, not war toys, and the association of boys with large machinery (and hence the outdoor world) underlies this whole area. It's quite unusual to see a picture of a girl in connection with the kind of toy I've just been describing. Also, amongst the racing cars, stunt cars, crash cars, dirt bikes and so on, the workaday world (of men, it must be said) is still fairly well represented. Construction site vehicles are quite common, and there are telephone repair trucks, refuse vans, various delivery vehicles and break-down trucks, the last usually called by the US name of 'wreckers', as most of these toys are from the USA. (It's a bad name for them but sounds more dramatic.) All of these are to do with earning a living and so are the models of enormous transport vehicles, though with these the ideas of size, power and aggression are much more to the fore. Most of the model manufacturers already mentioned have ranges of these and, in addition, the West German firm of Siku produce die-cast zinc models in 1/55th scale, some of them of amazingly large haulage lorries such as a mobile crane transporter and, unbelievably, a petrol station transporter. The US firm of Monogram produce plastic model kits, which snap together, for making enormous vehicles, two of them in 1/16th scale, 'to capture the spirit and undoubted appeal of trucking'.

Apart from the more immediate points about gender roles, there are overall political points to be made here, of a kind less obvious, perhaps, certainly as far as children are concerned. Real, gigantic vehicles, as opposed to models, are not — as yet — allowed in Britain, because of the damage they wreak on the environment. In addition, the models are of privately owned transport, here in Britain in competition with publicly owned British Rail for the carrying of freight. As far as these toys are concerned, therefore, children are emotionally aligned with privateering for profit long before they arrive at an age when they can consider the political arguments involved. Models, such as the one from Palitoy with the words 'Central City Fire Co.' on it, make a similar point. In this instance, a public service is, clearly, privately owned (and will, therefore, only operate if it makes a profit). Lastly on this theme (for now), it almost goes without saying that practically all the vehicles mentioned in this section are plastered with advertisements, thus signalling to children the messages of an economy based on private profit.

Model railways provide a peaceful and civilized contrast to most of what I've described up to now in this chapter. However, I have neither the space nor the knowledge to go into the subject as fully as it deserves. Anyway, the model railway manufacturers all deny that their products are toys. What does seem clear is that, usually, boys are introduced to this hobby by their fathers, though there's no reason why girls shouldn't be interested in it. What strikes an outsider most of all is the enormous stress put on detail and accuracy. For example, the West German Minitrix firm, which has a catalogue in English and Swedish available in Britain, claim to spend one-and-a-half to two years developing a new steam locomotive model. Making one mould for such a model, and several are needed, takes about 2,600 work hours. One of the smallest parts is a bolt, 2,000 of which will fit into a thimble. It's not only the models that receive such care and attention, either, though naturally they are of the greatest importance. The firm of Peco produces ballast of six kinds and the Richard Kohnstam company makes 22 different groups of trees, as well as 12 individual trees, including dark fir trees, small and large. This is a positive kind of hobby which obviously has its attractions and many of the models, especially the locomotives, are very beautiful.

Construction

Next, we come to construction sets and systems. These are usually thought of as being more appropriate for boys, though it's as well to bear in mind that there's a point of possibly even wider cultural significance. It's been said that the circle and, presumably, the sphere are more fundamental to the way of thinking of some native American peoples than the usual shapes, made up of flat surfaces and straight lines, which are found in construction sets. There are obviously very fundamental cultural implications here, which may involve other peoples, also (see p.169).

However, what's most noticeable about the marketing of the many sets available is the assumption that girls are less interested in these playthings than boys.

This can be seen very clearly in the Baby Castor range of sets from the Dessoy firm which is a member of the large Superjouet group. These seem to be intended for children of about two to eight years old and all consist of large pieces. (In construction sets, the general rule is, the smaller the hands, the larger the pieces.) The Casto Buggy and Giro sets, for instance, make trundlers big enough for children to ride on. The Jombo set also makes a trundler, as well as several other large items, such as a barrow and a trolley, while the Géant makes working vehicles and machinery of various kinds. These four sets all show boys on the boxes. However, Dessoy have not forgotten girls and have sets specially for them with pictures of girls on the boxes. The Casto Relax set is described in the catalogue as 'enabling little girls to make a pram, a cradle, and other accessories for playing with dolls'. No cranes or cars for them. The Castorine set is similar, says on the box 'construction for little girls' and you can make, for example, a high chair, a push chair, and a cot; while the Castorette set is similarly described and makes six objects for playing with dolls, including a dressing-table. Casto Relax and Castorine have parts with floral decorations and some of the bolts also have flower patterns on them. The nuts of the three sets are all flower-shaped. Furthermore, the sets intended for boys have parts mainly in the primary colours of red, blue and yellow (see back cover) while the girls' sets have colours either more subtly matched, such as orange and two shades of green on a white base in Castorine, or in more subtle shades. Casto Relax is mainly in pastel blue, lilac and pink (see front cover).

So, apart from being told, and shown on the packaging, which sex these sets are meant for, we have coded messages in the design, form and colour. And there's no need for any such distinctions at all! The Baby Castor range is attractive in several ways and doesn't have to be divided up like this. Another point is that the Jombo set, 'from 2 years', has tools while the Casto Relax set, 'from 4 years', hasn't.

We see a similar approach, and similar assumptions, in Pedigree's Playtime sets, new in 1984, for girls and boys from the age of three. The girls have a range of kitchen furniture, while the boys are provided with a range of truck, train and boat kits (see illustrations). Most of the boxes show pictures of either girls or boys, in case anybody should be in any doubt as to who should get what. The point is further emphasized in the catalogue, where a girl, encircled by the biological symbol for female, in pink, and a boy, within the male symbol, which is in blue, are shown playing with the sets.

12: Playtime Kitchens

13: Playtime Kits

Notice that the boys' things belong to the outside world. They move. They are either boats or vehicles with wheels. The girls' playthings are static and not only restricted to the house, but to the kitchen. (And then they say that girls have poorer spacial awareness than boys!) Moreover, the boys' toys are constructional kits. Though they're simple, you do have to fit them together. The girls' sets — cooker, washing machine, sink unit and so on — have a few knobs to turn and doors to open and close, and the items can be arranged in various ways, but you don't have to construct them. On top of all this, the boys' range has about twice as many items in it. So, there are quite a few assumptions bound up in these toys which are aimed at an age when children are beginning to put together some notions about the world and their roles in it.

Stepping down the age range even further, we can pick up some other attitudes. Building bricks, or blocks, must be the simplest construction toys of all and yet, as I've already pointed out, even simple geometrical shapes can carry ideological and cultural implications. It isn't long, however, in the life of a child, before such toys begin to have pictures or designs on them, or symbols such as letters. Then, more obviously, the values of a culture are being conveyed. It's more obvious still when we look back in time.

Reed's Sunday Toy, to be seen at the Abbey House Folk Museum in Leeds, may seem amusing now as the stern intention behind it (no doubt unquestioned at the time it was made) looks so obvious. It consists of a box of wooden building bricks with bible texts printed on them and also pictures of church windows. With these, you could build one church (on Sundays). This Sunday Toy dates from about the middle of the last century when similar sets seem to have been quite common. (The Noah's Ark was another toy you could safely play with on Victorian Sundays.)

You can still get a set of blocks for building a church, though there are some accessories as well, from the West German firm of Lorenz. This is in their World of Play programme for children of three years and upwards. It includes (1983) 18 sets and various supplementary packages and all the pieces are in wood, both brightly coloured and plain. There are simple blocks, some stamped with windows, doors and so on for making buildings, and also simple shapes representing people, animals, trees and vehicles. These are flat-sided and the emphasis is on shape and simple graphics. We can see the beginnings of construction proper — that is, when pieces are attached to one another — notably in the very attractive goods train which is built up by fitting blocks over pegs on wheeled platforms, which can be coupled together. The material and the basic way in which it's treated are so appealing that it's a pity that there's a zoo, with obviously unendangered species in it; that the circus set includes performing animals; and that the 'African Village' is the stereotyped kraal with thatched huts. All in all, the 'world' being transmitted to children here is that of western Europe about 50 years ago, and that's a pity.

By contrast, some bricks and blocks and other construction or building toys are about as abstract as it's possible to get unless, as I've already mentioned, the shapes themselves convey values. The large, hollow, wooden blocks, each with two open sides, from Community Playthings are in three sizes, the middle-sized ones measuring 14x28x28cm. The wood is plain but treated with preservative. These blocks can be used with ramps and boards to make simple climbing and balancing structures, or to make boats, cars and houses for playing in. One clear message with these is that they are meant for group play, which is a good message for small children. Perhaps, also, the warm naturalness of wood itself, in this case beech, has something to convey to small hands through touch, just as its appearance is pleasant to the sight. However, I know that children usually prefer the coloured and painted to the plain.

Two makes of interlocking, plastic, building bricks, about the size of real bricks, are available: Plasbrics from the educational suppliers Arnold and Lincabricks from Galt (who also supply the educational market). The first, in various colours, seem to me rather garish but they do have one face open with a bar across, so they're easy to pick up. The others, which I haven't seen, are similar but in brown and red and without the bar. Again, both of these are really meant for group and, hopefully, co-operative play.

Multilink cubes, available from educational suppliers and intended for children of about junior school age, are much smaller but, behind them, is a very determined effort to indoctrinate children — with mathematical principles! These hollow, plastic, 2cm cubes are in 10 colours. Each has a stud on one face and, on the opposite face, a hole which forms a socket. The other four faces also have sockets which means that the cubes can be snapped together, very satisfyingly, in all sorts of ways. A lot of accessories can be bought for many different maths activities, but it seems like fun to me. Unifix cubes, also available from educational suppliers, are similar but made of softer plastic and they don't make such a nice snap when put together. Also, they can only be fitted in a straight line unless the plastic retaining grids are used.

These examples of blocks, bricks and cubes show the large variety of products available and also show what can be done, in a positive way, in this sector of building and construction toys.

Next, we move more firmly to construction, as distinct from building, though still at a fairly simple and fairly abstract level.

The delightful Octons, available from Galt, are flat, octagonal, plastic shapes, about 56mm in diameter, which slot together at right angles. They are in six translucent colours so children can also experiment with mixing and blending colours. They're attractive, easy to work with and readily suggest things to make, including abstract, patterned constructions. Poly-Octons are similar, also coloured but opaque, and slightly bigger and stronger and therefore more suitable for younger children. The two kinds of Octons are compatible.

The well-known Stickle Bricks started in 1969 with the British firm of Denys Fisher. Now, having followed a familiar pattern, they're owned by the large US firm of Milton Bradley who market them under the Playskool trade name. Various boxes are available and the age ranges given go down to one or one and a half. Here, as usual, the desire for profit stretches the age range stated, but they may have some interest for toddlers. It's doubtful whether they'd maintain the interest of older children for long. I found them difficult to work with, difficult, especially, to align, and also garish. The packaging shows both boys and girls, all white, but, more importantly as far as race is concerned, there's the stickle boy, white with brown hair and eyes, and the stickle girl who's blonde and blue-eyed. Moreover, following a strange but common pattern in dolls and toy figures of various kinds, the girl has eyelashes but the boy hasn't.

The Connector construction sets originated in Denmark and have been on sale in Britain for twenty years or more. They are made of plain wood, the key element being rods with slits about 12mm deep in the ends so that they can be compressed to fit into holes in blocks. There are also pulley wheels in the sets. I mention this system here because of a report on construction sets in the magazine *Which?* of November 1964. This stated that children made a remarkable number of weapons with Connector sets. It's not that these have an especially military look but it just goes to show how powerfully children are indoctrinated and turned towards warfare. I was told (the information was unprompted) in each of two playgroups I visited in the course of one week, that the children, boys I presume, made guns with the construction sets.

It would be impossible, and not to the point either, to give a survey here of construction sets and systems available in this country. However, to give an idea of the international character of the toy industry, I'll simply mention a few from those I've seen and, to some extent, tried. Thinking about children from about three years old to 12, and moving up this age range, we have: Ringa-Majig from the USA for the younger ones, Reo-click from Belgium and Mobilo from West Germany for the middle years of the age range, Struts from Australia for children in the middle and upper parts of the range, and Ludoval from Switzerland for the older children. The Ringa-Majig I tried tended to fall apart but the others all seem to me to have their good points. Interestingly, in Reo-click, the method of joining pieces, with cusps and rods, is the same as that of a metal set called Kliptico, dating from about 1925, which can be seen in the Birmingham City Museum.

Before we get on to the really extensive and well-known construction systems which will take us into the field of engineering, I'd like to note an unusual development, and a good one, of recent years. We saw how, with the large wooden blocks from Community Playthings, there was an overlap with what's usually referred to as playground equipment. This has also happened in construction kits proper.

The West German firm of Quadro produces the kits of that name. Although they must be the biggest ever, they are still for quite small children. The basic kit consists of tubes of three lengths, the longest 75cm; various kinds of tubular joints or connecting pieces; and large panels. The tubes and joints are fixed together by a very simple locking device and the panels clip into the spaces between the tubes. Quadro is made of strong polypropylene, the tubes in red and the other parts in black, and can be used indoors or out as it's waterproof. Playhouses, climbing frames and slides, amongst other things, can be constructed and, with the addition of another kit which contains wheels, several vehicles to ride in, or on, can be made. The firm of Modulum existed to market Quadro in Britain. Then, renamed Genesis, and having got the idea, they started on their own with Gymbo, a similar construction system obviously derived from Quadro. The locking device, only, of Quadro was patented and Gymbo had a different one. While Quadro leaves play to the children's imagination, Genesis felt it necessary to include such things as a plastic shop awning, heraldic emblems and flags, and designs on the panels, all to suggest certain play settings or constructions. In 1987, the Gymbo system became the property of Milton Bradley who market it, under their Playskool trade name and with some modifications, as Pipeworks. Quadro now trade in Britain under their own name.

In 1901, Frank Hornby patented a construction system at first called Mechanics Made Easy but later to be known as Meccano. He had made the prototypes, in copper, for his own children. It wasn't the first construction system of its type, as one using nuts and bolts to fix together straight and curved strips of metal or whalebone, which were pierced with holes, had been patented in 1895.

Meccano, however, soon took hold in an age of scientific inventions and the *Meccano Magazine* first came out in 1916. There's always been an assumption that the system is a plaything and a learning tool for boys, as they are supposed to be 'mechanically-minded' and interested in science. There have been changes in Meccano, nevertheless, especially in recent years, and it's these changes I'll concentrate on.

The basic idea of Meccano, to do with how machinery works and how it's made, has persisted, though it now seems to be carried on mainly by men and to be concentrated in clubs. The kind of book commonly produced for boys between the two world wars, full of the 'wonders' and 'marvels' of science, reflected this basic idea. Alongside the wonder and excitement, though, there was still the firm belief that such things could be generally understood (by boys). A book, entitled *How it Works and How it's Done*, which seems typical of the period, although it appears to have been published towards the end of it in, I think, 1937 (it's undated) has chapters such as 'Miracle of Flight', subtitled 'How Man Grew Wings'; 'Servants of Transport', about railways, trams and buses; and 'Slaves of Steel', about machines that lift and carry. Although no doubt science is now much more difficult for the non-specialist to understand, certain construction systems, to be dealt with later, have kept to this basic idea of how machinery works or at least retained it in part. Meccano seems largely to have developed in other directions.

A Meccano leaflet from 1979 announces, ' "Today's Meccano" means action, with new motorised working models that introduce the realism and movement demanded by today's children'. Press information released in January of the following year states, 'Today, sets are for building dragsters, space ships, robots, stock cars, juggernauts — in fact anything of a contemporary nature, and a far cry from pre-war model traction engines etc!' In the same publication, with reference to new products, there's an even more specific statement: 'By emphasising the play-value of the toy rather than the constructional aspects, Meccano will attract many new users and establish a broader base for the whole range'. Even making allowance for sales talk, this seems significant. It shows, in fact, a complete abandonment of the original idea of Meccano.

Later in 1980, the Action Packs were introduced. ('Action' is a favourite word with toy manufacturers, especially where boys' toys are concerned.) Each kit makes one model. There are ordinary vehicles, such as a tractor and a cement mixer; several space vehicles and machinery (but with the accent on war); and a Mobile Rocket Launcher with a rocket that can be fired. Although they're meant as an introduction to Meccano, these are more like model kits than construction sets. (It's fair to point out that the military element wasn't new as there'd been, for example, a Meccano Mechanised Army Outfit in 1939.)

By 1982, and possibly it happened some considerable time earlier, Meccano had been taken over by Palitoy. Three more Action Packs, with wind-up motors, were available by then, for making racing cars, and there were also two Action Sets 'with extra moulded pieces for that final touch of realism' as it says in the catalogue. This is, again, obviously a move in the direction of model kits. Each of these sets makes several models. The first, called Trucker Fleet, makes transport lorries and the second, Deep Hyper Space, makes space craft — presumably military ones, as the catalogue tells us to 'control the galaxy'. The Action Packs had already been very successful commercially but the basic sets, called the 1000, 2000 and 3000, still continued and obviously allowed for skill and imagination. The second and third of these contained electric motors and battery units.

The following year, 1983, brought six new sets to 'give even greater realism', three of them containing motorized and electrical parts which could be used with models made from the other three sets. These are concerned with the principles of mechanics and several models can be made with each set. Altogether, therefore, these represent a return to the original idea of Meccano and a development of the range, if along a fairly narrow path. Two new items, a radio-controlled system and another electric motor, were added in 1984 but most of the Action Packs, and both Action Sets, had, surprisingly, disappeared from the catalogue. The six sets from 1983 and the two new items were all that remained in the price list, though the three Action Packs for making racing cars were still in the catalogue.

To sum up, the range dwindled after 1979 and became concentrated in the area of technology where, we'll see shortly, it was in competition with products from the well-established Lego and Fischer firms. The Action Packs and Sets showed a move towards the market for model-making kits, a market already well supplied, for instance by Airfix, also part of the Palitoy empire. By the end of 1984, it might have been thought that Meccano was on the way out but there were still the clubs and their publications — a Midlands Meccano Guild gazette was running, for example — and the regional Meccano exhibitions and the enthusiasts abroad. Even so, it seemed ominous when the *Meccano Magazine* collapsed. By August 1984, all that remained of it was a 'Meccano Corner', of two pages, in *Airfix Magazine*. However, such things really belong to the world of male adults, rather than boys. In 1985, Meccano was sold to a French company which kept on with the sets then in production but also, more significantly perhaps, produced several sets in the traditional Meccano style. So the story isn't ended yet. Meccano has for so long been thought of as the province of boys that it's largely gone without saying. The focus on machinery and science has been the basic point in this respect and although the emphasis on the actual power of machinery has been there all along, we've seen it take a more recent form in the Trucker Fleet Set. Speed and competition, though not important aspects of Meccano until recently, are thought of as being of especial interest to boys and the racing car sets are aimed at these targets.

In the Lego system, matters of gender are spelt out more clearly. At Billund, Denmark, in the 1930s, Ole Kirk Christiansen was an out-of-work carpenter who started making wooden toys with the name of Lego (from the Danish for 'play well'). It was his son Godtfred, however, who developed the Lego brick. According to a Lego booklet of 1977, 'A Brick and the story behind it', sales of Lego by that year covered most of the world apart from the continent of Asia, although there was a south-east Asian branch. At that time, three per cent of the Lego product was sold in Denmark and the rest exported. Almost one per cent of the total industrial exports of Denmark consisted of Lego. The Legoland Park in Denmark, which was opened in 1968 had, by 1977, about three quarters of a million visitors every year. The same Lego publication also gives the following statistics: 106 countries were importing Lego sets (by 1984, this had risen to 120); an estimated 50 million children were playing with Lego; 430 million Lego sets had been produced in Billund since 1955; and Lego leaflets were produced in 25 languages.

To give an idea of the main developments in this vast system, and in order to provide some framework for what follows, I'll set out some details from a Lego information brochure, 'Imagination and System', which was released in 1984. The first Lego bricks were sold in 1949 and these, or rather the stud and socket method of joining them, are basic to the whole system. It wasn't until 1955 that the first construction set, called the 'Lego System of Play', was marketed. From these beginnings, the system has grown and branched out, over the years, into several main areas. For instance, Duplo, for children up to five years old, was started in 1969 and Fabuland, for children from three to seven, came onto the scene ten years later. Both of these were major developments. In between, dolls' houses and furniture were introduced in 1971 and the first Lego figures reached the market in 1974. These figures, as we'll see, have by now taken several different forms. The most recent main development has been the Duplo Baby Line, in 1983. There have been other refinements and developments along the way.

Considered purely from a technical point of view, the Lego system is a good one. The sets do give rein to creativity and imagination, especially those for younger children, and especially when there are several sets to draw upon! However, we have to ask: what kind of world does Lego present to children? what's being conveyed to them by means of Lego?

To try to create some sort of order out of what must seem, to most people, a very confusing situation, I'll concentrate on the Lego products available in this country in 1983 (with one or two backward glances) before bringing matters up to date. I'll describe the main categories of products and draw attention to anything which seems to be of significance. Ideologically, and as usual, the main areas of concern will be gender, race and class.

In 1983, a year in which Lego planned to spend £1½ million in Britain on media advertising, we look first at Duplo. There are rattles, teethers and pull-along toys and, for children a little older, there are simple vehicles and simple construction sets, with big pieces for little hands, such as a Service (or petrol) Station, with a clicking pump, a School and Bus set and a Living Room set. These all contain peg-top people, women and men, the women (presumably) having the longer hair. Also, some male figures have moustaches. All the figures in the Duplo and Lego ranges described here represent white people. Figures of other racial groups have been long in appearing (see below). There are more men than women in Duplo and the men are in more active roles. It seems to be almost always men who are with or in vehicles, for instance, whereas women, at least in the catalogue illustrations, are often shown sitting in chairs. You could switch them around, but then the men often have non-removable hats attaching them, so to speak, to their roles. So, the pilot of the plane and the driver of the fire engine, both men, have appropriate helmets indicating that they belong in their machines. It can be said that, broadly, these gender distinctions show the pattern for the rest of the Lego figures. Towards the end of 1983, simple, articulated figures were introduced into the Duplo range. Most of these look like men in overalls and they're associated with trains, a tipper lorry and a crane. It could be argued that this is how life is. The point, however, is to change it.

Coming to Lego proper, there are three ranges of basic sets, to take us from three years old to 12. Over these ranges, in general, and as we go from younger to older children, the pieces get smaller, they increase in number, and the construction gradually gets more difficult. In the first range of basic sets, there's a different lot of peg-top people without such obvious gender distinctions as amongst the Duplo ones. There are simply two types of figure, one with short, brown hair and the other with longer, black hair. In the second range, the most typical and usual Lego figures appear. These have limbs and heads that move, and cusp-shaped hands that can be clasped around things. The men normally appear in hats or other headgear and the women have longer hair, and although the headgear and hair are interchangeable, the design of the dress is often gender-coded — there are necklaces, for instance — and often the headgear clearly goes with the rest of the dress which frequently indicates a particular job. These figures are actually yellow. The range of advanced basic sets, for children up to the age of 12, contains working models with moving parts — vehicles, cranes and aircraft; there are special items such as gear wheels and pulleys; and one set has a battery motor. With these, and with other sets in general, there are step-by-step instructions, normally just in pictures.

We have to go back to three years old again to take in the rather different Fabuland range. Here, there are simple houses and vehicles and articulated animal figures with tools or equipment, the idea being to promote stories. Once again, we meet the play and fiction link in a fairly specific way. The catalogue tells us how this is structured:

> The animal figures each have their own name and personality. They all have tools or equipment that indicate their personality and role in society ... . Big building elements make it easy for young children to make a setting for their FABULAND stories.

The bigger Fabuland sets include story-books with pictures which are also building guides. These seem to be also available separately, as I read one in W H Smith's in April 1983. This was *Edward's Skyscraper* and began with everybody saying how silly it was to live in a sky-scraper. Edward Elephant, however, spots a forest fire from the sky-scraper where he lives and after steps are taken to put it out, everybody concludes that sky-scrapers are good — especially, perhaps, if built with Lego as shown in the illustrations. There are about three times as many male as female figures in Fabuland, though something of an attempt does seem to have been made to encourage a creative and perhaps questioning attitude towards life. There's Hannah Hippopotamus, for instance, the head gardener, and Gertrude Goat with her painter's truck, ladder and paint pot. These are unusual roles for females but, on the other hand, there's also Marjorie Mouse 'the little housewife with her vacuum cleaner' and Paulette Poodle in her living room, also with vacuum cleaner, and these are more typical of the Fabuland figures in general. I don't want to suggest there's anything absolutely wrong about representing female figures with house-cleaning equipment. Rather, what's wrong is that it happens so often and males are practically never shown in such roles. Still, a start does seem to have been made with Hannah and Gertrude.

Now, we leave Fabuland for Legoland Town, pausing only to glance out to sea, or into the bath-tub, to note that the Lego ships are crewed by men.

Legoland Town is a conventional town with the typical, yellow Lego figures in conventional gender roles. There are far more men than women and there don't seem to be many children. There are service vehicles such as an ambulance, a post office van and a fire engine and these have figures to go with them and sometimes other accessories. There's also a medical centre, a post office and a fire station, and a strong police presence, in new headquarters. Certain themes can be followed up through separate sets: for instance, the set containing the road works barrow, road cones and barriers can obviously be linked with the excavator and dumper sets. You can get pieces of roadway to make up the Legoland Town, and also various road signs, and trees and flowers. As far as class is concerned, the town's accommodation includes a villa with a barbecue in the garden; a holiday home, with sliding patio roof and a grill in the garden; and a cottage, with a sunshade in the garden. All is order and calm, and all the people smile.

Legoland Space is another range, with about 20 sets of various sizes in it. Most of these are space vehicles and this is another all-male world — like Lego railways, another huge range with trains that can be battery-operated.

This brings us to the Technic sets, new in September 1983, which offer direct comparison with the less advanced stages of Fischertechnik, the system to be dealt with next. Lego had technical sets some years earlier, so Technic sets weren't a new departure altogether. Those in the 1979 catalogue were described as 'for the technically minded' and there was a photo of three boys playing with them. There were new technical sets, for making models, in 1981, and the matter of who they were intended for was made more explicit, in a folder describing the new products for that year, which said, 'these new models have technical functions which will appeal to older boys'. These were fairly complicated working models — that is, they had moving parts. The new sets were a tractor, a tipper lorry, a helicopter and a beach buggy, making nine technical sets in all available by the end of 1981. Some, at least, could be worked by batteries. It was also intended that boys should be able to make up their own models. Over the years, particular models are renewed, sometimes with only small changes. The helicopters of 1981 and 1983, for instance, were very similar. In 1986, Lego Technic brought out the Ski Chopper (see ilustration).

How have girls been faring with Lego? In 1979, several sets were available 'for girls from 6 years'. There were three large ones: a hospital, a bungalow and a hairdressing salon called 'Salon Colette', and girls were pictured prominently on the boxes. There were also smaller sets such as a nursery and, again, a 'Ladies' hairdressers'. With younger children in mind, it's intructive to compare two Duplo sets from the point of view of gender roles. The Figures and Furniture set contains six figures (four female, one male and a dog), six chairs, two beds, a table, six printed grocery bricks and 12 other bricks. In the catalogue and on the box the figures are all shown sitting in the chairs or beds and there's not much else for them to do. The Duplo Vehicles set, on the other hand, which includes six male figures, has 10 trolleys, six separate chassis and four trailers, all interchangeable. In other words, the set with mainly female figures is static while the one with male figures involves movement — a typical situation, met with in Pedigree's Playtime sets, for example.

These Duplo sets, amongst many others, are to be found in the Lego educational programme and although many of the sets in this have been designed for use with groups of six children, which is a good thing, it seems to me that teachers should have a close look before buying in view of the issues I've been raising.

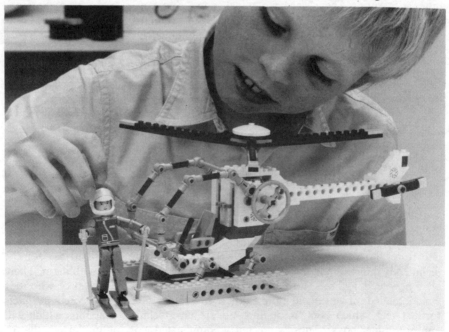

14: Ski Chopper with pilot

As regards the figures in the Lego system, overall, there are few children, women are largely invisible and mostly immobile, and as already mentioned, racial groups other than white have been late on the scene. I was told in early 1983, by a representative of the firm, that they were going to develop a multi-ethnic approach for their figures but the first multi-racial ones, the World People, didn't go on sale until the beginning of 1989, and then only in the Dacta range which is available solely through educational suppliers — that is, not to the general public. However, this is a start and these figures are very good, especially considering the difficulties of indicating racial features on such a small scale (see illustration). One set is available, of 18 figures in three racial groups of six — black, Chinese Asian and white.

As regards militarism, it's greatly to the credit of the Lego company that they do not, on principle, manufacture war toys. This has to be qualified slightly as there has been a castle set, with medieval knights, and in 1984, a new range, Legoland Castle, was introduced, featuring 'the good Sir Richard and the villainous Black Knight', according to the press release. (Villains tend to be black, in one way or another!) However, there's a certain distancing in such cases and these are obviously nowhere near as bad as toys drawn from modern warfare.

This account of Lego ends on the ever-present issue of gender and with something of a clash between the company and the consumers. First of all, here is Peter Eio, managing director of Lego in Britain, speaking in *The Sunday Times* on 23 January 1983:

15: World People

About 85% of Lego goes to boys. Girls have much less interest in construction, so we've brought out a new line — Fabuland — where the building aspect is greatly simplified and the emphasis is more on fantasy and playing with the models.

And here is Rupa Sarkar writing to Lego on 22 October 1982 from a London infants' school where her class had done a project on toys:

Dear Lego Person
we were Looking At A Book [the catalogue] caLLeD Lego 1982. we found 1 girL anD 5 Boy's. And I Dont think it is fair.
There shouLD Be A girL AnD a Boy in each picture. I am A girl anD I Like LeGo too. and I maDe A rocket too
From Rupa Sarkar (6)

Eleanor Ferguson also wrote:

Dear Lego person, Did a man make the lego book?
There are 5 boys so
there should be 5 girls
Don't you like girls? From eleanor Ferguson
age 5

The marketing manager, C A V Nicholls, replied on behalf of the company, thanked the girls for their letters and went on:

You ask 'don't you like girls?'. The answer is yes, we do, very much. The sad thing is that girls don't seem to like us very much. Some do, like you two, but not nearly as many girls buy LEGO sets as boys. ...

We have tried very hard to attract more girls, even going so far as to design products specially for girls, like furniture and dolls house sets. But none of them have been really successful.

So, come on girls, get more of your friends buying LEGO sets and then we can justify showing more girls in our leaflets, but when 96 out of every 100 Technical Sets (to take the most extreme example) go to boys we cannot show girls playing with them because that just does not reflect true life.

The last paragraph here shows what a deadlock exists, at least in the minds of the manufacturers. Rupa was not satisfied and wrote again on 30 November:

Dear Mr Nicholls
Why Do you think that girLs onLy PLay with Dolls and DoLLs furniture.
GirL's can make cAr's and rockets with LEGO
From RUPA

After some delay, this letter was passed to the consumer relations department and R M Williams replied on 14 January 1983 merely saying, however, that it was known, 'for a fact', that girls liked the train sets and Technic sets but that some preferred dolls' furniture. At this point, the correspondence stopped. It doesn't seem that much of an interchange took place, though this was through no fault of the girls.

Rupa and Eleanor might have seen the Lego Builders' Club advertised on the back cover of the catalogue and that, by joining it, they could compete for Master Builder Awards. They might have noticed the words, in brackets, '(yes, girls can become Master Builders too of course)', but I doubt whether they'd have been very much consoled by this.

Lastly, as regards Lego, we shouldn't forget that the messages embodied in their products — about gender, race, class and culture in general — go to about 120 countries.

The construction system produced by the firm of Artur Fischer is much less widespread in Britain and I know less about it, basically for that reason, though the British subsidiary has been very helpful to me. This system is very large and complete with a scope ranging from baby toys and very simple construction sets to sets for making what seem to be very complicated electronically-driven models. The plastic used in the manufacture of the Fischer products looks less bright and brittle than that used for Lego and a representative of the firm told me it was nylon. Certainly, it's pleasant to work with. There are metal rods in some of the sets but, apart from cords and a few rubber bands, these are the only non-plastic items used. The basic method for joining parts or pieces together, in most of the sets, involves small pegs which fit into slots or grooves. The pegs are either permanently fixed into pieces such as bars or cubes — that is, part of them — or they are loose and can be used to join pieces together. There are also small screws which fit into slots and have to be turned through 90 degrees.

For younger children, from about four to six years old, there are general sets and also kits for making particular models. The pieces are large and colourful and the method for fixing them together is simpler than the one described above. At this stage of the Fischer system, there are two kinds of figures. One kind consists of simple cone shapes with a round head on top. They have two eyes and a smile and are neither male nor female. The other kind are simple, articulated figures, with noses, who have a rather squarish look. They all look alike and seem to be men, though maybe this is largely because of their headgear. The vehicles they're associated with — a tipper lorry, a fire engine and an excavator, for example — are connected with male-dominated occupations. This points up the problem, really. Not many women drive fire engines — if any, in this country — but there are now women fire-fighters. As far as toys are concerned, the vicious circle has to be broken if children are to be allowed to realize their full potential.

After this stage, we move on to Fischertechnik and although there are sets for children down to the age of three, most of the sets seem to be described as being for children of six and over, 10 and over or 12 and over. These are mainly model construction kits for building the kind of vehicles and machinery we've met with elsewhere. However, great attention is paid to the engineering principles involved. The Fischer system is basically about learning, in a pleasant way. I made the merry-go-round in about two hours. I'm not very good at this kind of thing but I found the pictorial instructions easy to follow. The basic engineering principle involved in this set is the working of cog-wheels and this is clearly demonstrated by the model. The cogs might have engaged more firmly but this could have been something to do with the fact that I had two little pieces left over at the end. It seemed to me rather difficult for six year olds and I think they'd find the small screws, or locking devices, a bit fiddly. Also, for six years old and over, there are two starter kits, one for making 100 models and one for making 200.

Although the cone-shaped figures came with the merry-go-round, a third kind of figure is more associated with the models in the Fischertechnik range. These have articulated limbs and cusped hands and are more life-like then the other types but they're all alike, apart from the colour of their dress, and they're all white and male.

Moving up the age range, there are motor and gear kits, a kit to demonstrate the principles of pneumatics, one concerned with electromechanics, one to do with statics, and so on. There's also a special educational programme.

It seems to me that, with the reservations I've mentioned, the Fischer system is extremely good and well thought out. There are no houses or towns and there's no concern to reflect a way of life. In view of what I've said about two of the three sorts of figures in the system, I should add that girls are very well represented in the catalogue illustrations and on the packaging. As far as masculine gender roles of the more obvious kind are concerned, there's a whole series of sets based around racing cars. On the other hand, this firm does not, on principle, make any kind of military or war toys and for that they deserve our thanks.

Tool sets and science sets

We've been following a rather oblique line but I hope it's clear that this line, which runs through vehicles, machinery, building and making has everything to do with masculine roles in peacetime — even though it hasn't seemed very peaceful at times. In connection with the vehicles, especially, we've seldom been far away from the world of work, of breadwinning. Now, we approach the two main roles more directly; first, that of the handyman — Handy Boy, in fact, as that's the name of three tool sets which were being produced, by Randalls, over most of the years covered by this study. These sets are in window-boxes, they consist of basic woodworking tools, and differ only in the number of items in each set. The same firm also produced a similar set, Young Handy Man, this time with a large colour photo, of a boy using a tool, on the front of the box. Berwick take a harder line with their Tough Nut set. This contains tools and a helmet, here called a hard hat, the name construction workers have for it. The boy on the box is shown wearing this, with tools in one hand and making a thumbs up sign with the other. On one side of him, there's an oil rig and on the other there's some kind of building work going on.

There are usually a few sets of this kind around as well as sets of plastic tools for younger children. Sometimes, there are small work benches, usually with tools.

16: Chemistry sets

Science sets of various kinds are usually presented as being mainly or only for boys. Randalls produce a sizable range of these. There are five chemistry sets, for instance, differing in the number of experiments that can be done. These all follow the same general pattern of presentation, both on the front of the boxes and on the front covers of the booklets inside. This consists of a large colour photo of the head and shoulders (more or less) of a boy, together with a much smaller photo of a girl, so that the girl looks doll-like beside the boy. All are shown performing experiments. We see the same pattern of presentation in the Micro World sets, but the two Electronics Workshop sets don't show girls at all. The Merit Medi-Kit, at least, shows a boy and a girl in equal prominence on the front with the girl, in fact, in a more active role.

Salters have a huge range of science sets. Their junior sets, Electronics, Electrics, Chemistry and Microscope, all have boys only on the boxes, though a girl does get a look in, through the microscope, on a set combining the last three of these. She's flanked by two boys. The other Salter science sets, and there are a lot, mostly don't show children on the boxes (this is in the 1983 range) and the catalogue says of Electronics 1 and Electronics 2, that these were found by the Design Council 'to be equally attractive to both boys and girls'. Perhaps this was because these sets weren't gender-role coded or presented.

We shouldn't forget that there's another dimension, that of catalogue presentation, as far as gender roles are concerned. The Boots catalogue of 1982, advertising the Salter Microscope Set 1, shows only a boy using it, while only a boy is having fun with the Salter Fun With Magnets set in the Arnold 'Offspring' catalogue of the same year. There aren't any non-European children in sight.

In the Salters science range for 1984, there are 21 sets with re-designed packaging and endorsed by Johnny Ball, the BBC children's television and radio presenter. He introduces each science subject either on a floppy disc, 'free' with junior science sets, or a cassette, 'free' with senior science sets. On the boxes, overall, boys are featured about twice as many times as girls (see illustration, p. 113). Interestingly, girls are included where microscopes and chemistry are concerned (areas in which women have gained some sort of foothold). The idea of having a man, alone, introducing the sets must also play a large part in putting girls off.

Reference

1   Geraldine L Wilson, 'The Values Conveyed in Children's Toys', *Interracial Books for Children Bulletin*, New York, vol. 12 no. 6, 1981, p.4.

CHAPTER 6
THE FIGHTER

Now, we're going to separate the men from the boys — as overgrown boys, who are concerned about this sort of thing, keep saying. As usual, language gives a good guide to a society's gender roles. There are words for males who fall short of the expected gender role of fighter, such as 'softy' and, mainly in the USA, 'Milquetoast'. 'Sissy' which also originated in the USA and comes from the word 'sister', reminds us that males are expected to distinguish their behaviour from that of females. If they don't, they often actually get called by the names of girls which makes the point clearly. 'Nelly' and 'Nancy' or 'nancy-boy' are all terms of abuse for males, which carry, in these cases, strong overtones of homosexuality. 'Margery', however, a term from London slang of the second half of the last century, seems only to have meant effeminate. On the other hand, the expected masculine gender role here can also be exceeded in ways not acceptable to society in general, so we get words like 'lout', 'yob' and 'thug'. Thugs in uniform are all right, though, and then cease to be called thugs. Their behaviour hasn't changed. It's just that their violence has been sanctioned.

Toy soldiers and other figures
Nobody knows when toy soldiers first appeared on the historical scene, but it's possible to point out a few milestones on the way to the present situation.

Some of the earliest figures, in a recognizably modern form, were made by the Hilpert family of Nuremberg, around 1775. Prompted, seemingly, by the military success, or land-grabbing exploits, of Frederick the Great, they produced huge armies of small, flat, tin soldiers. Other German firms soon joined in and, in fact, Germany was the main producer of toy soldiers until late in the nineteenth century. By then, however, a strong competitor from this country, the firm of Britains, had developed and had, moreover, invented a new method of hollow-casting lead figures, in 1893. Previously, metal soldiers had been expensive and largely restricted to the upper, military classes. After this date, they were cheaper and large-scale commercial production could begin.

Britains early established a standard scale of 1:32, which is about 54mm high, for their toy soldiers, though they've always made them in several smaller scales and two or three larger. By 1914, toy soldiers had become a major part of the toy market in Britain and, following a lull due to the revolt against war toys after the first world war, trade in this sector was on the increase again in the 1930s. The firm of Britains followed the demand and was responsible for most of the supply. They made lead figures up to 1965 and then changed over most of their production to plastic ones. They have continued to produce 'metal based models', however, in an alloy containing zinc. The West German firm of O and M Hausser had made plastic soldiers from the 1950s. The most important thing, from the point of view of this study, is that plastic meant much greater possibilities as regards the articulation of figures and the militarization of boys.

Later in the chapter, after a survey of model military vehicles and other craft, and guns, we'll be concentrating on recent developments in military figures. Before leaving them now, however, there are some important points to be made.

For instance, although there were toy soldiers in warlike postures from early on, there does seem to have been a strong stress on military ceremonial and ceremonial dress, for a long time, even up to the second world war; after which this element gradually faded into the background. Britains still produce ceremonial figures but these are mainly for the tourist trade. (The rigidity of metal figures no doubt played a part in this emphasis on ceremony though I don't think it explains the situation entirely.) The first toy soldiers Britains produced were the 1st Life Guards and, even in the 1930s, they had sets such as The Changing of the Guard at Buckingham Palace. They also made a coach and retinue for the 1937 coronation. As might be expected, patriotism and royalism were always much to the fore but my impression is that the all-out concentration on the business of killing other people, to the exclusion of almost everything else, is a fairly recent development in the world of toy military figures in general, even though that's what soldiers are for.

Toy figures soon began to play their part in the matter of race. In about 1910, Britains were selling 'A Zulu Kraal realistically displayed (Native Village)', which contained thatched, beehive huts, palm trees and stereotyped warriors, with the whites of their eyes prominent, and carrying shields, spears and clubs. The same firm's Zulu Warriors of 1906 resembled these but also had prominent red lips. A similar image was presented, at about the same time, by the African Kaffir Warriors produced by the German firm of George Heyde. Cowboys and 'indians' were early on the scene, to perpetuate the racist myths of the 'wild west'. The 'red indians' often appear in a slinky, creeping posture with tomahawk or dagger raised. Cowboys don't go in for creeping about like this. Since I won't be returning to the subject, I may as well mention here that these myths have been kept very much alive up to the present day. In the period covered by this book, there's been, for instance, a How the West was Won set based on a television series; Wild West Action Models (toy figures) available separately; and a range of Wild West Vehicles, such as a stagecoach and a covered wagon; as well as several 'western' Snap 'n' Fix model kits, including a 7th Cavalry Gatling Gun. These are only from one firm, Model Toys, under their Timpo trade name. Marx Toys, in 1979, were keeping the Lone Ranger riding, with a large series consisting of articulated figures 24cm tall and other items such as a canoe, a wigwam and a wagon. Interestingly, El Lobo, 'leader of the Mexican raiders' is amongst this lot, giving another slant to the racist myth. (There's a Mexican Bandit amongst the range of 'western' Playpeople, as well.) Pedigree had a Lone Ranger assortment, with much smaller figures, in 1982.

Britains have a 7th Cavalry and Apaches series, all of them well armed, and there's even a Wild West Township range — a saloon, sheriff's office, general store, jail and so on — imported from the Danish firm of Hanse.

With dangerous ideologies in mind, and before leaving the historical background of this section altogether, we should take account of the large output of Nazi figures from the firm of Hausser between the mid and the late 1930s. These were marketed under the trade name of Elastolin which referred to the composition — basically sawdust and glue — they were made from. The SA (Sturmabteilung — Storm Detachment) which can be seen as the equivalent, in Nazi Germany, of the modern British SPG, were well represented in this output as were the SS (Schutzstaffel — Defence Squadron), all with Nazi insignia, giving fascist salutes and so on. Kurt Hausser, in a recent disclaimer from the firm about its Nazi period, has said, 'We were a commercial company trying to do business'. This is a particularly clear illustration of a point which underlies this whole book: profits and principles seldom mix.

Although it does seem that toy figures of the traditional, standard size are losing ground to the more recent, and larger figures, there are still a surprising number around. A look at some of Britains' ranges in 1982 shows the variety. There were series portraying historical adversaries, such as the American Civil War series and the Knights and Turks series, with the Knights in shining armour and the Turks clad mainly in black. British, German and US troops, mainly from the second world war it seems, were also featured, along with military vehicles and field guns with plastic shells. In the fictional future, there was a range of space models and figures in two groups, the Stargards and the Aliens, these last in black with red helmets.

Promotion and packaging are, as always, important. Britains send to children who write to them a round, fabric badge with a Union Jack design and the words 'Collectors' Award' on it, together with the company's name and its symbol, a guardsman. Matchbox, in 1979-80, were producing toy soldiers from the second world war in two sizes. The smaller ones, about 25mm tall, were in a world armies' range and the boxes of these, probably because of the size of the figures, showed groups of soldiers in combat. The other figures, which were about twice as big, were also in boxes showing battle scenes but this time the pictures on the boxes emphasized individual soldiers, in close-up, their faces grimly determined or twisted by snarls.

It's important to note the connections between historical events and toys, and the way in which they interrelate. Following their emergence into the light of publicity in recent times, it isn't surprising to note that the SAS have, by now, established a considerable bridge-head in the toy market. So, fresh from the Falklands/Malvinas conflict, you might say, they turned up in Palitoy's Airfix range in 1983, along with Modern US NATO troops and Modern 'Russians'. At the same time, Newfeld were selling their SAS Sabre Team figures, bigger, at about 10cm high, and with various items of kit. We now leave toy soldiers but we'll be meeting the SAS again.

117

Military models

I couldn't hope to deal here, in any thorough way, with the vast number of toy military vehicles and other craft, that are available, so I'll merely draw attention to certain significant points which relate to matters dealt with elsewhere. There are two main categories: ready-made models; and model kits, for making up and often for painting, also. When you look into it, these are rather different areas of the toy market. The first are the sort of models you might buy, for quite small children, at the local newsagent's. Details and accuracy aren't generally of very great importance and the vehicles need have no counterparts in real life. Kits, on the other hand, are more of a hobby and are for older children. Accuracy is very important and the models made are usually detailed, scaled-down versions of actual vehicles or craft.

To deal with the ready-made models first: Corgi have an interesting, futuristic vehicle, the Scanotron, which seems to be amphibious and which, according to the catalogue, 'operates in swamp areas where the earth's crust has been weathered by underground nuclear tests. Seals off exploding fissures'. This is a curious, and obviously deceptive and dishonest use of the word 'weathered', as it makes underground nuclear tests appear to be part of a natural process.

Matchbox, with their Adventure 2000 range, take us further afield, but without broadening our minds. 'The year is 2000 ...', they tell us,'re-enact [sic] the excitement of interplanetary conflict'. We have to tick the boxes in the catalogue as we collect these 'action packed vehicles'. Back on earth, Matchbox provide us with the Battlekings range of 'tough combat machines' and the Seakings range of warships. In the last chapter, we considered some of the more peaceful vehicles in Matchbox's Rough Riders range. There's also a Rough Riders military section known as OMNI Force. The initials stand for Official Military Night Invaders. With the US flag as emblem, they include a missile launcher, a tank, a jeep, a truck and a helicopter, all of which, we are told, with breath-taking arrogance, are 'ready for action in any part of the world'. According to *Fair News* of 29 January 1983, one of the most popular models in the Matchbox range is the Sea Harrier FRS51 aircraft, following its use in the Falklands/Malvinas campaign. We'll be returning to the relationship between war and war toys later.

Many of the models in this category are miniature, metal, die-cast vehicles and Dinky, as well as Corgi and Matchbox, is a well known brand name for this kind of toy. In 1979, Dinky, then owned by Meccano which was still a company in its own right at that time, had a fairly typical output of war toys with one unusual feature. There were 15 military vehicles and weapons — several fired shells, one fired rockets and one, the Junkers Stuka, dropped bombs containing percussion caps. What wasn't so usual was the fact that this last model was sporting the Nazi swastika. Although this might well have been realistic, in West Germany it could have given rise to a court case. Here, it's just one example, if a rather obvious one, of the process — which has been going on now for many years in comics and toys — of forgetting what fascism really meant, and means.

Although die-cast metal models, not necessarily to scale, are the main products in this part of the toy market, there are also plastic, scale models. The Japanese firm of Nichimo have a large output of these, including a vast array of warplanes, tanks and warships. As we'll see, Japan is strongly represented, also, in the military area of the model kits market, which is surprising in view of that country's role in the second world war. The West German response to war toys, referred to in the introduction, is very different.

We now move to model kits. Some differences between these and ready-made models have already been pointed out. Models made from kits are also often more for display than for play, interest being centred largely on the making. It's an adult hobby, as well. As with model railways, there's great stress on accuracy of detail and authenticity and there are various scales, particularly common ones being 1:32, 1:48, 1:72 and, for warships, 1:700. The larger manufacturers sell ranges of paints as well, and sometimes model-making tools. Such kits have been around for many years, and used to be made of wood. Now, however, they are in plastic, almost without exception. Sometimes, firms produce both kinds of model — there's a vast array of military vehicles, warships and warplanes in the Matchbox range of kits, for instance — but, more often, firms specialize in one or the other. There are usually a few kits for civilian models around, but these are vastly outnumbered by the military ones. The main focus seems to be on the second world war, and later.

One of the biggest firms I've come across, for model kits, is Revell. In 1979, when their largest range was of warplanes, their products were being manufactured in eight countries and sold in more than 80. In the same year, they claimed to have produced over 400 million kits in their 28-year history. About five million kits, they said, were made at their British subsidiary, in Potters Bar, in 1977. By 1981, Revell had 12 companies and licensees in the capitalist world. This sets the scene. In the area of model kits, a very few companies dominate the international market, though this is typical of the toy industry as a whole.

The Tamiya company started in 1958 and by 1981 were selling their products in 62 countries, including Czechoslovakia and Poland. In their 1982 catalogue, apart from a number of military figures and a collection of 84 military miniatures of every imaginable sort, they had 50 tanks, in two scales, most of them motorized and some with remote control. There were non-military models besides, amongst them a lot of speedway racing models. However, overall, military items take up 24 pages out of a 74-page catalogue and some of the illustrations of these are very small and there are sometimes 24 to a page. When you think that numbers are sold of each of these and that these are the products of only one firm, you can begin to get some idea of the extent of this rather warlike hobby.

The military output from two other Japanese firms, Fujimi and Hasegawa, is similar in extent and variety to that of Tamiya, so I'll just point out one or two things to try to give an overall picture. For instance, and as might be expected in this part of the hobby world where display is important, there are dioramas. These are tableaux of battle scenes with military vehicles and figures set in realistic terrain — the sort of thing you might like to have on your sideboard. Two of Fujimi's, for example, are Battle for Berlin and Invasion D-Day. There are, at least in Japan, modellers' clubs where the members produce their own dioramas. In their 1980 catalogue, Hasegawa show one made by the Shizuoka Cockpit Club. This same catalogue contains 115 model kits of aircraft, only one of which is classed as civilian and six as acrobatic planes.

The firm of Hales, which exists solely to distribute, test and service imported toys and games in Britain, handles Hasegawa's products and also those of the Monogram firm. This firm produces snap-together kits, rather than ones that have to be glued. Eighty of their planes are available in Britain, most of them warplanes and including the enormous US B36 called, in Newspeak, 'Peacemaker'. It has 80 bombs in the bomb bay.

The Airfix Modellers' Manual of 1983 shows the usual military ranges including, this time, a range of space vehicles and craft, mostly from the *Star Wars* film saga. The stress, throughout the manual, is on force, speed and power; the talk all of fighting and battles; the text peppered with words such as 'assault', 'attack' and 'combat'; and there's mention of all sorts of weapons. There's no indication of what all the fighting has been about. Actually, it just seems some kind of sport, especially in the article on air aces of the second world war where the German, Erich Hartmann, is picked out as 'the greatest of them all', presumably because he shot down 352 aircraft. Triple centuries are rare in cricket, also. In a gruesome combination of words which gives the game away, so to speak, we read that Werner Molders 'survived numerous sky battles to *score* 115 *kills* [my emphasis]'. There's no indication of what the Falklands/Malvinas conflict was about, either, though it's mentioned three times in this manual.

Guns

Guns speak for themselves and most people are very familiar with toy ones, so I don't want to dwell on them here, except to point out certain things which are not generally known or which might be overlooked.

Firstly, most guns are for killing people with, and most toy guns are imitations of these.

Secondly, they provide a good example of the interrelationship between actual life and the world of make-believe. Here's a man from a family of toy gun makers talking to Henry Mayhew around the middle of the last century:

> In war time, bless you, that was the time for my business — there *was* [emphasis in original] a demand for guns then I can tell you! I sold eight, then, to one that I sell now, though the population's increased so. ... I remember the first botched-up peace in 1802. ... My father ... thought the peace would do no good to him, but it didn't last very long, and the toy-gun trade went on steadily for years — with a bit of a fillip, now and then, after news of a victory.[1]

He's describing here the process I pointed to in the case of the Matchbox Sea Harrier model (see p. 118). Clearly, the demand for war toys is stimulated. The speaker is a London toy gun-maker who, according to his own estimate, was responsible for turning out 22,464 items per year. There was one other toy gun maker in London, he said, who made about the same number.

Certainly, there are a lot more toy guns now, and a greater variety. As well as all the military fire-arms which change gradually over the years, 'western' guns are still in plentiful supply and, in recent years, all kinds of space hand-weapons have been added. Then, just as there are cars, there are also weapons from television serials — James Bond and Kojak pistols a few years ago, for instance — as well as other detective guns and what might be called antique guns such as pirate and duelling pistols.

All of these kinds, except the space weapons, were being marketed by the Lone Star firm in 1979. As its name suggests, this firm had begun by producing 'western' fire-arms but over the years it spread its production to include the other categories. By mid-1982, it almost totally dominated the toy gun market, having bought up its main competitor, Crescent Toys. Presumably, it acquired Crescent's Sonic Space Laser, into the bargain, so to speak, and thereby also entered the space gun market.

Percussion caps, or amorces, as they're often fancifully called now, are less necessary for making loud bangs these days, and all kinds of gimmicks have been added. Bell's machine gun makes a 'loud staccato noise with red flashing sparks' without caps, for example. The same firm sells a Ping Pong Auto-Rifle and a Ping Pong Pistol for firing table tennis balls and to get children used to the idea of destruction early on. By saying that the pistol isn't recommended for the under fives, however, this manufacturer is being unusually restrained.

Packaging and the language used on it are, as elsewhere, important. Combex, in 1981, were selling a range of rifles and light machine-guns which included such weapons as the Combat 90 Tommy Gun, the M16 Red Devil, the Kick Fire 'vibrating gun' and the Attack Rifle. These were labelled, variously, as having 'realistic sound', flashing barrel' and 'recoil action'. The company clearly also felt it necessary to go in for a bit of recruitment, as the military guns had 'join the action commandos' banded across the corners of the boxes, or cards in the case of carded items. The illustrations on this packaging, with one exception, showed, not boys playing, but men, in the army, fighting. This, therefore, was the adult gender role presented as acceptable for boys to aspire towards. There were further inbuilt assumptions in these illustrations. The warfare pictured on the packaging, in several cases, was taking place in desert or tropical regions, and couldn't, therefore, be of a defensive kind as we have no such regions in Britain. So what would British troops be doing in such places, and why, and in whose interest, would they be doing it?

There are now SAS machine-guns, of undisclosed origin, for ages three and up, sold by the large retail chain of Zodiac Toys.

Action Man and other soldier dolls

Action Man wasn't the first soldier doll. There was a printed rag doll soldier in 1914, for instance, named Tommy Atkins, which was the general name for the ordinary British soldier of the time. Then, there were soldier dolls, that is, dolls just dressed in khaki uniforms, in the 1930s. However, Action Man did mark a new stage in the militarization of boys and greatly enlarged the possibilities for aggression. I'll give a brief historical survey first and then the situation in 1983 and later, before going on to questions of manufacture and marketing.

The doll we now know as Action Man was copyrighted as GI Joe in the USA in 1964 by the firm of Hassenfeld Bros which later became Hasbro Inc. In Britain, it was made under licence by Palitoy and first marketed here, as Action Man, in 1966. The present GI Joe figures sold by Hasbro in the USA are different and much smaller — more about them later — but the original GI Joe was similar to Action Man.

The front cover of the March-April 1966 issue of the trade magazine, *Toys International*, showed Action Man in frogman's outfit, knife brandished in one hand and sticks of explosive in the other. He was described, inside, as 'a fully-mobile, moulded plastic toy for boys which [could] be equipped for every phase of military service'. This marked his invasion of Britain. In the USA, there was a black GI Joe from quite early on, but there don't seem to have been any black Action Men over here. Army, navy and air force dolls were available in Britain from the beginning and it was intended to add more uniforms and equipment later.

Now, I'll describe the Action Man doll but I want to emphasize how important it is to refer to the descriptions of Barbie and Sindy and to the illustration (see pp. 66-68 and p.123), as a comparison speaks volumes as far as gender roles are concerned. Action Man is almost 29cm tall and made of hard plastic, except for the hands. The parts of his body are well proportioned, again except for the hands which are slightly large. His facial features have not been exaggerated in any way. He simply has a fairly straight nose and a mouth firmly shut. As with the fashion dolls, however, the eyes, which are blue, have come in for special attention, though of a very different kind. Since 1976, Action Man has had 'eagle eyes'. This means that, by means of a small lever at the nape of the neck, the eyes can be moved from side to side. The eyes of fashion dolls, in contrast, are just decorative. Another interesting touch is the scar over Action Man's right cheek bone, which shows that he's evidently seen some action. Typically, he has dark, close- cropped, fibre hair but has been available with brown and blond hair as well, and with a beard. Before 1970, he had moulded hair. His head is solid, though whether this is better than having an empty head, like Sindy or Barbie, is difficult to say. Possibly the weirdest design development in Action Man was the 'sharp shooter pose' which dates from 1981. For this, the head is pulled back and locked over a small projection at the front of the neck, so that the figure can shoot a gun from a prone position. As regards the torso, Action Man has a deep, muscular and well shaped chest and, for some reason — we can only speculate — he has moulded trunks. (They are, so to speak, part of his body.) As with fashion dolls, the hands and feet are of great significance. Since 1973, Action Man has had gripping hands — that is, they are made of a springy kind of plastic so that the fingers can be uncurled and then allowed to spring back to clasp

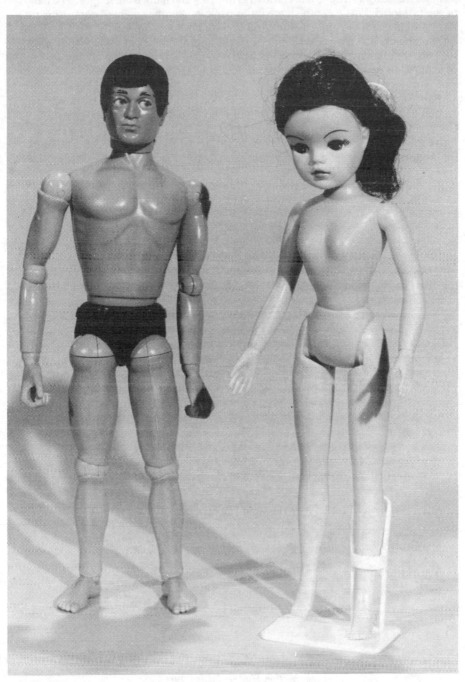

17: Action Man and Active Sindy

an object, usually a weapon. He can also grip string and hang from ledges. The hands of the fashion dolls, by contrast, are quite useless. Another pointed contrast is that Action Man can stand up, either unshod or with his boots on. Lastly, the figure has quite elaborate ball and socket joints at all the appropriate places which give a very realistic simulation of human movement. To sum up, it's a pity that all this care and ingenuity has gone, overall, to further militarism (see illustration).

Early in 1968, Action Man spoke — or, rather, the Commander did. The ordinary Action Man hasn't said a word to this very day and has just gone on obeying the Commander's orders such as, 'Action Man patrol, fall in' and 'Hold your fire until I give the order'. Regular modifications to the actual figures have been a feature of the Action Man concept over the years.

18: Action Man — basic figure

In November 1969, the magazine *Which?* reported that Action Man then had 22 outfits, together with equipment and other accessories, in three categories: military, sports and adventure. We'll follow the process by which he's become the almost entirely military figure of recent years. At about the time of the *Which?* report, there were three sports outfits: a footballer, a cricketer and an Olympic athlete. In the adventure category, there were Underwater Explorer and Treasure Hunter and, in 1971, Space Explorer. Even the military uniforms were not all particularly aggressive. In 1970, a series of British uniforms was started but several of these, of various guards' regiments, for instance, were of a ceremonial type. Amongst them, however, were Parachutist and Marine Combat uniforms. Four of this series were produced, ready kitted out, as souvenir items, in the hopes of starting a collecting craze, but this didn't work out. We can see, though, how the company was casting about and trying different approaches.

In 1971, the strips of five famous football clubs were reproduced for Action Man, and the intention was to add more. However, this didn't work out very well, either, not even when Sharpshooter Action Man came along, fitted with a device so that he could kick the ball.

What had come to be called the Famous British Uniforms series was still going in 1972 when a Calvary outfit, together with a horse, were added. You could get this series ready-dressed, or the uniforms separately. The military side, in a more warlike sense, had by then taken off well and truly and Action Man had a Scorpion Tank, along with other military equipment.

This outline gives the general background and sets the scene for later developments. We now move into the recent period dealt with in this book.

The Action Man Space Ranger outfits began to be produced round about the beginning of this period, or possibly a year or two before, but the enemy, the largely black-clad Captain Zargon, didn't appear on the scene until 1980. By that time, there were several space figures, space equipment such as a 'battle pack and laser', space arms which might be described as fantasy applied to weaponry, and two fantastic space craft. The following year, Captain Zargon was still on his own, although the catalogue said he was 'leader of the Space Pirates' and 'out to wreak havoc in the Universe'. It didn't say why.

In 1981, a Grenadier Guard, in ceremonial uniform, was in the catalogue, looking very much out of place. The following year, he'd vanished, and that was the end of ceremony.

Over the years, the figures have been grouped into various categories but, around this time, class was emerging quite strongly with most of the Action Men divided into 'The Soldiers' and 'The Officers'. German and US military figures had been added so that we get, amongst 'The Soldiers', a US machine gunner and a German Stormtrooper and, amongst 'The Officers', a Panzer Captain and a Luftwaffe Pilot, as well as a British Infantry Major. In 1982, there were 44 separate purchases available in the Action Man range, including figures, equipment, uniforms, vehicles and other craft. Some of these, of course, comprised several items. By this time, nearly everything was military, in a warlike sense. The only exceptions were a Police Motorcyclist, a Deep Sea Diver and a Mountain Rescue figure.

Things certainly got nastier over the years. New for 1982, were the three Special Team outfits, only available together, it seemed. There was Ground Assault, Arctic Assault and Underwater Assault. The Assault Copter was already there, in Transport Command, and was described in the catalogue as 'a helicopter bristling with fire power'. The Scorpion Tank was still going strong after 10 years and, amongst other things, there was an Armoured Jeep, 'equipped with swivel-mounted twin machine-gun' and the Pursuit Craft, which could be converted into four different transporters.

The Commander was still giving his 'five random commands' in 1982, but now the Space Ranger Captain chirped up with his 'five random "space" sayings'. He'd acquired 'Sharpshooter poseability' the year before.

The most significant new development in 1982 was the introduction of the SAS outfit, described in the catalogue as 'an authentic reproduction of the type used for undercover missions'. The dressed figure looks sinister enough, in black combat suit with black hood and gas mask, and rather like the ones seen on British television screens on the occasion of the Iranian embassy siege. Along with the outfit, you get a Heckler and Koch MP5 submachine-gun, a Browning pistol and a grappling hook.

We come to 1983. Spurred on, no doubt, by the Falklands/Malvinas campaign in mid-1982, Palitoy put their money on the SAS and their 1983 catalogue showed the development of a whole range of new SAS items. New to the catalogue, that is: I'd seen several of them during the second half of 1982. Following a marketing pattern developed several years previously, the firm had established a Key Figure in the SAS range. His outfit only differs slightly from that of the already existing one which, however, now became an SAS Trooper outfit in the Action Man Combat Division. It had also became a best seller, according to Palitoy.

Of the new military craft and outfits, SAS Beachhead Attack consists of an Assault Craft (a type of dinghy) with outboard motor worked by a battery. With this boat, you get a leaflet which has, on one side, instructions for putting the boat together and, on the other, a comic strip, entitled 'Night Attack', which begins 'on an enemy coastline' and ends with 'BOOM' and 'Mission accomplished!!' in the last panel. The Assault Craft is featured prominently in the strip.

As I've said before, play is close to fiction, especially dramatic fiction. To a certain extent, play is making up plays. Toy figures are very important in this respect, and those who manufacture them seem to understand this, in a dim sort of way. There are different sorts of fiction, however, and toy manufacturers, as in this comic strip and as, for instance, with the good versus evil conflict of the Space Rangers and Zargon, are usually only trying to prompt boys into mindless and aggressive role playing and ritual.

SAS Air Strike is a helicopter which, as they tend to do, 'bristles with fire power'. It has yellow markings on black which is the colour scheme of the whole range, the SAS insignia being in yellow. Then, there's an SAS Underwater Attack outfit and an SAS Parachute Attack outfit, which comes with a working parachute. 'How did the SAS get behind the Lines in the Falklands?' the catalogue asks us, and then tells us, 'By secret parachute drops from high altitude'. The SAS Secret Mission outfit reveals 'the way the SAS are supplied when deep in enemy territory' and comes with an inflatable rubber dinghy and other extras. Defence costs (or attack costs) go up and up. At Christmas 1983, the Action Man SAS Key Figure cost £7.99 and the Beachhead Attack (just the boat, that is, and without any batteries) cost £10.99.

The SAS were all the rage for 1983 and the ordinary Action Man got nothing, unless you count the Dog Tag ID (identity disc) which was a free offer with certain of the figures. (The offer also included a wrist identity bracelet for the purchaser.)

In other areas, the drive towards ever greater aggression and violence continued. A Commando outfit was introduced into the space range and the Special Team got a Missile Assault outfit, complete with missile launcher. Everywhere — in the promotion, packaging and in the names of the various items in the Action Man concept — you come across words such as 'action', 'force', 'assault', 'attack', 'combat', 'battle' and 'strike'.

This hectic atmosphere, offensive in both senses of the word, continued into 1984. 'How did the S.A.S get behind the lines in the Falklands?' the catalogue asks us again, and answers as before, while another reference to the SAS describes them as 'unsung heroes of the Falklands war'. The Parachute Regiment is also mentioned in connection with the Falklands/Malvinas campaign. It just shows, again, that war is good for this sort of business. I believe that the reverse is also true: this sort of business promotes war.

I've often heard it said, in tones of approval, that Action Man is a doll boys can feel free to play with and the speakers have usually gone on to mention the changing of outfits as being important. I think this attitude shows a terrible misunderstanding. Action Man, although more versatile, belongs in every way to the tradition of toy soldiers. Also, the best and most important feature about dolls (though not fashion dolls) is that they encourage caring for others. This is totally absent from the Action Man concept which is not about caring but all about killing.

Before leaving the Action Man juggernaut, I'll make a few points about promotion, sales and manufacture.

The identity disc dodge has already been mentioned. Another ruse, to keep the customers on the hook, was the poster which came with certain of the Action Man wares. This shows, on one side, a lot of the products in the range and there are little boxes to tick when you've collected them. The other side shows a violent medley of war machines and the usual heavily armed figures with grim or contorted faces. 'Join my team in military exploits both at home and abroad', Action man tells us. I wonder what exploits he has in mind at home. One corner of the poster advertises the star scheme which had been going since 1980, at least. The idea was to collect stars from the packets of Action Man outfits and accessories. You then stuck these on a card, answered certain questions to help Palitoy's production planning and sent it off, enclosing postage, to obtain a 'gift'. Twenty-one stars would get you an Action

Man basic figure, for example. These gifts were, it says on the card, 'rewards for distinguished conduct in the field with Action Man'. The explanation of this scheme begins with the words, 'Good news, men' and ends, 'Thanks, men. You've done well'.

Lastly (for now) on promotion — as we've seen in other cases, such as Sindy and Victoria Plum, fiction is produced as an offshoot of toys. Here, I'm talking about fiction in the usual sense, not the play fictions prompted by the toys themselves and their manufacturers. So, in Action Man's early days, Purnell published six adventure stories with Action Man as hero.

According to *Toys International,* a million Action Men were sold during their first year on the market. However many it was, it brought the manufacturer the National Association of Toy Retailers' Toy of the Year award which is given solely on the volume of sales. On the same basis, they voted Action Man Toy of the Decade, 1970-79. Taking all their products into consideration, my award for Most Socially Harmful Toy Producer Ever must go to Palitoy, though in the face of strong competition.

Palitoy claim, in their '1919-79 Diamond Jubilee' booklet: that Action Man is the biggest selling single toy concept in the toy trade; that, in 1978, the public spent more than £11 million on Action Man products; and that, in the years 1966-79, over eight million figures were sold and over 15 million outfits and accessories. It isn't quite clear, but it seems these figures relate only to Britain. In January 1981, *Toys International and the Retailer* reported that Action Man sales went up 13 per cent in 1980 and were worth £12 million at retail level. The magazine also reported that the space side had gone up 1,000 per cent.

Details of manufacture and international marketing show patterns similar to those we saw in the case of Barbie and Sindy. Much of Palitoy's output comes from the far east and, at one time, nearly all Action Men produced came from Hong Kong. Around the period 1977-79, Action Man products were either manufactured or sold, or both, in Australia, Belgium, Britain, Denmark, France, Greece, Hong Kong, the Republic of Ireland, Italy, Malta, Mexico, Spain and West Germany — amongst other countries. As with Barbie and Sindy, the general pattern is: manufacture in poorer countries and sales in richer ones.

After the foregoing account, it will no doubt come as a surprise that, in 1985, there was, suddenly, no trace of the Action Man concept in Palitoy's catalogue. The old soldier had faded away, at least from this part of the world, and only his logo remained, as if in memoriam, on the packaging of the Action Force range (to be dealt with very shortly). The abrupt disappearance of a firmly-established range seems baffling but it's noticeably the way Palitoy works. (Their Tiny Tears also met with sudden death, apparently late in 1983.) The only explanation seems to be that high-pressure promotion has to be kept up until the last possible moment, to sell off stock. After that, they keep as quiet as possible.

There have been, and there are, other dolls similar to Action Man, though none with anything like the same commercial success. Pedigree's Tommy Gunn was already established by the time Action Man arrived. An article about him in the magazine *Toy Trader* of May 1966 reports that he'd been ordered 'in quantity' by the army 'for use in recruiting demonstrations around the country'. (The army obviously believed that toys influence children.) At this time, Tommy Gunn had various outfits, including a grenadier one, and equipment and accessories in plenty. Two or three months later, Pedigree were reported to be bringing out playclothes for boys based on the doll's outfits and with the same equipment — a Sterling machine-gun, for example. However, Tommy Gunn was killed in combat, by Action Man — or, at least, so it seemed. Strangely enough, I saw him in the second half of 1983. He was being sold by Zodiac Toys and had been made for them in Hong Kong. There were various outfits and accessories and also a talking SAS officer, with four phrases. It just proves how true the saying is, that old soldiers never die.

Medium-sized fighting figures

We now move to several other ranges of plastic toy figures meant for boys. The majority of the figures in these ranges are considerably smaller than Action Man, though larger than standard size toy soldiers; they are moulded complete with clothing; they are all articulated to some degree; and, together with the many accessories that go with them, they are in bright or striking colours. Also, we now begin to move more towards fantasy and the links with fiction get closer.

In view of the change, in the USA, to the smaller GI Joe figure, it's interesting to note the arrival of Palitoy's Action Force in August 1982. These figures were called a 'mini Action Man range' in the catalogue of that year. They're articulated in a different way from the present GI Joe figures but, at about 11cm tall, they're of a similar size. To begin with, there were nine military figures, three other figures (two of them military) with accessories, and two convertible military vehicles. Palitoy claim to have sold nearly a million of these figures in less than six months. For 1983, five new 'teams' of figures, together with vehicles, were introduced. We should note, in view of the link with fiction which I've pointed to from time to time, that Palitoy talk of a 'strong theme storyline' behind Action Force. We'll see this emerging, as we go on. One of the five teams is called, simply, The Enemy and is described as 'a fiendish team of characters dedicated to overthrowing the world by using brilliant and strange sciences'. (It sounds like the present government of the USA.) Elsewhere in the 1983 catalogue, they're described as 'the deadly and feared enemy of the world' and we're told that 'only Action Force [here, that means the rest of Action Force] stands in the path of their aim of world domination'. It's important to note that the figures and vehicles in this Enemy group are largely red and that, although they have the skull and crossbones as their emblem, they carry several letters from the Cyrillic alphabet (the one used for Russian) on their vehicles. In a world threatened with nuclear devastation, this can only be seen as both dangerous and deliberate irresponsibility on the part of Palitoy. Another team, S.A.S. Force, includes several figures and vehicles, as follows: S.A.S. Boat Patrol, which is an Assault Boat with a commando figure; S.A.S. Para Attack, which is a parachutist with working parachute; the S.A.S. Panther, which is an Attack Jeep, together with a figure; and the S.A.S. Mobile Missile System. These small sets can all be bought separately and there's a separate set consisting of figures. The other teams follow the same general pattern. Z Force, known as the Heavy Brigade, includes, unusually, a blonde female despatch rider, on a 'rapid fire motorcycle'. The Q Force Deep Sea Team provides a 'full range of figures and accessories to fight the forces of evil under and on the sea', while the function of Space Force is 'to counter threats to the Earth's satellites and space craft'.

The overall impression is one of unending menace, from every quarter, which can only be stopped by totally ruthless forces using the deadliest of military technology. (And the market is swamped with toys which present this view of the world, or universe. There's no room for fun, or anything else.)

As regards advertising and promotion, Palitoy threatened 'a weight of support never before seen in the toy market', for the launching of the five Action Force teams in mid-1983. This was to include an Action Force comic and an Action Force Club.

I decided to follow the development of the comic and picked up the trail in *Battle*, a war comic, published weekly by IPC since spring 1975. The issue of 9 July 1983 had a section, 'presented by Captain Hurricane', for letters, competitions and so forth. (He had a long run, as hero of a comic strip in *The Valiant*, for at least five years — to my knowledge — up to about 1976.) Anyway, on this occasion he reminds readers of the Action Force story which had appeared in *Battle* a short while previously and tells them that, in the following weeks, the publishers would be giving away Action Force Mini Comics. On the back cover of this issue, there's a full page advertisement for the Action Force range. Later, *Battle* was renamed *Battle Action Force* and I studied the issue of 22 October 1983. The front cover shows Baron Ironblood, the leader of The Enemy, with some of his troops, and identifies him as 'the most EVIL man in the world'. (The inside front cover reveals, in small print, that Action Force is the registered trade mark of CPG Products Corporation, of the USA.) Three of the strips in this issue of the comic, all episodes in serials, feature three different, ('good') Action Force teams and The Enemy comes into one of these strips. In each case, the figures and vehicles in the strips are obviously drawn so as to resemble closely those of the Action Force range of toys.

This whole development is unusual because of the very close and specific relationship between toys and fiction in this instance and because, in connections of this sort, the movement is more likely to be in the opposite direction, from fiction to toys. However, we saw a similar process taking place in the case of Sindy and the Sindy annual. As far as Action Force is concerned, no doubt both Palitoy and IPC benefit from an arrangement which must increase their hold over the minds of boys.

In their 1984 catalogue, Palitoy reported that the comic had over half a million readers and that the Action Force club had more than 20,000 members. By the beginning of 1984, Palitoy had produced three million Action Force figures at their factory at Coalville, near Leicester.

Usually, the systems of aggression marketed as boys' toys can each be divided into four sections: figures and personal weapons; large weapons; transport — vehicles, vessels, aircraft and animals, often with weapons combined; and playsets. I'll deal with most of the toy systems to follow in this basic order.

First, I have to retrace my steps. In 1983, as part of my research into the history of Action Man, I felt it necessary to look into the GI Joe toy system. Fortunately, a friend was able to bring me a copy of Hasbro's then current catalogue from the USA. In view of later developments, the information I got from this turned out to be more important than I could have known at the time. The following account is based solely on Hasbro's 1983 catalogue and gives the picture as it then was in the USA.

Called 'a real American hero', GI Joe is said to be on a 'peacekeeping mission'. There are various military figures in a Mobile Strike Force Team and these are pitted against the 'evil enemies' or 'bad guys' such as Major Bludd and Destro who belong to Cobra Command. The figures are about 10cm high. In 1983, there seemed to be about 20 and these were sold separately, each with weapons, accessories and a file card with biography. The Ranger figure's Combat Command File card, for instance, says that he was 'warlord of a large, urban, street gang prior to enlistment', which seems to underline the point I was making earlier about thugs in and out of uniform.

The large weapons show something of a move towards fantasy. There's a vast range of them, including a Missile Launcher, a Flame Thrower and a Heavy Artillery Laser, known as HAL.

Amongst the vehicles, there's a Rapid-Fire Motorcycle (RAM); the Skimobile or Polar Battle Bear, which is a vehicle 'for G.I. Joe's arctic operations!'; and an Armored Missile Vehicle called Wolverine which, surprisingly, includes 'the former high fashion model COVER GIRL as the driver'.

As well as carry cases for the figures, there's the GI Joe Headquarters Command Center, a play set which includes a 'stockade' for imprisoning the 'COBRA Command terrorists'.

What looks to be a subsidiary company in the USA, Aviva Hasbro, manufactures GI Joe vehicles and large weapons in die-cast metal.

Words such as 'battle' (used as verb and adjective, as well as noun), 'action', 'assault' and 'attack' are everywhere and the whole system is backed by the usual massive advertising and promotion. There's also a fan club which over 30,000 children joined in 1982 and over 50 companies make GI Joe products on licence. (It's worth noting that GI Joe had disappeared from the scene during the post-Vietnam war era.)

Some time after examining this catalogue, I discovered that, from the spring of 1985, the GI Joe range, including Cobra Command, was to go on sale in this country, adapted for the British market. Thus, the later GI Joe followed in the footsteps of the original one. The range was to be sold under the Action Force brand name and would take the place of Action Force. I was able to examine the adapted GI Joe range at the Earls Court Toy and Hobby Fair in January 1985. Following the market strategy in the USA, the figures came with individual biographies but, as members of Action Force, these were changed. The Ranger figure, for instance, became Stalker, born in Marseilles. The GI Joe vehicles and larger weaponry, with a new livery and with the Action Force logo taking the place of the stars and stripes and GI Joe insignia, were mingled with the already existing Action Force ones. All this just goes to show the means and mechanisms of cultural imperialism carried out by a multinational firm in the pursuit of profit. (We'll be returning to this matter in the final chapter.)

Although there are fantastic elements in the systems I've already described, for instance the space aspects of Action Man and Action Force, the realistic elements have been more important. Now, however, we move over entirely into the area of fantasy, more especially space fantasy which, by the way, gives even more scope for aggression. I'll be dealing with Star Wars from Palitoy, Masters of the Universe from Mattel, Power Lords from the French firm Ceji Revell, and Transformers from Hasbro.

These all have features in common. The figures are either humans or superhumans, beasts of various sorts, or purely mechanical, that is, robots — or they are mixtures of any of these, in any proportion. The Star Wars figures are mostly about 11cm high, and Masters of the Universe and the Power Lords about 13cm, while the Transformers come in various sizes. Also, some figures have detachable parts, such as armour, and the larger ones, especially, are usually made so as to carry various weapons. In general, weapons range from swords and axes, to laser beams of various sorts, to those capable of destroying planets.

Vehicles and other craft vary from those based on animals, or derived from animal shapes, to more abstract, technological creations.

Playsets range from fantasy castles to science fiction creations, or they can be mixtures of the two. In fact, mixtures of all kinds are characteristic of these systems which, I might add, are continually being expanded.

Fiction is of great importance in these toy concepts and they all have fictional elements in common. First of all, it's a case of good versus evil on a galactic or, at least, interplanetary scale. This gives scope for massive aggression and violence. The goodies and baddies are clearly distinguished, not only by being either *very* good or *very* bad, but often by their appearance and dress, the baddies tending to look repulsive and to dress in black or, at least, dark colours. The goodies are of aristocratic stock or from some sort of élite. The hero (it won't be female, of course, or other than white either) will sometimes have a double personality, after the manner of Superman, Spiderman and others. The more human side of the personality is generally as weak as the other side is strong and this device, I suppose, aids identification. The hero often has a magic weapon, or talisman, to which he owes his powers. Female figures don't come into the picture much and, when they do, they tend to create problems by having to be rescued. Why the baddies are so evil or why they want to dominate the universe, as they usually do, is never explained. Rather, we just have to accept it as a kind of odd quirk they happen to have. There are strong connections here with the tradition of fantasy in children's fiction proper, especially as shown in the work of writers such as J R R Tolkien, Alan Garner and C S Lewis. These toy and fiction systems seem also to have drawn upon myths and legends. The Jedi knights of the *Star Wars* saga, for instance, recall the knights of the round table and the various magical weapons recall Thor's hammer and Excalibur, King Arthur's sword. Lastly, in this general outline, there's often a mystical, vaguely religious element somewhere in the background.

The Star Wars toy products arise from the three films in the saga and thus have a ready-made fiction, so to speak. Play, therefore, is more likely to take the form of rehearsing scenes from the films rather than anything more imaginative. In the process, the ideology of the saga is likely to be absorbed. The first of the films, *Star Wars,* which came out in the USA in 1977, has been an enormous money-spinner, and the toy products which arose from it and from the second film, *The Empire Strikes Back,* have had a comparable success in the toy world. The general background of these films must be fairly familiar to many people so only a few points need to be made before we move on to *Return of the Jedi* and closer to the present day.

By 1982, Palitoy had 45 Star Wars figures on sale in Britain. These include, of course, the main focus of hatred, the black-clad Darth Vader with his black helmet and mask, the hero Luke Skywalker, Princess Leia Organa and the two robots C-3PO and R2-D2 who, amongst other things, provide much-needed comic relief. Besides these, there's a large array of fighting vehicles and craft, including the enormous At-At (All Terrain Armoured Transport) based on a quadruped and about 56cm long. The Star Destroyer Playset is where Darth Vader can communicate with 'the dark side of the Force'. This is a mysterious, semi-religious power which the Jedi knights know how to use but they're on the other side of it, of course, and use it for 'good' purposes.

By the time *Return of the Jedi* was released, the film's sound effects department had more than 160 explosion noises. Earlier, the visual effects supervisor had declared that the film was going to be 'a two-hour roller-coaster ride'. Certainly I felt battered when I came out of the cinema. I hadn't been able to follow it very well and I doubt whether many of the mainly young audience could have followed it either. However, this seemed beside the point. The main object seemed to be to get drunk on violence. Also, the values embodied in the film came over quite well, mainly because they were familiar.

Several features were recognizable from imperialist fiction. The small, Furry Ewoks, for instance, who live in the forest on the moon of Endor, clearly play the role of 'native' 'tribes'. They're comical and not very menacing, unless frightened. True to type, they do a lot of chanting, they have a medicine man and a chief and are overawed by the golden robot, C-3PO and adopt him as their god. The robot's (and our) friends, however, are trussed up and seem bound for the traditional ceremonial death but a display of magic happily sorts things out. As well as being superstitious, loyal when you get to know them and so forth, the Ewoks are very expendable and, like 'natives' in other fiction, conveniently fight and get killed on behalf of the heroes. Richard Marquand, the director of the film, described his approach to them as showing 'a rather primitive and tribal kind of philosophy'.

In an episode with vague but unpleasant sexual overtones, Princess Leia is captured and made to serve, in a suitably skimpy dress, as dancing girl to Jabba the Hutt, a kind of giant slug with vaguely human features who runs the 'galactic underworld', or undergalaxy, perhaps. As if to underline the nastiness of this episode, there's a creature called Salacious Crumb, one of Jabba the Hutt's weird menagerie.

However, the princess is rescued and Luke Skywalker, farm boy become Jedi knight, wins through in the end, with some help from his 'lightsaber'. With Darth Vader dead and the enemy's gigantic battle station, the Death Star blown up, in the biggest explosion of all, the saga now seems to be at an end.

I've come across three fictional accounts — in book form, that is — of *Return of the Jedi,* one of them a 'special junior edition'.

As regards toy products, there were 77 figures available in 1984, some of them with cloth garments and removable helmets and most of them with weapons of one sort or another. Palitoy claimed that over 20 million figures had been sold in Britain by the end of 1983, at which time the National Association of Toy Retailers voted Star Wars the best-selling toy system, for the second year running.

I don't propose to deal here with the older generation of superheroes — Superman, Spiderman, the Incredible Hulk, Captain America and the rest — partly because I've dealt with their role in fiction in *Catching Them Young*[2] and the ideas they represent don't change in the different medium of toys, but also because I'd rather concentrate on bringing matters up to date. Let me just say in passing that the older generation of superheroes are still doing very well indeed in the world of toys.

The name, Masters of the Universe, points up very well the power-crazed and macho atmosphere of these toy systems. The main figure in this one — and there's often an individual who dominates the rest — is called, of all things, He-Man, and is described, on his blister-card, as the 'most powerful man in the universe!'. He's white, blond, muscular to the point of deformity and goes almost naked. (In fact, none of this lot bothers much with clothes.) His real identity is Prince Adam, the son of the king and queen of Eternia. On his side, amongst others, there's Ram Man, the 'human' battering-ram who has spring-loaded telescopic legs, Strata, the heroic winged warrior and Teela, the heroic warrior goddess. On the evil side is the skull-faced Skeletor (pronounced Skellytor), Lord of Destruction, and his gang which includes Beastman, Jitsu, who looks rather Japanese and has a 'chopping arm' for delivering karate blows, and the jokily-named Evil-lyn, Teela's nasty counterpart. Out of 20 figures altogether (1984), these two were the only females. (However, the point is certainly not to have more women represented in Masters of the Universe.)

Each figure has an articulated waist with a spring inside which enables him, or her, to deliver a 'power punch'. Almost all of the various male figures are obviously

19: He-Man

cast from the same basic mould and, as with all toy figures, the body language is very important. The arms have a swivel joint at the shoulder but are moulded in a fixed, bent position at the elbow which means that they can, virtually, only be moved into striking or thrusting positions. The legs are articulated at the hips but permanently bent at the knees, which gives the figures, when standing, a crouching, ready-for-action posture. Usually, one hand, sometimes the left, sometimes the right, is cusped while the other has the fingers outspread, as if ready for action. This is the basic pattern, though some figures have a hand formed into a fist. What the body language says, in fact, is 'aggression'. To add to this message, in He-Man's case the lips are drawn into a grimace (see illustration, p. 135). The figures are armed, mostly with various axes, swords and clubs, the weapons being pressed into the cusped hands or, in some cases, pushed into fists which have holes made through them, for this purpose. The two female figures are both clearly from the same mould, have a more upright stance and don't appear aggressive.

Larger weapons tend to be the laser type, but most ingenuity in this system seems to have gone into the vehicles, craft and animal mounts. He-Man goes into battle on a 'battle cat', a tiger-like animal with armour, or in any one of three science fiction machines, such as the Road Ripper which is for 'ground assault'. For the goodies, there's also Stridor, which is half machine and half horse and is 'equipped with deadly laser guns and protective body armour'. Naturally, the baddies have their own, evil transport.

The forces of good have to hold Castle Grayskull against Skeletor and his band because whoever owns it rules the mystical world of Eternia. The evil stronghold is Snake Mountain. Both bases are playsets, as you might expect and, following a growing trend, both are portable.

Another growing trend is for systems of aggressive figures to feature more and more in co-ordinated campaigns which can include film, television or fiction (in the usual sense and including comics) or any combination of these.

Mattel began to introduce the Masters of the Universe toys into Britain in 1983 and in early 1984 a cartoon series, *He-Man and the Masters of the Universe,* was running on commercial television. In this, Prince Adam is presented as very timid but, with magic sword in hand, he changes to He-Man. His 'battle machine', Attak Trak, can talk in the cartoon, and thus follows the current gimmick of talking or computer vehicles. Also, by early 1984, there was a Masters of the Universe annual and Ladybird had published two Masters of the Universe books. This was done by arrangement with a US publisher, and under licence from Mattel. The first consignment of these was rapidly sold out from my local branch of W H Smiths. Both books are lavishly illustrated. In *A Trap for He-Man,* the scantily-dressed and large-bosomed Teela has to be helped and rescued by male figures. In this crude fantasy, which is very much in comic book style, the writer can verbalize his way along as the words don't really mean anything. Skeletor, for instance, is said to generate 'a video-lens with his energy-blade' and Mer-Man 'use[s] aquapower to mind-scan the air and sky above'. In both this and the other book, *Castle Grayskull Under Attack!* He-Man has the 'guise of the weakling Prince Adam'. Between the toys and the books there seems some confusion over which of him is the 'real' one. In view of the strong fictional element in this system of toys, it's significant that, from early on, a small comic book has been supplied with each heroic warrior. In the spring of 1986, the *Masters of the Universe* comic, in the usual British format, went on sale. The editorial of issue number two said, 'if you have the toys featured in any of the adventures you have read, why not use them to re-enact the story?' This points up again the whole matter of ritual and rehearsal in play with such toy concepts, as opposed to the use of the imagination.

At the end of 1983, the National Association of Toy Retailers presented their award for the best new range of the year to Mattel, for Masters of the Universe, and by 1984 the range had risen to share top place in the best-selling list with Star Wars. At this time, it was being sold in over 30 countries.

In the same year, Ceji Revell introduced the Power Lords. These originated in the USA and appeared first in comics and very shortly afterwards on television. Soon they were toys. Some idea of the way these things are planned can be got from the fact that the first comic was published by DC Comics Inc. in the USA and dated December 1983 (though it might have come out earlier) and the first toys to appear in Britain were put on show here by a multinational French group in January 1984. These were six figures, an insect-based fighting mount, a Power Ship, and the Volcan Rock playset. It's a battle between good and evil again with the goodies led this time by Adam Power. (If you twist his head and upper torso around, he changes to Lord Power.) Four of the figures are fantasy creatures including Arkus, the evil dictator.

As the *Power Lords* comic books are in a series of three, they may have been produced specifically to promote the toys. Certainly, the figures, whether as comic-book characters or as toys, are licenced by the same US company and the toy figures are advertised on the back of the second comic book.

The first comic book is subtitled, 'To the Victor .... the Universe'. The battle between good and evil is already going strong and soon Adam Power learns that 'The entire universe is in dire peril!' He also learns that he's a member of 'the hereditary power-caste of the planet Toran' and that he is, in fact, the Power Lord whose 'awesome powers' are derived from a jewel. He learns, further, of the Power Lords of Toran, 'the keepers of the peace and of the law ... who have undertaken the perilous mission of safeguarding the peace-loving worlds of the galaxy against the threatening forces of war and evil'. (Here, substitute 'countries' and 'world' for 'worlds' and 'galaxy' and you have the role of the USA as seen by successive US governments since the second world war.) In the second comic, we meet the interesting question of balance which turns up quite often in a related but more respectable type of fantasy fiction which I've written about elsewhere.[3] Here, in the comic, we read 'the delicate EQUILIBRIUM of all the competing forces in the universe is maintained by an awesomely powerful cosmic MASTER'. As we might expect, nobody leaves matters to this mystical being and the usual dreary cosmic struggle takes place, with one mind-numbing power being matched by another until the baddies are foiled. As the third comic book reveals, a good trick, if you're in a tight corner, is to warp into hyperspace for a while. In business, a good trick is to

20: The A-Team

cash in on a going concern so, in this last comic, the Power Lords video game is advertised.

Another development in this line of fantasy is represented by the Transformers. This recent craze consists basically of robot-like figures made up, mainly, of a lot of articulated plastic parts. By twisting these about, rather after the manner of manipulating Rubik's Cube, you can change a robot into something else, usually a vehicle, though some change into dinosaurs, guns and other things. Then, you can change it back again — hence the name, Transformers. Some can be made into three different items. In spite of this new twist, or these new twists, and the rather bizarre figures and vehicles involved, the story-line is an old one, the familiar struggle between good and evil on a cosmic scale. I'll be returning to the Transformers, in a fictional context, towards the end of the book.

The last group of toy figures to be dealt with — the A-Team — are in a different category and first appeared here, from the US firm of Galoob, via Rainbow Toys, about the beginning of 1984 (see illustration). They arise from the well-known US television serial which, at first sight, may seem to have more in common with other serials such as *Knight Rider* and *Hardcastle and McCormick* than with the likes of the Power Lords. Admittedly, with so much killing and general mayhem, it's difficult to tell peace from war but the A-Team, at least originally, were full-time professional killers and so here they are, showing another aspect of the syndrome of aggression. Also, in the case of the A-Team, the characters have become important in the world of toys in a way that others from acted television serials have not.

The *A-Team* series already shown in Britain have been enormously successful. According to information from the Earls Court Toy and Hobby Fair, there were 14.5 million viewers for the first series which was surpassed only by *Coronation Street* in the popularity ratings. Certainly, *The A-Team* seemed to make a big impression on children, though mostly on boys, I'd imagine.

First of all, the word 'team' is important as it gives a clean, sporting image. Remember the teams in Action Force? 'A' is a good sort of letter and when attached to one of a group of some sort — say, teams, for instance — it normally signifies the best. So the A-Team start with an advantage in respect of language.

The four men involved, so the story goes, are commandos who were put in a military prison for a crime they didn't commit, and escaped. Now, they can be hired by nice, deserving, good little guys to sort out the nasties. Of the four, the black one, BA (standing for 'Bad Attitude') Baracus, alias 'Mr. T', has made the most impact and you couldn't get far at the Earls Court Toy and Hobby Fair in 1984 without seeing his picture. The television episodes are the familiar mixture of violence and wisecracks, with the accent firmly on violence. In those episodes I've seen, at least, I doubt whether children would be able to follow the story, except perhaps in a general way but, really, the stories are just there to link the bouts of violence together. As with the other systems of conflict and aggression described in this chapter, you don't have to work out the rights and wrongs of any situation. You know which side you're on from the start and you can see the others are baddies

139

anyway. They look it. The episodes I've seen have consisted of fist fights, gun fights, chases in various kinds of vehicles and craft, usually to the accompaniment of gunfire, and assorted explosions — all of which build up to a climax. Such goings-on would normally entail the spilling of a lot of blood, along with much pain and many dead bodies but these things — the results of aggression — are not really brought to our notice, particularly. Perhaps it would be better if they were. Instead, it's all presented as something of a game carried on in a rather genial fashion.

This, then, is the ideological framework within which children might be expected to play with the toys. The blister-carded figures (the cards have mock bullet-holes in them) come with the message, 'Soldiers of Fortune — Living on the Edge'. There's an A-Team Command Center Playset, based on a two-storey warehouse and containing a lift, a skylight or escape hatch, a heliport and a simulated computer control centre, together with other 'action accessories'. (Compare Barbie's or Sindy's houses and their contents.) Then, there's the Combat Headquarters Set with the four figures, plenty of weapons, two working parachutes and an 'assault boat'. There are many other sets including one of child-size Adventure Equipment with binoculars, walkie-talkie and other bits and pieces. Vehicles and other craft are very prominent in the A-Team range and include, for example, an Attack Tank with Laser Cannon and the Off Road Attack Vehicle, otherwise described as an All Terrain Vehicle with Trailer and Flame-Thrower Disc Shooter (whatever that is). Galoob have also produced four 'bad guy figures' who certainly look grim. One of them even has a black eyepatch, a sure sign of evil intentions. The muscular Mr.T, however, goes from strength to strength. As with the rest of the A-Team, you can get him in two different sizes, but he can also be bought in a 32cm high version, complete with necklace, medallion, bracelets, ear-rings and rings on every finger, as on television. The Combat Attack Set and the Fire Rescue Set are outfits and accessories for this figure. In addition, there's a talking Mr.T and two Mr.T rag dolls, the larger about 120cm tall.

It's remarkable how quickly popular television characters pass into everyday life. I hadn't heard of the A-Team before seeing the name on a T-shirt. In spring 1984, I noticed the toy figures of Murdock and Mr. T in the window of a local clothing shop, beside training shoes of the kind they wear. No doubt this was an attempt to achieve sales through an association of ideas. More to the point, as far as this book is concerned, was the news I heard at about the same time, from a London nusery and infant school. This was that 'A-Team games' in the playground had had to be forbidden because they led to such violence, and serious injuries were being caused.

Making money from promoting war

In this chapter, to give an overall picture, it may be useful to say something about the business side of things all in one section, although I've already mentioned one or two points along the way, in the case of Action Man and Action Force for example, where it seemed most telling to do so.

If good wine needs no bush, the toy manufacturers must have some very bad wine. In 1981, Palitoy planned to spend a third of a million pounds in promoting

Action Man sales. Detailed information on the campaign was available at the beginning of the year at the Earls Court Toy and Hobby Fair, to encourage retailers to place orders and to enable them to plan their sales tactics. The campaign was to include a nation-wide spring offensive on television consisting of a new 30-second film, featuring the Action Man Sharpshooter figure and a series of outfits, and two new 20-second films on national television in the autumn, featuring new items in the space and military ranges. These films, Palitoy claimed, would be seen by 50 per cent of all boys and their parents an average of four times. Then, there were to be two competitions run in comics, reaching, so it was claimed, over 70 per cent of boys aged five to 10; the Action Man Road Show was to visit about 90 outlets; a new star scheme was to be launched; merchandising displays were to be provided for retailers; and a display over six metres high was planned for Blackpool illuminations. This was just for Action Man.

As usual, there are profitable spin-offs to other companies through character merchandising. So, Dekker have an Action Man uniform in their range of play-clothes as well as a child-size Action Man accessories kit which includes a helmet, gun and hand-grenade. Some of the most chilling and depressing items I've come across, however, have been toiletries. I first noticed the Action Man Map Case Gift Box in Boots's catalogue for Christmas, 1982. It's produced by Bellair Cosmetics, under licence from CPG Products, and contains soap in the shape of sticks of dynamite, bath cubes labelled 'Depth Charge', a walkie-talkie design sponge and a compass. I didn't get there quick enough to see this gift box in 1982 — it was sold out — and I didn't see it the following year. However, I caught up with it at Christmas, 1984. (The gift box is on sale only during the season of peace and goodwill.) I should add that the dynamite soap was also available separately, at the fantastically exorbitant price of 89p for 100g. There's the Action Man Bubble Bath as well, which is liquid soap in an imitation military water bottle, called a 'Desert Patrol Bottle'. The package shows tanks firing, a train being blown up and Action Man with a gun. The products of Cliro Perfumeries, in their Operation Wipe-out range, should also be mentioned here. This firm has bubble bath containers in the shape of a hand-grenade, a stick of dynamite, a submarine and a walkie-talkie, and soap moulded in the shape of a plane, a tank and an aircraft-carrier. These things, to my mind, are the products of a sick society.

In early 1983, Palitoy stated that the world box-office takings for the *Star Wars* films, in a period of five years, had been $850 million and that there had been world merchandising sales of $1½ billion. Much of this would represent toy sales. Against such a background, Palitoy's plans for their Return of the Jedi output were well advanced, at least six months, to my knowledge, before the release of the film in Britain, and their toys went on sale to coincide with this. Such co-ordinated business campaigns ensure that children are deluged with a flood of products all carrying the same message. In the case of the *Star Wars* saga, there are, as you might expect, playclothes, this time produced by Acamas Toys and in two sizes: one for childen from three to six years old and the other for the five- to 10-year olds.

There are masks to go with these playclothes. There are also pencil cases, shoulder bags and rucksacks with scenes from *Return of the Jedi* printed on them, marketed by Character Products; and H C Ford and Sons have rubbery pencil tops of Star Wars figures made for them in Macau for the British market. On another tack altogether, though a familiar one, there was a Star Wars comic strip running in the *Sunday Express* in August 1983.

Let's take a traditional toy as a starting-point this time, instead of fiction, television or films. The kite is a very old toy and, you'd think, one of the most peaceful and satisfying. Mettoy's large Superman, Spiderman and Batman kites — with a 'Pow', 'Sok', and a 'Zap', as it says on them, respectively — seem to change all that. They have a Superman 'stunt kite' as well, with two control lines. The firm of Worlds Apart also have a 'stunt kite' in two versions, one with Darth Vader on, the other with the Millennium Falcon space craft from the *Star Wars* films. There are two strings for control, in 'action combat' with other kites. Use of these Star Wars properties is authorized by Lucasfilm, the production company for the *Star Wars* films. Of course, there's a Mr. T kite as well, produced by Wembley Playcraft.

Moving on to the A-Team now, the same firm sells a trundler and also a pedal-car featuring them. At least eight firms were showing A-Team merchandise at Earls Court in 1984, ranging from figures and vehicles to a projector and slides, to pencils, rubbers and various school bags. Some of these just involved use of the A-Team logo. By September 1984, there were three fiction publications based on the A-Team's exploits.

Salters, whom we last met in the context of science sets, have bought up character merchandising rights for some of the most popular films and television programmes. They have a strong line in transfers and got rid of over three and a quarter million of them in 1983, these being sold mostly as 'pocket-money' items, for example in confectioners' and newsagents' shops as well as toy shops. At present, they have series of transfers on Action Man, Masters of the Universe, *The A-Team* and *Return of the Jedi*. The ones of the 'cuddly Ewoks', they say, are 'particularly for girls.'

On that appropriate note, and as we come to the end of part one of this book, it's interesting to reflect on some of the differences between toys produced for girls and those produced for boys. All the various items mentioned in the last section, brought about by interwoven and often co-ordinated business strategies, go to show how boys are ideologically surrounded. Girls are also ideologically surrounded, but in a different way. Girls are narrowly hemmed in. You don't get Barbie and Sindy T-shirts, for example, and these dolls don't have the extensive connections, in film, television and fiction, that toys for boys have. These toys are more culturally visible and central and therefore, in a way, the values they embody are even less open to question. Boys may seem, at first sight, to have the run of the world — but what sort of a world is it? As we've seen, especially in this chapter, it's a world without care or compassion, where questions of causes or principles don't arise, and where power, aggression and violence are seen as good in themselves. And that's what most little, and big boys, are made of.

References

1 E P Thompson and Eileen Yeo (eds) *The Unknown Mayhew:* Selections from the *Morning Chronicle* 1849-50, London, Merlin Press 1971, p.293.

2 See *Catching Them Young,* vol. 2, London, Pluto 1977, pp.37-41.

3 *ibid.* pp. 150-51 and 152 for comments on this in the work of Ursula le Guin and Madeleine l'Engle.

POETIC INTERLUDE

AT NIGHT IN THE TOY SHOP

At night, in the toy shop,
the dolls all awake,
blink their eyes, nod their heads,
give stiff joints a shake.
And if you go softly
and if you sit tight
you might see what they're doing
— you might, you might!

A party was going on in Barbie's Dream House. Sasha and Gregor were in the living room, looking with wistful innocence at one another, and taking no notice of the disco. Strawberry Shortcake, Orange Blossom and their friends were all over the place, riding on the Clatterpillar, in and out of the doors and windows (that open and close) and knocking over the de luxe furniture. Snoopy was barking, for a change.

In the dining room, Tigger had just eaten Piglet and Mickey Mouse and was eying Baby Sarah. First Love began to cry. Tiny Tears wet herself.

In the sitting room, some Glamour Girls were playing strip poker with Superman, Batman (and Robin), Spiderman, the Lone Ranger and Worzel Gummidge.

In the kitchen, the Incredible Hulk was cutting the head off Girl's World.

The teddy bears were having a picnic on the balcony.

In the bedroom, Sindy's Disco Glitter Dress and Tender Touch under-wear lay scattered on the floor. By the Vanity Unit, there was a Carl Gustav anti-tank bazooka and a cluster of hand grenades. Sindy was in bed with one of the Action Men! (Both seemed disappointed.)

Barbie was stoned out of her mind, as usual. She'd had a row with Ken, her boy friend, who'd thrown the patio furniture into the Dream Pool and roared off in the Dream Vette, Barbie's de luxe sports car. He'd called at Barbie's Townhouse to collect his active and leisure world outfits, but there he found the rag dolls had a squat and wouldn't let him in.

Barbie was bored with parties, bored with her funtime fashions, her ultra-sophisticated costumes and her Pink 'n' Pretty outfit and its over ten absolutely dreamy looks and with all the other stuff that crammed her wardrobe.

She was bored with her beauty sets: her four shades of lipstick and four shades of nail polish, her two shades of cheek blusher and even with her nine eye-shadow colours.

She'd curled and straightened her hair and curled and straightened it again, and then curled it and then straightened it.

She was bored with her Starcycle Scooter, her Jeep 'n' Horse Trailer — yes, and also with Dallas, her golden palomino horse.

But most of all, she was bored with boring Ken, her boring boy friend, and his boring outfits, and boring smile.

She threw up, in the Beauty Bath.

Outside, the Action Men were hard at it, as usual, and the war was getting nearer. The Talking Commander, with the eagle eyes, was issuing his five random commands. The German Stormtrooper had blown up the Armoured Personnel Carrier with stick grenades and, with his Luger pistol, had finished off the British Infantry Major. The Panzer Captain, in his Armoured Car, was attacking the Action Force HQ when the Scorpion Tank appeared. The Luftwaffe Pilot, in his Assault Copter (bristling with fire power) swooped down and, releasing his four firing missiles, blew up the tank and the armoured jeep before the US Paratrooper could get his swivel-mounted twin machine-gun swivelled. The Copter flew off, pursued by the Pursuit Craft.

In the Dream Pool, the Underwater Assault Man and the Frogman, each mistaking the other for somebody else, were fighting it out with assorted weapons, amongst the patio furniture.

The night sky flashed and throbbed like a hundred discos. Shell bursts and explosions rocked the Dream House. Baby Sarah, First Love, Sweetie Baby, Tiny Tears and a crowd of baby dolls were crying, wetting themselves, and calling for their mothers. The SAS Action Man, with his Heckler and Koch MP5 submachine-gun, killed them all.

> At dawn, in the toy shop,
> the dolls all creep back
> to each box and packet,
> to each shelf and rack.
> And a stillness falls upon
> Barbie and Ken
> on Sasha and Sindy,
> on all Action Men
> — but they're only sleeping
> till night comes again.

PART TWO
GAMES AND PUZZLES

CHAPTER 7
INTRODUCTION

In and around 1982, just under a third of the money the British public spent on toys and games went on games. Two or three years later, the proportion would probably have been higher as the various kinds of games based on the microprocessor (often called computer or electronic games) had taken a bigger share of the market, and they were expensive.

Thinking on a wider scale, games cross national and cultural boundaries much more easily than books, which often have to be translated. Toys cross boundaries more easily still as they generally don't carry words, except as advertisements, whereas words are nearly always an essential part of games and therefore translation becomes necessary. However, the best-selling games are produced in many different language editions.

Another point to bear in mind at the outset of this study of games is the kind of appeal they have. David Pritchard, editor of the book, *Modern Board Games,* sums this up very well:

> Firstly, [the games] supply the spur of competition and the intellectual challenge which so many of us find stimulating. Then there is the escape they offer from the pressures of an often oppressive reality and, less obviously, the chance to assume the responsibilities of a Roman proconsul, a banker or a Head of State, if only for a few hours. Role playing and decision taking are powerful psychological palliatives in a society where the individual so often feels helpless to influence events. [1]

Another general point to note is that, once we get beyond the ones meant for small children and those usually described as family games, the games dealt with in this book and, in fact, most games of any kind are played overwhelmingly by males. Also, although there's a big overlap, children usually move from toys to games as they get older.

The last of these general points is that games can put across ideas more fully and precisely than toys so that, from games, children can learn more particularly about their society or, with games of foreign origin, another society.

The main features of puzzles and games

Puzzles are mainly for individual play and usually have one solution. They involve the use of skill or knowledge and, normally, there aren't any rules. Rather, if anything, there's just information on procedure and on what has to be achieved. Most games, on the other hand, are for two or more people and are competitive. Most of them are resolved or decided in some way: there's an objective and usually one winner. Games have rules and involve skill or luck, or some mixture of the two. Snakes and ladders depends entirely on luck whereas chess depends entirely on skill though, of course, good moves can be made by accident.

Competitive games, which means the overwhelming majority, can nearly all be placed in either of only two categories: race games and war games. With few exceptions, the first are played on tracks and the second on grids. I'll deal with the general characteristics of each of these in turn. First, race games.

The tracks, along which the competitors race, can be regular or irregular, that is, either set out in various geometrical forms — many of the early one are in spirals — or simply meandering about. Sections of track may likewise be regular or irregular consisting, for instance, of regularly-shaped panels, usually of equal size, such as squares, circles or ovals, or the track may be a path or road divided up into sections of unequal length. These sections are arranged in sequence and often numbered. To win, you usually have to be first to reach the end of the track, though sometimes you have to eliminate other players or gain a certain amount of money. Sometimes there's an element of capture in race games (though this is more typical of war games) and sometimes landing on an opponent's counter means it has to be moved back to the start. Although Monopoly is played on a track — a constantly changing one — the race here is to amass the most money, and the track has no end. Counters can be various miniature objects, as in Monopoly, but usually they differ only in colour. In race games, players most often have one counter each though in ludo, for instance, they have more. All players follow the same, or similar tracks, sometimes in opposite directions, and normally each player moves one counter, or one at a time, these moves being determined by the throw of a die, or dice. It follows that the outcome of most race games depends on luck. It's typical of race games that landing on certain sections or panels brings rewards or gains while landing on others brings penalties or causes setbacks. Most games are allegories — illustrations of human life as seen by certain societies at certain times — and this is especially true of games played on a track. Such games often embody the common idea of life as a journey, an idea which is embedded in language and frequently found in literature. In *The Pilgrim's Progress,* for instance, it's used with particularly telling effect.

Now, we turn to war games. These are played on a grid, that is, some kind of network which can be regular, as in chess, or irregular, as when a map is divided up into countries or regions, or both, for the more obvious types of war games. A regular grid, often a hexagonal one, can also be superimposed on a map and it's noteworthy that, even when there's no visible grid, as in table-top wargaming played with models over a terrain made to look as realistic as possible, there's still the invisible grid of a map, and rulers or, more often, slide-rules are used to regulate movement. (Incidentally, maps used for board war games are based on Mercator's projection — the one most of us were brought up on — which gives a very distorted representation of country size and which, on world maps, gives Europe the central position.) Board war games are usually played in the spaces of the grid, sometimes called 'cells' in books about games. Some games, however, such as the very abstract war game, Go, are played on the intersections of the grid which are usually called 'points'. These terms refer to regular grids, however. (More details will follow in due course — here, it's only important to grasp the general outlines and the similarities between different types of games.) In war games, the object is to defeat the opponent or enemy, most often by capturing all of their pieces, as in draughts, or by capturing a key piece, as in chess. Some people might balk at the idea of draughts as a war game and, of course, amongst war games, it is at the most abstract and least realistic end of the scale. Nevertheless, the main characteristics of war games — the idea of territory, of strategy, and of capturing — arc all there while, in the idea of crowning and the extra power involved, there's a vestige of the hierarchy typical of war games. Also, as you might expect in war games, the player is in command of a number of pieces, or troops, and not just one counter, or a very few, as in race games. As you move towards the more realistic end of the scale in war games, pieces (or pieces and pawns in chess) give way to tokens of various kinds until finally you have model soldiers. Different kinds, or ranks — pieces, tokens or soldiers — vary in value and powers, and move according to rules, one or more at a time. War games, in general, call for skill rather than luck and so, if dice are used at all, they're usually only used to decide matters (which would depend largely on chance in real life) such as, for instance, whether, in table-top wargaming, a bullet, fired at long range from an infantry rifle, will hit or not and, if it does, how severe the wound will be.

These are general characteristics of race and war games and, therefore, of most board and table games. However, I'll point out some exceptions here before moving on. A group of games, of which the best-known in Britain is Fox and Geese, involve animals, usually hunter and hunted. These are grid games, usually involve capturing and are strategic. Games of alignment form another group in which the object is to make a row of counters or symbols within a grid. These games are also strategic and may involve capturing, as in Nine Men's Morris; though sometimes, as in noughts and crosses, there's no capturing and it's just a matter of blocking an opponent who is on the attack. There are many games, world-wide, in these two groups and, as we can see, they share some characteristics of war games. As for other exceptions, Monopoly has already been mentioned as not being a race game in a strict sense, though there are similarities with typical race games. Again, Monopoly is one of a group of similar games, all commercial in this case and of recent origin compared with the traditional games just mentioned. What all these games have in common, along with most other games, is competition, or conflict, or both.

As this is the case, it's not surprising that many board games have been based on sports involving the use of pitches or courts which can be though of as grids, just as the games played on them can be thought of, though not too seriously, as war games. Similarly, many race games have been based on racing sports, such as speedway racing, and on track athletics. That apart, however, games seem to have been based on most human activities.

Now, in this broad survey in which I'm trying to pick out the main features for reference later on, we return to puzzles. We'll be spending most time on jigsaws and related puzzles, and with these the solution, obviously, is the completion of a picture or, say, a map or chart or something else attractive to look at. As the main point about puzzles is that there's a solution, and usually only one, I think that solitaire and the various kinds of patience would be better described, or at least thought of, as puzzles rather than games.

Puzzles involve skill, thought and physical co-ordination rather than luck. The metal puzzles, for instance, where usually two or three metal pieces twisted together have to be disentangled in a certain way, or the various puzzles in small boxes which involve rolling little ball bearings into holes, all demand the qualities mentioned, in some degree or other. The outcome of patience, however, is largely a matter of luck as it depends on how the cards turn up.

It might seem that, apart from jigsaws, most puzzles, especially of the manipulative kind just mentioned, cannot do more than merely help children to develop. It doesn't seem, in fact, that these puzzles can be used to indoctrinate children with any particular ideas and attitudes. How the puzzles are used, though, is a different matter and the way in which Rubik's Cube was promoted is a good example of how a dominating ideology can take over.

This manipulative puzzle was invented by a Hungarian, Ernö Rubik, as a mathematical aid. It became quite a craze in Britain around 1980-81 and it seemed at least harmless and at best instructive.

Then, the competitive element was introduced and players would race against the clock and against each other to see how quickly they could solve the puzzle. Don Taylor, in his book, *Mastering Rubik's Cube,* says:

> If you have worked out a ... solution, how fast can you do it? Can you break the three-minute barrier? If you can solve it in less than ninety seconds, you've joined the ranks of world-class professional cubists.[2]

This might seem a bit excitable and overstated but the book, which came out in Britain in 1981, was reprinted nine times in the same year. The following year, the world championships were held in Budapest and the winner was a sixteen-year-old youth from the United States who solved the puzzle in 22.95 seconds. All this just shows that bringing in a time factor can turn any puzzle into a competition and, when two or more people are involved, it can become something like a game. A similar process can happen with toys as, for instance, when children race toy cars against one another.

Since competition underlies most games, it might be as well to mark that fact now — but also to question whether this need be the case. In the annual publication, *The Good Toy Guide,* there was, over a number of years, a 'Development Guide' in which it was assumed that a child should 'become competitive'. This was the last item in a list of attainments and it was really in a different category from the others which were all to do with necessary physical and mental developments. The competition referred to here was at the simple and harmless level of snakes and ladders, (which depends entirely upon chance, anyway), draughts and noughts and crosses but such assumptions still shouldn't go without challenge. Certainly, the little daughter of some friends of mine didn't seem to have got the idea because, when we were playing noughts and crosses and she'd won a game, she told me it was then my turn to win.

At this point, I'll try to give a general background to games based on the microprocessor in order to avoid undue repetition and explanation in later chapters. We do, in fact, enter a recently-developed, confusing, ever-changing but important world. It's a world which depends upon complicated technology which has given rise to its own jargon and, while I want to keep away from this side of things as much as possible and concentrate on the games themselves, there are some basic matters to be sorted out. For instance, the everyday words, 'computer games' and 'electronic games' are used in a general way to cover different things, which is why I've used 'microprocessor' for an overall term. Having said that, however, all games based on the microprocessor have similarities, as we'll see.

During the period this book deals with, three main games-playing systems have been to the fore. These are hand-held or pocket games, video games and computer games. All have, as the main component, a microprocessor which can be based on a single silicon chip or a few chips and which carries out mathematical and logical functions. The three systems all have inputs, that is, some means whereby you can put in instructions or information and also outputs which can be either what a system gives out as a result of the input — how it reacts to input, in fact — or what it gives out simply as a result of the way it's programmed. The output, as far as games are concerned, is shown on some kind of screen. With these features, the main technical similarities end as the other main element, a memory (for storing information) isn't present in the simplest system, the hand-held game. The video game system is more complex and has an internal, or built-in memory which goes blank, or 'forgets', when the system is switched off and an external, that is, a separate, outside memory in the form of a cartridge — one of any number — which is slotted into the console (to be described in a moment). The cartridges are plastic cases containing silicon chips which carry video game programmes. A computer has both an internal and external memory but, in this case, the external memory is either a floppy (fairly pliable) or hard disc or a tape cassette, like the ones used in cassette players, usually for recording and playing music. Some computers take both or can be adapted to do so. As before, the word 'external' means something separate which is slotted into the system. Reference to the diagram will make these and other matters clearer as we go along (see p. 156).

Next, I'll deal with the three systems separately adding any other main points that need to be added.

The hand-held game is the least complex. It normally has a push-button input and, for output, a liquid crystal display (LCD), such as digital watches have, on a

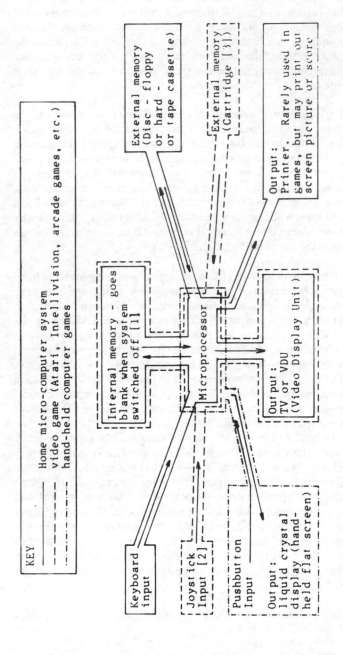

KEY

——— Home micro-computer system

– – – video game (Atari, Intellivision, arcade games, etc.)

—·—·— hand-held computer games

External memory (Disc - floppy or hard - or tape cassette)

External memory (Cartridge [3])

Output: Printer. Rarely used in games, but may print out screen picture or score

Internal memory - goes blank when system switched off [1]

Microprocessor

Output: TV or VDU (Video Display Unit)

Keyboard input

Joystick Input [2]

Pushbutton Input

Output: liquid crystal display (hand-held flat screen)

[1] This is called Random Access Memory (RAM) and can be changed or updated by the operator.
[2] One sort of 'controller'. Others are keypads (with about 12 keys), steering wheels and 'trackballs'.
[3] This is also called Read Only Memory (ROM) and cannot normally be altered.

21: The three main types of microprocessor games

156

small, flat screen. An off-shoot of this type is the table-top or home arcade game which, basically, compensates for being less portable by having a larger screen.

The console is the main part of a video game system. It's usually a box which needs to be plugged into an electric point and also into either a television set, so that the screen can be used for the game, or into a video display unit (VDU) which is, in this case, a separate screen for games playing. The console includes the slot for the cartridges and it also has the means of controlling the game which may be on leads attached to it. These controllers are the parts you hold in your hand to control action on the screen (or, in other words, to direct the input) and they are of various sorts: paddles, which only allow for simple movements; joysticks, resembling the control-levers of aircraft, which allow movement in various directions and which usually include a 'fire' button; and keyboards or keypads, rather like the ones on pocket calculators, which also provide for movement in various directions. There are other kinds of controllers such as steering wheels which are specially for guiding screen vehicles in driving games.

Computers can do many things and playing games is only one of them. Their greater complexity, however, does mean that the games played on them can be more varied and interesting, as we'll see. The memory parts of a computer have been described along the way but I need to add a very important point: the computer enables you to record and even compose games and store them on disc or tape. As far as input is concerned, the computer keyboard itself is used or, rather, some of the keys are, but joysticks and perhaps other controllers can be added. Output is onto the computer screen.

We'll be going into the historical development of the games in chapter 11 but I'd just like to make the connection with amusement arcades here as that's where the games originated. In fact, many of the games for the systems I've been describing are referred to as 'arcade games' because they are modified and usually simpler versions of popular games from the coin-operated video machines of the arcades. This process goes on as the amusement arcades spread. In 1979, there were 59 in London and towards the end of 1984 there were 186. The machines themselves have all the time been spreading into other places such as pubs, clubs, fish and chip shops and other take-away food outlets. At the end of October 1984, I explored an arcade near Leicester Square in the centre of London. It had pin-ball machines as well as very elaborate video games. With some of these, you climbed into a small cabin and sat down at the controls in front of a large screen. In these cases, you had, for example, to steer a car along a road avoiding other cars or guide a space craft while shooting down various 'alien' craft and avoiding their fire. The effect of moving forward was given by having the cars, space craft, rockets or other objects hurtling towards you on the screen. The people in the arcade were mainly youths and young men with a few older men and a very few — three or four — young women. It was fairly crowded and most machines were frequently in use.

Before leaving the technical aspects of these games, it might be useful to note that the basic idea of a grid is important here, also. Most screens are composed of small, rectangular pixels — picture elements — rather in the manner of a sheet of graph paper, and these are illuminated in groups and patterns to form the images seen. Proper curves, therefore, can't be formed and the emphasis is on straight lines and angles. It's not surprising, in view of this, that a large group of games, of which Pac-Man is the best known, are called maze games which means that the player is in the position of looking down on a maze. Another large group, of which Donkey Kong is perhaps the best known, are called platform games and have, as their main elements, multi-storey buildings, scaffolding and ladders. Structurally, the two groups are similar as a maze up-ended, so to speak, becomes a series of platforms. In other words, the difference is an angle of 90 degrees.

Within general frameworks such as these, there are many technical variations: two or three screens for hand-held and table-top games; improvements in colour, graphics and sound; the addition of speech, to instruct the player or make comments; and the introduction of gimmicks such as built-in clocks with alarms. The three-dimensional effect, in which objects seem to move towards the player and get larger, has already been mentioned in the case of arcade games. The same effect has been achieved in hand-held games, and in this case they are held rather like binoculars. Movement of a different kind is simulated by means of the scroll technique in which the background passes by on the screen as if seen from a train window. Also, games have been made more complicated and difficult as children have got used to them: the number of objects which can knock out the player can be increased and so can the speed at which they move (this often happens at different levels of a single game, of course); then, a time factor, for completing a certain task, can be introduced; or, complications can relate to particular games — in one, for example, a man, in the course of building an igloo, had to jump from one moving ice floe to another but if the temperature, which is shown on the screen, goes up, the ice floes melt and cause him further problems.

Moving on to general considerations of the games themselves, I have to say, first, that the various makes of video and computer are not compatible with one another as regards software — that is, the actual game programmes and their containers. However, software manufacturers often produce different versions of games to suit different makes. When I refer to microprocessor games in the following chapters, I won't mention which of the three main systems they are for or, in the case of video and computer games, which make of machine, unless this seems relevant. To give these details would be burdensome to a reader, I think, and in any case, the scene is changing all the time in this respect.

The content of most of the games can be summed up as kill or be killed and I'll be going into more detail about this in chapter 11. Here, let's just note some key verbs used in manufacturers' descriptions of the games: race; avoid, escape, survive; defend; destroy. The verbs in this list, for instance, were used by the US firm of Atari in a press hand-out of January 1984 which gave details of their then current, top ten best-selling video games. They were used — some more than once — in descriptions of nine of the games. The other game, Space Invaders, wasn't described. Other verbs commonly found in descriptions of the games on packaging and in catalogues are: save, rescue and (not so frequently) kidnap; catch, carry, pile, throw; and attack, bomb and shoot. These verbs are nearly always used as commands. In the war games on earth you have an enemy, whereas in space you fight 'aliens'.

Otherwise (this will give some idea of variations) you may, for example, be searching for treasure in a haunted house; destroying centipedes, scorpions and fleas; helping Snoopy fight the Red Baron; racing Donald Duck's speedboat through the obstacle course; playing chess or draughts; playing tennis or football; driving along a road or race track; or, in an old-fashioned, sexist, racist way, helping 'your hero save his beautiful maiden trapped by savages', who are described, also, as 'cannibals'. The game referred to here is Jungle Hunt, third in Atari's top ten video games (1984) and all the examples are from Atari's 1984 catalogue.

A separate category consists of games labelled 'educational'. I think all the games are educational in so far as they teach things to children. Whether these things are good or bad, however, is a different matter. Something to be noted here is that the games referred to as educational are meant for very young children. Atari's new 'educational video games' for 1984, for instance, were meant for children of three to seven years old and were to be played with 'a Kid's Controller specially designed for small and less agile hands'. Otherwise, most games meant to be played in the home seem to be aimed mainly at boys of about nine to 16 years old.

Lastly, as regards the subject matter of these games, most major sports and board games and even some card games and roulette have their microprocessor versions. Some of these, games of chess for example, provide various facilities such as self against computer, computer against computer and self against opponent. Often, you can choose from several levels of difficulty.

A very important, overall point about microprocessor games is that the vast majority of them are solitary — it's one person playing a machine.

The future of this part of the toys and games industry seems very uncertain. In 1983, the giant Atari firm was in financial trouble. At the beginning of 1984, the managing director of CGL (Computer Games Limited) stated that there was a constant increase in their turnover which almost doubled each year. They dealt, as distributors rather than manufacturers, mostly in hand-held and table-top games but also sold George, the programmable robot, a toy off-shoot of the microprocessor industry. Towards the end of the same year, I was informed by Richard Boulton, of Mirrorsoft, that the popularity of both video games arcades and computer games had been falling off in the United States and that 'utility', or, to use the US term, 'home productivity' programmes for computers were more in demand. These programmes are for learning how to do things or they allow the computer to be used as a tool, for example to produce music or pictures. It does seem likely that computer games will gain at the expense of hand-held and video games because computers not only provide for a greater variety of games but can do so many other things besides. In mid-December 1984, it was estimated in a BBC 2 programme that £30 million would be spent on computer games that Christmas.

Background history of jigsaws and board games

My purpose in this historical sketch is to show how jigsaws and board games were clearly used to indoctrinate children with ideas and beliefs convenient to the political establishment. Of course, this process still goes on but it's not so easy to detect from

159

close to. This glance back into history should help when we come to look at the situation nowadays.

According to Linda Hannas, in her book, *The English Jigsaw Puzzle 1760-1890*, John Spilsbury invented jigsaw puzzles, or dissected puzzles as they were called, around 1760. He would mount a map on thin mahogany board, cut it up along borders or boundaries and then sell it, boxed, for children to reassemble. By 1763, Spilsbury was established in business and was described in a London street directory as 'Engraver and Map Dissector in Wood, in order to facilitate the Teaching of Geography'. The earliest known puzzle is by Spilsbury and dates from about 1766. This is Europe Divided into its Kingdoms. One he produced the following year, England and Wales divided into their Counties, is remarkably sturdy and clear and shows the craft was already well developed. It's important to note the educational aim and also to note that, about the middle of the eighteenth century, there was a general attempt to combine amusement with instruction in children's books and playthings.

It was often the same people, or firms, who published both puzzles and games, as well as children's books, This isn't surprising, as the illustrations in the books could be used for puzzles and the puzzles, when put together, could become race games. A few family firms tended to dominate in all three areas and names well known in the history of children's literature, such as Wallis, Newbery, Darton and Harvey crop up again in the history of jigsaw puzzles and the history of board games. As we've seen, all the earlier puzzles were of maps and were meant to teach geography, and so it usually happened that the same firms, such as Wallis and Darton, made and sold maps also. The common link between all the different areas is printing. The firms mentioned were all producing puzzles in the last quarter of the eighteenth century. Output was large. The check-list, which is as complete as possible, in Hannas's book, *The English Jigsaw Puzzle 1760-1890*, shows that more than 560 puzzles were produced in the period covered.

Popular subjects show strong literary connections. For instance, there are, in the check-list, six dissected puzzles illustrating *The Pilgrim's Progress*, as well as many others on similar lines, and seven illustrating *Robinson Crusoe*. The first of these books is a key work of religious fiction and the second the blue-print for the whole imperialist tradition in fiction. One of the *Robinson Crusoe* puzzles from about 1835 consists of seven pictures illustrating the story, and two decorative panels. The central picture shows Robinson Crusoe with his foot on the neck of the submissive Friday.

A puzzle which fairly obviously derives from *The Pilgrim's Progress* was produced by the firm of Darton and Harvey (the two families were often linked in business, over the years) and is described on the box label as a Dissected Map of the various Paths of Life: A Lesson for Youth, 1794. This puzzle came with a descriptive sheet and the puzzle itself was clearly meant to be read, once completed. At the top of the puzzle is Parental Care Hall from which a number of coloured and interlinked paths lead down to Happy Old Age Hall at the bottom. Many dangers beset the unwary traveller who may go, for instance, via Temptation Gateway to Alluring Bower and so to Dangerous Seat. Others, such as 'tradesmen, much esteemed for their industry and sobriety', will pass by Temptation Gateway, so the description tells us, and get to Greatbargain Court. Other features of the map are Gaming Quicksands and Poverty Maze but there's still hope for those wise enough to go by Penitent's Pass.

A less abstract puzzle, printed for G Riley about 1790, is The Industrious Apprentice. It shows six hand-coloured woodcuts with a verse beneath each and it tells a story fundamental to establishment ideology — that of the two apprentices, one who is idle and ends on the gallows and the other who is industrious and ends as Lord Mayor of London. The industrious one marries his master's daughter on the way. This, or in some versions it's the master's widow, is the equivalent of marrying the princess in feudal fiction. The puzzle recalls a series of 12 engravings by William Hogarth published in 1747 and called Industry and Idleness, and one picture in the puzzle showing the former idle apprentice brought for sentencing before the former industrious apprentice, who's become an alderman, is very similar to one in Hogarth's series.

Another puzzle which shows the process of indoctrination going on has a long, but descriptive title: Bowles's Moral Pictures, or Poor Richard illustrated, being lessons for the young and the old, on industry, temperance, frugality etc. by the late Dr. Benj. Franklin. It was published by Bowles and Carver in 1795 and consists of 24 oval pictures illustrating proverbs and sayings such as 'Plow deep, while sluggards sleep: and you shall have corn to sell and to keep'. 'Poor Richard' or 'Richard Saunders' is the name under which Benjamin Franklin's *Almanacks* were published yearly from 1733 to 1758, inclusive. In these, the basic doctrines of an economic system are put forward in little verses and sayings mixed up with a lot of astrology and much about women and wives as chattels. Simplicity, prudence and moderation are recommended and Franklin points out the virtues of honest poverty and the snares of wealth. Naturally, charity is extolled. He tells his readers: 'Content makes poor men rich; Discontent makes rich Men poor'. This seems to be a quotation and it sums up a lot of what was no doubt seen as homely wisdom. It's not surprising to find him saying '*Mine* is better than *Ours*' thus neatly summing up the economic standpoint which gives rise to the 'moral' sentiments. There seems little doubt that the *Almanacks* were popular and influential in Britain's American colonies and they were also widespread in French translation. Following a common pattern, they turn up in puzzle versions.

In these examples of what was purveyed as everyday morality, particularly as affecting the working lives of the poor, it's important to note the cultural connections — between literature, art and dissected puzzles, in this case — since these show how people were surrounded on all sides by a uniform culture, a process which is even more pervasive today than it was in the past.

It's a fact that the prices of cultural wares, before mass production, would put them beyond the reach of most people — but there were ways around this. Prints of Industry and Idleness were probably hung by employers in their workshops and Hogarth noted that sales were particularly good at Christmas when merchants bought them as presents for their apprentices. He had aimed at cheapness in this particular series, anyway.

161

As far as the *Almanacks* are concerned, the editor of a modern edition says that great numbers were bought by noblemen and priests for distribution amongst poor tenants and parishioners. I think it likely that something similar went on in the case of dissected puzzles. There's a filtering process which takes place with regard to a dominant cluster of ideas, attitudes and beliefs which are linked together — an ideology, in fact.

Except when they were passed down as prizes, rewards or gifts, dissected puzzles, and the ideology they embodied, were meant mainly for the middle classes, as they were virtually the only people who could afford them. These puzzles confirmed the view of life of the bourgeoisie and also the principles by which they thought the lower classes should live. Following the usual social pattern, this ideology of the oppressor would be gradually dinned into the oppressed through whatever education they were allowed or, most of all, via religion. There was no shortage of puzzles which were specifically religious, in a biblical sense, and these all played a political role (or, you could say, the bible was used for specific political ends).

Further areas of indoctrination in dissected puzzles need to be pointed out before we move on to board games. Royalty was a very common subject for puzzles and was often in a historical context. In fact, history was seen as being almost entirely concerned with monarchs, typically as in the Historical Pastime or a New Game of the History of England from the conquest to the Accession of George the Third, which was published by John Harris and John Wallis in 1803. This is both a dissected puzzle and a race game on a spiral track. You assemble the dissected puzzle and then play the game, starting from the outside and winding round (largely royal) historical events and information, presented in medallions, to a large picture of George III, seemingly giving off rays of light, in the centre. This follows a common pattern, both in form and content. Edward Wallis around 1840 published the Royal Game of British Sovereigns on the same principle but with Victoria at the centre.

At this point, we go abroad to add racism and militarism to the ideological ingredients. Then, with a strong dash of patriotism, we have the stuff of which empires are made.

H M Stanley was mainly a journalist and explorer, though his exploring naturally led to fighting, in Africa, and he had previously fought on the Confederate side in the civil war in the USA. Stanley in Africa, published by Dean and Son in about 1890, consists of two puzzles with pictures on each side. There are seven pictures in all. One of these is captioned, 'During this period we lost 69 men from starvation and sickness' and shows us the intrepid Stanley tramping through a desert at the head of a column of black men several of whom have collapsed upon the ground. In the largest picture, 'Fight with Mazamboni's people', we see a rigid line of white soldiers shooting down a very inadequately-armed group of black men who are charging them. The divide and rule principle is also illustrated by this picture as there are many black figures fighting alongside the whites.

Similar attitudes can be seen in a set of puzzles called Soldiers of the Queen published by Thomas Nelson around 1900. One is 'Charge of the 21st Lancers at Omdurman' in which we see Sudanese men being mown down.

The jig-saw (tool) seems to have been invented about the middle of the nineteenth century and it was thereafter used for making the puzzles. By the end of the century, or shortly afterwards, 'jigsaw' was the common name for the puzzles and they kept this name even though most of them were made of cardboard and by the use of the cutting die following its development around 1900. Technical developments such as these meant that jigsaws, and the view of life they presented, came more within the financial reach of the working class.

I'll now sketch in a little of the historical background of board or table games from around the middle of the eighteenth century. From this time until about the middle of the next century games were printed on paper which was then mounted on linen or canvas. I have to emphasize the date I'm starting from as it was about this time that commercial games in the modern sense began to develop and these are what I'll mainly be concerned with in the following chapters. Of course, games with broad similarities to the ones I'll be describing had existed before — for some thousands of years — played on boards or on playing-surfaces scratched into rock or earth, but it isn't until the late period that we get games used as instruments of a particular ideology. To put it another way: chess is a war game, but whether it could be considered as propaganda for war is doubtful and of course it couldn't be said to put forward propaganda for a particular side. The ideas it embodies are to do with hierarchy and royalty, but in a fairly abstract way. Although the matter isn't simple, I hope I've said enough to draw a distinction here.

Considering the business background already touched on, with regard to dissected puzzles, and the strong desire, from about the middle of the eighteenth century, to combine instruction with amusement, it isn't surprising to find that the earliest dated game known in Britain (from 1759) is called A Journey Through Europe, or the Play of Geography. This is a race game over a map of Europe, with the usual kind of indoctrination built in. For instance, part of the 'Explanation' reads:

> He who rests on No. 77 at London, wins the Play, shall have the honour of Kissing the King of Great Britain's hand and shall be Knighted and receive the Compliments of all the company in regard to his New Dignity.

Anybody landing on a number where a king lived had another go. With other instructional games, such as the Royal Geographical Amusement (1774) and the Royal Geographical Pastime (1794), the word 'royal' meant little in terms of the games but just seems to have been tagged on to make a link with the establishment. This is a theme we'll be returning to later.

Religious and moral games, which might equally well be called political games, were usually in track form, the regular tracks consisting, typically, of a series of numbered panels showing pictures illustrating temperance, piety, pride, truth and so on. Spiral tracks, which can, apparently, be traced to ancient Egypt, became popular in the eighteenth century for this kind of game. In fact, most of the tracks at this time were spiral, with movement in an anti-clockwise direction, and this pattern continued for about 70 years from the middle of the eighteenth century. However, the track could, for instance, be in the form of a pathway, with marked and numbered sections, passing through a landscape. In this type, and very much in the manner noted in dissected puzzles, you could expect to find, for example, Industry Row, Poverty Path and the like. Systems of penalties and rewards apply in the usual way and the object will be to arrive at The Temple of Happiness, The Cottage of Content or some such place. It can easily be seen how *The Pilgrim's Progress*, with its allegory of life as a journey along a pathway, lent itself to this kind of treatment and also inspired other, similar games.

A popular moral game, played over a slightly flattened spiral track, was The New Game of Human Life published by Elizabeth Newbery and John Wallis in 1790. It was copied from a French game published in 1775. Although advertised as being for 'Youth of both Sexes', the 84 panels show different types of *males*, at different stages, from The Infant to The Immortal Man. Some are obviously bad, like The Thoughtless Boy and some good such as The Patient Man, shown bearing up under the aggressive onslaught of a woman, but some are neither — The Youth, for instance. Parents reading the commentary printed on the board under the title, 'The Utility and Moral Tendency of this Game', will find it suggested that they should stop children at each character to consider the moral implications, so as to contrast 'the happiness of a Virtuous and well spent life' with 'the fatal consequences arising from Vicious and Immoral pursuits'. Instructions are given about rewards and penalties and the paying of 'stakes'. There's more than a touch of hypocrisy, though, over the matter of gambling. A note at the bottom of the board tells the purchaser to mark a totum with the numbers one to six 'to avoid introducing a Dice Box into private Families'. Dice were held to be wicked because of their association with gambling. However, the totum, or teetotum — a small object like a top, usually numbered, and spun to give a score — is here used to carry out exactly the same function as a die.

In The New Game of Human Life women scarcely appear at all. They certainly appear in Le Jeu des Bons Enfans (The Game of the Good Children) but only to be crudely put down. This is a spiral race game published in Paris round about the end of the eighteenth century and in it all the players are presumed to be male. The object is to arrive at the festive table at the end. Two dice are used and anyone getting nine on his first throw lands on the marriage panel. He has to pay for this, from his tokens, and has to go and stay with the contented cuckold or the unhappy cuckold, according to whether his score was five and four or three and six. He can only be released from these prison-like conditions if someone else arrives to take his place. When that happens, he advances to the burial of his wife at panel 58. Those arriving on the marriage panel in more than one throw have to spit in the bowl, so it says, and start again. There are pictures of old women scattered around the board and players landing on these double their score.

However, perhaps the ultimate in this line was reached by the Indian emperor Akbar (1542-1605) who played Pachisi on large courts of inlaid marble around which members of his harem were directed to move. Around 1896, this game was modified, introduced into Britain and called ludo.

The New Game of Virtue Rewarded and Vice Punished, published by William Darton in 1818, gives us another line on gender roles. It's on a spiral race track and the player arriving exactly on Virtue takes the contents of the pool. With one exception, 'bad' and 'good' stages alternate, illustrated in circular panels, and players start with the House of Correction. Out of 33 stages in all, 31 illustrate good or bad attributes such as Honesty or Sloth, nearly all by reference to one sex only. Women overwhelmingly illustrate good qualities and men bad, with few exceptions. It's important to note this placing of women on a moral pedestal because it's been a means of keeping them in subjection politically. Also to be noted in these games is the way in which gender roles are inseparably bound up with questions of morality.

The first non-traditional, and commercial boardgame ever published in the USA was a moral one, The Mansion of Happiness, in 1843. This is a race game over a flattened spiral track on which just over half the panels are illustrations. It's interesting that, although, within the game, Idleness leads to Poverty, poverty is shown as a beggar-man with a wooden leg below the knee. In other words, poverty is alleged to be the result of a moral defect while it's pictured as the result of a physical mishap. This kind of illogicality, or hypocrisy, is common in these games. In the previous game discussed, poverty is represented by a woman who appears to have three small children. In the background is a cross, suggesting a dead husband. As a whole, the picture suggests that poverty is the result of misfortune, not vice. And of course — it need hardly be said — there's no suggestion that the social system may be to blame.

It's hard to see how children could have got much fun out of such games. However, the artist of The Cottage of Content or, Right Roads and Wrong Ways, has obviously made a good try to provide amusing illustrations. We see somebody falling into a pond and frightening the frogs, someone else being tossed in a blanket and various mishaps and chases. The game, which was published by William Spooner in 1848, is one of the 'cross-roads' type which began to appear about ten years earlier. In it, paths intertwine to form cross-roads and a teetotum is used to send the players forward or back, left or right. Even the names are rather less dire here because, although we have the likes of Punishment Path and Ruination Row, there's also the more light-hearted Sack Jumper's Lane and Plum Pudding Passage. The object, of course, is to arrive at the Cottage of Content.

Such moral (or immoral) games must have played a considerable part in reinforcing the established order of society. Even snakes and ladders was drawn into the struggle. The game was based on a very old religious game from India but, nevertheless, the earliest known British version, from 1892, has no moral framework. It has a spiral track whereas those to be described here are, like modern versions of snakes and ladders, played on a grid which serves as a track. The publishers of the following two examples are not known. First of all, the general idea with the moral versions is that you move from a good action or virtue at the bottom of a ladder to a reward at the top and down snakes from a misdemeanour or vice to a punishment. Usually, the crucial panels are appropriately illustrated and labelled. The example from about 1905, for instance, shows ladders leading from Honesty to Success, Punctuality to Advancement and Industry to Prosperity. The counterpart to this last ladder is obviously the snake down which you slither from Laziness to Poverty. Again, the most blatant lies about society are put forward. In the last example of a ladder, a pitman hewing coal represents Industry while Prosperity is illustrated by a very well-dressed man shown looking out of a window onto a huge factory. No pitman, however industrious, could climb ladders like that in our society and, even if such things were possible, there obviously wouldn't be enough prosperous situations to go round all the industrious workers.

In other words, there just isn't enough room on the top rung of the ladder. Only a few can succeed in a hierarchical society and that must be at the expense of others. To put it another way — and this applies to most of the games we've been considering — if society is organized as a race, most people will lose, no matter how hard they try.

The other example, from about the same time, is more obviously religious. In it, the tops and bottoms of the ladders and the heads and tails of the snakes are illustrated and most have labels. The first ladder represents Kismet, or fate, and the others represent virtues. At the tops of these there are pictures of a saintly-looking figure carrying some kind of light and going up a flight of steps. Kindness, Forgiveness, Faith and Self-denial, for example, are labels at the bottoms of these ladders while the heads of the snakes carry labels such as Unpunctuality, Covetousness and Depravity. The tails of the snakes mostly aren't labelled but the pictures here show beatings and various social misfortunes. Unpunctuality leads down to a building with the word 'Workhouse' over the door. Here then, within one game, we have a clear example of religion used to bolster a social order.

All these moral games convey the same basic message: if you don't accept your lot, and work hard and without complaint, you'll suffer hardship in this life and damnation in the life to come.

Moving on to historical games, that is, games dealing with history as a subject, we see another way in which the establishment consolidated its political grip on the country through cultural means. These games show an obsession with royalty just as dissected puzzles did. I'll give three examples of this kind of bias. The Royal Genealogical Pastime of the Sovereigns of England is a race game in which 'good' monarchs send you forward and 'bad' ones back. There have always been 'bad' monarchs, of course: it's the institution of monarchy which isn't questioned but is strongly promoted in these games. This one was published in 1791 by F Newbery and John Wallis. The track is mostly made up of shields giving the names of monarchs and the dates when they reigned, and the shields are surmounted by crowns. There are four portrait panels, one of them, at the end of the track, of the then reigning monarch, George III 'who will compliment the first player, who gets into his company, with winning the game'.

The New Game of Universal History and Chronology published by Wallis and Son in 1814 is in the form of a spiral race track of 137 circular panels, most of them pictures illustrating historical events. It begins with Adam and Eve and ends at the centre with a large, oval portrait of George, Prince Regent who is, seemingly, giving off golden rays of light. The usual kinds of rewards and penalties apply: moving forward or back; having another go or missing a turn; or winning or losing tokens. Some panels require the player to look up historical information in the book of rules provided with the game before gaining a reward. The spiral track with a large panel at the centre containing a portrait of a monarch is a common form for historical games to take.

In a later game, The Pyramid of History published by William Sallis, the playing area of the board is a pyramid of illustrations starting at the bottom left with the Creation and going, via various biblical and historical events, to Queen Victoria, Prince Albert and family who are at the peak of the pyramid and, presumably, represent the peak of creation. The very form of these games — the large panel at the centre of a spiral and the pyramid with the reigning monarch at the top — reinforces the message.

A very different kind of propaganda is put forward in the Jeu de la Révolution Française (Game of the French Revolution), a race game over a flattened spiral track, published in 1791 in France. This takes players from panel one, The Beginning of Liberty or The Taking of the Bastille, to the National Assembly or Safeguard of Liberty at the end. On the way, we see feudal rights abolished and judges elected by ballot of the people, amongst other historical events.

As with dissected puzzles, the price of these early games, as shown in the publisher's catalogues, would put them beyond the reach of most people. However, as I pointed out earlier, there were means by which the ruling class gradually spread its ideas throughout society. Also, technological advances continually had the effect of making cultural goods cheaper so that more and more people could afford them.

We now turn to look at the background to war games in the modern sense, that is, war games which are more or less specific and often partisan, unlike the ancient war games such as chess.

Russia versus Turkey was published by the firm of James Reeves in about 1854 and was inspired, if that's the right word, by the early stages of the Crimean War. Rather oddly, it's a race game in form, consisting of two linked spiral tracks of irregular sections. Equal numbers of players represent Russians and Turks and place their counters accordingly, in the Russian port in the centre of one spiral or the Turkish port in the centre of the other. They race in opposite directions, with the rewards and penalties mostly taking a military form this time, and the object is to capture the enemy port, by force of numbers if there are more than two players.

Several war games date from about this time but they don't seem to appear in any significant numbers until the years leading up to the first world war.

Unlike Russia versus Turkey, The Invasion of Europe, published by Chad Valley in 1910, is instantly recognizable as a forerunner of many modern board war games. Play is on a regular grid superimposed on a map of Europe and, although players don't have to side with particular countries, their aim is to dominate the continent. Even the pictures at each side of the playing area and the one on the box lid have all the main characteristics of present-day illustrations of games. There are battles raging, on land and sea — warships with guns firing, shell-bursts, smoke and flames. There's even a soldier with a typically contorted face.

The first world war brought further war games such as Chad Valley's Trencho in 1917. This was made under licence and is described on the box (incredibly) as 'the famous Australian war game as played in the camps and trenches'. It's based on Nine Men's Morris.

There were other kinds of military games not directly dealing with warfare, for instance, recruiting games. As far back as 1768, the Nouveau Jeu de la Marine (The New Game of the Navy) had been published in France. This was a race game with a naval slant and it was meant to encourage recruitment to the French navy.

Recruiting for Kitchener's Army, published by Valentine's Games in about 1915, is also a race game. It has a track of squares on a map of the British Isles and Ireland and the object is to reach Dover, obviously to board a troop ship. The physically fit are rewarded and go forward five squares whereas being underdeveloped, as well as drinking and smoking, send players back in the race. The board is decorated with a crown above crossed rifles, and with a cannon and a Scottish soldier.

From here, it's only a step to the use of games as war propaganda. Gioco [sic — misspelt] delle 3 Oche (The Game of Three Geese) was produced by Nazi Germany, in Italian, for distribution in Italy during the allied invasion of that country in the second world war. Players move around a spiral track towards the New Order in the middle. On the way, they may be penalized, for instance, when landing on an allied leader, or rewarded for landing on fascist flags. London is seen in flames and the invading forces are shown bombing a school and a hospital.

Games and puzzles in children's cultural surroundings

As we saw with toys, there are many links between games and puzzles and other aspects of the cultural surroundings of children. Here, we look at the process in broad outline, leaving more details to be picked up later on.

I drew attention to some early links with fiction in the course of the historical outline. Such links have continued and are, if anything, even stronger at the present time. So, we find Waddingtons, in 1985, producing both a board game and a card game based on the popular 'engine' series of picture books by W Awdry. The games are named after one of the books, *Thomas, the Tank Engine*. Several years before, in 1979, Whitman Publishing were producing 54 large-piece jigsaws based on this series of books. Waddingtons also produce board and card games based on *The Wind in the Willows* by Kenneth Grahame. Nor is it surprising to find, in Quicksilva's 1985 catalogue, a computer game version of Raymond Briggs's picture book, *The Snowman*. (There's also a television cartoon of it.) Quicksilva were then planning a computer version of the same author's *Fungus the Bogeyman* as part of a general move, on their part, in the direction of fiction.

The 1985 games catalogue from Waddingtons shows the kind of links between toys and games which have become increasingly common in recent years. There's a Superted board game and card game and also a Masters of the Universe board and card game. Both of these toy concepts were, as it happens, the subjects of television cartoon series, the first on BBC and the second on commercial television, and Masters of the Universe, as we've seen, also appeared in book form. A similar link-up is completed with the same firm's Mr. T card game.

There's a more general point to be made here about games, as well. On several occasions, when dealing with toys, I remarked on how they naturally gave rise to the playing out of stories. The connections between games and fiction are even closer. It's not only a matter of link-ups between games and certain books — we have to think about games *as* fiction. Compared with toys, games provide something less random and more definite, as fictions. They provide events in a certain order, all governed by rules. A game of Monopoly, for instance, could be very easily described in narrative fashion. Because of this general characteristic, games can present a very particular view of the world.

Controversies about games

As regards the general influence of games, there are several different aspects to be taken into account. I've already touched on how the form of a game can reinforce its message — a prominent final panel in race games, for instance. In a more general way, and as I pointed out in connection with construction sets (see p. 98), the circle for many people may be more basic than the straight-sided forms most modern games consist of. So it's intriguing to note that R C Bell, in his thorough and comprehensive book , *Board and Table Games from Many Civilisations,* remarks on how many 'North American Indian' games are based on a circle scratched in the ground. The form that games take, therefore, is the product of a culture and can play its part in reproducing that culture.

Turning to the actual content of games, I'll end this introduction with two examples showing some attitudes to them — attitudes suggesting that games do matter, do say something, and do, therefore, have an influence.

The first game, Bombshell, was one of Waddingtons' new products for 1981 and was meant for young children, perhaps of around ten years old. It had four funny, military characters — Serjeant Jimmy Jitters and Major Disaster, for example — and an 'unexploded bomb', with some kind of spring mechanism, in the middle of the board. Presumably, the idea was to try to defuse the bomb without triggering it off. I say 'presumably' because I've only seen an illustration of the game and read a brief description. In fact, the game didn't attract any particular attention until after the death of a London bomb disposal expert later in the same year. Then, there was a public outcry and the game was withdrawn from the market, at a reported cost to the firm of £200,000. I couldn't get any further details about the matter from

Waddingtons and they claimed they weren't allowed to divulge such things over the phone to people they didn't know.

So, to the second example. On 20 June 1982, *The Mail on Sunday* carried a front-page headline, in huge letters, saying, 'This insult to our dead'. It referred to a game called War in the Falklands which appeared in Britain shortly after the Falklands/Malvinas conflict. Illustrations, photographs and a small amount of text took up most of the rest of the front page and the article was continued in a full column on page four. The reporters were outraged by the fact that players could score points by 'sinking' British ships and went on to condemn Mayfair Games, the US manufacturer, and to misrepresent Games Workshop who, although they were Mayfair's British distributors, didn't import this particular game. On the same day, an MP said he was going to raise the matter in parliament with a view to getting the game banned. I had a look at War in the Falklands in a Games Centre shop in London. It was obviously aimed at older children and adults and was similar, in lay-out and organization, to many other war games.

The only difference was that it happened to be close in time to the actual events and, more importantly, close to home, in a patriotic sense. (*The Mail on Sunday* took the opportunity to indulge in a fair amount of jingoism.) Bombshell was also too close for comfort. I have no wish to defend either game but would like to point out that there's been no outcry about Arab-Israeli Wars, for example, a game from the US company Avalon Hill.

These issues raise a lot of points — about patriotism, about double standards and about how the press manipulates public opinion. Here, however, I want to stress that, apart from anything else, these examples do seem to show that games are important and influential. It's quite possible that the very same people who were offended by Bombshell and War in the Falklands would dismiss Arab-Israeli Wars as only a game — but that's another matter.

References
1   David Pritchard (ed.) *Modern Board Games*, London, William Luscombe 1975, p.6.
2   Don Taylor, *Mastering Rubik's Cube*, Harmondsworth, Penguin 1981, p.24.

CHAPTER 8

GAMES AND PUZZLES FOR VERY YOUNG CHILDREN

Although children begin to play with toys when only a few months old, it isn't until later, at about the age of two, that they begin to play with puzzles. Later still, they come on to games. Of course, this is because even the simplest puzzles and games demand logical thought.

The simplest puzzles are usually similar to jigsaws, in some way or other, and they fall into various broad categories. In raised inset puzzles the pieces fit into a picture or plain background and stand out in relief from the base board. Peg-board puzzles or peg puzzles are similar except that the pieces are lifted by means of pegs or knobs. In both these types of puzzles, each single piece usually represents an entire animal or object. There may be about six of them and they fit into separate places on the board. Sometimes, there's a picture underneath as well. For instance, you may lift up the front of a garage and see a car 'inside'. In another type of puzzle, a few pieces simply fit together to form an object or figure, that is, without a frame or background. Some of these are in very thick plywood so that the objects or figures can be stood up. With these, there are usually no more than three pieces. Then, moving closer to proper jigsaws, there's the type of puzzle which consists of several pieces that fit together inside a tray or frame. Naturally, there are variations within these main categories.

The pieces themselves vary in size and number from one puzzle to another. Generally speaking, the smaller the child the larger and fewer the pieces in each puzzle. Also, with very young children, shape seems to be more important than colour or line in deciding where the pieces fit.

For the age range dealt with here, puzzles will normally be in wood. Later, children move on to the familiar jigsaws with their typically-shaped and interlocking, die-cut, cardboard pieces.

Simple puzzles and games

The puzzles are pictorial and present children with a particular view of the world. Not surprisingly, the ideological features I've noted in connection with other playthings turn up again here.

The Family Inset Board from Galt, for instance, presents the usual gender stereotypes. In fact, the family itself, consisting of father, mother and three children, in descending order of size, is rather stereotyped. More importantly, however, the mother wears an apron and carries a mixing bowl and a spoon; the boy is in football kit and carries a football; the girl, in a dress and with her hair in pigtails with bows, has a doll; and the baby boy has a ball and a train. The father wears a suit and tie but carries nothing. Here, socially conditioned roles are presented simply but forcefully to children. Another inset board on the theme of Home, one of a range available from Nottingham Educational Supplies in 1982, shows a three-storey house and girls, only, doing various chores.

People in working roles appear in the puzzles quite often but usually only in a fairly narrow range of occupations. Postmen and milkmen can often be seen — usually, as in the Helpful People series from Spears — along with another very familiar figure, the policeman. Rubbing shoulders with these are figures symbolizing the establishment such as beefeaters and, of course, guardsmen. What was really surprising was to find a guardsman included in the National Costumes series made by Willis Toys around 1979 and 80. Presumably, his uniform was meant to be the English national costume! as the other puzzles all represented countries or regions, including Wales and Scotland. The Scottish figure, however, also had a rather military look. I'm glad to say this series has now been discontinued.

Otherwise, amongst these puzzles, there are plenty of animals, though often in zoos or performing in circuses, and plenty of vehicles by means of which the major oil firms get in their usual bit of advertising. Then, of course, it's a mostly male and almost entirely white world.

The usual link-ups are made with other areas of popular culture, though this happens with proper jigsaws rather than with the types of puzzles I've been dealing with up to now. Salters, for instance, in 1984, were marketing three A-Team and two Knight Rider jigsaws and also two My Little Pony jigsaws, in this instance latching on to what had become a very popular toy concept for girls.

As usual, there are examples which show alternative ways of looking at the world, and presenting it to children. There's the puzzle in the People at Home series from Willis Toys which shows a man in an apron doing the washing-up. However, as far as puzzles are concerned, most progress seems to have been made in the area of race.

Lambeth Toys have a range of puzzles made from colour photographs and showing scenes from Britain's multicultural community. There are eight puzzles of which four have seven pieces, cut in a simple way, two have nine pieces and two have twelve. These last four are cut in the traditional jigsaw pattern, Obviously, the range is meant for younger children, round about nursery and infant age. These puzzles are made from birch plywood and are supplied in strong wooden trays. The pictures, for example 'Indian Dinner', 'Sunflowers' and 'The Band', will provide plenty of things for children to talk about (see illustration).

22: *Sunflowers jigsaw*

A range of jigsaws called Celebrations was produced for children of primary school age by the Learning Resources Branch of the Inner London Education Authority. The puzzles, made from wood-fibre board, show full colour photographs of special occasions in the cultures of various ethnic groups living in Britain and there are nine scenes in three different sizes, the larger ones having 99 pieces each. The basic aims of the puzzles are to foster mutual respect amongst children from different cultural backgrounds and to encourage them to talk and share ideas.

The Just Like Us jigsaws are also from the Learning Resources Branch of ILEA. They are meant for children aged four to seven and are made from 12 colour photographs showing everyday scenes in the lives of children from a variety of ethnic backgrounds. These wooden, interlocking puzzles are mounted on hardboard bases with the unbroken outside edge of each picture forming a frame. There are three levels of difficulty — nine-piece, twelve-piece and twenty-piece — and the harder puzzles tend to have more figures, and therefore smaller ones, in them. The pictures present children with an interracial community and some of them will also help children to question gender-stereotyped roles. A very lively picture entitled 'Football', for example, focuses on a girl kicking the ball while 'Building Things' shows both a girl and a boy, black in this case, actively at work with a construction set. Clearly, all the puzzles have been carefully thought out, as learning materials from the ILEA usually are.

The Face Play series of eight wooden inset puzzles come from the same source. These show photographs of the faces of four women and four men from four different ethnic groups, including European; a man and a woman from each group. The puzzles are meant for children aged three to five and each consists of six straight-edged pieces which fit into the middle of the puzzle, the outside forming a frame. Each piece shows a separate feature, such as eyes or mouth. There's a teachers' leaflet with each puzzle suggesting games and other activities through which children can explore facial differences, and more comprehensive notes are also available.

The Children of the World series from Willis Toys is similar, in materials and design, to the Face Play series. This time, however, as well as pictures of four heads, of children from various ethnic backgrounds, there are also four puzzles each showing the whole body. Hispanic children are included in the range.

In the ideological area of class, the general rule, as might be expected, is for rather well-off life-styles to be represented in jigsaws and similar puzzles. Houses, for instance, tend to be detached and set in spacious grounds, as in children's fiction. However, it's good to be able to record an exception. The Fischer peg-puzzle house is a big one but it seems to be divided up into flats, like many large houses in the older parts of London, and it's part of a terrace. There are also lots of lively things going on in the picture.

We now move on from jigsaws and related puzzles to a very varied assortment of playthings, most of which might be said to involve early learning activities. There are simple games involving pictures and alphabets; picture/letter and picture/word games of all kinds; domino and lotto-type games; and games to do with shape and colour recognition. What are the most common attitudes and values presented to children by means of these playthings? The general picture has already begun to emerge through other toys and puzzles dealt with so far.

Nearly all the activities mentioned involve pictures of some kind and, first of all, it has to be noted, as usual, that females and people other than European are under-represented. Otherwise, it's very much the mixture as before: symbols of royalty and patriotism — kings, queens, crowns, flags and guardsmen; aggressive symbols — there are guns of all kinds; and a remarkable number of 'red indians'. All these are particularly noticeable in the very comprehensive catalogues from Galt, who are countrywide educational suppliers on behalf of other manufacturers as well as manufacturers in their own right. I'd like to emphasize that the examples I've given all carry symbolic meanings unlike, for instance, the other pictures they usually appear with; pictures of apples, dogs, cats, cars, buses and household objects. To present children with recognizable subjects or ones they can identify with is sound educational practice but neither a crown nor a gun is a familiar object from a child's everyday surroundings. It isn't hard to see at what point obvious, ideological manipulation begins to intrude. Nevertheless, I should add that I don't believe the manufacturers of these playthings consciously set out to indoctrinate children. I doubt whether they're aware of any such object — but that's the first problem. A few particular examples should be enough to give a general idea of this group of playthings.

The Picture Word Maker, supplied by Galt in 1979, was meant as a pre-reading activity. Amongst the pictures in it, and several times there are different pictures of one item, are ones of animals, toys and everyday objects but only four human beings appear, all native Americans and all with the letter 'i' which presumably stands for 'indian'. Thus, these much-abused people are reduced to the level of things and (non-human) animals. There are 60 pictures in all, amongst them several guns.

In the same catalogue, Pair-it Lotto invites children to associate a wigwam with a half-naked 'indian', dancing, tomahawk in hand (as well as a pen with a bottle of ink). In other words, we have a racist stereotype.

Again, from the same catalogue, My Picture Word Games, which are reading aids, show us somebody labelled 'man' who happens to be white, wearing a collar and tie, carrying a brief-case and with a rolled newspaper under his arm. Compare the 'indian' from Pair-It Lotto above.

Find It, from the Galt Early Stages catalogue of 1982, is pre-reading material in the form of a kind of picture lotto. From it, children get a strong dose of gender stereotyping. Of the four picture boards, one shows us a mother and daughter (presumably) in the kitchen, the mother rolling pastry and surrounded by pots and pans. Another scene is set in the garden where father (I'm sure we're meant to assume), surrounded by garden implements, is mowing the lawn. The boy is playing with the dog. In the bedroom picture, the girl is shown playing with a doll in a cradle while the boy plays with some kind of building blocks. The fourth picture board, however, which shows a bathroom scene, isn't stereotyped along gender lines.

Examples like this, showing the same tired old attitudes where matters of gender, race and class are concerned, could be added to indefinitely.

Traditional, commercial and co-operative games

Moving on to games proper, in a traditional sense, we move also to a different ideological area, the one that has to do with competition and its opposite, co-operation. This is a very big issue and most of the rest of this book will be taken up with it in one way or another. On the other hand, we won't lose sight of attitudes and values concerning gender roles, race and class. As we'll see, they are inseparably bound up with the idea of competition and with what it leads to in the end — aggression. We've already seen a lot of aggression in boys' toys, and this brings me to a further point: notions about gender roles will now underlie almost all the material to be analysed. I've already said that games are mainly a male concern. To put it another way, games involve both competition and an aggression which is psychological if not physical — and competition and aggression are thought to be male characteristics.

Almost as soon as children can begin to relate to one another, they're taught to compete. As far as games are concerned, children, in Britain at least, usually seem to be introduced to the traditional ones first; games such as noughts and crosses, draughts, and perhaps Fox and Geese and Nine Men's Morris. I should say at once that I think these are good games but it's important to recognize the implications in them, especially in view of the commercial games to be described shortly.

First of all, these are games for two people and, usually, one wins and the other loses. (Sometimes it's important to state the obvious.) Even so, it doesn't matter much unless the same person loses all the time or most of the time.

All these games are played on grids and have some elements in common with war games, whether it's capturing, or simply blocking moves or both. All involve strategy or simple tactics, in varying degrees.

Other games played by small children, such as snakes and ladders and ludo, are clearly race games and therefore also involve competition. However, in snakes and ladders this doesn't matter as the outcome depends entirely upon luck. In all the other games, players have to use their skill to win — and this also applies to the version of draughts in which the object is to lose pieces!

I've drawn a distinction between traditional and commercial games and, of course, the main difference is that commercial games are invented, usually by individuals, and then produced by manufacturers under the protection of copyright laws. There are, however, commercial versions of the traditional games, even of a game such as noughts and crosses, which really only requires something to make marks with and a suitable surface. Yet, in 1981 Susan Wynter was producing wooden noughts and crosses, and grid; in 1982 Galt was producing a board with wooden pieces; and in 1981 the House of Marbles had a version played with marbles on a board. There might be a place — in a car or sick bed, perhaps — for magnetic noughts and crosses but I don't think a very strong argument could be put up for it.

Traditional pencil and paper games are always being commercialized in this way, which not only shows that games in our society are, in the end, about profits but also that the creativity of children suffers in the process. I'm reminded of the hopscotch pitches that are painted on school playgrounds, and of a reference I've seen to commercially produced plastic conkers, of all things!

The following four examples of commercial games (in the usual, proprietary sense) all give rise to important and typical ideological considerations.

There's Belt-a-Mole, for instance, described by Marx Toys in their 1979 catalogue as follows: 'Moles' heads appear at random from a simulated mole hill, inviting the participant to knock them off with a small hammer'. (Compare Slap Sticks on p. 23.) Aggression, a disregard for life, for the environment even, are all here presented as good fun.

Around the same period, Spears were offering something similar but on a grander scale. In their game, Wildlife, players 'travel the world and share the adventurous life of the animal catcher', according to the catalogue, and 'compete to stock their own zoos'. This is a 'family game' with two sets of rules for children in different age ranges. It obviously draws upon children's interest in animals, as do all the other zoo and circus playthings but, for the most part in toys and games, there's no actual respect shown for animal life. The animals are just there to be imprisoned for people to gawp at or taught tricks for the amusement of an audience. But then, there's not much respect for human life either in most board games — and there does seem to me to be some connection between the two.

The next two games provide a shift of focus. As we'll see in the following chapters, a remarkable number of games are about obtaining money or wealth. Waddingtons' African Star, basically a race game, is one of these. The firm announced it as new in 1982 and, strangely, claimed at the same time that over a million had been sold in Scandinavia. It was presented as a family game with a minimum age limit of seven, and was described on the box as 'a thrilling diamond hunt through darkest Africa'. Nor is this reference the only pointer to a lingering imperialism. The whole idea that Africa is there simply for white people to range about in is reinforced by the fact that only white people appear, and that prominently, on the front of the box. The whole thing is reminiscent of the novels of H Rider Haggard, first published about a hundred years ago, though there were other, similar novelists, both before and after him, and their heroes usually ended up rich. Waddingtons repackaged the game for the following year, renamed it Diamond Hunt and announced it in their catalogue as 'new for 1983'. (This is a common practice.)

Milton Bradley's game, Operation, has been on sale over a period of seven years, to my knowledge. It's presented in a joky manner and the idea is to perform 'operations' on the figure pictured inside the box. However, if you make a slip a buzzer sounds and the nose lights up. (Batteries are needed.) The object of the game is to make money, by carrying out successful operations. You then 'collect the highest fees', as it says on the box. No doubt this is the way the medical profession works in the USA, where Operation originated, but the marketing of the game in

23: *A Beautiful Place (the picture includes both the square cards showing 'good ecology deeds' and the yellow plastic pieces)*

Britain, where we still have a National Health Service, can only be seen as open, political propaganda, and this directed at children as young as six years old.

The examples up to now in this section must suffice to give some idea of the range of attitudes usually presented to very young children through board and table games. The picture can be filled out, however, if we now consider some co-operative games, as they present alternative attitudes — ones not found in the games described up to now.

Two-Step was invented by D C Stedman of Harmony Games. It's played on a grid of squares, four by seven — so not all games played on a grid need be war games or even competitive. To begin the game, the four blue and four green pieces are placed, not in any order, in the two rows at one end of the board and the same numbers of red and yellow pieces are placed similarly at the other end. The object is to move each set of pieces to the opposite end. Up to four can play, and there are several variations, but players have to co-operate and plan their moves in order to succeed. I can think of some possible improvements, to do with the size of the board and the differentiation of the pieces, but the game is produced on a small scale, a fact which, I imagine, would make these difficult to implement. Besides, this is carping, really. Two-Step is a very good and basically simple game which is both co-operative and intriguing. Also, like most co-operative games, it encourages positive discussion, whereas most competitive games involve close secrecy, or bargaining, or give rise to arguments.

A Beautiful Place is one of the many co-operative games of all kinds produced by Jim Deacove at his firm, Family Pastimes, in Canada (see illustration). I'll describe the version copyrighted in 1981. The 'beautiful place', a pleasant country scene, is pictured at the centre of the square playmat and it's covered, at the beginning of the game, by eight cardboard rectangles which make up a picture of the same scene, heavily polluted and turned into an 'ugly place'. Around this central scene are spaces for 12 dark clouds. These, known as 'bad deeds', are pictured on 12 smaller cardboard rectangles. At each corner of the playmat, there are three spaces for suns, or 'good deeds', which are represented by yellow plastic pieces. A large die, with black and yellow dots on it, determines whether dark clouds are filled in or whether suns are collected. Players combine together and three suns can be used to remove a panel of the 'ugly place'. One sun can remove a dark cloud and the object is to reveal the whole of the 'beautiful place' before the dark clouds ring it round. People combining together is the essence of this simple and outstanding game. However, there was room for improvement in this early version — the playmat was made of paper, for instance — but, in this connection, it's important to understand that games such as Two-Step and A Beautiful Place haven't millions of pounds or dollars behind them, in development and promotion, as the games of the multinational companies have. Nevertheless, A Beautiful Place would get five- to eight-year-olds used to the idea of co-operating in a very enjoyable way. Younger children, as well, can manage this game. A friend of mine tried it out with her nursery class where it was very popular. The later version of the game has a board and there are small square cards instead of yellow plastic pieces. These cards illustrate deeds that are good from an ecological standpoint. One card, for example, is I Tidy Up.

179

Some of them, though, such as, I Recycle Metal and Glass, will tend to put the game beyond the reach of the smaller children, which is a pity in a way.

A Beautiful Place is available, in Britain, from the Earthcare Co-operative in Durham city. They also distribute other co-operative games from Family Pastimes, amongst them two, Max and Harvest Time, which are equally outstanding and for a similar age range.

The East Anglian Resource organization, which is the educational publishing unit serving Cambridgeshire, produces Peaceable Pastimes by Peter Brimblecombe. These are four co-operative games which come in a box together and are for children aged nine and above. (One is a classroom game of the moving-about kind and it therefore falls outside the scope of this book.)

Another, Urgent Delivery, is for seven players (though there can be doubling up) and is played on a track, though it isn't a race game in the usual sense. In this case, the track is a roadway which zigzags along a plastic strip four and a half metres long. Five vehicles, each of which can repair a single kind of breakdown, such as a flat tyre or a failure of lights, together with another vehicle, the 'wreck truck', which can repair any breakdown, are moved along this road but the object of the game, for all players alike, is to get the van carrying medical supplies from the drug company at one end to the hospital at the other. At the hospital, there's a patient who will die unless these supplies arrive. The roadway is divided into sections on certain of which breakdowns or crashes happen. On other sections, there are lay-byes, and vehicles arriving on these can choose to move into them to leave the road clear. Each vehicle in turn is moved along the sections of the road according to the throw of two dice. There are other subsidiary rules which we needn't bother about here. What is important is the overall strategy, which is to co-operate in such a way as to let the medical van get on ahead and to keep the other vehicles behind in case it breaks down. Obviously, players must plan and discuss moves in order to ensure that the medical van gets through. If, for instance, the electrical van has a flat tyre and the tyre repair truck doesn't stop to repair it, then the electrical van won't be able to repair a lights failure in the all-important medical van. The wreck truck could save the situation but only if it happens to be behind, as turning back along the road isn't allowed. This is a well thought out and original game which demands good judgment and which gives rise to plenty of involvement and discussion.

Leapwalker, another of the Peaceable Pastimes, is a game played on the points and corners of a grid within an overall triangular playing area and the idea is to get four differently-coloured pieces at the base of the triangle onto places at its apex. Although various ways of moving are possible, the only way to make progress is by jumping over a piece directly in front, and the players must co-operate to succeed. As you can see, there are some similarities with Two-Step but this is a distinct and intriguing game in itself. There's also a harder version.

In the game called Waterhole, the water-hole itself is a circle at the centre of four concentric rings or tracks. These have radiating spokes, giving a spider-web effect, dividing the tracks into sections and, at the same time, making a kind of grid. Players take the parts of six herbivores (plastic animals are provided for this game) who start in the outer ring and who have to get to the water-hole and then back to their home territory. However, they have to avoid being eaten by the three carnivores, one in each of the other three rings, who are moved forward automatically at each round of the game. If an animal is eaten, the game is lost. There are rather complicated rules about how the herbivores can move and under what conditions they are safe. However, the general principle is that there's safety in numbers, so they must act together. This is an original game but an adult friend and I (admittedly, playing three animals each) found it too hard and, after we'd played and lost about four or five times, we felt like giving up, and did so.

This illustrates a fundamental point about co-operative games. All the players can win but they can all lose, as well. The games must be balanced, so that they're neither too hard nor too easy.

Peaceable Pastimes give rise to other general points. In a way, Waterhole and Leapwalker are rather like puzzles — there are definite solutions in which luck need play no part. Players have to co-operate to solve problems which are built into the games themselves. In competitive games, problems are often posed (and, in war games, usually posed) by other players, though luck often enters in to some degree or other.

As with A Beautiful Place, the actual materials of Peaceable Pastimes could be better. For instance, the playing surfaces for Leapwalker and Waterhole could be of board of some kind, rather than, respectively, paper and plastic. However, that would make them dearer to produce, no doubt, and they're cheap compared with the general run of commercially produced games. The sheer length of the road in Urgent Delivery presents a problem but, even though it does zigzag, it's hard to think of another way of setting it out which wouldn't be less realistic. But, to make a different point about materials, it's really asking too much when you have to provide your own vehicles for this game! and, what's more, you don't know this until after you've opened the box. Surely, all games should come with the equipment necessary for playing them.

On the whole, however, these games in Peaceable Pastimes represent outstanding and well thought out attempts to produce co-operative games which will involve and stimulate children. And, after all, competitive board and table games have been developed over several thousand years whereas co-operative ones have only appeared recently. (This is less the case with the more active kind of games in which some cultures have shown strong co-operative traditions.[1])

It will be useful to bear the above co-operative games in mind in the chapters to come as they show that there are alternatives to most of the games available.

Microprocessor games, mainstream and alternative

Still within the early age range, we have to take microprocessor games into account. Although it's a fact that children, very early on in life, get caught up in the more destructive and warlike sort, I feel it's best to deal with these, all together, in chapter

11. In this section, therefore, I'll be dealing with other types of popular games and also pointing to some alternatives.

Frogger began as an arcade game and a hand-held version was first marketed in Britain by CGL in 1983. In it, the player has to guide frogs through various dangers to safety. They have to cross a road without getting squashed by lorries and cars, they have to avoid getting eaten by snakes and they must cross a river by jumping on logs and turtles' backs. As it's about preserving life, Frogger is unusual amongst the commercially popular games. However, like most such games, it's made competitive by having a system of scoring points.

The game of Pitfall! was designed by David Crane, produced in the USA by the video software manufacturers, Activision, and first marketed in Britain in 1983 by CGL. In it, you guide 'pitfall Harry' through the jungle in search of lost treasure; avoiding tar pits, crocodile-infested pools, cobras and scorpions, amongst other things. Although this game has a very different setting, there are broad similarities with Frogger — the main object is to avoid danger in a world full of menace.

Perhaps the best-known of all microprocessor games is Pac-Man, a game originally produced by the Japanese firm of Namco. In the Atari video version, the player guides a small, round figure with a large mouth — this is Pac-Man — hither and thither in a maze. The object is to score as many points as possible while avoiding the four ghosts who are out to catch him. He has four lives in a game. To score points, Pac-Man gobbles up the dashes which line the passageways of the maze as he moves over them. They are worth one point each. He scores five points each time he gobbles up one of the 'power pills' which are in each of the four corners of the maze and these also give him extra strength which enables him to turn on his pursuers and eat them up. They are worth quite a lot of points but this strength soon decreases and Pac-Man has to flee again. From time to time, 'vitamins' appear briefly near the centre of the maze and, if Pac-Man can get to these and eat them, he adds 100 points to his score for each one. This is the basic game. I should add that sources of extra energy, such as the 'power pills' in this case, and objects affording bonus points, like the 'vitamins', are common features of these games. Here again is the world of menace but in this case, and unlike Frogger and 'pitfall Harry', Pac-man can do more than just avoid danger. He has a chance to fight back. However, along with this feature, a distinct element of aggression has now entered upon the scene (although in a lighthearted way) and this is typical of these games as a whole.

It's also typical for these games to be centred upon male figures, as we've seen in the last two examples. Sexism takes a more decided turn, though, in the very popular Donkey Kong, a platform game which originated from the Japanese firm of Nintendo. (Japan and the USA are the world's leading producers of microprocessor games.) In this one, the idea for which was taken from the film *King Kong,* a gorilla grabs a woman and, in the first screen — a 'screen' means background or picture setting — climbs to the top of a structure of girders. (The structures in each screen get more and more difficult.) Mario, a carpenter, has to try to rescue the woman while avoiding various dangers including barrels rolled at him by the gorilla, Kong. The basic framework here is the familiar damsel in distress, or helpless woman, and the rescuing hero. The woman is a chattel, to be fought over, and a sex object. In fact, there's a hint of sexual danger here which is particularly offensive. The important difference between the game and the fictional tradition it draws upon is that Mario never brings off the rescue. As in most of these games, the player always loses, no matter how many points are scored. Mario, of course, is collecting points, as is usual with such games. In fact, this is the real object of the game.

We now pass to alternatives again. Most of the following games are marketed as educational and although I don't think it's very valuable to put certain games into such a category — because children can learn things from all games — there are clearly some important differences between these and the ones just described. I'd just prefer to think of the following as better games.

Mirrorsoft, the software publishing division of Mirror Group Newspapers, have produced some interesting computer games for very young children. The ones I'll describe were copyrighted in 1984.

Hi Bouncer is one of several cassettes which feature the Mr Men from Roger Hargreaves's picture books. There are four main screens and various levels of difficulty, which is common practice as it helps to keep up an interest. Once a stage, or a game, has become familiar and easy there's not much point in going on playing it. Here, you control Mr Bounce in his efforts to help his friends — by retrieving a lost scarf, for example — but you have to stop him bumping into certain other Mr Men characters by bouncing him over them. So the emphasis is on helping. I found the easiest level of the practice programme difficult enough but quite small children seem to manage these things without much trouble.

Here and There also features the Mr Men and the four games on the cassette are designed to teach direction and simple route planning to children aged four to eight. In the first one, which is really a kind of jigsaw puzzle, you have to put Mr Tickle together by using the keys of the computer to direct pieces up, down, right and left. In the second game, you have to direct Mr Tickle's very long and elastic arm into Mr Grumpy's house to tickle him. This can be done one move at a time or a complete route can be planned before you direct the arm to move. Complications can follow when Mr Grumpy starts blocking up the entrances to his house with chairs. In another game, with delightful graphics, you have to direct a friendly worm up a tree to the red apple which it then knocks down for Mr Lazy. The game gets more complicated as the tree grows more branches but if you get to the end the worm sings a song for you. Lastly, on a chessboard, the player controls four Mr Men who have to trap Mr Tickle. He's controlled by the computer and is trying to get past them. This time, you can move the four Mr Men to your right or left or to their right or left.

Look Sharp, according to Mirrorsoft, is a cassette meant 'to test and train children's powers of observation in an amusing way'. The basic method is to get the player to remember and compare scenes in a variety of games, some based on Old Macdonald's Farm. Here, for instance, we see a collection of animals and, after studying the picture, we have to start from a blank screen and reconstruct it, as parts of it are played back, by choosing the correct parts in the right places.

These three cassettes from Mirrorsoft are enjoyable and show some simple, non-violent and useful forms that computer games can take. There's no scoring and therefore no competition in the usual sense. Instead, the child is just trying out and developing her or his own skills. Moreover, in these games the player can succeed. The colours used and the sounds accompanying the games are attractive. A serious drawback, however, is that girls would be at a disadvantage in the all-male world presented in these programmes.

Caesar the Cat, which Mirrorsoft imported from Hungary, is different from the foregoing games and is, in some ways, like the usual type of game. However, it's more original, genuinely funny and technically better — but also difficult. The setting is a pantry and you have to steer Caesar round the shelves to catch mice which appear, bewilderingly, at any point on the screen to nibble the food. You have to direct Caesar to pounce on them and dispose of them by carrying them through the door which appears whenever he catches one. You lose points if he knocks crockery off the shelves and this can also end the game. The graphics are outstandingly good, especially the busy, nibbling mice.

The Applied Systems Knowledge firm (ASK) which, at about the beginning of 1986, became part of the Living and Learning company, specialize in what they describe as 'creative learning' computer programmes for children from three to 14 years old and they state that 'great care is taken to ensure that nothing in a program can be interpreted as violent, racist or sexist'. In this, the company is to be congratulated. Some of the programmes might be considered as puzzles, rather than games, but several of the items in this section, generally, tend to stretch definitions.

Podd, by Don Walton and produced by ASK in 1984, is one of these. A dumpy little figure who knows 120 words turns up on the screen with the information, 'Podd can ...'. If you type in 'jump' or 'run' on the computer keyboard the figure carries out the action, but if Podd doesn't know the word typed then you see 'Oh no I can't' appear on the screen. So the game is just a pleasant way of learning action words and how to spell them.

Facemaker, a drawing game by Gloria Callaway, was also produced by ASK in 1984. At each stage in the programme, the player has to choose between two options, such as fair or dark hair and short or long nose. Although these are simple distinctions, they can be modified as a face is gradually built up on the screen. Several people can combine together to play this game of construction.

These few alternative examples from Mirrorsoft and ASK must serve here to give some idea of the variety that's possible, especially in computer games. It's heartening to note that things may be moving in a more positive direction. In February 1985, Mirrorsoft stated that, according to market surveys, educational software sales would be overtaking arcade game sales by about 1987 or 8. This seems to confirm the general trend noted in the last chapter. Mirrorsoft also pointed out that over 80 per cent of schools have computers and that parents buy hardware and software to continue education at home. It'll be interesting to see what happens.

Most microprocessor games are for older children and will be dealt with in the following chapters. However, the positive examples here should be kept in mind as they show that things can be different.

Reference

1   See Terry Orlick, *The Cooperative Sports and Games Book:* Challenge Without Competition, London, Writers and Readers Publishing Cooperative 1979, pp.75-7 (originally published: New York, Pantheon 1978).

CHAPTER 9

WHAT'S THE GAME?

In the games to be dealt with in this chapter, children are further introduced, and in a more specific way, to the main ideological and economic foundations of their society. We now move up the age-range and adults play a bigger part. In fact, many of the games to be considered are marketed as 'family games'. Also, as in the last chapter, we move between the family and the education system. Schools — quite naturally — play a major part in transmitting the values of society.

Board and table games and money

There are many games based on various aspects of business or economics and the usual object in these is winning money — imitation money here, of course — from other players. Practically all these games are played on some kind of track. However, the race isn't necessarily to be first to get to the end of the track. The main concern is to make money or to force other players into poverty, or both. A remarkable number of games from the capitalist world are about getting rich, in fantasy of course, and it's easy for those who grew up within the system (which means most of us) to overlook this obvious fact. The significance, I think, isn't far to seek. Most people, in real life, have very little money but they can find some psychological compensation for this through games in which, even if only for a short while and in a world of pretend, they have the chance to possess wealth. Paper 'money' aids the illusion and now takes the place of the tokens of earlier games. For a society with vast inequalities in the distribution of wealth, such games provide a safety-valve, though one of many.

Monopoly is the most typical and the best-known game in this section. The object of the game is to amass the greatest amount of wealth at the expense of the other players and although you just go round and round the track it's important to note that it's always changing as players gain or lose property. In other words, there's no real end to the track.

The game was developed in the USA around 1930 by Charles B Darrow who was unemployed at the time. A game with many fundamental similarities had been patented by Elizabeth M Phillips of Virginia in 1924. In fact, there are so many similarities that Darrow simply must have based his game on this earlier one and he may have known of another, again very similar and earlier still, called Brer Fox an' Brer Rabbit, which was copyrighted in Scotland in 1913. It also seems possible that he knew of a game actually called Monopoly. This one, however, was 'designed to show the evil resulting from the institution of private property'. Darrow took the street names of *his* Monopoly from those of Atlantic City, where he and his family used to go for holidays, and the original counters (usually called 'tokens' in this game) are supposed to have been imitations of charms on a bracelet belonging to his wife. In other words, they are quite arbitrary and have no particular significance. Demand grew for Darrow's home-made game and when shops began to order it, he took it, sometime in 1934, to the US firm, Parker Brothers, to see whether they would manufacture it on a bigger scale. At first they refused but later they took it on, modified it, and launched it in 1935. Soon afterwards, Waddingtons were granted a licence to manufacture Monopoly and produced their British version with London place names and with pounds instead of dollars. In other countries where Monopoly is manufactured, similar changes have been made and the tokens have also been changed from place to place and from time to time. However, even though, over more than 50 years, there have only been small alterations in the game, sometimes these do seem significant. For instance, a comparison of the version of the game as first produced by Parker Brothers with one produced by Waddingtons, copyrighted in 1972, shows that super tax (called 'Luxury Tax' in the earlier version) is the only thing visibly to have gone up in cost.

In early 1985, Waddingtons brought out a new version of Monopoly for the fiftieth anniversary of the game. Basically, nothing was changed, but a booklet telling the story of the game was included and all was contained in a new black and gold commemorative box.

As David Parlett remarks in *Modern Board Games,* Monopoly 'will probably remain popular for as long as people remain fundamentally greedy'. Its popularity cannot be doubted. In 1985, it was being manufactured on licence in 32 countries and it had been translated into 23 languages by 1989. Parker Brothers estimate that they've sold over 90 million sets since 1935. In Britain, Waddingtons estimate that they've sold 15 million sets. They also export the British version to 67 places abroad, though this figure includes some very small islands, colonies and dependencies. Computer versions of the game were planned for 1985. In many countries, national Monopoly championships are held and Parker Brothers organized the first world championships in 1975. At the world championships, which were held in Palm Beach, Florida, the 14-year-old British champion was competing against contestants from 26 countries.

The political aspects of the game are of great importance. Even the fact that it originated and became very popular in the midst of an economic depression is highly significant. Monopoly, it has to be said, is a good representation, if a simplified one, of the way property speculation works and this is in spite of certain oddities such as the fact that being in jail can often be an advantage, and the matter of collecting £200 when you pass Go. The most unrealistic aspect of the game, however, is that players start off with equal amounts of money. (Most money games are the same, in this respect.) In real life the case is very different. Other aspects of the game can best be seen as political propaganda, and of a kind I've noted before in toys and games from the USA. The two Community Chest cards, 'Pay Hospital' and 'Doctor's Fee', point to a private health system just as the Chance Card, 'Pay School

Fees' points to the private education sector. Likewise, the Electric Company and the Water Works are clearly not under state control. However, these aspects just indicate more obviously the private enterprise system the game represents. Not surprisingly, perhaps, Monopoly has been banned in some countries, such as the USSR and Cuba, though it seems to me that it shows up the worser aspects of a private enterprise system very well. The drawback, but also the strongest propaganda point, as far as capitalist countries are concerned, is that it suggests there's no other system. Notwithstanding this, a Russian version had been produced by 1989 and it was poised to go on sale in the Soviet Union.

In spite of the popularity of the game, children feel upset at losing, as with most strongly competitive games. They probably wouldn't be consoled if they realized that greed and ruthlessness are the characteristics (or defects) needed for success in Monopoly — so strong is the desire to win by the time they've reached an age when they're able to play it.

Before we move on to other, less familiar games in which the object is to amass money or wealth, some further general points should be noted about this group of games as a whole. Usually, players are invited to take on the roles of managers or directors or they have to play at being the owners of factories, mines, transport systems and so on. In short, players take the parts of bosses, and big bosses at that. They're never asked to run a newsagent and confectioner's or a fish and chip shop. That might be too near reality and it's fantasy the games manufacturers are after. Nor are players asked to take the parts of workers, the ones who actually create the wealth. In fact, it's typical of these games that workers are usually absent altogether.

On the technical side, the games are normally played on tracks, as I've mentioned, and on these there are panels inflicting penalties or bringing rewards in the traditional manner. There's often a banker, or equivalent, which makes for easier money transactions and the games depend upon some mixture of luck, skill and low cunning.

A report in *Money Which?* of December 1978 gives a good idea of the various types of games in which the object is to become rich, in fantasy. Seventeen games, mainly from Britain and the USA, were reviewed after being played by families which included children from the nine to 13-year-old age range as well as older teenagers. The games consisted of: five about buying and selling stocks and shares: four which could be described as general business games; one about personal or domestic finances; and seven others which were, separately, about business speculation in hotels, about mining and transport, oil (three games), property, and railways.

One of the largest producers of games is the Avalon Hill company and a glance at the game titles in their 'Leisure Time' catalogue (which is undated but of 1981, I think) gives a further idea of the range of games in the fantasy wealth category: Acquire, Rail Baron, Business Strategy, Executive Decision, Stocks and Bonds, The Stock Market Game, Gold! and Foreign Exchange. Four of these were in the *Money Which?* report and Avalon Hill claim that they can all be enjoyed by the whole family. Two of them, Business Strategy and The Stock Market Game, have variants to enable them to be used in the classroom and one, Foreign Exchange, allows players to use 'dirty tricks' as part of their strategy. (I'll have more to say about this aspect in chapter 11).

A more detailed examination of three further examples will probably be enough to suggest the general atmosphere, and political assumptions, of this group of games.

In 1985, Waddingtons re-issued the board game, Ulcers, in a newly-designed version, describing it on the box as 'the hiring firing business game'. The players manage firms and gain or lose money in various ways as they move around the board. One panel, for instance, says, 'Picket violence — pay £10,000 damages'. This seems to be the only way in which the workers make their presence felt, as the object of the game is to employ staff — administrative personnel, that is, not the workforce — and have enough money to pay them, and you win when your firm has a complete staff. The game is, therefore, rather unusual in that it isn't directly concerned with personal gain. On certain panels, players are instructed to pick up 'ulcer' cards and, when in difficulties, they can 'poach' staff from other players. The game is meant for ages 12 and upwards.

Spears's game, 5 Star, is described as being for children of 10 years and upwards. It was developed in the USA and launched in Britain in 1985. A press release describing the game states that 'the dynamic young executive and entrepreneur has to develop a travel/tourist chain of enterprises and, at the same time, amass a 100 million dollar fortune'. The 'enterprises' consist of 'Luxury Hotels, International Airlines, Holiday Clubs for the rich, and Gourmet Restaurants'. The combination of these to be collected varies from player to player and depends on the 'objectives' card each draws at the beginning of the game. It's interesting that the currency is dollars or, that it hasn't been changed to pounds.

Poleconomy, sub-titled 'The Power Game', was first published in Australia in 1980. It was invented by Bruce Hatherley, a New Zealander who was at the time unemployed and is now a millionaire living in New York. Compare Darrow, who became a multi- millionaire on the royalties of Monopoly, a game likewise invented by an unemployed person during an economic slump and likewise a game of fantasy wealth. In 1983, the British version of Poleconomy was published by Woodrush Games who, at the beginning of the following year, stated that three quarters of a million copies had been sold 'worldwide'. It's a rather complicated game, with three levels of difficulty, but I doubt whether 10-year-olds, as claimed, would find much of interest, even in the basic game. The difficulty arises not so much because of new elements but because of the sheer number of different elements. However, there are many games which are much more complicated and this only shows the lengths people who are interested in games will go to. There are tracks, dice, gains and losses and a banker — but there's also inflation, insurance and, most importantly, an added political dimension. In the advanced game, players are, rather ominously, and at the same time, both business people and politicians, an arrangement sure to guarantee injustice. Woodrush describe the game as being 'all about government finance and industry interacting with private enterprise in a political democracy'. An interesting feature is that panels on the board are sold to actual companies in each country where the game is published. These panels are of two kinds, called 'company squares' and 'advertising squares' in the rules of the game but, of course, the purpose of both, from the companies' point of view, is advertising. In Britain, 49 companies and organizations are involved and have their names on panels around the board. Poleconomy has been endorsed, not surprisingly, by the Institute of Directors in Britain and, much more surprisingly, by the Department of Education in New Zealand. Presumably, it's in use in schools there as it is in Australia, though I doubt whether either country would admit to the political indoctrination of children.

A broader point about the political implications of these games needs to be made before we move on to games presenting alternatives. As I've pointed out before, imperialist attitudes linger on, for instance, in a fairly specific way in some games such as Business Game which used to be called Mine a Million. It's made by Gibsons on licence from Waddingtons and was copyrighted in 1976. In it, as the rules state, 'players are the owners of tin mines in [a] newly developing country', so the game is based on a big assumption about who has the right to be where and doing what. It's true that, within this neo-colonial setting, the activities of multinational companies are accurately reflected. The point I wish to make is that such activities aren't questioned. We're told, 'the winner of the game is the first player to acquire one million dollars from his [sic] exports'. This sounds very much like exploitation but the interests of the 'developing country', or its inhabitants, don't enter the picture.

However, probably the best way of showing up the narrowness and bias of such games is by considering alternatives which present a different way of looking at the world. Of necessity, these operate in a wider social context and, as you might guess, there aren't many of them. Class Struggle, though, is a good example. It was invented by Bertell Ollman, copyrighted in 1978 and produced by Class Struggle Incorporated in the USA. Avalon Hill bought the US licence for it round about 1981. In this game, players represent classes: either the major ones, workers and capitalists; or the minor ones, farmers, people with small businesses, professionals and students. Players throw the 'genetic (or luck-of-birth) die' to decide which class they represent and then throw two ordinary dice to move around the track of 84 panels. Capitalists get 'assets' or 'debits' when they land on blue panels, as workers do when they land on red panels. These panels announce stages in the class struggle. For example, number 15, 'Police and army protect capitalist interests' and number 46, 'Increase in government spending on arms' bring assets to the capitalists; while number 16, 'Workers organize a working class political party' brings assets to the working class and number 75, 'Capitalists throw many workers' leaders in prison' (a much later stage in the game!) brings debits to the workers. Some panels are half red and half blue and favour both of the major classes or one and not the other. There are also: 'confrontation' panels which are mostly general strikes and elections; panels giving the opportunity for alliances between classes (but never between workers and capitalists); and panels requiring the players to take 'chance cards'. A chance card from the workers' pack, for example, reads:

191

> You have just been laid off from work. If you blame yourself, or foreign competition, or the Blacks, or Jews, move two spaces back. If you blame the Capitalists, move two spaces ahead.

A chance card from the capitalists' pack reads:

> Coal mine disaster caused by absence of safety equipment that you refused to put in because, you said, it was too expensive. Send roses to the funeral, and move back 3 spaces until the public outcry blows over.

The object of the game is to get to the last confrontation panel, 'Revolution', and to call for one to take place at the most favourable moment. Then, assets and debits are sorted out to see who wins. If the capitalists win, the result is 'barbarism' and if the workers win the result is 'socialism'. However, if the capitalists land on panel 81, they start a nuclear war and destroy the whole world. This brings an automatic end to the game and nobody wins. If the workers land there first, then this particular end is avoided for the rest of the game. Class Struggle can be played according to beginners' rules, full rules and tournament rules and is meant 'for kids from eight to 80'. I don't think children under about 12 would get much out of it, however. Explanations of the four kinds of confrontation and of why particular assets and debits are handed out are provided with the game, along with hints for classroom use and a reading list.

Ollman, in his entertaining book about how Class Struggle was developed and marketed, sets out the wider implications of the game. His account also provides us with some rare and telling insights into the games industry.

Class Struggle is quite openly biased, unlike most games which are covertly biased — usually because they only present a small part of the subject they deal with. Games, like people (including those who devise the games) cannot be neutral. We can ask, at least, that children shouldn't be hoodwinked and that, at least, they have access to debate.

Beat Unemployment!, a game for two to six players aged six onwards (though six is far too young, in my opinion) was produced by the small firm, Staplemoon, in 1982. This game takes the argument further as it's more one-sided than Class Struggle. It says on the box and on the box sleeve, 'combine strategy and luck to survive monetarism gone mad' and an introduction to the rules describes the game as follows:

> A Miner, Teacher, Shipworker, Engineer, Shopkeeper and Company Executive meet in a survival game, the winner of which is the player who at the end, overcomes the monetarist system and remains employed.

Players start with unequal amounts of money and take turns at throwing the die and moving the Monetarist Fiend around a circular track. According to the space he lands on, players have to pay money to one another or pay into the Monetarist Fiend's Cosmetic Economic Policies Fund. There are cards to be picked up which bring rewards or penalties. These are Pay As You Lose cards which can do either and Survival cards which provide some defence against the Monetarist Fiend. One survival card reads: 'You organize a workers' co-operative to survive and trump imminent shutdown threats'. Given that the vast majority of games with a business or industrial setting simply ignore the workforce altogether, you'd think this was innocent enough. (One Pay As You Lose card, which states that the Red Party comes to power, causes players to lose their bonuses, so the game isn't altogether one-sided.) However, on 4 August 1982, *The Daily Star* devoted most of its front page to attacking the game. Under a massive headline, 'Game of Shame', there was a short article in which the interesting line taken by the reporter, Carole Malone, was not that the game was anti-monetarist but that it made fun of the unemployed. This was either a deliberate misrepresentation or the result of inexcusable ignorance. Malone also managed to get Doug Hoyle, a Labour MP, and David Williams, a leader of the union COHSE, to condemn the game. These people should certainly have known better than to lend their weight to members of the gutter press, especially if, as I suspect, they hadn't seen the game for themselves. *The Daily Star* had another go in its 'Comment' inside the paper where it ridiculed and abused the firm (which it repeatedly called 'Stablemoon') making a particular point of the fact that players ended up unemployed. (The fact that players end up penniless in Monopoly must be all right, I suppose.) I wrote to Malone and also to the managing director of the firm and co-designer of the game, Ricki Chavez-Muñoz — who, in his reply, explained that, 'From an ideological viewpoint the object of the game is to expose the "consequences of a despairing economic system" by placing workers within the structure of Friedmanite monetarism'. In a meeting we had later, I learnt more about the background to this affair and got a copy of a letter written by Chavez-Muñoz to the editor of *The Daily Star* on 4 August, the day of the paper's attack on the game. This stated:

> We made it clear to Ms Malone in our telephone conversation yesterday that our aim is not to exploit the unemployment situation ... and that moreover we would be donating 75% of the profits generated from the sales of the Beat Unemployment! game to any project dealing with unemployment.

I had no reply from Malone. The whole episode shows, firstly, that resorting to ridicule and abuse is easier than making out an argued case based on the facts, and secondly, that the gutter press will exaggerate, misrepresent and lie about any threat to the establishment, however small. As a result of the attack, the game failed and, ironically, jobs were lost at Staplemoon.

Before leaving this section, I should point out that there's a whole category of money games which have nothing to do with business or the activities of multinational corporations and which are so familiar that few people stop to consider the ideology involved. These are gambling games such as lotto, bingo and roulette. We've already seen variations of lotto and bingo in connection with pre-reading activities. In the games for older children imitation money is used. Such games are important because they get children used to the idea of gambling; and gambling as a whole, in the adult world, provides an important safety-valve in a society with massive inequalities in the distribution of wealth. So, in 1979, Spears were producing lotto and bingo 'for your home' and Randalls had seven versions of roulette and two of bingo. In their 1982-3 catalogue, Gibsons had six different roulette sets, including a 'junior model' and a 'junior de luxe model'. Various accessories were available separately and there were also six bingo or lotto items. In 1983, according to the British Toy and Hobby Manufacturers' Directory, there were six firms producing roulette. By 1985, the number had dropped to four but perhaps these four had just cornered more of the market. Gambling games often have a touch of class and Berwick's Casino sets from 1982 are presented in a typical kind of way. The logo, containing the words 'High Society' and showing a top hat, cane and pair of white gloves, appears in a corner of each box lid along with a large picture of a (nuclear) family, in evening dress, around a table on which the games are spread out. In the case of the 'luxury set', which contains roulette, a horse race game and craps along with other gambling games, there's a large candelabrum on the table.

Gambling on the stock exchange, which we've seen in games mentioned earlier, isn't really any different in principle but it's usually called 'speculation' or it comes under the general and less offensive term of 'investment'.

Path of life games

The games to be dealt with now are allegories of human life or, at least, of people's working lives. Money usually comes into them but this is because, to some people, so it seems, life and work are largely about making money. Some early games of this kind have already been described, in chapter seven, and later in this section I'll be filling in a bit more of the historical background as it helps us to understand the present situation. First, we look at three board games which are popular today.

A lithographer from Massachusetts named Milton Bradley invented The Checkered Game of Life in 1866 or thereabouts and, with it, started the very large firm which still bears his name. In structure, it was a track game played on an adapted draught-board, called a checker-board in the United States. Hence, the name includes a play on words. In content, The Checkered Game of Life was a typical moral game of the period in which the object was to reach Wealth or Happy Old Age and avoid Disgrace, Prison and Suicide. (I should mention that, in spite of the similarity of the names, there's no particular connection between this game and The New Game of Human Life of 1790 which I analysed in chapter seven.)

The present-day descendant of The Checkered Game of Life is simply called Game of Life and is very different from the original. Here, we look at the version copyrighted by the firm of Milton Bradley in 1978. It says on the box lid, 'Skill and chance for all the family — an exciting journey through life!' This is meant as a kind of description of the game. Two other quotations from the box lid help to fill out the picture: 'Start with money in your pocket and a fast car. What more can anyone ask for in life — except a little luck?' and 'Buy wisely, speculate shrewdly and gamble with flair. Success depends on luck and skill — just as in real life.' The object of the game, as given in the instructions, is 'to have accumulated the most money on your journey through life after all players have reached either the Retirement Home or Millionaire's Mansion'. Plastic parts, mostly buildings, have to be fitted into the board and you have a little plastic car into which pegs can be inserted, pink ones for females and blue for males. You go around the track, each panel you land on, with few exceptions, affecting your finances. Sometimes the

RATRACE

24: Ratrace — the box lid

25: Ratrace — part of the board with playing materials

track forks and joins up again later so you have certain options. The first choice, for instance, is between business and university. You get married, in a little plastic church, and add your spouse '(blue or pink peg)' to your car. Certain panels bring children to the family and you add more blue or pink pegs to the car. You can borrow from the bank (and pay interest), sue people for damages, buy shares, take out insurance, win on the horses and buy status symbols —such as a Rolls Royce, a private jet, a villa in the south of France, a luxury yacht, or an art collection — just as in real life! On the other hand, you may be 'Blackmailed by your butler. Pay 10,000'. (The currency isn't named.) You may find yourself climbing Everest, for 50,000 or inventing an automatic cocktail shaker, for 20,000. Everything has its price. Even having a son or daughter brings you 1,000 from each of the other players. All this may not be everybody's cup of tea, or way of life but, in such a setting, it isn't surprising that, some time before 1978, one panel used to say, 'Disgraced — reduced to living on social security'.

Ratrace was copyrighted by the Canadian company, House of Games, in 1967 and is produced in Britain by Waddingtons (see illustrations, p. 195). It's described on the box lid as 'the game the social climbers play' and it presents, albeit in a joky way, a totally cynical view of society. The board consists of three separate tracks within a square: the outer one is the working-class track, the middle one is for the middle class, and the inner track is 'high society'. There are fewer panels in the middle class than in the working class and fewer still in high society. At the centre of the board is the Racetrack Tote Board and the Stock Exchange. Landing on certain panels enables you to gamble on these by throwing dice. The object of the game is to be the first player to get enough money to retire on. This is a stated sum which can be decided by the players. To achieve it, a player moves upwards in the class system 'sniggering at the opponents he [sic] has left behind', as it says in the rules. All players start on the working-class track with their little plastic rats, equal amounts of money and a business each, and then move around it, according to throws of the two dice; the basic idea being to collect three status symbols, enough money and a 'night school diploma' or 'country club membership' (these are equivalents) in order to move into the middle class. However, if you haven't managed to get one of the last two qualifications in the usual way, by landing on the appropriate panels and paying the required fees, you can buy it on the black market. On the other hand, if you land on the Society Wedding panel you can move straight into the middle class, regardless. There are telling distinctions between the classes: the middle-class equivalent of the country club, for instance, is a yacht club. You can buy status symbols when you land in various shops, and again there are distinctions between the classes. At Rose's Clothes and Furs, for example, a member of the working class can buy the 'latest style suit' for 100 (the currency isn't named). On the middle-class track, and at the same shop, there's a 'designer jogging outfit' on offer for 500, while in high society, Rose's have a 'mink coat for Pamela' at 3,000. Class distinctions such as these are made throughout the game. The working class get wages, for example, while the middle-class player gets a salary and people in high society get dividends. The game is also sexist. I've already mentioned Pamela's mink coat. In addition, on the middle-class track, Royal car sales have a 'chic runabout for Jane' at 500 and on the high society track they have a 'sports car for Diana' at 3,000. It seems to be assumed that men, who are not named, give these status symbols as presents and, in fact, that it's men who are playing the game. An overall point to note is that the game portrays moving upwards in a class-based society as a natural process and, moreover, as being much easier than it is in life.

The game of Careers was invented by James C Brown, a social psychologist, and was first marketed by Parker Brothers in 1957. I've examined what I take to be the British version, which was copyrighted by Waddingtons in the same year, and also another version copyrighted by Parker Brothers in 1978, by which time they were part of Palitoy. I bought this in 1984. I'll describe the first of these and then note any significant differences in the second. The careers on offer, then, in the 1957 version, are: University, Big Business, Going to Sea, Politics, Hollywood, Uranium Prospecting in Peru, Expedition to the Moon and Farming. The board has an outer track and the careers tracks branch off from, and return to it. At the beginning of the game, each player decides on a personal success formula which is expressed as any combination of Money, Fame and Happiness adding up to 60 points. A thousand pounds equals one money point so that, for example, a player mainly interested in money might have a formula of £50,000, five fame points and five happiness points, which adds up to 60. With such a formula, certain careers, such as Big Business, will be more important than, say, Politics which offers more in the way of fame. The first person to achieve her or his own success formula is the winner. Most of the panels on the tracks bring rewards and penalties and these are in terms of money, fame and happiness. During the course of a game, a person may complete several careers. Any one career may be completed several times and each time, an 'experience card', which gives an advantage, is gained — except in the case of University where you don't collect an experience card on completion but instead 'score an automatic salary increase of £2,000 and select a degree as you leave'. When you've gone through any career three times, you can 'retire'. This means you can 'take Bermuda vacations at will'. Some particular panels require a few comments. First, those on the outer track. Landing on one of the so-called 'penalty squares', Hospital and Park Bench (on the Park bench 'you are unemployed'), brings serious disadvantages, rather than just an interruption in following careers. It's a case of blaming and then punishing the victim, a strategem often resorted to in strongly competitive societies. There's also, on the outer track, the opportunity to gamble on the stock market. On the careers tracks: if you enter Politics, you can 'lunch with royalty' and also judge a beauty contest; if you enter Hollywood, you can 'marry foreign prince(ss)'; and if you go on an Expedition to the Moon you can rescue a stewardess from a jammed air-lock. These all bring rewards.

In the modern version of the game, there are six, not eight careers. Big Business and Politics are still there and also University, though, as in the earlier version, this is somewhat in a category of its own. The other three are Show Biz, Art School and Sports. Practitioners of the six careers are pictured on the board but only one of them, illustrating Show Biz, is a woman. A similar bias is shown on the box lid. All are white. However, whether women or men (other than white) would want to be mixed up in this sort of thing is a different question. There are no comparable illustrations in the earlier version of the game, but such as there are show a white and male bias. The device of the success formula is the same in the present-day version but the word 'Fortune' has now replaced the cruder word, 'Money'. Other differences between the two versions are small but significant. Unemployment is no longer called 'Park Bench' but is illustrated by a man fishing. That is, unemployment is seen as a period of peaceful leisure (though it still carries penalties). The Big Business career now includes a panel which says, 'Eliminate coffee breaks. Bonus: £1,000'. This is unusual, in such games, as it gives us a glimpse of opposing interests in society. One person gains: others lose. However, in our quest for Fame, Fortune and Happiness, we can't stop to think of other people and, anyway, it's only a bit of fun, really; only a game. In this connection, it's interesting that all the careers are ones which offer individual success or they're presented as doing so. In Politics, for instance, there's no mention of parties or policies, and the sport represented is tennis, which allows for more in the way of individual success than most major sports.

Game of Life, Ratrace and Careers all represent certain aspects of society, or society seen from a certain ideological viewpoint. To put it another way, they tell stories: they profess to give some account of life. For this reason, it's important to take note of what they are saying. The most important message is found in the object of each game: to make the most money in Game of Life, to be the first to reach a certain sum of money in Ratrace, and to be the first to complete a success formula in Careers. The first two games are about money, class and status, to the exclusion of almost everything else, while Careers presents life in terms of fame, money and happiness, to be gained through individual competition.

At this point, a glance back into history should help towards an understanding of both business, and life and career games. The older games we now look at will also make a link with the games described in the historical account in chapter seven and provide some interesting comparisons with them. We'll consider three examples, all of them simple race games in which the overall system is that players are sent either forward or back depending on the panel they land on. All originated in the late nineteenth century and all are for and about white males.

Office Boy was first published by Parker Brothers in 1889. Brian Love, in *Great Board Games,* quotes the description of the game given in the Parker catalogue of that year as follows:

> It shows the haps and mishaps, the hazards and accomplishments in the career of a business man from his start as an office boy, gradually working his way up to the head of the firm. If he is careless, inattentive or dishonest, his progress is retarded and he is sent back or kept in low positions: if capable, ambitious and earnest his promotion is assured.

In the 1920 edition of the game, Laziness, Carelessness and Dissipation send players back while Carefulness and Ability bring promotion. The object is to be the first to reach the central panel and so become head of the firm. What seems to stand out here is the moral framework of the game, something which has entirely disappeared from modern games, to be replaced, all too often, by simple greed or by what some people would call the profit motive. On the other hand, in Office Boy the morality of the game isn't set within a religious context as, almost invariably, it would have been in earlier games. In fact, in none of these three games is the moral system sanctioned by religion.

The Game of District Messenger Boy was first published by the US firm of McLoughlin Brothers in 1896. In this one, players begin as messenger boys and the winner becomes president of the telegraph company. Laziness and Carelessness (again) together with Untidiness send players back, while Promptness, Accuracy and Neatness bring advancement. Brian Love comments that the game 'reflects the contemporary belief that the American capitalist system would reward merit and enterprise'.

The game of Cash, which has the words, 'Honesty is the Best Policy' in large letters on the box lid, as a kind of sub-title, was published by J H Singer in the United States towards the end of the nineteenth century. The object of this game is to be the first player to reach the last panel and become a millionaire. Basically, Cash operates in the same way as the two games just described, if in a rather more crude manner. The rewards and penalties, for instance, are sparse and show little relationship to one another. And the illustrations on the playing-board — all three boards are illustrated — are less detailed, although more direct. In this case, a large picture in the middle of the board shows an alert, eager-looking lad striding along, carrying a parcel. Below this, a smaller picture, labelled 'discharged', shows a sad youth dragging his feet as he moves along. Behind him, is a counter with a position marked 'cashier'. Players are sent to this picture as a punishment.

Comparing these games with the modern games described above, the most striking thing about the two groups is that they exist in different worlds. You wouldn't find a modern game putting forward the idea that honesty is the best policy, for instance. On the contrary, nowadays underhand methods are often part of the game. Not that I favour the simple moral world of the older games. It was patently false, if in a different way. In any hierarchical society, virtue and effort won't necessarily be rewarded, and certainly can't often be rewarded. There's not enough room at the top of the ladder.

We couldn't expect children, either in the late nineteenth century or now, to gain any real understanding of the world from playing such games. No doubt the manufacturers would claim that that wasn't their intention but they can't produce value-free games: they can't avoid presenting some view of society in games such as these.

Anyway, it's refreshing to turn, for an unusual alternative, to a game which isn't an allegory in a direct sense but which does seek to increase understanding of society and in an area very much neglected in the foregoing games — that of relationships between the sexes. Woman and Man is a game for older children and adults which was published in the United States by Communications Research Machines in 1971. In the rule and question book it's described thus: 'Woman and Man plays to stereotypes: but only by confronting our myths and assumptions about the sexes can we be free of them'. Women are warned that, in the game as in life, they're at a disadvantage but players can choose to take the part of either sex for the purposes of the game. In structure, Woman and Man is like most games played on a track. There's also a system of cards, some of them given out and some acquired during the game, and these influence the course of play. For example, a man or 'male' player may pick up a card saying, 'You stop paraphrasing your girlfriend whenever she opens her mouth. Lose five STATUS QUO points and admit she actually speaks pretty well'. Another card, for someone playing a 'female' role reads: 'You are the only woman psychologist on your research team. At staff meetings, the men assign you the tasks of taking notes and serving coffee'. The player has to agree to this and loses points as before. There's also a collection of questions when a confrontation is called for in the course of the game. For example: 'True or false? In 1971 there were only two women in the US Senate'. (This is false as there was only one woman.) The fact that the game gives males, or those playing masculine roles, an unfair advantage might have made it tiresome except that a strategy called 'teaming up' is available, to players of feminine roles only. This helps to restore the balance without hiding the bias. Phase two of the game gives a framework for discussing any of the issues raised and there's a bibliography of useful books on the subject at the end of the rule and question book. Altogether, this is a lively game which has plenty of humour — if sometimes of an ironical kind — and which increases the awareness of the players at the same time. It's strongly based on US society and although it can be played here with interest, a version based on British society would be even more interesting.

Microprocessor games and the values of a social system

A picture should be emerging by now of the ways in which a society, through the traditional kind of board and table games, passes on to children its basic assumptions about the relationships between people, both in an economic and a social sense. Naturally, we find the same process going on in the world of microprocessor games. In the next few examples, we'll be concerned both with the themes of the games and with how they are presented by manufacturers. The way the games work in detail isn't important.

Acornsoft is a firm which produces programmes for the BBC computer. One cassette, from the education section of the autumn 1982 catalogue, contains two business games, Stokmark and Telemark. In Stokmark, 'players compete in buying and selling shares. The first to turn his [sic] initial capital of £1,200 into £5,000 is the winner'. The object in the second game is 'to make the largest total profit or to win more than half the total market for televisions'. Clearly, this is the familiar world of the business games already examined, but here presented in a different medium. Also, it's clearly thought of as a world for males. The cassette case shows a picture of three men in an office.

In Business Game (Mine a Million), we saw the exploitation of a 'newly developing country'. In Planet Miners, a computer game from Avalon Hill, we see that imperialism knows no bounds. The object of the game is:

> to stake valuable mining claims throughout the solar system in the year 2050. Each player must decide which ships to send to which planets and when to try 'dirty tricks' like a sabotage and claim jumping.

As we see, 'dirty tricks' are part of the game.

Individualism, competition and imperialism are all part of the same ideological complex and aggression is a part of all of them. The social system from which such games arise is inherently aggressive and naturally aggression is very much to the fore in many games and not necessarily only in war games, as the next two examples show.

Death Race is an arcade game which was produced by the US firm of Exidy in 1976. It's one of a largish group of microprocessor games in which the player guides a vehicle on the screen by means of a steering-wheel. In other words, it provides a simulation of driving. However, in most such games the idea is to avoid oncoming traffic and survive for as long as possible. In Death Race, on the other hand, the player has to see how many pedestrians he or she can run over in a minute. They try to flee from the car and each time one is hit a scream can be heard and a graveyard cross appears on the spot. At least this, apparently, was how things were when the game first came out at which time it was called Pedestrian. Not surprisingly, the game aroused opposition, which is probably why Exidy made the scream into something more like a squeal (though it seems it could still be adjusted to give a more human-like sound). They also started calling the figures 'gremlins' and, in a later version, Super Death Chase, they became skeletons. A representative of the firm remarked of the first version of the game, that if a lot of people got fun out of running over passers-by, then you had to let them.

Mattel's car-driving video game, Bump 'n' Jump, which was being advertised in the *Power Lords* comic of January 1984, is less sadistic. The object is to become 'king of the road' and you do this by bumping other cars or jumping over them. The advertisement says, 'nice guys finish last. If they finish at all'. As so often in this study, we see how the cruder, less human side of human nature is being appealed to.

Aggression, as in these games, helps to fill out the ideological picture I'm trying to describe here. Naturally, the whole picture includes war which I'll be dealing with in chapter 11.

The next game requires more detailed treatment as it operates in a wider political sphere. It also gives an inkling of some of the possibilities of computer games while showing that the drawbacks are the result of human, rather than technical limitations. The game of Kingdom comes in the introductory package with BBC computers and is dated 1981. In it, the player is king over a number of subjects in three villages. The people have a certain number of baskets of rice. On one side of the villages, floods threaten the lives of the people and the destruction of their crops: on the other, thieves come from the forest to plunder. As king, you have to decide, each season, how many people you put to work on the dikes, to try to prevent flooding; how many you send to work in the fields; and how many have to defend the villages from attack by thieves. Having decided, you set the game in motion and floods and thieves come in as determined by the computer. At the end of such a 'season', a balance sheet appears, which includes a census and, short of complete disaster, you proceed to the next year of your reign. Several interesting assumptions are built into the game. The villagers' life is presented as variable but fundamentally unchangeable. Nor have they any say in it. On the one hand, they're at the mercy of nature: on the other, there's a human menace. They're also at the mercy of their king who makes all the decisions. They never seek to overthrow him, even when he makes bad decisions. The king never thinks of having a permanent dike made or of clearing out the thieves once and for all or, better still, rehabilitating them. (A few do join the villagers, from time to time.) Matters of this kind don't enter into the game. Furthermore, as king you can be very detached — you don't see your subjects as people like yourself. It's true you have to think, rather than just react as in other kinds of microprocessor games but, as we can see, this is only within narrowly-prescribed limits. Of course, all games work within limits though the limits can be set so as to challenge assumptions rather than reinforce them.

Woman and Man was an example of a board game which challenged assumptions. There are also microprocessor games which do this, one of them in precisely the same field as Woman and Man, that of gender roles, This one is Mrs Mopp, a computer game by Tina Billet copyrighted by Atlantic Software in 1984. It's a pity the title brings to mind a stereotype and although I can see this might have been the intention, I still think it detracts from the game by allowing people to think of it as flippant. However, the game itself is very good. Mrs Mopp has to move around the screen clearing up after a very untidy family. She has to have the right container or utensil — a laundry basket for dirty washing, for example, or a tray for dirty crockery — and when she's collected 10 items she has to take them to the right place; the washing machine or the sink in these instances. Colour coding (things that go together are the same colour) helps in the whole process and there's a system of scoring. From time to time, Mrs Mopp can use magic spells but, although they help, they also sap her energy. As she works, she gets 'tired' and then 'very tired'. (We read the words on the screen.) At such times, she can refresh herself from the bottle in the corner but, if she has too much, she gets first, 'tipsy' and then 'drunk'. In this case, it's more than ever likely that she'll be unable to cope with the fast-appearing items around the kitchen. The game ends when she's hemmed in by them and can't move; or when, after 'very tired' and without refreshment, she leaves home and we read, 'A woman's work is never done'; or, when she gets drunk and falls down. This is an unusual game which makes its point in a humorous way. The young people who played it for me, both girls and boys, were as much taken by it as I was.

Role-playing or simulation games

We now turn to a completely new group of games. In these, the general pattern is that players take the parts of people confronted by a problem or task in a given situation; usually military, commercial or social. On the basis of information provided, they make decisions and the outcome is regulated by a referee. Role-playing games are distinct from board and other table games, though you usually need to be at a desk or table to play them. They take us a lot nearer to drama, especially improvised drama, and some of them, or parts of them, work in much the same way as plays. Another important point is that the ones designed for young people are used almost solely within educational institutions of one sort or another.

First, we return to the business world. Simulations of business strategies and operations grew out of war simulations and the fact that they have now become established in education is largely owing to the efforts of the American Management

Association which began developments in this area in 1956. In England, application in the classroom was begun in 1968 when the Esso Students' Business Game was first tried. The Society of Academic Gaming and Simulation in Education and Training (SAGSET) was established the following year and is still very much a going concern. In 1969-70, 243 schools in England and Wales took part in a business game organized jointly by the Institute of Chartered Accountants, International Computers Limited and *The Financial Times*. A computer centre dealt with school decisions. As far as I know, there were no complaints about political indoctrination in our schools. A teacher wanting to introduce peace studies, however, is almost certain to run into problems.

A few examples will help to show the usual type of simulated business games which are played in schools but organized from outside. Two projects were afoot in Kent schools in the autumn of 1974. In one, the Folkestone Junior Chamber of Commerce organized a Stock Exchange Game which was sponsored by the Victory Insurance Company of Folkestone. Forty-eight teams entered and were each given an imaginary sum of £15,000 to invest in stocks and shares. The winner was to be the team which made the greatest profit over a six-month period. The other project was a business game organized by the Institute of Chartered Accountants. In this, sixth formers acted as boards of directors (you normally start at the top of the ladder in these games) and their decisions were monitored by computer to find out the 'company' with the biggest profit and most efficient 'board'.

In the winter of 1983-4, the Royal Bank of Scotland ran an investment game, called Capitaliser, in which 337 'syndicates' in 161 Scottish schools took part. Each 'syndicate' had a fictional £10,000 to invest in the stock market and the winner, of course, was to be the group making the biggest profit. Each member of the winning 'syndicate' was to get a £25 voucher and a two-day trip to the London stock exchange and the school concerned was to receive £500 and a trophy.

Not that the schools need any help from outside in these matters. I have a copy of an Iron and Steel Role-Playing Game which came from the geography department of Forest Hill School in the Inner London Education Authority. It dates from about 1969-71, which shows how quickly such games got into schools here. There's a variant of the game for the first form which begins, typically, 'You are members of the Board of Directors of [an] Iron Manufacturing Co.', but I'll concentrate on the game as meant for older school students. The aim of it is to understand how different factors, such as the presence of raw materials, transport and changing technical developments, have influenced the location of iron and steel industries; to understand also how management decisions are reached; and finally, to relate the hypothetical locations of the game to actual ones in Britain. The whole project is meant to go on for three lessons, at least. First of all, information is given out together with a quiz based on it. Then, as it says in the instructions, 'top marks give top people — CHAIRMEN OF COMPANIES'. The rest of the class is divided up into about five company boards and the stage is set. Three sessions follow, each called a 'round', in which the children, using maps dated 1820, 1880 and 1969, discuss and decide upon the location of their iron and steel works at these dates. At the end of each round, the teacher announces the relative suitability of each location and allocates profits and losses accordingly. Finally, the overall winner is declared on the basis of total profits. And this, profits, is all it's about, apparently. There's no mention of social benefits or of the consequences, in human terms, of the decisions made. Although there's a realization that skilled labour is needed, this is just another factor, like transport. At no time are the children asked to identify with the workforce or even to consider society's needs in general — and this is typical in such games.

Another geographical game I've seen is A Herefordshire Farm which, I suspect, is an adaptation or copy of one with a similar name, devised by W V Tidswell. It begins:

> Mr Brown is a farmer at Canon Pyon and is going abroad for five years. Imagine that you have been appointed to manage the farm whilst he is away. He has instructed you to make as much profit for him as possible.

Instead of going into the details of the game, which is a wearisome permutation of crops and fields (with the teacher announcing the weather for each year) and a grand total of income at the end, I'll suggest an alternative to show things in a different light:

> You are a worker on Mr Brown's farm and live in a tied cottage. You do a job which has long and variable hours and which is frequently dangerous for three reasons: because of the machinery you have to use which often doesn't comply with the safety regulations; because of having to work with harmful chemicals; and because of possible attack by bulls. As an agricultural worker, you are amongst the lowest-paid in the country while farmers, who are generally very wealthy, have just had a 45% rise in their income. You are the local branch secretary of your union.

I think a good game could be worked out from such a start. It could centre on branch meetings such as an emergency one following an accident to a member or one to discuss a loss of jobs. The game could take several interesting directions and deal with, for instance, factory farming, soil erosion or the use of chemical fertilizers, and the relationship of any of these to profits and human welfare. Could it be argued that children would learn less from such a game? Could it be argued that children should not have the chance of playing such a game, even if just in addition to A Herefordshire Farm?

Role-playing games, meant for use in schools or by youth groups, have been produced both by large companies, such as Coca-Cola and Shell, and by various social agencies.

Spring Green Motorway is produced by one of the latter, Community Service Volunteers. It first came out in 1972 and the revised edition of 1980 was reprinted in 1984. The problem the game concentrates on is to do with the proposed construction of a new motorway and the social impact this will have on the village of Spring Green. The role playing culminates in a public meeting in the village hall. Within these limitations, the game is well worked out but the main issues, politically — why roads instead of railways? and why private instead of public transport? — aren't raised, though they might, by chance, be introduced in a small way. In this game, children are not asked to question the system: they are only invited to accept its assumptions and work out solutions to the problems it creates. However, unlike the other games just considered, Spring Green Motorway does present us with ordinary people who are affected by decisions rather than just with decision-makers. Nor is the main point of the game making profits.

Another game dealing with an important social issue, this time housing, is called Tenement. Shelter, the organization which campaigns for the homeless, published it as part of their youth education programme in 1978. It's been updated since and, according to the most recent information I've had from Shelter, there's still a big demand for the game from schools. The introduction to Notes for [the] Controller sets the scene:

> 'Tenement' is a simulation concerned with the problems of families living in a multi-occupied house in a large city. The idea of the simulation is to make young people aware of some of the difficulties and frustrations of living in such a situation and to point to ways in which some of those difficulties could be solved by the introduction of agencies concerned with such problems.

Children take the parts of people living in the house and people working in the agencies, such as the local authority housing department and the Department of Health and Social Security. There's also the part of the landlord (a racist, though the word isn't used) who lets the house out, furnished. Parts are allocated, information given out accordingly and soon the game, or play, can begin. As with Spring Green Motorway, there's no hint that things could be radically different. All is played out within the limitations of society as it is at present. There's an argument which goes: this is the way things are here and children should know how the system works — and that's fair enough in its way. But unless, at some stage and in some way, it's put to children that housing problems are political problems, that the 'housing stock' of the local council represents a different approach to a human need, and that you don't have to have landlords, good or bad — then surely the most important educational dimension is left out. Looked at another way, the game teaches children that the situation in Tenement is the way things are, and have to be. This isn't true. As my informant at Shelter told me, the game is meant to be part of a course or project and teachers could raise the kind of points I've mentioned. The suggestions for discussion provided, however, don't really give any leads here.

Starpower, by R Garry Shirts, goes much deeper. This role-playing game for about 25-30 players and a 'director' was copyrighted in 1969 by the Western Behavioural Sciences Institute in the United States and is available in Britain from Oxfam. In the game, a rigid society divided into three classes is built up through the distribution of wealth represented by 'chips'. Then, the wealthiest group is given the power to make the rules of the game. I'll now describe the main outlines of Starpower. Firstly, a random assortment of chips of five colours is put into three bags and each player draws out five. The colours have different values and these are explained to the players by the director. Secondly, bargaining takes place during which players try to increase their scores. This bargaining system has fairly complicated rules. Thirdly, according to scores, players are divided into three groups, though some adjustment may have to be made by the director to ensure that

205

these are more or less equal in number. Fourthly, the three groups are given badges — squares for the highest scorers, circles for the middle range and triangles for the lowest scorers — and they now sit separately. In the second round, chips are drawn as before but this time the director has distributed them in the three bags and given these out to the groups so as to favour the squares who get the chips with higher values. Another session of trading follows and the rich get richer. Then, the director announces that the squares, because they've done so well, henceforth have the right to make the rules of the game. They may, and probably will, for instance, change the rules of bargaining so as to favour themselves. The circles and triangles can suggest rule changes to the squares but the squares don't have to accept, or even consider them. The likely outcome is that the circles and triangles will either give up or become hostile and subversive. At this point, the director stops the game and a discussion follows. In Starpower, the lesson is plain and applies to all class-based societies: the people with wealth will make rules (or laws) to protect their privileged status, and other classes will react in predictable ways. It's a lesson which underlies most of history.

In this chapter, we've looked at board games, microprocessor games and role-playing games, and we've seen how children, both at home and at school, are introduced to the dominant ideology of their society. This ideology has, as its main elements, individualism, competition and aggression. These are mainly characteristics of the masculine gender role, so games, at this stage, are becoming more and more the province of boys and men. As the whole ideological complex is rooted in the economic system, it's not surprising, really, to find that the object in so many games is to acquire wealth, in one way or another. To attain the object in these and in most games, players have to be individualistic, competitive and aggressive. I hope I've done enough, by pointing out alternatives, to show that games don't have to be like this.

CHAPTER 10

THE GREAT ESCAPE

From now on, in this and the next chapter, we move to games which are played mainly by older children and adults and almost entirely by males.

In this chapter, I'll deal with what have come to be called fantasy role-playing games. As regards the role playing, there's a link with the simulations described towards the end of the last chapter but there the resemblance ends. In the games to be described here, the stress isn't on learning, at least not in any specific way. The stress in these games is on fantasy and escapism, together with butchery.

Also, a very important part of these games is the acquiring of fantasy treasure and this aspect seems to me particularly significant as the games began and became enormously popular in the depths of an economic slump. From this point of view, it's interesting to draw a comparison with Monopoly which is solely about fantasy wealth and which began in similar circumstances about forty years before.

The structure of fantasy role-playing games

Fantasy role-playing games are extremely complicated. Here, I only want to give a general idea of how they work in order to get on to the more important questions of what they are saying and doing.

Usually, a group of players are involved — say, four or five — of whom one is a referee. This person can make up an adventure or use a ready-made one. The other players choose from certain types of characters available, such as warrior or magician, and then make up individual characters by rolling dice to give scores for particular attributes. Usually, three ordinary dice are used so that a player gains scores out of 18 for attributes such as, for example, strength and wisdom. Dice are rolled again to give the amount of money the characters have and with this they buy weapons and other equipment and supplies to go adventuring — usually in a dungeon where they will have to fight various monsters in order to gain treasure. Goods and what they cost, which is usually given in gold and silver pieces, are set out in tables and all the details about each character are recorded on a card or piece of paper. The adventures usually take place in a vaguely medieval setting but one in which magic is very important. Combat with monsters is conducted by throwing dice.

Ian Livingstone, who played a major part in introducing fantasy role-playing games into Britain, has called them 'the most serious alternative yet to reality'. A description of one of them, Valley of the Four Winds, which was produced by Games Workshop in 1980, seems to bear this out and it also gives a good idea of the atmosphere of these games. The description is from a Games Workshop catalogue which appears to be from early 1981:

> The game is full of the very stuff of legends — wizards, dragons, evil mages, heroes, armies of undead skeletons, and loathsome swamp creatures. Players take the roles of Good and Evil with the King of Farrondil trying to hold back forces of evil whilst sending his champion knight on a quest to find the magical Swan Bones to help turn the tide of the battle.

Most of the games have this kind of setting, though there are science fiction ones as well and, as we'll see, the role-playing system can be extended to war games. However, those who play fantasy games and wargamers are usually in two distinct groups.

More details can be filled in from a Games Workshop leaflet which explains role-playing games to those who might be thinking of taking up the hobby. (They are also known as 'hobby games'.) It says that character selection and 'dicing-up', otherwise known as 'generating' characters (i.e. the process outlined above) are common to all such games; it says that the games appeal to people between the ages of 11 and 35; and that there are no winners or losers in these games. Certainly, if your character is killed you can roll up another one, though this hardly seems a cheerful task, and characters usually combine together against the adversaries set upon them by the referee. On the other hand, in spite of this kind of co-operation, the games are full of conflict.

Before the game, the referee designs an adventure, often called a 'dungeon'. This is drawn to scale on graph paper or on a honeycomb grid of hexagons, called a 'hex', which can be bought. Basically, the dungeon consists of a number of rooms connected by passages or tunnels. There can also be steps to different levels. The referee arranges for a good supply of monsters, usually guarding treasure, and builds in other devices such as secret doors and traps. Normally, also, there will be magical items or phenomena. All this can be invented and prepared according to guide-lines. On the other hand, there are ready-made dungeons available just as, with some games, there are 'ready-rolled' characters.

A feature of such games is that they have detailed rule-books, or series of them, full of tables and statistics. Another feature is the use of many-sided dice to give various scores for different purposes. These can range from four-sided dice, with sides numbered one to four, to 20-sided, numbered nought to 19 or nought to 9 twice. Two of the latter, one to give tens and the other units, can be used for percentages — or one of these could be thrown twice.

Dungeons and Dragons, produced by the US firm Tactical Studies Rules (TSR), was the first fantasy role-playing game and, I should think, is still the best-known and most widely played. The following account of it should help to draw some of the foregoing information together.

Each player chooses a character from one of seven 'character classes'. Four of these are human — cleric, fighter, magic-user and thief: and three are 'demi-human' — elf, dwarf and halfling. The characters' attributes or abilities, for which scores are rolled out of 18, are: strength, intelligence, wisdom, dexterity, constitution and charisma. Most of these can be modified in various ways but those with a high score in strength, for instance, are advised to consider being fighters while those with a high score in wisdom are advised to think of being clerics. Further, player characters, and monsters also, must belong to one of three 'alignments' which give more general characteristics. These are: lawful, chaotic and neutral.

Players begin at the first experience level and reach new levels by acquiring points which are awarded by the referee according to the rules and usually for killing monsters, gaining magic items or treasure and for practising skills. Basically, Dungeons and Dragons is about winning treasure and killing monsters so here we have, in another form, the masculine breadwinner and fighter roles.

Combat is long and complicated, and has many rules, with the 'non-player characters', which are usually monsters, being controlled by the referee. All characters have 'hit points' which stand for the amount of damage they can take before dying. At an encounter, throws of dice will decide which character strikes first and whether a hit is made. Then, the difference between the scores, at each subsequent throw and after possible adjustments for various reasons, is taken from the hit point total of the losing party and when this is reduced to nought the character is dead. (However, retreat is possible.) The whole process can take several rounds or throws and, at each stage, all sorts of adjustments may be made. Armour will reduce the amount of damage, for instance. I should add that, in fantasy role-playing games, monsters commonly carry weapons.

Throughout the game, the referee can roll a die or dice to decide the outcome of any other event. What happens will depend upon the score and often the referee will have to refer to the various tables in the rule book. Again, modifiers of different kinds may be applied. For instance, a character may be particularly resistant to a spell.

An extract from a sample dungeon expedition given in the Dungeons and Dragons basic rule book will help to provide some further idea of the atmosphere and method of play of fantasy role-playing games. First, however, I should point out that the generally masculine nature of these games is shown by the fact that the referee in Dungeons and Dragons is known as the Dungeon Master (DM). (Runequest, a similar game system, has a Game Master.)

> THE SITUATION: This party includes four 2nd level characters and a 1st level dwarf: Morgan Ironwolf, a female fighter (the *caller*); Silverleaf, an elf; Fredrik, a dwarf; Sister Rebecca, a cleric; and Black Dougal, a thief. After equipping themselves, these characters have journeyed to the

26: *Dungeons and Dragons (and other) products*

Haunted Keep ... . As caller, Morgan relays the party's actions to the DM after the characters decide what they want to do. ...

[The party comes upon a door behind which Black Dougal hears voices.]

Morgan: We're getting ready for combat. Fred and I will force the door.

Dougal: I'll guard the rear!

DM: OK. The party is set, with Black Dougal guarding the rear. *Rolling to see if the door is forced.* It opens. You see half a dozen goblins.

Fredrik: Let me at them!

DM: You can't be surprised, but they can be. *Rolling for surprise.* No. Roll for initiative please.

Morgan: Fred rolled a 2.

DM *rolling:* The goblins have the initiative. *Rolling reaction for the goblins.* They must have heard you, Fred. They charge, yelling, 'Kill the dwarf! Chop them to hamburger!' (*Combat is now resolved, morale checks taken etc. The goblins fight until all are dead. It is now time to check for wandering monsters, but the DM's roll indicates that none appear* [sic].)[1]

This passage gives a good idea of the role playing involved and also shows how close these games are to fiction. In the game's rule book, the authors state that a good Dungeons and Dragons campaign is 'similar to the creation of a fantasy novel, written by the DM and the players'. (I'll be dealing with the fictional background of the games later.)

In this context, the word 'monster' means any non-human creature or other non-player character (NPC) handled by the referee. Monsters are of central importance in fantasy role-playing games and over 14 pages in the Dungeons and Dragons basic rule book are taken up by descriptions of them together with statistics. The list, from Acolyte to Zombie, includes four sorts of bears, as well as a Bugbear, and dragons of six different colours. These last have 'breath weapons' of various types such as acid, chlorine gas, lightning and fire, each of which appears as one of three different shapes: a cone, a line or a cloud. Surprisingly, there's a Normal Human in the list but, for the most part, it's a weird and outlandish mixture. There's a Gelatinous Cube (of about three metres in dimension), Grey Ooze, Green Slime, three kinds of Living Statue, a Wererat and Weretiger, as well as a Werewolf, Medusa, Ochre Jelly, Orc, Pixie, Skeleton, three kinds of Giant Spider, a Thoul (which is 'a magical combination of a ghoul, a hobgoblin, and a troll') and a Wight. This last is described as 'an undead spirit living in the body of a dead human or demi-human'.

Many developments in the game have now taken place and all sorts of aids and accessories have been marketed (see illustration). Players reaching the third level of experience provided for in the basic game can move on to Expert Dungeons and Dragons or Advanced Dungeons and Dragons. The first of these provides more of the same kind of thing but the second brings further complications such as a greater variety of characters and many more rules. John Butterfield, David Honigmann and Philip Parker in their book, *What is Dungeons and Dragons?*, state that the three books of rules for Advanced Dungeons and Dragons contain over 250,000 words. One of these books is the illustrated *Monster Manual* in which over 300 creatures are listed and described and their statistics given. The *Fiend Folio* gives over 200 more creatures, and treasure tables as well. Of course, all this is best regarded as reference material for playing the game. Nobody has to know it all, though the Dungeon Master, at least, has to be familiar with the main outlines. In late 1984, the Companion Set, which takes Dungeons and Dragons to the 24th level, was published in Britain, having come out two or three months previously in the USA, and the Masters' Set, taking the game to the 36th level, was published here in mid 1985. The Immortals' Set, meant to be the last one, is — at the time of writing — yet to come. All these extend the scope of the game — or game system, it might be better to say. There are plenty of other accessories. Livingstone, in his book, *Dicing with Dragons,* which was published in 1982, lists 36 playing aids for Dungeons and Dragons and 51 for Advanced Dungeons and Dragons, most of them 'scenarios', that is, adventures.

As the above account shows, it would be difficult to imagine anything further from reality than fantasy games, and this is the main point about them.

Origins

Some account now of the history of the games will help to bring other points to light.

Dungeons and Dragons and all the other fantasy games so popular now have originated from two sources: one is fictional, from which the games have taken their content, or subject matter; and one is wargaming, from which the form or structure of the games has developed. The main literary influence is from Tolkien's books; *The Hobbit,* first published in 1937, and *The Lord of the Rings,* first published in three parts over the years 1954-6. These signalled a revival of fantasy and soon gave rise to a cult. The fictional and wargaming strands of development came together and became intertwined round about 1970 in the town of Lake Geneva, in Wisconsin in the USA, and although it's true that fantasy had been creeping into wargaming some years previously, in Britain also, we have to look to that time and place for the beginnings of Dungeons and Dragons, the first of the fantasy role-playing games.

It was then and there that Gary Gygax was trying out a set of fantasy rules with his local wargaming group. These were published in 1971 as a fantasy supplement in *Chainmail,* the group's rule book for medieval wargaming. The supplement included a section on 'man-to-man combat', a necessary development on the road from battlefields to dungeons. Using this material, Dave Arneson extended the idea of individual role playing and added the idea of the development of characters which was to become the system of levels and experience points already mentioned. He also added the dungeon setting. Then, working together, Gygax and Arneson developed the rules for Dungeons and Dragons and the game was published at the beginning of 1974 by TSR.

Although there were difficulties and inconsistencies in the rules, the idea caught on and several other fantasy role-playing games were brought out in the USA such as Tunnels and Trolls from Flying Buffalo in 1975, Chivalry and Sorcery from Fantasy Games Unlimited in 1977, Runequest from Chaosium in 1978 and Dragonquest from SPI (Simulations Publications Incorporated) in 1980. Science fiction role-playing games came along slightly later, making use of the same basic structure but with a space or futuristic setting. In this line, TSR produced Metamorphosis Alpha in 1976 and Game Designers' Workshop, another US firm, published Traveller, the most popular science fiction game, in the following year. In 1978, TSR produced Gamma World, described by Butterfield, Honigmann and Parker as follows: 'The game postulates a world in which a nuclear holocaust has devastated much of civilisation. ... Players play the roles of normal (pure-strain) humans, mutated humans or mutant animals'.[2]

All this happened in the USA, but Britain was soon to follow the lead, largely through the activities of Games Workshop, a firm started by Steve Jackson and Ian Livingstone in 1975 with the express purpose of importing Dungeons and Dragons. The firm opened a retail shop in 1977 and by the end of 1985 there were seven shops, and a wide distribution network for fantasy and science fiction games from the USA had been developed. Amongst other activities, Games Workshop began publishing *White Dwarf,* the fantasy and science fiction games magazine, in 1977; opened a factory for making metal miniatures in 1978; and published the first four of its own games in 1980. The monthly circulation of *White Dwarf* at the beginning of 1985 was 42,000 and at the end of that year Games Workshop brought out the first issue of a quarterly magazine, *The Good Games Guide.*

Out of 12 fantasy and science fiction games manufacturers listed by Livingstone in *Dicing With Dragons,* 11 are in the USA. The other is Puffin Books and their entry is for the *Fighting Fantasy Gamebooks* (to be discussed later). Initiative in this field has clearly remained with the USA, in spite of the developments in Britain. In fact, these developments show how the cultural influence of the United States spreads to other countries.

A word needs to be added here about miniature figures or models. At first, these weren't used in fantasy gaming — in fact, there weren't any — and characters and monsters just existed as statistics on paper. However, in view of the development of the games, structurally, from table-top wargaming with its armies of metal soldiers, it was to be expected that players would want to use figures. At first, they made do with substitutes but then, in about 1976, manufacturers of metal figures began to provide them for the fantasy games market. Soon, a small industry grew up around the designing and making of such figures. Normally, they aren't provided with the games but are sold separately and usually unpainted. In fact, painting them has now become a hobby in itself and, by the end of 1985, Citadel Miniatures were producing their own colours amongst which I noticed 'skull white' and 'chaos black'. A lead or tin-based alloy is generally used for making the figures but some plastic ones are also available. Most are either 15mm or 25mm high.

Citadel Miniatures is the division of Games Workshop which was set up to produce figures, and their output is very largely for fantasy gamers although they do make some ranges of historical military figures. They have licensed manufacturers to produce their figures in the USA and Canada and they themselves produce miniatures, under licence, for other game systems besides Dungeons and Dragons.

The Fantasy Tribes range in the 1982 Citadel Miniatures catalogue shows mainly the most common figures from mythology or folklore — trolls, goblins, dwarfs and orcs — though there are plenty of skeletons. Most figures are armed. Fantasy games players don't bother about consistency so you can get some very odd mixtures of figures from different mythologies, legends and cultures. Certainly, there's variety and in the Citadel catalogue Count Dracula rubs shoulders with the Anglo-Saxon hero, Beowulf, as well as with a Djinn from Arabia, Robin Hood and even the historical figure of Rasputin. In the way of fiends and monsters, you can include in your dungeon, for example, the Wraith Rider on Undead Horse, the Minotaur, an Amazon Berserker, a Tentacled Crawler and a Mummy, amongst others. Things are a whole lot nastier, however, in Citadel's range of Fantasy Specials designed to bring 'realism and flavour', so they say, into fantasy role-playing games. Here the female figures, in particular, give rise to concern. The Serving Wench and Seductive Wench (she goes with Large Tavern Bed, Unmade) point to stereotypes. In a rather different category, however, are the captive and naked females, such as the Naked Girl Bound Hand and Foot and the Naked Girls Bound to Post, Cross and Yoke (three figures). Worse still are the figures of women being punished or tortured, such as the Naked Girl in Restraining Device, the Naked Girl in Stocks, Naked Girl in Pillory and the Naked Girl Roasting on Spit over Brazier. There's also the woman as victim — Necromancer with Female Sacrifice on Altar — and, as if to show that females do get the whip hand sometimes, the Dungeon Torturess with Whip. I'm glad to say that such figures are not common and nor are such matters typical of fantasy role-playing games. I'm pleased to add, also, that a representative of Games Workshop told me, at the beginning of 1986, that such figures had been discontinued by his firm. In other words, it was no longer lending active support to fantasies of sexual sadism.

Some account now of other fantasy role-playing games will bring further points to light and also give an idea of the range of such games.

Tunnels and Trolls was devised by Ken St Andre who liked the idea of Dungeons and Dragons but found the mechanics of the game needlessly complicated. He therefore kept to the basic structure but simplified the game. However, people not familiar with fantasy role-playing games will find the Tunnels and Trolls rule book, of over 60 large pages, quite complicated enough. A feature of this game is that it caters largely for the solo player. This means there are fewer options and, since this is the case, the game is further along the road towards fiction proper. (A novel with alternative endings, say, would be the first step towards games from the direction of fiction.) A typical solo adventure is best looked upon as several interwoven stories divided into sections. For example, section 14C from Buffalo Castle (a Tunnels and Trolls 'adventure') reads:

> You have stumbled into the falling rocks trap. Dozens of rocks fall on you
> from the ceiling. Roll one die to see how many hits you take. Your armour
> may take hits for you in this case. After you climb out from under the rocks,

you may go back the way you came (go to 13C) or you may search for secret doors (go to 23D).

Runequest, by 1986 owned by Avalon Hill, is another massive game system basically the same as Dungeons and Dragons. In this one, however, the game takes place in the fictional world of Glorantha, and so the Game Master doesn't have to devise overall settings. According to Livingstone in *Dicing With Dragons,* Runequest appeared to be — judging from surveys and awards — the third most popular role-playing game in Britain, after Advanced Dungeons and Dragons and Traveller.

These fantasy games, and fantasy games in general, are all for older children and adults (Livingstone gives an average age of 13) but, following familiar business strategies, manufacturers not in the market at this age level have been quick to involve younger children.

The Sorcerer's Cave, in fact, is described on the box as a 'family game of fantasy' for two to four players of 10 years and upwards. Solo play is also possible. It was designed by Terence Donnelly, copyrighted in 1978 and is now produced by Gibsons. Here, large 'area cards' are laid down on the floor, one by one, and these together form a simple map of the sections of the cave that have been explored. Players choose parties of adventurers from a motley crew consisting of ogres, dwarfs, trolls and priests but also men and women and a hero and a 'woman hero'. These have various abilities and characteristics and are moved around the cave, happenings being brought about by information and instructions on smaller 'action cards' which are drawn when a party enters a cavern that hasn't already been explored. For the rest, it's treasure, monsters and magic, and the mixture very much as before. The two kinds of cards carry out the function of a referee, in a simplified way.

The Mystic Wood, described in the rules as 'a family game of exploration and adventure', was also designed by Terence Donnelly and is published by Gibsons. It was copyrighted in 1980. Here, the setting is more in romance literature than in fantasy. The section on the literary background at the end of the rules informs us that the game was inspired by the sixteenth century courtly romances *Orlando Furioso* by Ludovico Ariosto and *The Faerie Queene* by Edmund Spenser. In structure, the game is very similar to The Sorcerer's Cave and here again the use of cards is a main feature. The map of the wood itself is made up of a grid of 45 cards which, except for the two gates and the tower, are laid face down. Each player takes on the role of a knight who has to set out from the Earthly Gate to fulfil a 'quest'. You win by either fulfilling your quest and leaving the wood by the Enchanted Gate, or by defeating the king and occupying the castle. The female 'knight', Britomart, however, isn't allowed to win by defeating the king, which looks like discrimination. The players 'explore' the wood as cards are turned over revealing paths and 'denizens' such as a dragon, a troll, a wizard, the king and a Saracen. These have to be 'encountered', some encounters resulting in fights which are decided by throws of dice and by taking various powers and factors into account. Knights can joust with one another. Items in the game include a lance, a potion, a ring, the grail and a golden bough. (It's acknowledged that the game owes something to J G Frazer's

The Golden Bough, as well.) Thus, the game is simpler than Dungeons and Dragons and less vicious but it clearly draws upon the first fantasy game for its basic structure.

Swords and Wizardry, also produced by Gibsons, but undated, is a game for two players aged nine and upwards. In structure, it shows another interesting approach as it's played on a board of 100 squares — that is, on a regular grid. On this, an imaginary land of castles, forests and a lake are shown. The pieces used in the game differ in the way they can be moved and in their value. This recalls chess, while the method of capture is similar to that in l'Attaque (see p. 231). However, while the structure moves us towards wargaming, the atmosphere of Swords and Wizardry is one of fantasy. The game is set in what are called 'the Dark Ages' and the largely military force of each side includes a hero, a wizard, a king and a princess as well as monsters and peasants. The object of the game is to rescue the princess held by the opposing force. She has no attacking or defensive powers and cannot be rescued by monsters, which would be 'too frightening' or by peasants, which would be 'too demeaning'. Therefore, the traditional gender and class roles of fairy stories are upheld. It might be argued that these are appropriate to the setting of the game but how appropriate is the setting of the game for the children of today?

While other firms, such as Gibsons in the case of the last three examples, are ready to cash in on an established trend, the manufacturers of the major fantasy role-playing games try to hook children as consumers at an ever more early age.

So, we get Dungeon! from TSR, first copyrighted in 1975, and for two to eight players aged eight to adult. The board is like a dungeon floor plan with the usual tunnels and rooms, and play is focused on the usual activities such as fighting monsters and collecting treasure. You can be a hero, a superhero, an elf or a wizard and the object is to be the first to return to the start with a certain amount of treasure.

Other games drawing upon the same fantasy source have been manufactured for children down to about five years old. Fantasy Forest, for example, also from TSR, is stated to be 'a family game for 2-4 elves, ages 5 and up'.

It's as well to remember that science fiction role-playing games are part of the general picture outlined in this section. However, I'll not deal with them here as they have by no means the same sort of following amongst children as fantasy games. I suppose this is because, unlike fantasy games, they depend on a technical knowledge which most children don't have. Traveller, for instance, a game of extraordinary complexity, isn't really meant for children at all. On the other hand, children are familiar with fantasy in some form or other from their earliest years and the fantasy games draw upon this background. Because of this, I would suppose that nostalgia for childhood forms some part of the attraction these games have for older players.

The spread of fantasy role-playing games

We now focus on popularity and sales.

Early in 1983, on a Friday, I bought the basic Dungeons and Dragons set at a local shop. It was the third one they'd sold that week. The man who sold me it said the game was enormously popular and that local schools bought it for their pupils to promote 'imagination'. These straws showed which way the wind was blowing.

Livingstone, in his book *Dicing With Dragons,* says that a million copies of the game were sold in the first six years after it came out. At the beginning of 1981, *British Toys and Hobbies* stated that sales of the basic set alone in the USA were 'reported' to have been over a quarter of a million in 1980 and that Dungeons and Dragons was the most popular hobby game in the world. In 1982, the same magazine stated that annual sales of Dungeons and Dragons were more than 200,000, again in the USA. (They're very careless about facts and figures in the trade, so the apparent drop in sales isn't significant. You have to get a general impression from different sources.) In Britain, at the beginning of 1983, the managing director of TSR's subsidiary here was predicting an increase of 50 per cent in turnover for the year — to £800,000. As yet the interest in fantasy role playing games has shown no signs of abating and there's no sign of sales reaching a peak. Moreover, the interest in fantasy tapped by and, in turn, created by the games has found other channels, as I'll show in the following pages.

Other developments or spin-offs show the growth of interest in this field. TSR first published their 'monthly adventure role-playing aid', the magazine *Dragon,* in 1976. It deals mainly with Dungeons and Dragons, as might be expected, and Gygax was a frequent contributor especially over the first few years. To an outsider, the subjects of the articles in *Dragon* can only seem amazing and the detail in them bewildering. An article on vampires, for instance, describes 14 of them from different parts of the world. Another article is entitled 'A Look at Lycanthropy'. The word, as its origin implies, should refer to the kind of insanity in which those afflicted imagine themselves to be wolves (the were-wolves of legend) but here were-rats and were-bears are included, as well as other fantastic creatures. A link with wargaming is shown in a very different article by Gygax, 'The Nomenclature of Pole Arms' in which 24 kinds of these weapons are described. *Dragon* has been and, at the end of 1986, was still available in Britain, though not in large numbers. In about 1982, the British subsidiary of TSR brought out its own magazine, *Imagine,* in which articles from *Dragon* were reprinted alongside home-grown ones. However, the parent company in the USA were never really behind *Imagine* and publication ceased in 1985. *White Dwarf,* which I've already mentioned, changed from bi-monthly to monthly publication in 1982 and at the end of 1985, circulation stood at about 50,000. Again, as with the games themselves, so with the magazines, the overwhelming influence of the USA is very marked. In *Dicing With Dragons,* Livingstone lists 13 games magazines, eleven of which originated in the United States. One is British and the publisher of the other magazine isn't given. As might be expected, most of the publishers are games manufacturers. Of these magazines, one deals mainly with Tunnels and Trolls and one entirely with Traveller while another concentrates largely on Runequest.

Amongst the rather strange offshoots of role-playing games, especially the fantasy ones, are 'fanzines'. These are magazines put together by fans of the games and, for the most part, they come and go in an ever-changing scene. Livingstone lists 13 in *Dicing With Dragons* (1982) but 23 were reviewed in the February 1984 issue of *Imagine*. These included two on war games, three on science fiction gaming and one on a game called Car Wars. The other 17 were on fantasy games.

Many clubs exist for those who play the games and, following the lead given by my Dungeons and Dragons supplier, I traced one at a local boys' comprehensive school and arranged to visit it. This club met weekly, after school, for an hour and 50 minutes to play Dungeons and Dragons and, on the day I was there, there were 22 boys of all ages in attendance. One told me he had started playing at the age of nine. The teacher who ran the club acted as Dungeon Master in one of several games which were being carried on at the same time. Some of the boys had brought their own rule books, dice and miniatures and seemed very familiar with the game. I was struck by the extent to which the younger children, especially, were caught up in the games, in some cases excitedly acting out the parts of their characters through exclamations, gestures and so on.

Following the pattern that usually develops with popular toys and games, there's a British Dungeons and Dragon Players' Association with broadsheet, badge, special offers and other benefits.

Other activities and events keep up the interest in role-playing games and fantasy games in particular. Games Workshop organized their first Games Day in 1975 and this has been an annual event ever since. I went to the 1981 Games Day (or one day of it — it was a two-day event, actually) which took place in London on a Saturday and Sunday in late September. About 5,000 people attended on each day, most of them young men between the ages of about 18 and 25. As I arrived, costumed warriors were having a battle outside, watched by a crowd, while inside, amongst the many trade stands, there were various demonstration games going on, as well as games in which it was possible to take part including prize competition games. There was also a figure- painting competition. Although many kinds of games were represented, including chess and computer games for instance, the stress was very much on role-playing games, with Dungeons and Dragons and Traveller very much in the forefront. Such games, however, are even more the concern at the Dragonmeet event started by Games Workshop in about 1977 and organized by them annually ever since. Until 1985, it was held in London but in 1986 it was due to take place in four other towns as well, on different dates.

One of the weirdest offshoots of fantasy role-playing games was Treasure Trap, a system of live role play which was started in mid-1982 at Peckforton Castle in Cheshire and went on for about two years. Two men leased the rather derelict castle and people joining their club would go there to have adventures. The organizers reported an overwhelming response from all over the country. Tricks and traps were contrived, treasure provided, and monsters laid on. Parties, appropriately costumed and armed, and accompanied by a referee, ventured into the castle, each person having a number of 'life points'. Monsters, with dyes of various colours on their teeth, claws or weapons, would try to daub the adventurers. Each colour of dye represented a certain amount of damage and at the end of an encounter the referee would inspect each player to see how many life points were lost. There were other features besides these basic ones but the game had to come to a stop when the lease of the castle ran out and the firm collapsed.

A very different kind of development has been the production of microprocessor games based, very loosely in most cases, on fantasy role-playing games. At first, it mightn't seem that these games could be adapted to such technological means and this is true to a considerable extent. It's clear that the usual interaction between the players can scarcely be reproduced, though the 'play-by-mail' games set up by various companies and run on a central computer are a move in this direction. Of necessity, however, almost all microprocessor games are for solo play. Also, while a microprocessor, carrying out the function of a referee, can obviously deal with all the complications quickly and efficiently (but without the flexibility of a human referee) it might be argued that there's not much left of a game such as Dungeons and Dragons after that. On the other hand, it can be said that the basic features of fantasy role-playing games are the same as those of many typical microprocessor games, especially the simpler, hand-held ones. Going on a quest to obtain treasure, avoiding traps, and killing monsters to gain points has the same features — seeking, avoiding, destroying and scoring points — as several of the microprocessor games already described.

Mattel's Advanced Dungeons and Dragons video game, called Cloudy Mountain, shows some of these features. In it, the player goes on a quest and has to gather the proper tools and weapons in order to overcome the dragon and gain the treasure. Obviously, there can't be much in the way of role-playing here. It's just the usual kind of video game. In fact, with this as with most microprocessor versions of fantasy games, it seems to be mainly a case of cashing in on an established interest or a name, such as Dungeons and Dragons.

However, there has been another development, and one that takes us very close to fiction again. Computer programmes called 'text adventures' have been produced and, with these, what you see on the screen is very like a section from a solo adventure (such as I've quoted on pp. 214-15) or from any of the 'gamebooks' (such as the ones in the next section). Structurally, the text adventures work in the same way, only you press keys to make choices instead of turning pages.

The fictional background and other links

We now turn to consider the fictional background to fantasy role-playing games and also the way in which fiction and these games have become more and more interrelated. In fact, fiction and games here are so closely connected that, at times, it becomes difficult to say which is which. We'll also be glancing at links between the games and other aspects of children's popular culture. All this should give further insight into what the games are saying.

Tolkien's work has, without a doubt, been the major influence on the content of the games dealt with in this chapter. Other writers whose names tend to appear in lists of fictional source material for fantasy games are Alan Garner, Robert E

Howard, Ursula le Guin and Michael Moorcock. The name of John Norman also turns up now and again. He's a special case to be dealt with shortly. These writers, along with several others, are commented on in the book *Fantasy Wargaming* which was compiled and edited by Bruce Galloway (and which, incidentally, has an interesting title as it points to the connections between two main types of games playing). Galloway mentions, in particular, *The Weirdstone of Brisingamen* and *The Moon of Gomrath* by Garner and le Guin's *Earthsea* trilogy, all fantasy novels written specifically for children.[3]

The books can be used in various ways. Although Gygax has said that *The Lord of the Rings* is 'quite unsatisfactory as a setting for a fantasy adventure game' (because it's so detailed and complete), the game, War of the Ring from TSR is, apparently, an attempt to recreate the major features of the book and Galloway argues that it's precisely because most dungeon adventures take place in a vacuum, without any coherent setting, that they become boringly repetitive. Nevertheless, the games generally draw upon fiction in a haphazard sort of way, using certain aspects — ideas perhaps, or characters — at random. An article in *White Dwarf*, for instance, deals with the incorporation of the rings of power from *The Lord of the Rings* into Dungeons and Dragons. The general mish-mash is well illustrated by Tunnels and Trolls in which the wizards are modelled on Tolkien's Gandalf or on Merlin from Arthurian legend while the warriors are based on Howard's Conan, the popular barbarian whose violence has recently been transferred to film. The rogues in Tunnels and Trolls are drawn from yet another author.

I'll now deal with some of the fiction in more detail to show the characteristics of the authors and what, in their work, has inspired the gamers. Of the later writers, Moorcock undoubtedly seems to be the most important, as stated in *Fantasy Wargaming*:

> If one contemporary writer of fantasy fiction can be said to have influenced fantasy wargaming or 'dungeons and dragons' [sic] more than any other ... the 'Oscar' must assuredly go to Michael Moorcock.[4]

The three Moorcock novels I'll refer to were all published in the early 1970s, that is, in the few years just before Dungeons and Dragons came out. It might be said that the setting of *The Sleeping Sorceress* is vaguely medieval but that's probably too generous. Really, the story isn't set in any particular time or place and, as there's magic at will, that means there are really no rules and not many problems for the writer. No wonder that, by 1981, Moorcock had written over 50 fantasy and science fiction novels. In this one, we meet Lord Elric and 'the huge runesword Stormbringer, the source of his strength and his misery'. Magical and doomladen weapons are typical. We learn that war is imminent between Chaos and Law (compare the alignments in Dungeons and Dragons) but, really, wholesale carnage goes on throughout the book along with plenty of gruesome details. The general pattern is that contestants call up, by spells, talismans and the like, ever more powerful and often unintentionally comical creatures which are then overcome by still more powerful creatures which are vanquished, in turn, by yet more powerful ones, and so on, very much in the manner of the superheroes of the comic books. It's also typical that some nasty being wants to dominate the earth 'seeking to destroy the equilibrium of the Young Kingdoms'. The social background is aristo-cratic and hierarchical though, of course, there's no reason why this should be the case in fantasy writing. In Moorcock's *The Bull and the Spear* there are more features which are typical of both fantasy fiction and fantasy games. Here, Prince Corum, a god-like figure, goes to help the Tuha-na-Cremm-Croich (strange names are also typical) who are being attacked by seven 'misshapen giants' with 'strange powers'. First, however, he has to go on a quest, or two quests, to get a bull and a spear, in order to defeat them. It's all about fighting, very graphically described, with the usual questions of 'balance' and 'order' in the background. In *The Oak and the Ram,* which is 'The Chronicle of Prince Corum and the Silver Hand volume the second' there is, if anything, an even greater emphasis on aristocratic hierarchy and kings, together with more quests and more treasures conferring special powers. Not surprisingly, the language has an archaic air about it partly from the use, not always accurate, of obsolete or obscure words. Apart from the general influence of Moor-cock's work upon games, there are also particular examples. A board game called Elric, produced by Chaosium, is set in the 'Young Kingdoms' of *The Sleeping Sorceress,* as is a role-playing game called Stormbringer from the same firm.

This escapist mixture of mysticism and butchery, however, appears harmless enough when compared with the work of Norman. It does appear as if the nasty Citadel miniatures mentioned earlier, featuring naked women captive or being tortured, were made for fantasy games based on Norman's novels. These in general seem to represent a warped backlash against the advances towards equality made by women in recent times. *Fighting Slave of Gor,* which is volume 14 of the 'Chronicles of Counter-Earth', was first published in the USA in 1980 and appears to be fairly typical. It's noteworthy that Norman chooses to set his fantasies on another planet. Early on in the book, we're told that, 'In every woman there is a slave, in every man a slaver' and we're given to understand that this represents 'a fully natural biological relationship'. According to Norman, the men of earth are fit to be the slaves of women because they're not real men. However, as could be foreseen in the novel, Jason, the man taken to Gor from earth and made a slave to Lady Florence, eventually makes her *his* slave — which was to be demonstrated. And slavery here is no figurative expression and neither is it the kind known from history. Here, it has a particular sexual bent. So, amidst the whipping and branding and the chains and collars, there are various types of bondage and a lot of leather, usually black. This goes on for over 370 pages and, where it isn't boring and repetitive, it's just sick. Women undergo continual and prolonged humiliation and degradation and are frequently raped. One passage must suffice to illustrate the attitudes promoted in this book. (The context isn't important — in fact, it could be almost anywhere.) 'How fit she seemed, in her place in the order of nature, naked, kneeling before a man. At this point it is common to rape the female.'[5] Such fantasies need treatment, not publication, and it's unfortunate, to say the least, that they have, apparently, found a corner in role-playing games.

So far, in this section, I've been dealing with the influence of fiction on fantasy role-playing games. In turn, the games seem to have influenced the production of a vast array of fantasy novels, often very thick ones, often in series by individual authors and having a named fantasy setting or centring on a particular hero, or both. However, there's been a more technical move into fiction from the games side and it's this that we should concentrate on here, more especially because it's been directed specifically at children.

The Warlock of Firetop Mountain by Jackson and Livingstone was published by Penguin under their Puffin imprint, in August 1982. It looks very much like any other Puffin book but, in fact, it's part story and part game and you need two dice, a pencil and a rubber to play it. (Such books are now generally known as game-books.) There are rules, basically along the lines of those for Dungeons and Dragons, but very much simplified. The referee is, in effect, replaced by the book in which the reader is addressed as 'you'. The text of the book is divided into 400 numbered sections each of anything from a couple of lines to a page in length. At the end of most of these, and if you're still alive, you're told which section to go to next or given a choice or, where you go can depend on a throw of the dice. This is the basic structure and, as can be seen, it doesn't differ in any essential from that of the solo role-playing games described earlier in this chapter. In *The Warlock of Firetop Mountain,* as in the games, there are many encounters with monsters, though here they are resolved in a simpler manner. If your quest is successful and if you don't get killed or fail in any other way — for instance, by not having obtained necessary items — you arrive at the last section of the book. Here, you take possession of the warlock's treasure and also his spell-book which gives you 'unlimited power'. For the first few months the book was on sale, there were leaflets inside each copy advertising a competition — to draw and decorate a map of the labyrinth beneath Firetop Mountain using the information given in the book. The first prize was a model of a dragon about 60 cm long from Citadel Miniatures.

The Warlock of Firetop Mountain soon caught on and about 300,000 copies were sold in 1983. By the end of that year, four more titles had been added to what had become the *Fighting Fantasy Gamebooks* and, altogether, nearly a million copies of this series had been sold. Also, at around that time, rights had been sold for the publication of the first book in France, Holland, the United States and West Germany. In Britain, a magazine, *Warlock,* was started for followers of the series. And so it went on. By the end of 1985, 18 *Fighting Fantasy Gamebooks* had been published, all of them, incredibly, either by Livingstone or Jackson or by both. Not all the books had the familiar dungeon settings. There were science fiction, 'horror film' and other scenarios, as well. Sales were expected to reach four million by Christmas of that year, so the editor of the series told me a few days before. However, this was only English language sales in Britain and the Commonwealth. By that time, also, several books in the series had been translated into 13 languages, and sales were particularly good in France, West Germany and Japan.

All the books in the *Fighting Fantasy* series require the same simple equipment — dice, pencil and rubber — and all have the same basic structure. Naturally, given this structure, they are all meant for solo play. There's the same limitation, in fact, as with the fantasy microprocessor games touched on earlier. In the absence of a referee, choice is restricted and sometimes none of the options on offer is attractive (to me, at least) and other possibilities aren't mentioned. Also, for purposes of combat, several monsters, for example, have to be treated as one or you have to fight each one in turn and it's not very little likely that four zombies, even, would fight the adventurer one at a time instead of all at once. However, it's a relative problem. A referee can't deal, simultaneously, with several battles.

At the end of 1985, there were all kinds of series of gamebooks from several different publishers and there were all sorts of structural variations. In one of these, for example, you have a table of random numbers and make a choice (or take a chance) of where to go next by closing your eyes and placing a pencil on it. In the *Zork* series, which Penguin got from the USA and published here in early 1984, the reader simply makes a choice from the ones available at the end of a section and, according to the choice, is told where to go next. There are no dice and therefore there's no combat as it's normally understood in fantasy role-playing games. This series is meant for children of about eight to 10, say, whereas the *Fighting Fantasy Gamebooks* will probably appeal to children up to about 14 years old. At the opposite extreme from these examples of gamebooks with a very simple structure, fantasy role-playing games, of something like the complexity of Dungeons and Dragons and catering for several players, are now being produced in average paperback format and are sold in bookshops and in book departments of larger stores like any other books. An example is the *Fighting Fantasy* role-playing 'gamebook' by Jackson, which is basically a rule book for a referee but which also contains two short adventures. The *Dragon Warriors* series published by Transworld under their Corgi imprint is also of this type. For books like these, dice and other accessories usually have to be bought elsewhere. Apart from the smaller size, these are not really any different from the rule books found in the boxed games along with various accessories and, in this connection, it seems a natural development that the Tunnels and Trolls rule book, as well as several of the solo games, have now been published in the normal Corgi format.

As we return to gamebooks (that is, fiction involving choice on the part of the reader) as opposed to rule books (that is, compilations of tables and instructions for playing the games) it's interesting to note that the basic structure, of numbered sections with alternatives, has been applied to different kinds of content, and various attempts have been made to move away from the usual fantasy and science fiction subjects. The main reason for this, rather than any particular attraction of the gamebook structure itself, seems to have been that the usual subjects didn't appeal to girls. Not very surprisingly, given their social conditioning, girls show little interest in venturing underground to kill monsters and win treasure (or in other variations on the roles of fighter and breadwinner).

In an attempt to reach girls, aged about 11 to 14 in this case, Penguin brought out six books in a series called *Starlight Adventures* in 1985. The subjects were to do with careers — ice-skating and radio journalism, for example — and one book centred on ponies. However, the editor of Puffin gamebooks told me that the idea was to stress facts rather than glamour in the treatment of these typical 'girls'' subjects. In these books, dice could be used to decide moves or the reader could simply make a choice without using dice. In spite of all this, by the end of the year sales had not been good and it was doubtful whether the series would continue.

We'll be returning to this point but take a short step back in time now as Penguin weren't the first in the field with gamebooks, not even in Britain. TSR began publishing the *Endless Quest* series of gamebooks in the United States, apparently in 1982. At any rate, imports of these were on sale in Britain before *The Warlock of Firetop Mountain* came out in August of that year. Naturally it was to be expected that US firms would continue to make the running in this particular field. Also, as I've noted before, it's part of normal business practice to hook children, at earlier and earlier ages, into a profit-making concern. The *Endless Quest* series was intended for children of eight and over. No dice were needed. At the end of a section you just decided, for instance, whether to stand or run and were directed accordingly. Twelve books in this series were on sale in Britain before 1984 with titles such as *Dungeon of Dread* and *Revenge of the Rainbow Dragons*. At the beginning of 1984, TSR released two further series in Britain: *Fantasy Forest,* designed for children aged seven to 11, and the *Heartquest* series, aimed at girls from 11 to 16 years old 'who like romance with their adventure' as the press hand-out put it. Here, then, was another attempt to reach girls, if from a different angle, but this didn't succeed either and the series was discontinued in 1985. The *Endless Quest* still goes on, however, and numbers 13 to 29 in the series were in print at the end of 1985. Some have science fiction themes, some feature Conan and some Tarzan but most draw upon the Dungeons and Dragons type of fantasy. At the same time, TSR had five other series of gamebooks, with different variations on the basic structure, on sale in Britain.

It seems that this structure is now applied to practically any sort of children's fiction. In December 1985, I noticed that there were gamebooks based on Enid Blyton's *Famous Five* stories. Games have never before had such an influence on popular culture.

Other developments have followed on from the commercial success of fantasy role-playing games and these show the usual pattern of business strategies.

Perhaps the most obvious spin-offs, after fiction, were toys. In 1984, TSR introduced their range of Advanced Dungeons and Dragons Adventure figures derived from the *Monster Manual* and *Fiend Folio*. There were 24 main figures, in coloured plastic, which varied in size up to about 10 cm and the intention, according to TSR, was to 'introduce ... adventure gaming to a new young audience', in this case the four to 10-year-olds. At the same time, Matchbox were producing Advanced Dungeons and Dragons figures under licence. Their range consisted of coloured, plastic, articulated figures in two sizes along with smaller 'collectables'. There were also three steeds for the figures to ride on and a play setting, the Fortress of Fangs. The figures were carded and labelled 'good' or 'evil', the evil ones tending to be dressed in black. These products were not for use with the game but were simply meant as toys. In fact, it's very noticeable how similar the range is, in its main features — figures, steeds, playset and the 'good' and 'evil' framework — to other toy ranges already dealt with such as Masters of the Universe. Also in 1984, Acamas Toys jumped on the bandwagon with their Swords and Sorcerers range of toys and playthings. There were figures, a fantasy vehicle, a dragon steed and a playset, as usual, but also playclothes together with masks, weapons and shields, and an inflatable dragon to ride on.

The American Publishing Corporation of the USA have produced jigsaws, for sale in Britain, from the cover pictures of *Endless Quest* books and also from the illustrations on the boxes of the Dungeons and Dragons basic set and expert set. In Britain, Waddingtons and Games Workshop have also produced Dungeons and Dragons jigsaws and presumably all three firms were acting under some arrangement with TSR. Such developments are to be expected but this one also shows the importance of artwork in the world of fantasy role-playing games.

Fantasy of this new kind has also found its place in films and television. *The Dark Crystal,* released in Britain in 1983, was perhaps the first major film to show this and it included all the main elements as seen in the fantasy games, and also the fantasy toys, dealt with in this book. The film is set on another planet, which is obviously more convenient, but it features the usual struggle between the forces of good and evil, represented in this case by the wise and gentle Mystics, on the one hand, and the vicious and cruel Skeksis, on the other. The original rulers of the planet had been split into these two types of beings following a disaster in which the mysterious and powerful crystal, around which their society revolved, was broken. All these fantastic creatures are vaguely reptilain in appearance but they look their good and evil parts, especially the Skeksis. Jen, a Gelfling (rather like an elf) has to go on a quest to find the missing fragment which will restore the crystal to wholeness and the planet to harmony. There are other weird and fantastic creatures and some light relief is provided by the Podlings, simple peasants who live in the forest and counterparts of the Ewoks in *The Return of the Jedi.* Some further connections can be underlined. Jim Henson, co-producer and co-director of *The Dark Crystal,* is the inventor of the Muppets and Gary Kurtz, the other producer, also produced *Star Wars* and *The Empire Strikes Back.* The credits included 'special thanks' to Garner whose work, as I mentioned earlier, is used as source material by fantasy role-playing gamers.

As part of the ceaseless round that makes up the world of children's popular — and commercial — culture, *The Dark Crystal,* in its turn, gave rise to toys. Aviva Hasbro had, in its 1983 catalogue, a range of the main figures from the film.

The third television cartoon series based on Dungeons and Dragons was being shown in the USA at the beginning of 1986. The first series was shown over here by the BBC in 1984. In turn, these feed into one of TSR's gamebook series, the *Dungeons and Dragons Cartoon Show Books.* And so it goes on.

I'll end this section of links and connections with a junior counterpart of Treasure Trap. In the summer of 1985, Dolphin Adventure Holidays were running, amongst other activities for children, a fantasy holiday called The Forest of Doom. This was based on the Puffin *Fighting Fantasy* book of the same name and was run in conjunction with Puffin Books. It took place, either on a day or residential basis, at 13 centres in England, Scotland and Wales.

Language

As usual with toys and games, the language which surrounds them can give some good clues about attitudes. This is particularly the case with role-playing games which involve a lot of words both printed, in the rule books, scenarios and so forth; and spoken, amongst the players in the course of a game.

Clearly, there's a great deal of aggression in these games but, as elsewhere with toys and games involving violence, there's an evasion, in this case through a kind of verbal side-stepping, of the real results of violence. For instance, Ken St Andre uses the expression 'toasted dwarf' of a dwarf burnt by a dragon's breath and refers to 'hobbit purée' as the result when a hobbit gets clubbed to death by a giant. Examples such as these, of words which mean either a wounding or a killing, sometimes with the manner of death implied, are common in descriptions of adventures. The following examples, from *What is Dungeons and Dragons?* illustrate the point well. In the adventure given in the book, one of the player characters, Slammer, describes an incident: 'Gripper trod on a cave locust, hidden in the rubbish. It spat on him, but I cooled in and creamed it with one stroke.'[6] (I've heard the expression 'creamed' used by a wargamer also.) Later in the adventure Slammer comments, after being wounded in the arm by a Lizardman, 'he wouldn't have mincemeated a fly, normally, but he ketchuped my arm'. Later still, we read, 'The sword twisted in his hands and diced the monster's stomach./ "Did you see that?" shouted Slammer. "I hamburgered it!"'[7] We last came across a hamburger, used in a similar context, in the Dungeons and Dragons basic rule book (see p. 211). In this connection, a point to note is that if players nearly always encounter non-player characters that are either non-human and repulsive or human and unspeakably evil (as they tend to do) then this provides a licence for violence. Moreover, such opponents are nearly always ready to attack without question.

Looked at another way, this kind of language can be seen as a means whereby the players can avoid seeming to take such games too seriously. This comes out also in the names of some of the spells in Tunnels and Trolls: for example — Knock Knock, which is for opening locked doors; Poor Baby, for the healing of wounds or injuries; Freeze Pleeze, which throws a sheet of ice at enemies; and Upsidaisy, which allows the player to levitate and move objects. There's a tongue-in-cheek quality here as if the intention was to let the players be seen as laughing at themselves to forestall other people from laughing at them. They're not really taking this childish pastime seriously, seems to be the message. However, I should add that there have been objections from some fantasy gamers to the frivolous names of these spells.

It's difficult, and perhaps too soon, to draw any overall conclusions about fantasy role-playing games. It does seem to me that escapism is the main element and certainly it would be hard to find anything more removed from the problems which beset the world today than the average dungeon adventure. Then, the scope provided in these games for the amassing of fantasy wealth must be of some significance in a society which attaches great importance to the acquistion of real wealth but where most of the people haven't any, to speak of. As we've seen, many other games have this as the main objective. To my mind, aggression is a central factor in fantasy gaming in spite of the disclaimers made from time to time by supporters. They say that the main thing is the development of the characters created by the players. A comment by Livingstone seems to show a more accurate reflection of what goes on

226

in the games. He sees them as an alternative to war games: 'Playing killing human beings is one thing but when it is monsters or dragons or humanoids in outer space, it doesn't matter so much'.[8] This is a valid view but exactly how much, and also whether, such killing matters can be disputed.

To discover what attracts people to these games, it might be better to look to the only new factor they have introduced, that of role playing itself. This provides a greater degree of participation than can be found in other comparable games. The players, perhaps relatively powerless in their daily lives, can exert some kind of control over events, albeit in fantasy. This view really brings us back to escapism again and it seems a good point at which to stop.

References

1   Gary Gygax and Dave Arneson, *Dungeons and Dragons* (Basic Rule Book) 2nd ed. Lake Geneva, USA, TSR Hobbies 1981, p.B59.

2   John Butterfield, David Honigmann and Philip Parker, *What is Dungeons and Dragons?* Harmondsworth, Penguin 1982, p.153.

3   There's an account of related fantasy novels for children in vol.2 of my book, *Catching Them Young*, pp. 145-61.

4   Bruce Galloway (compiler and ed.) *Fantasy Wargaming*, Cambridge, Patrick Stephens 1981, p.74.

5   John Norman, *Fighting Slave of Gor*, London, W H Allen (Star Books) 1981, p.271.

6   John Butterfield and others, *op. cit.* p.86.

7   *ibid.* p.98.

8   Quoted in: Dennis Barker, 'The Profits of Fantasy', *The Guardian*, London, 25 September 1981, p.6.

CHAPTER 11

PLAYING WAR

I've already mentioned that games are mostly played by males. War games are almost exclusively played by males and, more than any of the other categories of games dealt with in this book, they are played by adult males. This is especially true of table wargaming which is the most complicated branch of war games.

Here, I'll deal firstly with board war games (but including two role-playing games) before moving on to table wargaming and then microprocessor games.

Board and role-playing war games and an alternative

Games with a long history, such as draughts, chess and Go, are basically neutral, that is, we're not asked to take sides which are ideologically opposed or which can be identified with particular countries. Nevertheless, it's easy to imagine that people playing these neutral and fairly abstract war games might pretend that the opposing sides represented real enemies in conflict, and in modern times, as I'll show, players have been helped along in this respect. Games originating later in history tend to relate more to the real, political world and therefore are in a different category. The game of Transvaal, for instance, which came out in about 1900, puts players on opposing sides in the Boer War. Even so, there need be no great involvement, in partisan fashion, as the game is essentially like Fox and Geese. Closer to our own times, players are more and more called upon to take sides in a specific way until, with a game like Merc (to be described later in the chapter), they are politically aligned, on the far right, and can play out their warped fantasies.

Returning to traditional games — a few more details about chess and Go will provide some interesting pointers in a military context. Shaturanga, dating from about the fifth century in India, seems to be the ancestor of the chess family of games. In it, the pieces represented the four corps of ancient Indian warfare: elephants, cavalry, boatmen and infantry. Naturally, over the centuries, and as the game moved from culture to culture, it took on different forms and the European descendant, certainly, became less specific in a military sense. More precise elements can always be brought back into the game, however. Amongst many stone chess sets on offer from Gibsons in 1983 was the Civil War set, with Roundheads and Cavaliers in opposition, and the Rorke's Drift set which, according to the catalogue, symbolized 'one of the most heroic stands in British history'. (This refers to an occasion in South Africa in 1879 when a small band of British soldiers held a much larger group of Zulus at bay for about 12 hours. Doubtlessly, the British had vastly superior weapons, though it doesn't say that in the catalogue. It does say that a full description of each individual piece is provided.) By such means, chess can be placed in particular military contexts.

Go is the Japanese name for a game of Chinese origin called Wei-Ch'i. The first reference to it in Chinese dates from about 625 BC. In Japan, it became popular in the eleventh century and in the sixteenth century a state academy of Go was founded which awarded degrees.

The game is played on a regular grid of squares formed by 19 lines criss-crossed with 19 others. This is empty to begin with. One player has 181 black, disc-shaped 'stones', as they are called, and the other has 180 white ones. These are placed, one at a time and in turn, onto any of the 361 points, that is, the intersections or junctions of the playing area. The object of the game is to surround or, at the edges of the board, shut off the most territory, or points. Stones can be captured but, as in chess, capturing isn't the main object of the game. However, whereas in chess, pieces and pawns are captured when an opponent displaces them by moving to the square they are on and in draughts, pieces are captured when an opponent jumps over them, in Go, stones are captured and removed when completely surrounded or shut off by those of the opposing colour. These are the main features of what can obviously be a complex and absorbing game. It's also a game of military significance in spite of seeming rather abstract at first sight. This appears to have been recognized at an early date in Japan where it was popular with the Samurai caste in the thirteenth century and where, until 1600, there was a compulsory course in Go at the military academy. These are early instances of connections between games and the military. There'll be more to come. It seems strange that Bell, in *Board and Table Games from Many Civilizations,* while (correctly) putting draughts and chess into the chapter on war games, should nevertheless classify Go along with 'games of position', in the subdivision 'territorial possession'. Apart from anything else, the method of capture in Go is more realistic, in a military sense, than that in the other two games. Also, Bell uses military terms to describe the game, as does the British Go Association in its folder explaining how to play.

We now turn to games of more recent times while linking up with the historical section in chapter seven and overlapping with it.

From the first world war onwards, board war games became popular. A small group of these, produced by Gibsons, will serve here to illustrate games of the period between the two world wars.

The first one was, as a matter of fact, invented in the 1880s or soon after in continental Europe but it only reached the British market, introduced from France by H T Gibson, in about 1925. This was l'Attaque. Like other games of the period such as Transvaal, it has obvious similarities with traditional games, in this case chess. L'Attaque, however, is simpler than chess and more explicitly a war game. It's played on a grid of 100 equal squares, ten by ten, which is superimposed upon a simple terrain. A river with five bridges runs across the centre of the board and on either side of this the two players deploy their armies which consist of pieces representing various army ranks together with two spies, one on each side. Each player also has four mines and a flag. These pieces, made up of small cards, printed on one side and slotted (in the most recently available version) into plastic bases, are placed on the board with their backs to the enemy so that their identity is concealed. When a player moves a piece back to back with an opposing piece and calls, 'attack', the ranks (or point values) are revealed and the one of lower rank (or value) is removed. The winning piece is replaced with its back to the opponent. Memory is involved, therefore, and tactics at a simple level. The object of the game is to capture the enemy flag, though stalemate situations are possible.

The idea for Dover Patrol, invented by the Gibson brothers around 1928, was suggested by l'Attaque and the basic structure is the same. As with l'Attaque, there's no reference to any events in military history and sides are not identified. The action of Dover Patrol takes place at sea.

Working along the same lines again, the Gibson brothers went on to produce Aviation which dealt with air warfare; and then in about 1935, combined the three games, and therefore land, sea and air warfare, in Tri-Tactics.

Several points need to be borne in mind about this group of games. Firstly, they are relatively simple. For l'Attaque and Dover Patrol, the age range is given as nine years and upwards, while for Tri-Tactics the lower limit is 11 years. Secondly, they don't relate to any actual events or countries — at least, the versions I've examined don't. In this respect, they are not a lot less abstract than chess, for example. Thirdly, and most significantly, after quite a long period on the market, for commercial games, they were clearly on the way out by the beginning of 1986. Aviation had already been replaced, in 1980, by Battle of Britain, a structurally similar game but one based on a historical event. It only remains to say that, compared with what's to follow, these games almost have an innocence about them.

Certainly, there's nothing innocent about Diplomacy, described on the box as 'the classic game of political intrigue and military power in imperial Europe'. The inventor, Allan B Calhamer, says that it 'has pioneered, among games of [its] type, the introduction of ... permitted deception [and] ... conflict on a continental scale'. The game is of US origin and was first produced in 1954, since when it has been associated with several firms in both the USA and Britain. Latterly, Diplomacy has been marketed in Britain by Gibsons for players of 12 years upwards, though Calhamer calls it an 'adult' game. Its popularity may be judged from the fact that, up to 1975, magazines devoted to the game had been published in Belgium, West Germany and Italy as well as in English-speaking countries. Fans play the game by post and national championships are organized.

The board shows a map of Europe in 1901. There are seven 'great powers', each of a different colour and each divided, rather arbitrarily, into regions. The surrounding seas are also divided into areas. Each 'great power' has pieces of its own colour representing armies or fleets. These used to be short and long blocks, respectively, but are now in the shape of bullets and warships. Dotted across the board are 'supply centres' and, in the full length version of the game, the winner is the first player to occupy the majority of these. Alternatively, a certain number of moves can be decided on beforehand, in which case the winner is the one who has most pieces (armies or fleets) on the board at the end. There are other variations, according to the number of players — it's best with seven, though fewer can play — but, in all cases, the overall idea is military conquest. The game consists of fighting a series of spring and autumn campaigns each of which is in three phases: diplomacy, in which players negotiate; planning deployment, in which players secretly write down orders for the movement of their pieces; and actual movement, when these orders are read out. Complicated rules govern movement and the resolution of conflict, though the latter is basically the same as in l'Attaque. Play depends upon strategy and deceit, rather than luck, and the writing of orders takes the place of the throwing of dice.

Basically, this game is about gaining territory, and therefore power, at the expense of others: to use words Calhamer often uses in his description of Diplomacy — about 'grab' and 'stab'. Such bland and open cynicism in a game was something rather new in 1954. Of course, there's nothing new about cynicism in politics. The new element is to accept this as normal, standard practice and to present it as such in a game. However, worse is to come.

Another of the many wearisome games about domination — on a global scale this time — is Risk. 'The world conquest game', it says on the box. Risk is based on a French game, La Conquête du Monde (World Conquest) invented by Albert Lamorisse, and was first produced by Parker Brothers in 1957 as a result of collaboration with the French Miro company. In recent years, it's been marketed (under the brand name Parker, however) by Palitoy.

The board shows an irregular grid superimposed on a map of the world: the six continents are subdivided into 42 regions, in a haphazard sort of way — for example, 'Siam', which ceased, finally, to be the name of what is now Thailand in 1948, stands for the whole of south-east Asia. Although Risk is about world domination, the basic game (there are variations) presents players with more modest goals such as to 'Conquer the continents EUROPE and AUSTRALIA plus a third continent of [their] choice' or to 'Destroy all GREEN ARMIES'. (Players' armies are differentiated by colour.) Instructions such as these are on 'mission' cards dealt out at the start of a game. Other cards determine which regions players occupy to begin with and onto these territories each deploys equal numbers of plastic armies. Further armies are acquired in various ways but always on a the-more-you-have-the-more-you-get basis. Conflict is resolved by throwing dice.

The rules, as is quite common with such games, are badly written and confusing which perhaps explains why the copy I bought had a leaflet in it advising people to write in with any queries about how to play.

An advertisement for Risk in the *Sunday Times Magazine* of 20 November 1983 is very revealing. It shows the game, as if in progress, spread out on what looks something like a table. A boy of about 12 is leaning over this in a menacing posture and looking out of the photograph at the reader as if at an opponent. The caption reads, 'Even if you double my pocket money, I'd still wipe you off the face of Africa'. This conveys very well the atmosphere of the game and the aggression the manufacturers are angling for. Apart from that, why Africa? Whose Africa? The blurb below the photo and caption stresses unprincipled conduct in diplomacy:

> Treaties and pacts will be signed, then before the diplomatic ink dries you'll find yourself on the wrong end of a full scale advance by a brother-in-law you've loved and trusted for 15 years.

Sounds great fun!

The next game has a very interesting background. It shows, in a particularly direct way, the connection between the prevailing political ideology of a country (in this case the United States) and its cultural products. First, we look at how this game is presented. The Game of Nations, as it's called, is described on the box as 'a political strategy game for adults and older children' and also, in the words of Miles Copeland (more about him later), as an 'amoral and cynical game'. These words are printed over a design which shows, prominently, a black attaché case with a combination lock. The case is partly open — inside we glimpse a bunch of keys and a tape cassette — and rests upon an Iranian passport and a copy of *Pravda*. Beside the case is a copy of Copeland's book, *The Game of Nations*, showing the front cover with the publisher's blurb on it.

The rules tell us that the main object is to 'remain in the game' and, of course, this is essential in order to play it but, after that, the object is to gain power through the possession, manipulation and exploitation of imaginary oil-bearing countries. The large board, in two halves, shows eight of these which are given a middle eastern tang through their names, pictures of camels and so on. Each of the two to four players has a set of 'character pieces' comprising 'leaders' — two politicians, two kings, a dictator and a guerrilla — along with a secret agent, a number of tankers and pipelines and seven million in money (the currency isn't specified). Leaders are placed and then moved on circular tracks within the countries, from which, at certain points, they can launch attacks on their neighbours. All this costs money. Players make money by co-ordinating tankers and, for greater advantage, pipelines, with the oil derricks in the countries they control. 'International incident cards' such as, 'Loan from I.M.F. approved/Receive 3 million in revenue' or 'Guerilla killed in ambush/Remove your guerilla' add another element to the game. Players must drop out when they have no more money.

Again, it has to be said that the above features bear some resemblance to part of the international political scene but it has to be added — as with so many games on the market — that this game gives no hint of any alternative. The kind of political behaviour portrayed, in which greed is the motivating force, might is right and humane considerations have no place, is put forward as the only kind of behaviour there is. The game says, in effect, that this is the way things — and people — are.

We now turn to the background of The Game of Nations. As a game, it's the result of the efforts of a small group of people who worked in, or were connected with, the Washington Games Center in and around the early 1950s. Here, experts with the necessary information played out the moves national leaders were likely to make in response to then current international events. In other words, they played out simulations to try to predict what would happen. The supervisor of this centre, having worked in the USA's intelligence organization during the second world war, moved on to the Central Intelligence Agency (CIA) soon afterwards. Copeland, author of the book, *The Game of Nations* (sub-titled The Amorality of Power Politics) worked at the Games Center and also helped to organize the CIA when it was formed, in 1949. He's also the author of a leaflet, 'The Armchair Strategist's Introduction to The Game of Nations', which comes along with the game and in which he extols the 'game player attitude'. This he had adopted from the supervisor of the Games Center (also called the Peace Center in the leaflet) when they worked together there. Briefly, the 'game player attitude' is one by which political problems are regarded as problems to be solved rationally, without any consideration for moral principles. (Copeland seems to think there's necessarily a conflict between being rational and being moral.) Looking at the matter in another light, we may well ask whether it is this 'rational' approach which has taken humanity to the brink of destruction.

Copeland's book, which is actually a study of President Nasser of Egypt, contains some interesting assumptions which throw light on the 'game player attitude' and the attitudes which lie behind many of the games to be examined here. First is the assumption that might is right which, in the book, means that the USA has the right to interfere anywhere in the world. In this connection, Copeland blithely writes about changing the leaders and governments of other countries. Following on from this is the idea that he and his like know what's best for other people, but a better way of putting it might be to say that they know what's best for themselves and what they take to be US interests. The other main cluster of assumptions in the book is to do with what some people call 'human nature'. The sort of political skulduggery Copeland deals in arises from a view of life as being competitive and based on self-interest, and a view of people as being basically evil. In other words, it's the ancient notion of original sin.

It seems only a short step to Apocalypse, described as 'The Game of Nuclear Devastation' on the box, and intended for two to four players aged 10 to adult. The game was produced privately for several years under the name of Warlord before it was taken up by Games Workshop and produced in 1980 as Apocalypse.

As often happens, more attention has been devoted to the front of the box than to any other part of the product. It shows a huge, phallic gun being fired. Inside the box, apart from a lot of empty space, there's a board in two halves which don't fit together properly. This shows a rough and inaccurate map of Europe, the seas round about, and north Africa, and over it is superimposed an irregular grid which divides both land and sea into areas all of about the same size. Britain and Ireland, for example, are divided into 14 regions including two cities. As all the dividing lines are the same thickness, including those dividing sea from land, it's very hard on the eyes and the colours don't help in this respect, either. Armies are differentiated by colour and each player has 140 of them. They are represented by small squares of thin card which are painfully difficult to pick up and move. Radioactive markers and city markers are similar. These items, together with 36 small, plastic missiles, a leaflet of the rules and a die for which you have to supply your own cup or cover (a necessity in this game), cost me £7.95 in 1983 and if I mention the matter of cost and materials here it's not because Apocalypse is altogether very unusual in this regard.

As is common in war games, a player's turn consists of phases, in this case three: firing and exploding missiles; adding further armies; and moving and attacking, building up new missiles or reconstructing. The die is for resolving conflict. I should add that players are not asked to side with particular countries in this game. They merely play at being 'ambitious and unscrupulous politicians' as it says in the catalogue.

This is the basic outline of Apocalypse. Its implications are serious. First of all, we've arived at a different aspect of wargaming now. This is not a historical war or a war fought over imaginary territories: this is the next war, centred on Europe — a theme in games which will become very familiar by the end of this chapter. Even more serious is the idea put forward in this game that regions which have become radioactive owing to the explosion of missiles can, under certain circumstances, be 'reconstructed'. Lastly, no people are mentioned. The most important fact about war — that people get killed and maimed — is left out. However, this is usual in such games.

Having heard, with some astonishment, that Mike Hayes, the inventor of Apocalypse, was a member of CND, I wrote to him about what, in my opinion, were the disturbing implications of this game. Accepting responsibility in a very creditable and unusual manner, he wrote me a long and considered reply on 21 January 1984 and it behoves me here to present his case as fairly as I can.

He begins his defence by acknowledging some difficulties:

> Many people have raised the question of whether Apocalypse is in extremely bad taste — in particular players are tempted to 'win' by using nuclear weapons not only on their direct enemies, but also on neutral parties or allied territory where, for example a radioactive buffer zone is thought desirable to hold back superior conventional forces.

He then moves on to a more general question, familiar from the last three games dealt with here: 'the game is so structured to tempt players into dirty tricks, double-dealing, breaking of promises and ratting on friends'. In view of these features, Hayes says, he had to ask himself a 'key question' when designing Apocalypse. This was (he puts it in capitals): 'HOW DID THE ADOPTION OF "IMMORAL" BEHAVIOUR WITHIN THE GAME AFFECT PEOPLE'S ATTITUDE IN REAL LIFE, PARTICULARLY THEIR REACTION TO THE NUCLEAR ARMS RACE?' Hayes then goes on to mention five 'observations' he's come up with in response to this question. Firstly, he says that the games player, through being at different times in the role of victor and victim, (and more often in that of victim, given the number of players and the fact that there's only one winner) eventually develops a 'detachment from the objective "to win by smashing others" '. Secondly, Hayes claims that it's better if military strategies are widely known and rehearsed by games players; in which case the element of surprise is lost and the real thing is less likely to be put into practice. Thirdly, there's the point about the devastating effect of nuclear weapons:

> In Warlord *no* reconstruction was allowed, and a superbomb — creating wider devastation was introduced. At the end of Warlord there was no doubt that any victory was utterly hollow. Because Apocalypse was played over a smaller area, with fewer players, the rules had to be simplified, and Reconstruction was introduced.

Fourthly, in his letter, Hayes makes the point that, although the game allows all kinds of nasty behaviour, players don't necessarily have to indulge in it and can even win without doing so. He admits that people rarely take this option but thinks that those who do are mature. Lastly, he contends that games players 'sublimate their innate violence' into games and are mild in their personal lives. Concluding his letter, Hayes writes: 'The threat to the world comes from politicians who play war games for real, and who feel obliged to play on our behalf'.

I don't want to argue, point by point, the matters raised in this fairly comprehensive statement and I'll be dealing with the one about sublimation later, in any case (see pp. 273-74). However, I would just like to draw attention to the alterations the publishers made in this game after taking it over (the third point above). It's not often we get a peep behind the scenes like this. My only comment is that Hayes must have agreed to the changes, most importantly to the bringing in of the dangerously misleading notion of reconstruction, so the final responsibility is his.

Although it was described in the August 1980 issue of the magazine *Military Modelling* as 'a work of genius', Apocalypse had been dropped from production by the beginning of 1985.

Nuclear warfare is at least a possibility in the next two examples which are produced by Victory Games (part of Avalon Hill) and intended for adults and older teenagers. The first, Nato, subtitled 'The Next War in Europe', was copyrighted in 1983 and imported into Britain around the end of 1984. The second, Cold War, subtitled 'The Game of Global Politics Influence Peddling and Double Dealing' was copyrighted a year later than Nato and arrived correspondingly later in Britain. Here, they are marketed by TM Games which shares an address in north London with Avalon Hill.

As regards the materials and method of play in the case of these games, there aren't any particularly unusual or significant features (they are played on large paper sheets rather than boards as such, that's all) and I haven't thought it necessary to go into any great detail. Much more important are the assumptions the games are based on. Also, these two illustrate disturbing developments in war games in recent times.

First of all, there's the actual setting and framework within which play takes place. Nato, which is played on a map of central Europe, is described by the manufacturer as a 'simulation of a Warsaw Pact invasion of West Germany during the late 1980s'. In this case, therefore, we're given the immediate cause of the action;

we're told what triggers it off. This is something new amongst the games examined so far in this chapter. The blurb on the back of the box goes into greater detail:

> Throughout the 1980s, tensions between NATO and the Warsaw Pact allian-ces escalate to dangerous levels. Repeated, large-scale Warsaw Pact ma-neuvres keep NATO constantly at the verge of full alert. Suddenly, the game changes as Warsaw Pact airstrikes thunder into NATO's forward airbases; at the West German border columns of Soviet and East German armor have jumped off along the entire front, churning their way toward the Rhine. ... The next war in Europe has begun.

Another thing is that the opposing forces are specifically named here in a projected conflict. (There are special rules for chemical and nuclear warfare.)

So, the next war takes place in Europe and is started by a deliberate and unprovoked attack from the Warsaw Pact. The saddest thing about the crass and wanton irresponsibility shown in the marketing of such a game is that it's not altogether unusual these days.

Cold War is less specific but it promotes the 'game player attitude' again, which certainly has its own dangers. This game is played on a map of the world divided into 27 regions and the four players, who represent North America, the Soviet Union, China and Western Europe, have to try to control as many regions as possible in order to derive income from them. 'Nice guys are very likely to finish last!' the Victory Games catalogue says. However, if players are good at 'instigating insur-gencies and coups to disrupt opponents' and at 'seizing every opportunity to benefit by someone else's loss', they'll probably do very well. It's 'fun to play', into the bargain, so the catalogue says.

This same catalogue, dated spring 1985, has in it 11 'military simulation and strategy' games, one of which has two additional and separate modules. All are available in Britain.

With the last two examples, we've been moving into the area of board war games for adults, though it's not a very well defined area and there can't be any clear dividing lines. Another way of putting it would be to say that these are the sort of games which wait at the boundaries of childhood. Those interested can easily move on to them. The problem over age suitability is highlighted by the Avalon Hill firm which doesn't seem to be sure whether its games are for children and adults or just for adults, or whether such descriptions are just misleading anyway. Certainly, board war games for adults were pioneered by Charles S Roberts who founded the firm in 1958. Now, it seems to be easily the largest producer of board war games, with about 70 on offer, most of them available in Britain. (In recent years, Britain and Japan have been major importers of Avalon Hill games.)

The last board war game to be dealt with here helps to complete the picture, as far as this type of game is concerned. Superpower, a game for two to six players aged 12 and upwards, came out, after much publicity, in early 1986. It was invented by two Canadians, E Bruce Hollands and Daniel R McGregor, who called it Foreign

Policy. Games Workshop, however, which took it on, changed the name as they had done with Warlord (Apocalypse) but, this time, made no major changes in the game itself. Superpower is subtitled 'The Game of Global Exploitation'. (Cynicism and exploitation seem to have become strong selling points in recent years.)

Although the design of the box lid identifies the Soviet Union and the United States as superpowers, players don't take the parts of any named countries. The board, in four pieces which join together, shows maps of four regions in the third world and the object is to dominate 12 countries in each of these regions. A player (superpower) dominates a country in three stages: by economic influence, then by military influence and, finally, by military fortification. There are counters, pieces and various cards. The players' counters, called 'representatives' in the rules, are adult, male figures about 3 cm high and of different colours but otherwise identical. These are standing, bent slightly forward and to one side in a friendly posture, and each carries in one hand in front of his chest, a bundle with a tiny dollar sign on it. This is, presumably, economic aid. Behind their backs, however, they hold revolvers, or pistols. In other words, they symbolize hypocrisy. According to the throw of a dice, players move these representatives around a track, the panels of which relate to happenings in the countries on the maps. Very small and fiddly plastic pieces are used to show the stages which the third world countries go through in the course of being dominated: a piece with a dollar sign for economic influence, one in the shape of a tank for military influence, and a symbolic fort for military fortification. Conflict and other matters are decided by throwing dice or voting. The game ends when all the countries have been dominated and, presumably, exploited. Then, the superpowers reckon up their 'victory points' (awarded for various achievements in the game) to see who's won. Some other features of the game are worth noting. Military fortification involves the unavoidable loss of 'world opinion cards' which means that other countries disapprove. The loss of world opinion over invasions, military coups and military responses, however, can be withstood by the use of propaganda. Even so, it didn't seem to me that the loss of world opinion mattered very much — with two playing, anyway — nor was revolution or guerrilla warfare likely to upset the superpowers unduly. Diplomacy may be used, and a vote called, to cause the withdrawal of an opponent's military influence but this may be reversed by the use of a veto.

Overall, the implications of the game are clear. Third world countries are there to be exploited, with total disregard, by stronger countries. World opinion is to be ignored or manipulated. Some people argue that this is the way powerful countries behave and that one's as bad as another. In fact, Stewart Parkinson, Games Workshop's European Sales Manager, takes this attitude. He says:

> People need to be more cynical and see that governments are doing wrong under an ideological banner. The game has no political bias, all governments are seen to be as bad as each other.[1]

I'd have some important disagreements here. It doesn't seem to me that this is the way things are and it doesn't seem useful to pretend that it is. Certainly, it's not the way things have to be and the game neither presents any alternative nor suggests that there's anything wrong in a cynical, might-is-right approach to world politics.

(In this, of course, Superpower resembles most of the other games dealt with in this chapter.) Also, the suggestion of conflict between the United States and the Soviet Union, made by means of the box design and described to me by a representative of Games Workshop as a 'marketing ploy', is, to say the least, unhelpful. Then, in spite of Parkinson's remarks, quoted above, there is no ideological conflict in the game — there's only a struggle for power in military terms. Furthermore, I'd have thought we'd need less cynicism, not more — if we're going to survive, that is. Lastly, it's very difficult to see how 'wrong' can be exposed by inviting players to take on the role of wrongdoers. Yet Hollands, one of the inventors of the game, makes the following claim:

> [Superpower] is ... designed ... to reach out and inform the public about the plight of the Third World and the realities behind superpower conflict. ... Superpower demonstrates the illegal, unjust actions and policies performed each day by the world powers.[2]

At least, there's an acknowledgement here that games can transmit ideas and attitudes. Superpower, Hollands says, is 'a game which challenges and teaches'. However, whether it teaches what he says it does is very much to be doubted. I think that only games played from the point of view of the wronged, not that of the wrongdoers, can achieve what Hollands is aiming for.

We now come to the role-playing games mentioned at the beginning of the chapter. The first is Merc which was copyrighted by Fantasy Games Unlimited, in 1981. No indication is given of age suitability. On the box, Merc is described as 'a modern role playing game of counter insurgency' and as 'a role playing game of modern mercenaries carrying out missions for their employers anywhere in the world'. The structure is basically like that of the role-playing games described in the last chapter. Here, 'The Corporation', that is, the mercenaries' employer, takes the place of a Dungeon Master or Game Master. Here, also, as in other role-playing games, you can 'roll up' a character, his (in this game) physical appearance and physical and mental attributes, and choose weapons according to the weight he can carry (which depends on physique). Tables are used to decide the outcome of combat and you get experience points and monetary rewards at the end, as in the other games. The content or subject of Merc, though, is vastly different. In this game, you can, for example, choose to go on an 'undercover mission' to assassinate somebody, in which case the maximum number of points is awarded. However, the 'Introductory Mission' given in the rule book involves killing on a larger scale and takes place in 'Rhodesia'.

In this 'mission', some historical notes at the beginning tell us that 'by 1975, only two nations in Africa could still boast of a White Power Control ... [omission mark in original] and both were under attack'. The nations in question are South Africa and Rhodesia, of course, but the most important cues here are the word 'boast' and the racist notion of 'White Power'. We're told that 'Rhodesia was in political turmoil and under embargo', that 'this situation was opportune to Communist interests' and that 'soon terrorists appeared ... armed with Soviet weapons'. Mercenaries also appear, hired by the 'White Government' to train and lead 'loyal' troops. The people labelled 'terrorists' (in their own country!) have been causing

239

disruption and a particular group of them has been traced, allegedly, to a certain village. The 'team orders', that is, the object of those taking part in the game, are 'to terminate [i.e. kill] the entire terrorist band, and village if necessary'. Amongst the (ready-made) team are: Vladamir Hutov who, despite his (misspelt) Russian, first name, is from Hungary; Dubra Chatowski who is described as a 'Polish freedom fighter who had to leave Poland ... with Soviet hounds at his heels'; Charles Toby, a white Rhodesian of English descent 'who is fighting for his home'; and Toko, a 'loyal black Rhodesian', who is, in fact, the 'loyal native' stereotype so familiar from imperialist fiction. Toko is the driver and has a dog-like devotion to Toby.

This may be a fantasy world but it's none the less vicious for that. Merc represents another aspect of wargaming — that of the far right politically.

Games from this end of the political spectrum are by no means rare and, with the next one, The Price of Freedom, we pick up again the line that we were following in the board game Nato — one that we'll pick up twice more (when we come to table wargaming and computer war games) — the line that presents NATO and the Warsaw Pact countries, or the United States and the Soviet Union, as enemies.

At the very end of 1986, The Price of Freedom, a role-playing game by Greg Costikyan from the US firm, West End Games, went on sale in Britain for, so it was claimed, ages 12 and upwards. Though it was possibly the most vicious and irresponsible game around at the time, it was an obvious development from what had gone before. In this game, which is quite complex but, in structure, very similar to Merc, players take on the role of guerrilla fighters in a USA in the process of being occupied by the Soviet Union.

The title logo on the box involves the stars and stripes and the hammer and sickle while the illustration on the front of the box shows three young adults bursting through what, seemingly, is the flag of the 'United American Soviets'. All three are armed and the middle one, a white man with the slogan, 'Better Dead than Red' on his T-shirt, is flanked by a black man and a white woman. Over them towers a bust of Lenin.

A leaflet labelled 'Freedom File A' sets the scene:

> A gutless President has been elected.
> America has signed international agreements
>   prohibiting 'Star Wars' defenses.
> The Soviet Union has developed a shield
>   against nuclear attack.
> The Soviet Premier demands American surrender.
> The President complies.
> Soviet troops are landing in your hometown.
> In this, its darkest hour, America needs heroes.
> Are you willing to pay... [omission mark in original]
>   THE PRICE OF FREEDOM?

The Player Book is notable for some amazingly bad attempts at Russian in the section headings and some very dubious slogans, which are scattered here and there, such as: 'The Right to Own Guns is the Right to be Free', 'My Country, Right or Wrong' and 'Peace Through Superior Firepower'. A passage from the introduction gives us the general tone of the game:

> Throughout its existence, America has stood for liberty and the rights of man. The struggle between America and Russia is not one between two super-powers of more or less equal moral weight, but between freedom and slavery; between light and darkness; yes, between good and evil.

Some people might think this rather tongue-in-cheek, especially as it appears under the sub-heading, 'Some Propaganda', but such a view would be mistaken. West End Games describe The Price of Freedom as 'a serious and sophisticated military roleplaying game' and draw a distinction between it and their 'humorous games'. As if to make sure the other players get the message, and despite the overwhelmingly inflammatory tone of the printed text of the game, the gamemaster is advised to motivate them by having the Soviets do 'something completely despicable, evil and *wrong*' at the beginning of each adventure.

It's a relief to turn to a peace game as an alternative to all this warmongering. The south Yorkshire branch of the Campaign Against the Arms Trade produced Choices in 1982 or thereabouts. This is a role-playing game of the simulation kind — along the lines of Spring Green Motorway and Tenement, analysed in chapter nine — rather than of the kind represented by Dungeons and Dragons.The makers describe it as 'an arms trade role-play game for schools and interested groups' and it's for 15-30 participants, in the middle to late teens I'd say. Included with it are 31 copies of 'Live and Let Die', a short leaflet about arms sales to the third world, and also a pamphlet explaining the background to Choices. The game itself consists of 30 individual, different role-playing cards divided into three sets of 10. One set is for the arms buyers — the government ministers of the central African state of Balandia. This country suffers under an extremely repressive régime propped up by foreign aid and arms and very much subject to the influence of Transworld Investments (which has bought up a factory in Britain and proposes to make the armoured cars called Slamvans there for export to Balandia). There's a revolution-ary movement in the country. Another set of cards is for the arms sellers — British government ministers who have to decide on arms sales, issue licences and so forth. The third set of cards is for the arms makers — workers at a declining British firm bought up by Transworld Investments. It's rumoured amongst them that armoured cars are to be manufactured by the new firm and that this will make for fewer redundancies. The idea is for these three groups to discuss separately, taking roles — the first two meet in cabinet, the third in the works canteen — and then to come to group decisions. Afterwards, a general discussion can take place. As the expla-natory pamphlet makes clear, the game should take place within a context of background information or as part of a relevant course. A serious drawback in Choices is that we don't have the revolutionaries' point of view represented. Therefore, the players are likely to have their attention focused on the symptoms of the disorder only, rather than its cause. The information missing couldn't come from any other source in the game.

Table wargaming

The hobby of table or table-top wargaming (which seems to have started on the floor) is largely an adult activity. George Gush, in his book written with Andrew Finch, *A Guide to Wargaming,* mentions that the limited surveys that have been carried out suggest that those following the hobby tend to be male and in their teens and twenties. We need to pay some attention to this branch of wargaming because the picture would be incomplete without it. There are connections here both with the military and with toys. In fact, it's just a complicated way of playing with toy soldiers — I don't care what its followers say!

Of course, it's made as realistic as possible and involves models — of soldiers, vehicles and larger weapons — deployed on the battlefield or, rather, on the sand-table, a basic item of equipment for hobby wargaming on which sand can be arranged, and other features improvised, to look like various kinds of terrain. A lot of military knowledge and research usually goes into wargaming and, most importantly, there are books of rules. Dice are used to cover the element of chance and slide rules to calculate movement. There are opponents, so all the main elements of a competitive game are there — but it's still playing with toy soldiers.

A brief look at the history of table or miniature wargaming — which is usually just called wargaming — is very revealing. Toy soldiers first appear on the scene as the playthings of princes, to help train them for command. The future Philip IV of Spain, for instance, had a very detailed wooden army in 1614 and Louis XIV of France had silver armies round about the middle of the century. In the late eighteenth century, a game was invented at the court of the Duke of Brunswick. It had pieces representing military units and also rules for movement, and it was played over a grid of 1,666 squares. This, along with a good number of games from the early nineteenth century, owed much to chess. The invention of Kriegspiel (War Game) during this period in Switzerland was a most important step. It was played with blocks representing armies, field guns and so on which were moved about on a map instead of on squared terrain, and it was used for the instruction of military cadets, first of all in the Prussian army. It was introduced into the British army after the Franco-German war of 1870. Kriegspiel became the standard and, while its use and development for military instruction continued, a separate development took place leading towards the hobby of today. Soon after Kriegspiel was taken up by the British army, the Oxford Kriegspiel Club, probably the first wargames club in Britain, was founded, in 1873. This showed a move away from a wholly military context.

Further developments in the direction of wargaming as a hobby took place in this country with the involvement, in the period up to the first world war, of two leading literary figures.

Robert Louis Stevenson spent the winter of 1881-2 convalescing at Davos, in Switzerland, where he spent much of the time playing soldiers with his stepson, Lloyd Osbourne. Their game seems to have owed nothing to previous war games but, from very simple beginnings, it was taken to a fairly advanced stage, as Osbourne records in *Scribner's Magazine* for December 1898:

This game of tin soldiers, an intricate 'kriegspiel', involving rules innumerable, prolonged arithmetical calculations, constant measuring with foot-rules, and the throwing of dice, sprang from the humblest beginnings — a row of soldiers on either side and a deadly marble.[3]

As Osbourne makes clear, the game was closely based upon actual warfare, the battles and manoeuvres taking place across a map drawn on the attic floor with chalks of different colours.

However, it's not known to what extent Stevenson's game, as reported by Osbourne, influenced the development of the hobby. The influence of H G Wells, on the other hand, cannot be doubted and his book, *Little Wars,* which grew out of two articles of his in *The Windsor Magazine* and which was published in 1913, is the first book on wargaming in its modern sense.

Wells seems to have been unaware of Stevenson's games and therefore to have re-invented floor war games. Basically, *Little Wars* is about the application of rules to playing with toy soldiers and in the book Wells gives an account of the development of these rules into a comprehensive system. For instance, rules were laid down governing movement: it had to be decided how far soldiers and vehicles might be expected to move in a given time. Using these rules, a player was allowed to do as much as possible with his or her army in, say, five minutes. A way of dealing with combat had to be decided on, also. Wells and the friend he played with at first tossed a coin to decide who was dead, if one soldier touched another from the opposing army, but later they decided that the two would kill each other. More rules were added as the game developed and a method was worked out, to be applied over several games, whereby points would be awarded for each soldier killed, field gun captured and so on. In Wells's system the main thing was hitting and knocking over soldiers, and this kind of game only became realistic with the invention of the toy 'spring breech-loader gun', as it's called in *Little Wars.* (Stevenson and Osbourne, once they'd progressed beyond marbles, had used cufflinks and letters from a toy printing press as ammunition, and these were thrown.) It's interesting that here, at the start of the hobby, we find Wells putting forward the excuse made by all apologists for wargaming: 'how much better is this amiable miniature than the Real Thing!' he says, as though the two were alternatives.

I should point out a few more landmarks of historical interest before arriving at the hobby of today. The framework of the modern game was established by Wells but further major developments, mainly to do with rules and model figures, were to take place. There seems to have been something of a lull in table wargaming between the world wars (though this doesn't seem to have happened with the less realistic board war games). Perhaps people had had enough of the 'Real Thing' and anything with a fairly close resemblance to it. However, the British Model Soldier Society was started round about the mid 1930s and, after the second world war, wargaming centred on this group. They organized wargames championships for which J C Sachs, a military man, drew up the rules, basing them on those in *Little Wars.* He also tackled a problem wargamers have had through the years — that players can normally see far more of the battlefield than a general would be able to in actual warfare. Sachs's answer was to raise the terrain to round about eye level, though this does seem as if it would create other problems.

A big step was taken with the publication of the first wargames magazine, *War Games Digest*, in 1957. This took place in the USA, though many of the early subscribers were British and, in fact, for a few years, it was published from Britain and the USA in turn. Once the magazine was started — others were to follow, of course, and I'll be referring to one or two of these — wargamers could meet and organize more easily.

At about this time, an advance happened on the models front, as well, when Airfix brought out their sets of 20mm high plastic figures. The lead soldiers from the firm of Britains were rather too big for most table wargaming and too dear, as wargamers needed lots of them.

Another important step was taken when Don Featherstone, who had been involved with *War Games Digest* at the British end, organized the first national convention of wargamers in Britain, in 1961. Since 1966, these have taken place every year. Featherstone did much to promote the fast-growing hobby. His book, *War Games,* was published in 1962 and had run into seven impressions by 1973. Peter Young, another wargamer in the military, claims in the foreword that it's the first addition to the literature on the subject since Wells.

The next big step was the commercial production of rules and the Wargames Research Group was set up in 1968 for this purpose. Their Ancient Rules, published the following year, became almost standard for wargamers and the group's modern rules have been adopted by the US army as a training aid. This is just one of the many connections between war games and warfare.

Table wargaming has continued to grow. By 1976, there were over 200 clubs in Britain, and Featherstone, in his book *Wargaming* published in 1977, was able to list 21 books on the subject. *A Guide to Wargaming,* which was published in 1980, lists 65 sets of wargame rules, commercially available and arranged according to various periods of warfare.

Realism has always been important to wargamers and, over the years, a lot of effort has gone into making all aspects of wargaming more realistic. The amount of detail, and the attention to small particulars, is bewildering to people not involved. As regards figures, there's now a great variety, representing practically all historical periods and in several different sizes, to suit all warlike tastes. For instance, in the first issue of the magazine, *Miniature Wargames* (undated but bought in the spring of 1983), there are advertisements for late Roman legionaries as well as Austrian musketeers — in both shakos and helmets — from the Napoleonic wars. These are tiny, just over 6mm tall, and such figures are usually sold in batches on a single base. More than twice as big, at 15mm, there are 10 different types of French infantryman advertised, from the period 1490-1530. Turning to a different kind of detail, an article in the same magazine is entitled, 'A Plain Man's Guide to 15mm Figure Painting' and contains the sentence, 'It is well worth the effort of researching horse colourings'. Another article deals with the question of whether Hittite chariots (of, say, the thirteenth century BC) carried two or three men.

In the end, compromises have to be made somewhere between realism and playability. A whole army can scarcely be deployed on the table top, not even if the figures are tiny, and military units are usually represented by a proportion of their real numbers, often in the ratio of one to 33. In general, the more realistic the game, the more details, and the more details, the more calculations. Another problem is time. In half an hour of play, wargamers will normally expect to get through about two to four minutes of historical time. Computers can be used to cut down on bothersome calculations but, as with fantasy wargaming, these are, up to a point, an essential part of the whole business.

At this stage, it'll be useful to step back and look at the wider context. The fact is there's been a boom in table wargaming since the late 1950s. Technical developments, some of which I've noted here, have played a part but it seems to me more important to look at the matter from another angle.

From such a vantage point, we can see that wargaming is only part of a military culture, a culture very much orientated towards, and obsessed by, war. After that, a good question to ask is: which countries have been most involved in the wargames boom? The answer is already evident from the historical outline above but some further details from Featherstone's work will help to underline the point. In the first of the two books of his I've drawn on (published in 1962), he lists 'the world's principal suppliers' of model soldiers and wargame vehicles. Britain is at the top of the list with 12 suppliers, the USA has five, Western Germany four, and Spain and Sweden have one each. Fifteen years later, in *Wargaming*, Featherstone lists the 'principal makers of wargames figures'. (It isn't clear whether vehicles are included here but they could scarcely be separated off and, anyway, it doesn't alter the point). In this later list, suppliers in Britain have increased to 19 and there are 12 in the USA and five in West Germany, while Spain and Sweden still have one each and two suppliers have appeared in France. The increases here just follow the pattern of the growth in popularity of wargaming. It's more important to note which countries are most heavily involved. (Sweden is a rather peaceful country and its presence in the list — even with only one supplier — is something of a surprise.) We should, I suggest, look at wargaming and kindred pursuits against this international background.

The collecting and the painting of military figures are practically hobbies in themselves, and are catered for by the magazine, *Military Modelling*. The issue of October 1982 gives us further evidence of warlike inclinations and connections. Here, there's an advertisement for 'commemorative' models called 'heroes of the Falklands', comprising three 'character heads'. These are almost busts and represent the marines, the navy and the Parachute Regiment. In the same issue of the magazine, there's an advertisement for a series of military figures, numbers one and two of which are, respectively, the Parachute Regiment and the marines. These are said to be 'also commemorative models of the Falklands campaign', though they seem to have been made before it happened. Again, in the same issue of *Military Modelling*, there's an account, entitled 'The Battle of South Georgia', which is part three of 'The Falklands Memorandum'. All this seems to show an undue interest in the 'Real Thing' on the part of those who tend to claim their hobby is a harmless alternative.

Clubs have been mentioned in passing but it's now time for a closer look. In 1983, on St George's day, I went to the exhibition of the South London Warlords, 'Salute 1983'. (Their first 'salute' had been in 1972.) There was a queue to get in and I estimated the attendance at something like 700. These were mainly young adults of about 20 to 35 years old. A sprinkling of those present were older and there were also some younger people, down to the age of 12 or so. About three per cent were women, who were helping rather than participating, and there were just a few black people. Some of those attending had dressed up for the occasion: three were in first world war uniforms; one in a colonial type of uniform, with a pith helmet; one in what appeared to be a nineteenth century uniform, with a scarlet coat; and one person, who had a whitened face and 'blood' coming from the corner of his mouth, was wearing raggy jeans and a 'shot- through' shirt, with the holes outlined in red.

The South London Warlords were hosts to 20 other clubs and all had games going, spread throughout three halls and a foyer. Also, 22 traders in war games had stalls. A tape was playing war noises in one corner and there were plenty of drawn maps and charts in evidence, and lots of slide rules. There was great variety amongst the games in progress. One club was playing out a siege according to the Ancient rules of the Wargames Research Group while another was staging a well-researched historical battle between British and German colonial troops in east Africa. Two clubs had made-up battles set in Vietnam, one of them involving a referee. However, I found most disturbing the two encounters between NATO and the Warsaw Pact. There's not a lot to say about the first of these as much of it had been carried on by post and phone, and although the players had started in 1980, they hadn't reached the end of day one. In the other, though, the 'Russians' had parachuted into Norfolk and were opposed by British and US troops. Some 'Russians' were disguised as US troops, but this ruse had been found out. Apart from the general and worrying issue — that so many people are fixated on war — these particular examples, and the attitudes involved, seem very unlikely to bring disarmament and peace any closer, to say the least.

Other clubs have interests that go beyond just wargaming and a look at them can reveal some interesting connections. One such club is the Society of Ancients, formed in 1965, which is concerned with the study of military history in the ancient and medieval periods and also with wargaming in the same periods. It runs a wargames championship and produces the bi-monthly magazine, *Slingshot*. Another society, not concerned with games in the first place but having a wargaming section, is the Victorian Military Society. It publishes a quarterly magazine, *Soldiers of the Queen*. The focus here is clearly on an imperial past, and a historical dead end.

A different approach to military history is taken by the battle re-enactment societies whose members dress up, arm themselves according to the period in question and stage historical battles. In *White Dwarf* for August 1982, there was an advertisement for recruits to join the Blue Regiment of the (Roundhead) London Trained Bands of the Sealed Knot English Civil War Re-enactment Society. The Sealed Knot, incidentally, was a secret royalist organization in the time of Cromwell's Commonwealth. We've now entered the role-playing area again and several other connections spring to mind here: the fantasy adventuring (Treasure Trap) at Peckforton Castle, for instance; the clubs where would-be cowboys can play out their fantasies; and those where men play soldiers in a more modern sense and run around shooting one another with dye pellets.

If you feel like a week's holiday after all this, you might like to spend it in the village of Folkton in Yorkshire. There, at the Wargames Centre, they have enormous tables and vast armies of model soldiers, and you can play wargames to your heart's content.

The hobby of wargaming must seem very weird to those who have no leanings in that direction. A remark made by Wells, however, in one of his articles, already referred to, in *The Windsor Magazine,* can give us some idea of what it's all about at a personal level. He writes: ' "Little Wars" is the game of kings — for players in an inferior social position'. In other words, wargaming, like fantasy role-playing games, can provide some compensation for powerlessness in real life. Players take on the roles of commanders and generals (much as, in business games, they take on the roles of bosses) and not, it need hardly be said, the roles of infantrymen. Wargaming excludes that possibility, even.

Another, overall point needs to made before we leave this short survey of wargaming. I remarked, at the beginning of this section, that wargaming was playing with toy soldiers and there does seem — I can't put it more kindly — a strong element of immaturity, of childishness in it. Featherstone called Stevenson and Wells 'eternal boys' and thereby, unwittingly perhaps, put his finger on a crucial point.

Microprocessor games and war, and alternative games

Microprocessor games have, generally speaking, a younger following. They also have a shorter history, but a very revealing one. We should note when and where they started and the extent of their success as well as the values bound up in them and the attitudes they call forth and encourage.

Nolan Bushnell and Ted Dabney produced a coin-operated, that is, an arcade, video game called Computer Space in 1971, in the United States. It was described by Bushnell as 'a cosmic dogfight between a spaceship and a flying saucer' but, for all that, it wasn't a success. Then, with Al Alcorn, they designed Pong (based on table tennis and for two people) which Bushnell and Dabney, as the firm Atari, marketed in 1972. This, the second game to be based on the microprocessor, was a success. From then on, such games were established and were soon to find their way into the home, where we'll follow them. (Arcade games continued, of course.)

Home video games, originally, were for playing only on a television screen by means of a console. Later, for some systems, video display units (VDUs), which are, basically, just separate screens, were developed. The first home video game system was produced in the United States by Magnavox in 1972. It was 'dedicated', that is, just one game could be played on it, though with variations; a game might have, for instance, a table-tennis or tennis variation, a variation derived from squash and so on. In 1977, Atari introduced the first successful home video system and called it the Atari Video Computer System (VCS), though it wasn't a computer in the usual sense. Various games could be played on this by putting in different cartridges. In other words, it could be 'programmed' and was not tied to one game, or dedicated, like the arcade machines and the Magnavox system.

The general pattern of development has been that games are produced first for the arcades and then, possibly, in home video, hand-held and computer versions depending on popularity. In general, arcade games appeal to young adults and older children; hand-held versions are for younger children, say of about nine on average; and video and computer versions are for those in between. However, some of Atari's home video games, such as the war games, Asteroids, Defender and Missile Command, include versions for younger children. It's difficult to be precise in such matters; I've seen a four-year-old boy playing an arcade-type game. The very popular games, Pac-Man, Galaxian and Space Invaders, all began in the arcades, in Japan as it happens, where Space Invaders was so popular that it created a national shortage of the 100 yen coin. (Japan, it should be noted, has played a very big part in this sector of the games market.) Space Invaders continued its success in the United States, where it was produced on licence, and probably did more than any other game to spark off the craze for such things round about 1978. All you have to do in Space Invaders is shoot as many 'aliens' as possible before they land on you.

It's against this background that we have to look into games of war and aggression, to find out what ideas are bound up in such games and what messages they hold for those who play them. Basically, this is a simple matter. What most of the games say is: kill or be killed, destroy or be destroyed and eat or be eaten. Aggression is explicit, virtually in all of them, whether they are war games or not. However, most of them fall into the war category and no doubt manufacturers would claim to be catering for a demand. As a publicity leaflet from CGL in 1983 says, 'the "shoot them down" principle is without doubt the most popular concept — particularly with the younger age groups'.

The groups in question aren't likely to include girls, as these games, based on advanced technology, are generally thought of as being for males. The exception proves the rule: Centipede, a game from Atari, was actually programmed by a woman, Dona Bailey, who declared, 'I'm convinced my game is a woman's game'. In it, the centipede, and assorted insects, snails and so forth take the place of the usual alien spaceships or enemy missiles and all wind their way down from the top of the screen through lots of mushrooms. At the bottom is a 'bug-blaster', which takes the place of a gun and with this you shoot the animal invaders. This one can be seen as something of an improvement on the general run of games. However, we're not concerned with relative merits at the moment but with gender roles. Another example, also from Atari, gives us a further insight into this matter. The very fact that it was thought necessary to have a version of Pac-Man — called Ms

Pac-Man! — for girls, says a lot in itself. However, a demonstrator at the Earls Court Toy and Hobby Fair amplified the matter to a journalist as follows:

> In this version, she [Ms Pac-Man] has a little bow in her hair, and the ghosts which chase her are slightly less intelligent than in the male version. She's supposed to be cleaning her house, and after she scoops up all the dust on one floor, she goes up to the next.[4]

These examples show us how microprocessor games are regarded from the point of view of gender roles and, by implication, how aggression and war are regarded, from the same point of view. Many of the games simply take imperialist ideology into space. Racism in an earthly context, for example, becomes the anti-alien factor in space.

Nevertheless, there are differences, apart from the obvious ones, between micro-processor games and others. In most board and table games, apart from some very simple ones, players have a certain amount of choice and, within limits, they can decide what to do. This is true of some games for the computer, as the large amount of information computers can store allows for more complex games and more choice, if the programmers want to build it in. However, in most microprocessor games there's no choice and the players are not only given roles but told what to do: 'You're the tank commander. ... Watch out for land mines! Ready, aim, fire!' and 'your mission is to save the human race'. Time and again, as in these typical examples, the wording on the packaging and in the catalogues sets the scene.

Naturally, and as in other war games (and business games) players take very important parts. They are commanders or generals or, without a named role, they may simply be saving the human race. In any case, whatever the packaging says, the role is obvious once you step into the game.

Usually, players don't know who they're fighting, much less why, as an enemy (other than the vague but menacing 'aliens') is seldom named in these games. It's probably even worse when the enemy *is* named, though, as then it's always — without exception, I believe, in imaginary as opposed to historical conflicts — the Soviet Union. When it comes to the second world war, the Soviet Union, usually called 'the Russians', also appears as the enemy and the player is then cast in a German (not Nazi) role, as in Avalon Hill's Tanktics where he or she is a German tank platoon leader on the eastern front. Worse still are the imaginary games set in the near or not-very-distant future.

One of these is Raid Over Moscow, a computer game produced by the US firm, Access Software, copyrighted in 1984 and distributed in Britain by US Gold, in the same year. An analysis of this will bring out some important features. The game loads to the sound of the US national anthem, The Star-spangled Banner, and the background of the title screen is the US flag. In the game, the USSR launches nuclear missiles against seven US cities and one Canadian city in turn. The player's task is set out on the cassette inlay card:

249

27: *Theatre Europe*

As squadron leader, you must lead your commandos on a virtual suicide mission; knock out the Soviet launch sites, and then proceed into the city of Moscow. Armed only with the weapons you can carry you must seek and destroy the Soviet defence centre to stop the attack!

Elsewhere, the player's role is referred to as 'squadron commander of the U.S. Defence Space Station' so both antagonists are named in this game. The first task is to manoeuvre planes out of the hangar. Then, you have to shoot your way through various defences, on different screens, to get through to destroy the launching sites at Saratov, Leningrad and Minsk and then the defence centre at Moscow. This all has to be carried out within a certain time in order to stop the nuclear missiles which are represented on the map screen as clusters of small white dots moving gradually towards their targets. 'Play it like there's no tomorrow!' the cover advises.

Some very serious assumptions are made in this game. The Soviet Union is the 'enemy' and is referred to as such; it makes an unprovoked, first-strike nuclear attack; and the USA is in the position of being forced to retaliate. There seems little basis in reality for such assumptions, to say the least. I suggest we should ask: is such a game more, or less, likely to bring about a climate of opinion in which the final war could take place? Also, suppose, in the USSR, they were selling a nuclear war game called Raid Over Washington and with the roles of the two antagonists in Raid Over Moscow reversed. What would the reaction in the USA be, to that? It only remains to add that the game ran into a lot of opposition in Britain, especially from CND, but about 100,000 copies were sold within a year or so.

Some people might want to argue that Raid over Moscow isn't very realistic and that there's a lack of particular details. Another computer game, called Theatre Europe, is much more specific and, as it's also a strategic game overall, whereas Raid over Moscow was a 'zapping' game, it calls for a more detailed analysis (see illustration). Theatre Europe was invented by Alan Steel and produced by Personal Software Services (PSS) in 1985. Like Raid Over Moscow, it can be played at three levels of difficulty. The instruction booklet that comes along with the game tells us, in a matter-of-fact sort of way, that it 'covers the first 30 days of the next war in Europe'. You can choose to command NATO or the Warsaw Pact forces, though the instruction booklet assumes you choose NATO. As in all such games, the computer takes the other side. It's claimed that the game is a fairly realistic simulation based on military statistics and that these show the Warsaw Pact as having a massive military superiority over NATO. (The truth seems to be that there is rough, overall parity between the two but, of course, this is without counting the USA's military strength around the world in non-NATO countries.) The main screen shows a map of Europe with army units — blue for NATO and red for the Warsaw Pact — in position, most of them confronting one another along the border between West and East Germany. (There are also off-screen air units in the game.) Interestingly, the aims of the two antagonists are different: the Warsaw Pact has to take over West Germany while NATO has to prevent this. In other words, the Warsaw Pact has an offensive role and NATO a defensive one. So, if you take the Warsaw Pact side you have to play more aggressively. You can choose to have 'action screens' in a game, in which case you have battlefield scenes and can take part by fighting in the familiar zapping way. However, the basic game with its different phases — moving, attacking, rebuilding — is, in structure, rather like some of the more complicated board war games. In an attack, the stronger unit wins, though this can be modified by use of the action screens. At the end of the game, you get a percentage rating which represents your ability as commander.

We can now go on to some particular features of Theatre Europe. A 'special missions' phase allows you to use chemical and nuclear warfare. In the case of a 'strategic chemical launch', there's no control over where the gas will go but, while the game was being demonstrated to me, one such launch from NATO, for instance, landed on Moscow, which afterwards became uninhabitable. By taking this option, however, you do run the risk of one of two kinds of nuclear response. In the case of a 'strategic nuclear launch', the scene changes from the map to a city skyline, the missiles rain down and a mushroom cloud rises. I saw Paris destroyed in such an attack by the Warsaw Pact (played by the computer in this case). I also saw the Warsaw Pact put 'Fire-plan Warm Puppy', the other kind of response, into operation. This involves the launching of most missiles from one side or the other (as opposed to a nuclear strike on one target) and you are warned that the 'enemy' reaction will be extreme. In this instance, the nuclear exchange led to the 'probable onset of nuclear winter' and the 'end of twentieth century civilization'. However, you could 'press space bar to try again'! (This is the least realistic feature of the game.)

The whole matter of nuclear weapons is significant in Theatre Europe and obviously some effort has been put into making their use less attractive than it might be, and less of an easy option. This doesn't seem to me to be the main problem, or the only one. However — to continue. I've mentioned nuclear attacks carried out by the computer in retaliation. If, on the other hand, the player wishes to start one, there's a certain procedure to be gone through which is part and parcel of the approach to nuclear weapons taken by the inventor of this game. In order to gain access to the 'nuclear fire missions', the 'nuclear authorization code' has to be tapped into the computer. You can get this by phone and the number — which is (0203) 668405 — is given on the screen. However, it isn't quite as easy as that. When you ring up, you hear a recording which begins with the music of John Lennon's song, 'Give Peace a Chance'. (This is also played over the title screen.) Then, a man's voice interrupts the 'programme' to announce the breakdown of the Geneva talks aimed at preventing the escalation of the 'northern war' into a nuclear confrontation. He adds that there's a strong possibility of a nuclear strike on Britain and goes on to tell us, amongst other advice on what to do, that 'non-essential personnel' (who are they?) should remain indoors. He, in turn, is interrupted by a grinding noise and then we hear a baby crying. Lastly, a woman's voice says, 'if this is really what you want', and gives the nuclear authorization code, 'midnight sun'. I believe that, at first, the code was only available by phone but now it appears, not very prominently, in the instruction booklet. This, I understand, is because owners of the game abroad can't really be expected to ring the number, which is in Coventry. (By December 1986, the recording had been changed, though not in any very significant way.) Further, on the attitude to war taken in the game, there are two or three references in the instruction booklet whereby the inventor and manufacturer seek to avoid the possible, or probable, accusation of irresponsibility. For instance, the game is 'dedicated to the people of the world in the hope that the game is never played for real'. To me, promoting war games and making profits out of them and at the same time claiming a moral purpose seems like having your cake and eating it.

I discussed Theatre Europe with Richard Cockayne, the managing director of PSS. He agreed on the 'implicit assumptions', as he put it, in the defensive and aggressive roles allotted, respectively, to NATO and the Warsaw Pact, and said that Europe provided a 'convenient scenario' for the war. In line with the face-saving attitude to war just noted, he claimed the game was 'educational'.

When Theatre Europe first came onto the market, there was hostility in some sections of the press, where the game was regarded as dangerously irresponsible, and three national chain stores — Boots, John Menzies and Woolworths — wouldn't sell it. W H Smiths, however, had no such scruples and they, along with independent traders, helped to sell over 10,000 copies of the game during a period of about a month after it first appeared. Later, Cockayne told me that Theatre Europe had been a 'fairly comprehensive success'. It did get good reviews in trade and hobby publications and, as 'best strategy game of 1985', it won the Golden Joystick Award of the magazine, *Computer and Video Games.* Newsfield, the publishers of three other computer magazines, awarded it the same title in the same year and also in 1986. By the end of that year, five versions were available for different computers.

With regard to the way in which the Soviet Union and the United States (or the Warsaw Pact and NATO) are cast in the role of enemies at war in microprocessor games, we should note that the board game, Nato, presented us with a similar scenario. I might add that, apparently, the Soviet Union can still be the 'enemy', even if not named as such. In *The Winners' Book of Video Games,* which is frantic, childish and reactionary, and all the more disturbing for that, Craig Kubey, the author, writes that there are 35 million, mainly young men, in the USA fighting against 'aliens, flying saucers and World War III attacks from Russia'. This is in spite of the fact, which he acknowledges, that manufacturers — of arcade and home video games in this case — seldom name an enemy. Atari uses the word 'sputniks' for its satellites in Missile Command but there are few pointers of this sort. Nevertheless Kubey is determined to believe he's fighting 'Russians'.

Next, we turn to the ideological influence that may be brought to bear through the actual mechanism of these games; the way they work, as distinct from the subjects or themes they deal with, their form rather than their content. With certain categories of computer games — what might be called strategic war games such as Theatre Europe, for example, as well as games like Kingdom, described in chapter eight — thinking on the part of the player, at least to some degree or other, is necessary. With virtually all other microprocessor games, thinking in any meaningful sense isn't even possible and all that players have to do is react. Adeline Naiman, in an excellent article on home and arcade video games, puts this very well. Having stated that 'video games control children', she asks, 'What do these games teach their avid players?' and answers:

> they teach automatic responses. With almost no accompanying text or instruction, they lead the player into responding to a stimulus, like a mouse repeated-

ly pressing the pleasure button. The player hasn't time to think, only to respond. You develop eye-hand reflexes that are amazingly quick. This is useful in warfare, doubtless. So is automatic obedience.[5]

The point has not been lost on those with a special interest in warfare, as Ronald Reagan disclosed in a speech he made in 1983:

> I recently learned something quite interesting about video games. Many young people have developed incredible hand, eye, and brain coordination in playing those games. The air force believes these kids will be our outstanding pilots should they fly our jets.[6]

Bound up with this question of unthinking responses is the fact that — except for the categories of computer games just referred to — microprocessor games happen in 'real time', that is, time within a game is the same as actual time and what takes five minutes, say, in a game would take five minutes if it was happening (and if it could happen) in real life. This is very different from the situation in table war games, for instance.

While the games — again the real-time games — can be said to control the players, that doesn't mean the players feel powerless. There's the sense of power that comes through being at the controls and making things happen. This seems to me to be an important factor in these games. In practice, it's the power of life or death or, rather, just of death. Do we take the next step and say it's a joy in killing that these games provide?

Of course, such games envelop the player in a menacing and hostile environment, but things don't have to be like that. Put very simply, you could say that each of these games involves bringing illuminated shapes on a screen into contact. It doesn't follow that one shape has to eliminate another. Touching can involve caresses as well as blows, construction as well as destruction, after all.

Sound effects make up a distinctive feature in microprocessor games and manufacturers pay considerable attention to this. A 1980 press release from CGL, for instance, referring to Galaxy Invaders, says that 'a "strike" by missile on invader results in a suitably satisfying "explosion" ' and that, in general, 'a veritable orchestra of sound effects adds to the excitement'. The sounds are usually those made by weapons, bullets, shells and missiles and all kinds of military vehicles and craft. However, as we've seen with the US anthem in Raid Over Moscow and 'Give Peace a Chance' in Theatre Europe, music has its contribution to make within the general framework of the games. Lighting effects, often in connection with explosions, are also peculiar to microprocessor games and both light and sound are used to reinforce the messages of the games. Also, both operate at a semi-conscious kind of level and help to bring about the complete absorption of the player in the game, which is a characteristic of real-time games in particular. Related to this is the fact that the player is occupied non-stop, and frantically, from start to finish. You don't have to wait your turn, as in most games, and there's no time for reflection. These factors all help to explain how the drug-like effect is brought about.

Kubey, whose book I referred to earlier, can perhaps give us an inkling of this effect. He says that, when firing at a flying saucer in Asteroids, 'it has been found useful to yell, "Die, Fat Boy!" ' Otherwise, he describes the enemy as 'disgusting perverts', 'creeps', 'weirdos' or 'aliens'. His attitude is partly joky and tongue-in-cheek but how else could a 32-year-old man pass off such stuff? On the whole, Kubey may be too outlandish to be typical. I hope so.

We now consider the social context of these games: first, the immediate context of clubs, books and magazines; then, the economic background; and lastly, moving further away from the games themselves, the links with other aspects of children's cultural surroundings.

The clubs connected with microprocessor games, like the fashion doll clubs, are concerned, above all, with promotion and profit. They are normally run by the manufacturers who seize on some well-tried dodges likely to catch the interest of children in this society. So, in 1983 for example, the CGL Fun Club was running schemes involving the award of Master Gamer certificates for a qualifying score, or time, and this was for each game they dealt in. After qualifying, you could go on for the British record in the game of your choice. In the same year, the Parker Video Games Club, in its first news-letter, was advertising T- shirts, cartridge holders and score pads (as 'free', 'special' or such-like offers); also printing information from young players and photos of them; running competitions; and giving news about forthcoming games. Still in 1983, the Atari Owners' Club had over 200,000 members and produced bi-monthly news-letters, and there was also as Intellivision Game Club.

It's neither possible nor necessary to give an overall picture of the books and magazines that have been published as a result of the boom in microprocessor games, but a couple of references in passing will help to cast more light on the subject. One book, *The Player's Strategy Guide to Atari VCS Home Video Games* by Arnie Katz and Bill Kunkel was published by Penguin in 1982 and is of interest for two reasons, apart from the information it contains. Firstly, it's a surprisingly specialized book for such a popular imprint, which shows what a following the games had attracted by then and, secondly, it had been published, earlier but not long before, in the USA, and so indicates which way the prevailing winds of popular culture were blowing. *The Winners' Book of Video Games,* referred to above, was also published in Britain in 1982 and also published first in the USA a short time before.

At about this time, the boom in these games was reaching its highest pitch. Some idea of the extent of their appeal internationally — and an even better idea of the amount of money spent on promoting them, perhaps — might be gained from the fact that world Pac-Man championships were held in Paris in 1982. (The winner was a 16-year-old boy from Manchester.) We shouldn't forget that demands are created, and that the size of the demand bears a relation to the amount of money put into creating it. In each of the years 1982 and 1983, Atari spent over £4 million on advertising and promotion. There's also a relationship between such expenditure and the price you have to pay for the products. Prices and, therefore, profits are high because so much is spent on advertising and promotion. *These* costs are large in order to sell highly-priced goods. Such relationships are particularly true when it comes to microprocessor games. So, for instance, the retail cost of Galaxy Invaders, the hand-held game mentioned earlier in connection with sound effects and in which the player defends the earth against invaders from space, was £22.95 at the beginning of 1980. Since then, of course, defence costs have gone up enormously. The first two Star Wars video games — Star Wars: Jedi Arena and Star Wars: The Empire Strikes Back — were produced by Palitoy under the Parker brand name in 1982 and cost £29.95 each. Two more cartridges were to follow, based on *Return of the Jedi*.

This brings us to the question of wider links with other aspects of a child's surroundings. We've just seen the link with films but, in this case, it should be noted that, before the official Star Wars video games, the films had had a considerable influence on space war games in general. Then, making a link with toys, it's interesting to meet with an old soldier in an unusual role: Action Man in the Palitoy video game, we're told, 'takes on his arch enemy in the form of a giant COBRA snake'. There are even links with food. In 1985, tins of Heinz Invaders (pasta shapes in tomato sauce, resembling space craft) were on sale in the supermarkets. This might seem rather frivolous but it's all part of the surroundings, the cultural atmosphere. Certainly, links with the US military aren't at all frivolous. We've met with Reagan's view of the usefulness of video games enthusiasts. A more direct link is the fact that Atari works with the US army in adapting video games for training purposes.

At this point, we look at alternatives again. Airbase Invader is a computer game produced by CP Software, in 1984. It's described on the cassette inlay card as 'non-sexist, non-violent, satirical, arcade adventure'. (Here 'arcade' means that the game is of the type found in arcades. The word is often used in this manner.) The card also gives us a summary of the plot:

> President Raygun clones are on the loose amongst the bunkers beneath USAF airbase Greenham Common, with one thought only upon their collective minds — to find the red nuclear attack button and signal the end of the world. Fortunately for humankind, our hero, Annie, has worked her way through the barbed wire and armed guards into the complex of bunkers and is set to use her feminine charms on the president Raygun clones and save the world from Armageddon.

The player takes the part of Annie, the 'peace woman'. Ranged against her are Harry Hardnose, 'photographer of the gutter press'; Old Bill who is trying to 'nick her'; the Iron Lady; and the 'squaddies', all called Tommy Gunn.

The main features of the game are simple. Annie blows kisses (red hearts) to destroy her opponents while they kill her by bumping into her or, in the case of Tommy Gunn, shooting her. She has three lives and can gain points by gathering food, drink, maps and secret documents, though these don't seem to help her in her overall objective. A dubious feature of Airbase Invader is that the Iron Lady can't be disposed of at all.

A representative of the firm told me that this game was an 'inspiration' and a 'one-off', and that CP Software has no general policy for producing such games. On a different occasion, another representative of the firm told me that the big stores said this game was 'political' and wouldn't take it. I hope it's clear by now that all games embody ideas about life and society and therefore all are political, to some degree. At least, the politics are on the surface in Airbase Invader and thus are open to question whereas most of the other microprocessor games — most games, in fact — are full of assumptions taken for granted.

There are other matters that need our attention in this game. For instance (and it's perhaps already apparent) the main elements of Airbase Invader are the same as in typical zapping games. There's a conflict which involves the elimination of opponents; there are missiles, which are kisses in this case; there's shooting; and there are the familiar collisions. Furthermore, Annie has a number of lives and she scores points by collecting various items. Even though these elements are used towards what is, for games, a very unusual end — the prevention of nuclear war — there must, I think, still be some question of whether it'll be just another zapping game to children or whether they'll actually be struck by the fact that, for a change, they're on the side of peace, so to speak. In other words, does the mechanism of the game, the medium, carry the message or, rather, does it carry a different message? Is this new wine, but in old bottles? All this may seem grudging, in the face of an original and praiseworthy game, and the young lad who demonstrated it to me was aware of its novel implications — they could scarcely be overlooked — but I can't say what effect they had. Even if I could, it wouldn't prove anything, as different individuals heed the messages conveyed by games to varying degrees and it's the general effect on a large number of people that matters. Looking at the question in this way, the important point is that, for every game that says 'peace' there are clearly thousands that say 'war'.

Deus ex Machina, produced by Automata in 1984, is something quite unusual. It consists of two cassettes, one audio for a cassette player and one, carrying the graphics, for a computer and these have to be synchronized. The result, which lasts about an hour, is a game but much more besides. On the audio cassette there's a play in which Ian Dury, Frankie Howerd and E P Thompson take part and this, along with the music and lyrics, is the work of Mel Croucher, one of Automata's directors. Andrew Stagg wrote the computer programme which is the visual part. In a handout on Deus ex Machina, Croucher says, 'It is non-violent, non-sexist, positive, provoking and funny: the antidote to the numbing "games" of computer-simulated destruction which I personally find sickening'. The text of the play is provided with the game and part of it reads, 'Killing is wrong, even pretend killing on little screens. And people that sell violent games to children should be put away somewhere safe, till they get well again'.

As a whole, the text is based on the speech, from Shakespeare's As You Like It, beginning with the words, 'All the world's a stage' and going on to describe the 'seven ages' of 'one man' from 'infant' to 'second childishness'. In the game, the

257

player has, first, to bring about conception and then to nurture the subject through the various stages from conception to death. The cursor on the screen has to be guided, sometimes, very interestingly, nudging and caressing the subject to maintain life and at other times protecting it from the police who are trying to hunt it down.

Not many children, or only older ones, would be able to gain much from this extraordinary attempt to stretch the bounds of what can be done through computer games. Most importantly, Deus ex Machina proves that microprocessor games in general don't have to be restricted to conflict and destruction and that the form of the games, as well as the content, can be changed. The way the cursor is used is the crucial factor here.

Unfortunately, although Deus ex Machina was very favourably reviewed, it never really took flight as the wholesalers wouldn't give it the necessary backing. Automata had an overall policy of producing non-violent games. At the beginning of 1986, the company was struggling to survive and Croucher had left.

The boom times have gone, for microprocessor games, and they now occupy a more modest corner of the games market (though a casual check I carried out, in February 1989, revealed no fewer than six magazines devoted, wholly or mainly, to *computer* games, which shows how things are developing). In 1982, when microprocessor games, as a whole, were just about at their peak, the average life of each new hand-held game was about two months, a situation which led to a constant search for gimmicks but all too seldom to genuine creative approaches. Towards the end of 1984, Croucher noted, in a Play for Life newsletter, that the proportion of overtly violent games amongst the best sellers was falling. The writing was on the wall. Nevertheless, this part of the games industry showed itself unable to develop beyond the basic idea, albeit with thousands of variations, of zapping the 'enemy' or 'aliens'. What happened to Deus ex Machina is very much to the point here, as it illustrates what was wrong. As if to underline the writing on the wall, the trend away from violent games has continued and still fewer, in proportion, are being bought. And if most manufacturers have been unable to rise to the occasion, it's encouraging that the consumers have, in the end, got fed up with their wares.

References

1   Reported by Camilla Berens in *City Limits*, London, 7-13 February 1986, p.11.

2   Bruce Hollands, 'Superpower: A History of the Game of Foreign Policy', *White Dwarf*, London, no. 74, February 1986, p.5.

3   Lloyd Osbourne (introduction) 'Stevenson at Play', *Scribner's Magazine*, New York, vol. 24, December 1898, p.709.

4   Reported by Simon Hoggart in *The Observer*, London, 6 February 1983, p.27.

5   Adeline Naiman, 'Video Games: Mindless, Macho, Militaristic', *Interracial Books for Children Bulletin*, New York, vol. 13 nos 6 and 7, 1982, p.27.

6   Ronald Reagan, speaking to students in Florida, 8 March 1983, quoted in Mark Green and Gail MacColl (eds) *There He Goes Again:* Ronald Reagan's Reign of Error, New York, Pantheon 1983, p.45.

PART THREE

PART THREE

CHAPTER 12
CONCLUSION

Here, in this chapter, my task is to try to draw together the main threads of this study. As I see it, there are five main aspects to be considered: cultural imperialism; the international character of the toys and games industry (these two are closely related); the modern marketing strategies of the larger toy and game manufacturers; the links between children's playthings and the wider world of culture and politics; and the all-important matter of aggression. The ideology carried in toys and games (the word will be taken to include puzzles) is, overwhelmingly, expressed in terms of gender roles and the most crucial of these is the masculine, aggressive role.

Cultural imperialism
By cultural imperialism, I mean the export of an ideology from a rich and powerful country to a number of other countries, in this case by means of children's playthings. Naturally, the country concerned must dominate the other countries economically (which usually means militarily, as well). In fact, there's a sense in which economic domination almost inevitably involves cultural domination.

As far as toys and games are concerned, there are only a few countries — perhaps five or six — which are major producers, with the United States being the main one by far. Others are Japan, France and West Germany. Britain is also a major producer which, according to information put out by the British Toy and Hobby Manufacturers' Association in 1978 and again in 1984, was exporting toys and games to over 150 countries. It should be noted, however, that such exports would not necessarily originate in Britain. They could be made here on licence from a US firm, for instance.

The firm of Spears, for example, which could hardly be thought of as a multinational, in 1979 had agents, representatives or distributors in 18 countries and in seven Caribbean islands. In 1982, Fisher-Price claimed that their toys were sold in about 80 countries. The ideological implications can be seen if we take a particular instance. Palitoy reported in 1983 that they were selling a lot of 'traditional British-style dolls' in 'Korea' (I presume South Korea is meant), Nigeria and Papua New Guinea. It's impossible to say how many of these were bought by white residents and it's doubtful whether many of the people of those countries would be able to afford them. In terms of race and cultural identity, however, this must have some significance. More specifically, Palitoy reported that Tiny Tears, their white, toddler doll, was popular with the Chinese in Hong Kong, as well as with European residents.

Of course, other major ideas, values and attitudes, as well as those to do with race, are carried from one country to another by means of toys and games and I've indicated what these ideological strands are in the course of analysing particular playthings, such as Barbie, Sindy and Monopoly. In these cases, and in some others, I've given details of the extent to which playthings are marketed throughout the world. It can be assumed, however, that most of the present-day toys and games I've dealt with are sold widely throughout the capitalist world and this should be kept in mind. Something else that shouldn't be forgotten is that cultural imperialism takes place in other fields also — in films and television programmes, for instance, and in all kinds of popular entertainment.

And another thing! We shouldn't overlook the fact that, in countries with a class structure, there is such a thing as internal cultural imperialism, by means of which the dominant or establishment ideology is dinned into the have-nots to get them to believe that they are undeserving. The actual process is always the same and involves the destruction of a native or folk culture and its replacement by a commercial culture. Toys and games play a big part in this process.

Multinational manœuvres

I've said that only a few countries dominate the market. It's just as true to say that only a few firms do, and we now come to focus more strongly on the international character of the toys and games industry and the ways in which the multinationals work.

Even the larger firms in the industry are usually part of still larger commercial concerns which basically have nothing to do with toys or games. So — to take examples from the end of 1982 — the Ideal company was part of the Columbian Broadcasting System, Fisher-Price belonged to Quaker Oats, and Palitoy was owned by General Mills Inc. The picture is continually changing, at least amongst the subsidiaries and smaller or not-quite-so-enormous firms. Parent companies change in their composition, though they are not so likely to be taken over. However, the general rule — bigger fish eat smaller fish — applies. It so happens that most of the bigger fish, like the three I've just mentioned, hail from the USA.

If we narrow the focus still further, and look at the Palitoy/General Mills connection, we'll be able to see some important details. First of all, a few years before 1982, Palitoy's Action Man products were being manufactured or sold in over 13 countries (see p. 128). Palitoy itself made Action Man under licence from the CPG Products Corporation, a subsidiary of General Mills Inc. (Palitoy was a 'division' of General Mills.) At that time, the parent company had 71 subsidiaries, and subsidiaries of subsidiaries, in 22 countries, including Bermuda and Hong Kong. General Mills was concerned with food mainly (one firm appeared to specialize in shrimps) but its interests ran also to insurance, textiles, crafts, jewelry, wallpaper and, as we know, toys and games.

I've been careful to specify the date, the end of 1982, because of the ever-changing situation. By mid-1986, Palitoy had gone and so had the interest in toys and games. These changes throw more light on the subject — but first we glance back. In the late 1960s, General Mills decided to go into toys and games and started to buy up firms which produced these, such as Parker Brothers in the USA and Palitoy, Denys Fisher and Chad Valley in Britain as well as companies in Australia, New Zealand, Canada, Mexico, France, West Germany, Holland and Belgium. For the most part, the firms taken over continued to trade under their own names. Palitoy itself acted in much the same way as its parent company, gobbling up Airfix in 1981. (Airfix had swallowed Meccano which had swallowed Dinky.) Then, mysteriously, at the end of 1985, General Mills decided to move out of toys and games and, by the beginning of 1986, Palitoy had become Kenner Parker (UK), a division of Kenner Parker Toys International based in the USA.

At this same time, to give some further idea of the sort of thing that goes on, Salters, which had been described by *Toys International and the Retailer* in January 1984 as 'one of the few wholly independent and wholly British toy companies that remain', had just been bought up by Peter Pan (seemingly another British company, however). Also, Hasbro and Milton Bradley had become associated under a holding company, Hasbro-Bradley, although they were to continue operating separately, at least for the time being. Still with the focus on early 1986 — Pedigree was in danger but was eventually bought up by a consortium, thus ensuring a future for Sindy who, as we've seen, was later to fall into the hands of Hasbro.

The general point here is that most toys and games are the products of a system over which the general public has no democratic control, an irresponsible system motivated, not by children's needs, but by profit. No wonder most teachers and other educationists have ignored the world of toys and games. It's had very little to offer them. I think they are wrong, however, in not, at least, recognizing its negative aspects, the way in which it makes their work more difficult.

Commercial developments on an international level, such as the ones just noted, are not new, except in scale. Through toys and games, these developments threaten to impose, on children throughout much of the world, a uniform culture, narrow and limited, selfish and shallow, and aggressive.

This culture reaches into every corner of children's lives, as never before. One of the mechanisms which help to ensure this is character merchandising which I've already mentioned. Here again, however, it's necessary to note that this is now on a never-before-seen scale. In the three years to the end of 1983, for example, character merchandise overall grew by 300 per cent and toys played a significant part in that growth. One character or concept — Mr. T, say, or Masters of the Universe — can have as many as 200, or even more, spin-offs. My Little Pony was a best-selling toy for girls throughout 1985. Over 65 manufacturers held licences to produce over 200 My Little Pony items in a range of categories as diverse as confectionery, clothing, party paperware, household furnishings and crockery. As for the ponies themselves — we know how children don't like to feel left out of things and it must be very hard on a little girl to be the only one in her class without one. Parents, however enlightened, are placed in impossible situations over matters such as this and the general My Little Pony atmosphere, created through character merchandising, makes it all the worse.

Against this background of commercial structures and developments, and as an example of cultural imperialism, I'll cite the inroads that have been made into the British toys and games industry by US firms. (I should perhaps add that this is not out of any patriotic motives — Britain doesn't differ all that much, ideologically, in any case — but just because I happen to know more about this particular example.) What concerns me, overall, with the necessity for urgent changes in the toys and games industry in mind, is that the more the industries in any given state are foreign-owned the less influence that state has over its own future. In other words, foreign firms are less answerable to public control.

As regards Britain and the United States, the commercial connections go back a long way, and some of them have been mentioned in the course of this study. Here, however, I'll concentrate on recent years. According to an article in *The Economist* of 25 December 1982, it was estimated that, by 1981, 21 per cent of the British toys and games market had been taken over by five US companies: Palitoy, Fisher-Price, Ideal, Milton Bradley and Atari. As we've seen, the first three of these were then part of multinationals. The general picture at the time was of a sales slump in which a few big industrial enterprises got even bigger. Revell was another US company well established in Britain at the same time. It had claimed in 1979 to be the world's largest manufacturer of plastic model kits. The previous year, so it was claimed, the British subsidiary itself was selling to over 60 countries. Mattel, with Barbie, was also well established here in 1981 and they brought us He-Man in 1983. Since that time, Hasbro, with My Little Pony and The Transformers, has also become very much part of the toy scene. More recently, in 1985, the very large US firm of Coleco has set up in Britain. The company's enormously profitable Cabbage Patch Kids had already been on sale here for about two years and in 1986 they brought us the macho, militaristic and vicious Rambo range.

Thinking more particularly of games, the Parker range was introduced into Britain in 1970 and, after one year, had gained 10 per cent of the market. Of course, certain games, such as Monopoly, had been produced here on licence for many years. At about the same time, Milton Bradley began to expand into Europe. In the four years up to, and including 1980, they captured about 30 per cent of the games market in Britain. Avalon Hill, with its vast assortment of board war games, first exhibited at the Earls Court Toy and Hobby Fair in 1979. They now seem to have become established.

If the United States can do this in Britain, which is a wealthy country and which already had a strong toys and games industry, how can most other countries hope to survive the economic and, of course, cultural and ideological onslaught of the USA? The pattern outlined here has happened in other industries, as well, but in the case of toys and games we are, in the end, talking about children's minds.

Marketing strategies

The overall marketing strategies used by the companies concerned, and the implications of these, should also be noted. First of all, let it be said, there are large purses to be won. During the period covered by this study, the amount spent by the British public on toys and games steadily crept up to approximately £922 million in 1987. It could reach £1 billion in 1989. Likewise, the stakes are high. Palitoy claimed that, in 1984, they would be spending over £10 million on promotion. In 1986, Mattel said they would be spending the same amount on promoting toys and that the sum represented 35 per cent of all toy advertising in Britain in the first half of the year. Of this amount, £7.7 million was to go on television advertising. No doubt Barbie would be heavily involved. Thus, Mattel aimed to boost retail sales of their products to over £100 million, twice that of 1985. Several of Hasbro's products were permanently in the best-selling lists in 1985. The company attributed this to heavy year-round promotion. At the beginning of 1986, Frank Martin, the group marketing director at Hasbro-Bradley, said they were intending to invest even more heavily in television, 'because [their] results have proved it is possible to create wide and virtually immediate demand by this method'. The important word here, I think, is 'create'.

It's sometimes easy to miss the obvious so we shouldn't fail to note that, in this illustration of the process of cultural imperialism, children's needs don't enter into the picture. We can develop this point further by considering a particular business tactic. Optimus Prime, a leading figure in the Transformer concept, was so much in demand for Christmas 1985 that supplies ran short. Nevertheless, by early 1986 it had already been decided to replace the figure by Ultra Magnus, in accordance with the tactic of killing off toys when they reach a sales peak. This, it can be said, is catering for children's *wants* (which are created by advertising and publicity). But then these wants are displaced by other wants (artificially created again) the whole operation being designed to set up a puppet-like consumerism, and a condition of endless dissatisfaction. To state the obvious again, the overriding motive is increasing profits, not catering for children's *needs* which — let's not forget — are not the same as children's wants.

A word about recent developments in marketing strategies will complete the picture, as far as the operations of the toy and game industry are concerned.

The trend in toy manufacturing over the last 20 years or so and where figures of any kind are involved, has been towards complete toy systems, or concepts. We've seen how these work, in the case of Strawberry Shortcake and the fashion dolls, for example, and with Action Force and Masters of the Universe. This is the most vital area to look at in the toy world because children can identify with figures and because an ideology can be readily presented to children through such means. (In fact, it would be impossible to have figures which didn't embody ideas and values of some kind.) The toy concept ensures that a more comprehensive view of the world can be presented and therefore this recent development is potentially a very powerful force in the shaping of children's minds. It's time now to summarize the main features of this approach to the selling of toys, and ideas.

28: Glitter 'n' Gold Jem

One main figure will probably be at the centre of a toy concept. It will, most likely, be made of plastic but it can be a soft toy made up of a variety of fabrics and stuffings or, it may be made of rubber, or there can be versions in any or all of these materials, or mixtures of them, and there may also be different sizes in each. Then, there can be: other figures and perhaps domestic or pet animals, especially dogs, horses or ponies; outfits, neverendingly, for any or all of these; playsets; vehicles; and accessories for any or all of the items mentioned. The figures, these days, are likely to come with names and characters, and clothing to match, and probably with a place in a ready-made story as well. Sometimes, such marketing tactics are foisted onto the most unlikely toys, so, for instance, we get the ready-made, free-floating fantasies of My Little Pony and, even more unlikely, the fond whimsy of the Care Bears. Such toy concepts leave very little to the imagination and they are likely, if anything, to give rise to ritual, rather than play. I say 'if anything' because it's difficult to know what children can do when they've got a concept toy; except get another, of course — which is just what the manufacturer wants. So children go on collecting, or consuming, and the profits mount up. (Once it was quite usual for a doll to come without name, character or story, and probably with little or nothing in the way of clothing either, and it was up to the child, and the child's family, to provide whatever was needed.)

Nowadays, toy systems such as the ones I've mentioned often start at a fairly advanced stage. Hasbro's fashion doll concept, Jem, for example, which first went on sale in late spring 1986, began with: eight different, clothed dolls with figure-stands, which came with extra outfits or accessories, or both; 24 additional outfits, eight of them convertible (by removing, reversing or re-arranging garments); two playsets which included various accessories; and a car (see illustration). A cassette of 'Jem music' came with every doll except the main one, Jem, but, in this case, it could be obtained, as a limited offer, by sending proof of purchase. There was also a competition to win videos of 'fabulous Jem music'. The whole was held together by a storyline with an already will developed conflict situation, set in the world of pop music.

The fictional element in toy concepts deserves further attention here. Conflict, of some sort, seems to be the germ of all fiction and, with toy concepts, it's usually of a simple good versus evil kind. However, it's important to note the form this takes. Such a good and evil conflict situation in the case of the Jem concept, for instance, is on a small scale, as this is for girls. In fact, it's more a matter of nice against nasty than good versus evil. Simply, Jem — who has a dual identity, by the way, like Superman, Batman and others — leads her nice pop group, the Holograms, against their nasty rivals, the Misfits.

The fiction which sustains the Transformers is on an altogether grander scale, as usual for boys — the heroic Autobots battle against the evil Decepticons for possession of the world. This is a framework familiar from comic books, and the object of the struggle is the same as that of certain board games. In so far as the story-line involves the invasion of the earth by robots from a distant planet, it recalls the basic set-up of many microprocessor games with their alien invaders. Even these recent toy concepts, therefore, having nothing really new to offer, in the way of fiction.

267

Returning from the fictional element to the general summary of toy concepts, we should note that it's easy for manufacturers to expand these, either just by adding more figures, by introducing different categories of figures or figures in supporting or parallel groups. So, we get 'teams', as in Action Force or, developing from Masters of the Universe, the Evil Horde and (for 'little girls') the Princess of Power collection. Further vehicles, playsets and so on then follow.

A club with badges, newsletters and competitions is a possible development, of a different sort, in connection with a toy concept.

If a given concept didn't start in films, or in a television series or fiction, in the first place, then it's likely — in the case of a popular success (which, these days, means one heavily advertised, especially on television) — that it will have a further lease of life in these areas. The move from toy concepts to full-length films is a very recent stratagem seen, for example, in the case of My Little Pony and the Care Bears.

A popular success in the toy world, whatever the origin, will be promoted further, as we've seen, by character merchandising, and the likeness, name or logo, or, more likely, all of these, will be licensed out for use in the production of, for example: other toys, games and puzzles, including trundlers, tricycles and bikes; clothing, especially T-shirts, playclothes and nightwear; jewelry, cosmetics and toiletries; watches; school equipment, including pencils, pencil sharpeners, rubbers and rulers, together with holders for these; stationery; food and drink containers and crockery; food cartons and wrappings, especially those for snack foods and confectionery; clocks and tape recorders; bedclothes; wallpaper; and practically any other products that children are likely to meet with in their everyday lives.

Thus, what the toys stand for, the way of looking at the world presented to children through them, and especially what they have to say about gender roles, is reinforced and repeated at every turn.

Games, of necessity, follow a different pattern. An overall summary of the main aspects, from a manufacturers' and social point of view, will complete the picture here. Commercially successful games will be produced in de luxe and travel versions and will be redesigned, repackaged or updated in some way from time to time (as fashion dolls are, for example). Also, there will be foreign language versions. However, the main line of development will be through clubs and via competitions and tournaments at local, national and international level. A game with all of these aspects would be fully developed commercially. Magazines might accompany this process, though it isn't usual for a game to have a magazine all to itself.

From the foregoing, it's clear that there isn't much point in asking, in general, whether children are influenced more by their friends or parents, by television, by comics and other fiction, or by games rather than toys; or — you might as well add — by bubble-gum wrappers, rather than cereal packets. Or, more particularly, if children are obviously influenced by He-Man, can we say it's the He-Man toy figure and not the He-Man in comics or the one in television cartoons? It isn't possible to make distinctions of this kind, broad or narrow, and children can be influenced by any or all of these.

A war culture

The complex of ideas, attitudes and values — the ideology — bound up in children's playthings, and carried by the process of cultural imperialism, has been analysed in this book as a whole. It's now time to begin to move towards the major aspect of this ideology — aggression — and to see it in a wider context.

Children in Britain, and male children in particular, are brought up in a war culture. This is part of a general atmosphere of aggression, which is closely based on the masculine gender role. The aggression, in turn, grows out of a system of competition which shows itself in every corner of society. This situation is, it seems to me, even more intense in the USA, and has its counterpart, to a lesser degree, in other capitalist states.

I've used the word 'atmosphere' because I think that aggression is just as pervasive as the atmosphere and, for the most part, just as unnoticeable, or unnoticed — that is, until you start looking into children's culture! An experience of mine will illustrate this. One day in October 1983, I was checking on the advertising of toys and games on television, during the children's programmes. One advertisement was presented in the form of a television news bulletin and called 'Action Force News'. It featured the Action Force figures in the style of news items about the early stages of the Falklands/Malvinas conflict. They were pictured as if embarking for the war zone and some of them were given the names they had in the *Battle Action Force* comic at the time. After this, I lingered a while and got caught up in the following part of the programme. This was a short play, lasting about 20 minutes, in which the boy hero constantly and proudly refers to the fact that his dad has been in the SAS. The boy is also shown as being strongly attached to his Airfix model kit which happened to be for making a Nazi German dive-bomber, the Stuka, from the second world war. One scene, quite incidentally, shows the boy and his father playing a video war game. This had nothing to do with the plot. In fact, there wasn't much of a plot at all but there was a strong emphasis on the interests, mood and thoughts of the boy. He thinks he might join the army when he grows up but, he says, his dad has told him that Britain probably won't have an army then and that they'll probably 'throw stones at the Russians and run'. That's about all there was to this play — but let's go over these two items, the advertisement and the play, to see what they add up to. The advertisement was for aggressive toys, it drew upon the real-life Falklands/Malvinas conflict (possibly giving an extra boost to army recruitment on the way) and it glanced at fiction in the form of a war comic. The play aligned us favourably with the SAS (another boost for recruitment, perhaps), gave prominence to a war toy with Nazi associations (free advertisement), and presented a video war game in an attractive light. The boy's leanings were towards the army but this part soon turned into cold war propaganda with the 'Russians' as the enemy. The theme running through all these elements is war, which we see in a male context and presented, very largely, through the masculine gender role of fighter. It all took place, on an ordinary day in an ordinary year. I have no reason to believe it was unusual or exceptional and no public outcry followed about the indoctrination of children or about bias in television programmes.

This is part of what I mean by war culture — the ordinary, everyday atmosphere of aggression — but there are other areas to be filled in, and connections to be made, in order to give a clearer picture.

With regard to aggression, we've already seen a good few connections between the world of toys and games and the adult world, most of them of a more direct kind than the ones just mentioned, which were to illustrate a general background of aggression. The Falklands/Malvinas conflict, in particular, has provided specific examples of the impact of actual events on both toys and games. Let it suffice here to add, in order to underline this kind of link, that the Palitoy catalogue in 1983 included a reference to the Parachute Regiment as 'winners of 2 V.C.s and many other awards in the Falklands war' as a selling point for Action Man's Parachute Regiment outfit.

At school, the pressures on children are generally more subtle, but not different. The war culture is here also. *Deadly Persuasion,* a penetrating and informed booklet by Greta Sykes, Helen Mercer and Jan Woolf, gives a telling analysis of school history textbooks in relation to the cold war. The authors express the overall problem as follows:

> the simple idea of the Soviet Union as 'enemy' and 'attacker' and the U.S. as friend and defender ... seems to be the message which the textbooks perpetuate. With few exceptions they operate with a scheme which moralistically determines the world as good and evil. The post-war world is basically divided into two sides and a rigid model established to interpret events.[1]

The 'message' here is the same as that of several board and computer games I've described, while the good and evil model is basic to all the major toy concepts: Star Wars, Action Force, Masters of the Universe and Transformers, for example. Such toy concepts are for small boys. Do they, I wonder, when they grow older, simply substitute actual states for the factions labelled good and evil in their toys (and comics)? History textbooks would seem to encourage this and it certainly makes for easy thinking. At the end of a shocking recital of lies, misrepresentations and omissions in school history textbooks, the authors conclude, 'to educate for peace is not indoctrination, far from it. The indoctrination already practised subtly educates for war'.

Other kinds of indoctrination in schools are not so subtle. The CND magazine, *Sanity,* reported in October 1982 that a missile regiment had taken a Lance missile, which can carry a nuclear warhead, to Matthew Humberstone Upper School at Cleethorpes in Humberside, to show to the children there. Presumably, the army had been invited to put on this display. At midsummer the following year one of the local free newspapers, in the district where I live, carried an article with the heading, 'Assault Course at Fun Day'. Contrary to what anyone might have expected, following such a title, there was no trace of irony in the article. It described how a battery cadet regiment had put on a display for the Tubbenden Infants and Junior

School, in the London Borough of Bromley, on the school's fun day which had been organized by the parents' association. The cadets, of course, were children as well, one who was mentioned being 13 years old. The article was illustrated by a large photo which showed cadets, and children from the school with their headmaster.

Again, I've no reason to believe such happenings are exceptional. I've made no effort to seek out material of this sort, nor have I checked on how many secondary schools still have cadet corps of their own.

There isn't space here to go into other aspects of the war culture that surrounds children, on television in general and in films, for example, but I've given particular instances along the way in this study, especially in chapter six. As for war comics, I analysed this very important aspect in *Catching Them Young* and the picture hasn't changed much since.[2]

The number of war toys and games, and the war culture of which they are part, reflect national, economic priorities, as might be expected. In Britain, in 1983, the Ministry of Defence was running 30 research establishments, and 40,000 scientists, out of 100,000, were working in 'defence'. In comparison with five other western European countries, Britain was bottom in all areas of government spending except defence, where it was, massively, top.

In Britain, systematic co-operation between governments or the military establishment on the one hand, and toy and game manufacturers on the other, is either not very common or kept very quiet. Such co-operation was taking place long ago, however, in the United States, as Carol R Andreas tells us in a very revealing article, 'War Toys and the Peace Movement':

> A Detroit [toy] buyer informed me in the spring of 1964 that military men from Washington attended the toy fairs to help promote military items and to offer their consultant services to those who wished to produce or display authentic military toys.[3]

Articles in the trade periodical, *Toys and Novelties*, pointed out that 'these services were available as part of the Defense departments's mandate "to promote wide public understanding of its objectives and accomplishments" '.[4] The toy manufacturers returned the help. Andreas, using information from *Toys and Novelties*, records that the Defense Department regularly purchased military toys for use in training and also that Mattel was 'expanding its line' to manufacture real weapons under contract to the United States government. Andreas also quotes a representative of Hassenfeld Brothers (later to become Hasbro), makers of the original GI Joe figure, as follows:

> Let me say that the United States government is extremely cooperative at all levels of its military structure, in helping any organization in any manner that it can. We ourselves have been working in close contact for a number of years with local officials in our own National Guard and Reserves, as well as military officials up through, and including, the Pentagon.[5]

Contacts, such as the ones referred to in this article by Andreas, are indications, I would say, of a fully developed war culture.

From this, it can be seen that banning war toys has to be considered as part of a much wider problem. Also, the argument which manufacturers of war toys put forward — that they're only catering for a demand — has some truth in it, but they also help to create that demand. It's a chicken and egg situation. In any case, this is a poor argument. Dealers in hard drugs also cater for a demand but not many people seem to think that that excuses them.

Aggression

Toys and games reflect this war culture and also play a large part in reproducing it; by socializing children into gender roles, in the first place, and then by conditioning boys into being aggressors.

We must now concentrate on the masculine role of aggressor, as a matter of urgency, I suggest, because if we don't manage to change it altogether it's likely to bring proceedings on the earth to a halt. Apart from the fact that this is an urgent matter, enough to justify all our attention at the moment, I must say that the question of male conditioning, in general, has been very much neglected. It isn't widely enough recognized that boys, and men, are emotionally crippled through the imposition of the role of fighter, or even that they are killed and maimed because of it. There may be other reasons for fighting but this has all too often been the only one — fulfilling a role. (It's worth noting, as well, that men also suffer when the breadwinner role is no longer available to them, as the suicide rate amongst unemployed men shows.) What I have to say here will, I hope, help to rectify this neglect of male conditioning.

We now, therefore, settle firmly on the theme of aggression and, first of all, I have to deal with some beliefs that have a bearing on the matter, especially since they are likely to get in the way of any new approach to children's toys and games.

Inevitably, aggression looms very large in the nature/nurture controversy which, in various aspects, has been going on for many years now. Briefly, it's a question of how much of human psychological make-up we inherit genetically — that is, how much is inborn; and how much we owe to influences in our environment — that is, our cultural and social and even our geographical surroundings. This is a vast area of knowledge and research and the subject of aggression, within it, is itself far too large to be dealt with here in anything like a thoroughgoing way. So, I'll merely point to the features which have a bearing on the matter in hand, which is the aggressive, masculine gender role as presented to boys through playthings.

The part of the nature/nurture controversy which relates to aggression has gone on largely within the fairly new study of ethology. This deals with the behaviour, especially of an automatic or instinctive kind, of animals, including humans; and especially as this behaviour is affected by their environment, social and otherwise. It is very much, I would say, the study of how animals relate to one another and of the factors which have a bearing on this. At the outset, however, it's important to

272

recognize that a definition of such a thing as instinct in humans, or even its existence, is very much open to question. Also, there's nothing in the way of undisputed scientific evidence to show that aggression is inherited.

Certain books have been at the centre of the debate about aggression: Konrad Lorenz's *On Aggression* (first published in English in 1966), Desmond Morris's *The Naked Ape* (1967), Robert Ardrey's *The Territorial Imperative* (1967), and *The Imperial Animal* by Lionel Tiger and Robin Fox (1972). I'll give some account of these books, after first making some general points.

These authors, while writing about human nature (whatever that is), usually base their arguments on other than human, animal species. Their opponents, while continually exposing these arguments, base their own views mainly on human behaviour. As this is the case, it's best to start with a summary of the situation amongst non-human species. As regards conflict between species, though 'conflict' is perhaps too strong a word, we have to take hunting into account; the fact that certain animals prey upon others. Also, different species compete and sometimes come into conflict over territory, though the reason is the food supply the territory provides rather than the territory itself. Within a species, certain groups or individuals may compete for territory, either — again — because it's a source of food or because it's a way of securing mates, or both. It isn't often that killing occurs within a species, as there are many inbuilt signals animals use to stop encounters short before they reach this stage. A dog will acknowledge defeat, for instance, by putting its tail between its legs.

Lorenz's theories are firmly based on animal behaviour, especially on the behaviour of the greylag goose. He believes that aggression is instinctive in all animals and, furthermore, that without necessarily being stimulated, it wells up from time to time and has to be expressed and so drained off. Because of the draining-off process, this idea of aggression has come to be known as the catharsis theory. It is, in fact, a widely held and seldom questioned view. There's evidence of it, for instance, in *The Good Toy Guide 1983*, where it's said of two punchballs that they are, respectively, 'wonderful for letting off steam' and 'great for releasing tension and energy'. Of course, children need exercise and need to use their plentiful energy but the words here, especially the 'letting off steam' figure of speech, do seem to point to the cathartic model of aggression. (It should be added that the punchballs are at least as likely to *prompt* aggressive behaviour.) Antonia Fraser, in her book, *A History of Toys*, gives unthinking support to the same notion. She 'feels', she says:

> that children are better off provided with safe guns, *to drain off their natural aggressiveness*, [my emphasis] than sheltered from things which will soon be apparent to them in the world around.[6]

Another instance of this widely held assumption about aggression came when, during a phone call to the British Association for Early Childhood Education in January 1982, I mentioned my concern about war toys. The woman I was talking to gave a superior chuckle and asked me, 'How do you cater for children's aggression?'

This common belief about aggression was obviously around for a long time before Lorenz came on the scene, but he did, by adding evidence based on his own observations of (non-human) animal behaviour, give it the status of a theory. However, things have now moved on. Apart from the dubious practice of drawing conclusions about humans from the behaviour of other animals, and apart from the question mark over instincts, especially as regards humans, the catharsis theory itself no longer stands up to serious examination. Firstly, aggression can be taught or copied, a matter which Lorenz seems to have ignored very largely but one which is soundly documented, mainly by reference to experiments with people, in Albert Bandura's book, *Aggression:* a Social Learning Analysis, in which he gives a very good overview of research in the subject. Secondly, much evidence, both in this book and in *The Child's World of Make-Believe* by Jerome L Singer and others, which likewise takes in many research studies, goes to show that aggression, far from being reduced when vented, is generally increased, at least for a time.

I should add that the catharsis theory of aggression is, to all intents and purposes, the same as the idea of sublimation as put forward by the inventor of Apocalypse (see p. 236).

Taking a common-sense approach, and returning to toys and games in general, we may ask: is it an accident that the most aggressive state, the USA, produces the most aggressive playthings? And we may wonder why, if such playthings serve to drain off aggression, the USA is not the most peace-loving of states. To look at the question from another angle, let's suppose, for a moment, that aggression is inborn in boys and that playing with toys which stimulate aggression works it out of their systems — according to the popularly held belief. Supposing also that there's a maternal instinct in girls, shouldn't it follow that playing with baby dolls would work the desire for motherhood out of girls' systems?

Judging by the popularity of his book, Morris, in *The Naked Ape,* must be telling a lot of people what they want to hear. (The title, which refers to human beings, gives the basic attitude.) Otherwise, and in spite of the insights in it, it's difficult to account for the success of a book which contains so many careless statements, contradictions and generalizations. As far as aggression is concerned, Morris maintains that, in humans, it takes place over questions of hierarchy, over territory and in defence of the family. Since there's no proof, this is very much a take it or leave it kind of proposition. More to the point for present purposes, however, is Morris's extraordinary assertion that co-operation causes war! The argument goes, that men had to co-operate with one another in order to be successful in hunting, that the bonds of loyalty thus established became in-built, and that they developed into notions of patriotism and other group loyalties for which men were prepared to fight. The aggression in such cases would, presumably, according to Morris, arise over questions of hierarchy, territory or the family, as already mentioned, though there don't seem to be any obvious links. Nor can this theory account for odd details such as the fact that Innuit peoples (Eskimos), who have been hunters well into modern times, are both co-operative and very peaceful.

Ardrey's arguments, in *The Territorial Imperative,* are even more astonishing but they've found a ready acceptance in many quarters and they are representative of writers who base their views on non-human animal life and biological inherit-ance. At the outset, Ardrey tells us that his starting point is the urge to own and defend territory (this soon comes to mean the same thing as property) and he says that this urge is 'fixed in our genetic endowment'. Patriotism he regards as an 'open [modifiable] instinct' and as the equivalent of territorial behaviour in other animal species. I've already mentioned the reasons for territoriality in the rest of the animal world — where it occurs, that is. Many species are not territorial at all and amongst those that are, there are huge variations, and even considerable ones within single species, depending on such environmental factors as the density of population and the season of the year. But the whole approach of arguing from what other species do is fraught with danger because, in any comparison, there comes a point where the differences are more important than the similarities. At one point, Ardrey instances slime moulds in support of his argument! Clearly, he's free to believe that he has a lot in common with slime moulds, but he shouldn't speak for the rest of us.

For me, the crux of the book is when Ardrey (a US citizen) describes his outrage on hearing of the Japanese attack on Pearl Harbour in the Hawaiian Islands (a US colony) which brought the USA into the second world war. To be fair, he wonders whether his response was something he'd been born with or something he'd been taught. But how can there be any doubt? Even supposing we agree for a moment that he was born with some kind of territorial instinct, why should we suppose, further, that it could extend to the Hawaiian Islands? which are about 3,700 kilometres distant from the USA, over the sea; which the USA took from Spain in 1898; and which Ardrey would never have heard of but for modern, human means of communication. The factor of distance alone makes this a totally different matter from territoriality in other animal species which only claim what they can physically range over. Japan, I should add, is even further away from Pearl Harbour. Also, I wonder what happened to the Hawaiian 'territorial imperative'. They must have one, if it's instinctive, even though the big beasts do win.

Finally, on this particular line — since the USA now seems to look upon the greater part of the globe with a very possessive eye, we should be extremely wary when biology is used to justify such an attitude, even though it is called a 'territorial imperative'. In similar fashion, religion was used in the nineteenth century to justify British imperialism.

Amongst other things, Ardrey also asserts that the 'biological nation' is one of 'outward antagonism', that the 'normal condition' for humankind is one of 'mutual animosity' and that 'war ... has been the most successful of all our cultural traditions'. This, he says, is because it satisfies what he singles out (perhaps correctly) as the 'needs' of all animals — identity, stimulation and security. How war could satisfy such needs in any meaningful or positive way is quite baffling.

It's worth adding a point or two on the whole question of using evidence drawn from the behaviour of other animal species. Apart from the fact that such an approach is full of pitfalls, it should be added that evidence from the same source can be used to support views directly opposed to the ones put forward by writers such as Lorenz, Morris and Ardrey. For instance, in one very impressive experiment, kittens brought up with rats became attached to them and rarely attacked them.[7]

275

Another experiment has shown that, when the breast of a female chaffinch was painted red, like that of a male, the males treated her as if one of them, and then her behaviour changed and became as aggressive as theirs. Also, in an experiment on pigeons lowest in the pecking order, the male hormone, testosterone, was insufficient to increase aggression, but it could be increased by conditioning.[8] Such work shows that behaviour presumed to be instinctive can be modified by environmental factors. However, those wanting to learn about human behaviour should study people.

The views of Tiger and Fox, in *The Imperial Animal,* are less outlandish than those of Ardrey. For one thing, their arguments are based less on behaviour in other animal species. Central to their approach is the claim that the social relationships appropriate to the hunting stage in the development of human societies have been built in, genetically, and determine social relationships (and roles) now. Some crucial assertions, of a political nature, are based on this claim (which, of course, cannot be proved). They state, for instance, that 'the basic economic group is the hunting group or its analogue, and basic economic activity is on the predatory model'.[9] This statement, which isn't very clear, does, however, seem to ignore the fact that other animals don't prey upon members of their own species. Hunting is carried out by one species upon another, or others, whereas all economic activity, of whatever kind, only takes place *within* the human species. Other species aren't involved. Therefore, the activity of hunting (an affair between species) can scarcely have led to war (a problem within the human species) as Tiger and Fox contend.

In the area of gender roles (though they would call them sex roles) Tiger and Fox have quite a lot to say which has a bearing on aggression. What is adds up to, in their own words, is that 'war is not a human action but a male action; war is not a human problem but a male problem'.[10] Just suppose, for the sake of argument, that what this statement implies is true — that aggression, of the sort involved in warfare, is innate in human males. Why, then, aren't more men willing to leave home to go and fight in wars? Why do we have conscription and why were there press-gangs before that and, earlier still, the military obligations of serfs under feudalism? Why has compulsion been necessary if what Tiger and Fox say is true?

The deeply reactionary framework of *The Imperial Animal* is revealed in a comment on sexual activity and killing, both of which, the authors say, 'were part of the package of original sin and therefore of human nature'. The doctrine of original sin — the belief that people are inherently evil — must surely be the most psychologically damaging idea ever to be inflicted on humankind. 'Human nature' stands in as its everyday representative, the familiar resort of people arguing against the possibility of change. It's comforting, and an easy way out, to base your argument on human nature, as it means you don't have to do anything. In fact, it means that nothing can be done because, in the well-worn expression, 'you can't change human nature'. That is, in effect, what all these writers have been saying, and they've been saying you can't change it because it's underpinned by biology and you can't argue with biology. In this, such writers both reflect and reinforce popular belief, However, we need to keep on asking: what is human nature? unless we're satisfied with the answer; biology. We need to take note, as well, of other answers such as the one put forward by Bandura: 'From the social learning perspective, human nature is characterized as a vast potentiality that can be fashioned by social influences into a variety of forms'.[11] As the term suggests, the social learning approach, which Bandura favours, puts the emphasis on environment, in the nature/nurture debate. As far as aggression is concerned, he says:

> the specific forms that aggressive behaviour takes, the frequency with which it is expressed, the situations in which it is displayed, and the specific targets selected for attack are largely determined by social experience.[12]

However, the book which gives an overview of the whole subject I've been dealing with in this section is *Not in Our Genes:* Biology, Ideology and Human Nature by Steven Rose, Leon J Kamin and R C Lewontin. This is a recent, thoroughly researched and carefully argued book in which the focus is firmly on human, social behaviour. The authors reject biological determinism — the view that genes determine the behaviour of individuals — and also the closely-allied views of the sociobiologists who maintain that genetics determines society. They also reject the view that the social environment, alone, determines human behaviour, which is a stance they call 'cultural determinism'. They even reject the interaction between genes and environment as determining the organism because, they contend, this implies a distinction between the organism (animal or plant) and its environment and supposes that the second makes the first — that environment dominates. Also, they hold that this 'interactionism' puts the emphasis on individual rather than social development. Instead of these various approaches, they propose 'interpenetration' between the organism and the enviroment. This means 'a dialectical development of organism and milieu in response to each other'. In other words, the environment changes the organism but the organism, especially in the case of the human species, also changes the environment which then, again, changes the organism — and so the process goes on. This is very much the core of the book which the authors sum up as follows: 'The theory of this dialectical relation, in which individuals both make and are made by society, is a social theory, not a biological one'.[13] It could scarcely be otherwise, as they dismiss all theories based on biology:

> up to the present time no one has ever been able to relate any aspect of human social behaviour to any particular gene or set of genes, and no one has ever suggested an experimental plan for doing so. Thus, all statements about the genetic basis of human social traits are necessarily purely speculative, no matter how positive they seem to be.[14]

It's against this background that we have to see the problem of aggression. Up to now, I've talked about it in general terms but with the accent strongly on war which is what concerns me here. However, it's important to recognize that there are, amongst humans, different forms of aggression. At an everyday, individual, personal level, it can be verbal or physical but it always involves anger, to some degree or oher, and perhaps hatred. The collective aggression which we see in warfare is quite different and, I might add, peculiar to the human species. Anger and hatred, at least at the outset of a war, if not later on, are absent. Rose and his co-authors put the matter well:

warfare among state-organized societies has little to do with prior individual feelings of aggression. War is a calculated political phenomenon undertaken at the behest of those in power in a society for political and economic gain. 'Hostilities' begin without the least hostility between individuals except as deliberately created by the organs of propaganda. People kill each other in wars for all sorts of reasons, not the least of which is that they are forced to do so by the political power of the state.[15]

As regards the causes of war, here we need only concentrate on greed (though it's a fairly comprehensive cause). The greed has usually been for greater power and wealth (often in the form of territory) and this brings us back to children's playthings again. It has to be noted that toys and games for boys are, overwhelmingly, about power and wealth. Furthermore, the idea of power is strongest in toys — in figures and vehicles, for instance — while wealth enters more into games. Think of all the games concerned with money, treasure and property, amongst the ones not directly concerned with war, that is.

With the question of aggression still in mind, as it relates to the masculine gender role of fighter and to boys' playthings, we now move to another field of study, anthropology, to have a very brief look at actual societies.

Margaret Mead's book, *Sex and Temperament in Three Primitive Societies,* is an account of the Arapesh, Mundugumor and Tchambuli peoples of New Guinea. She describes their societies, respectively, as follows:

> In one, both men and women act as we expect women to act — in a mild parental responsive way; in the second, both act as we expect men to act — in a fierce initiating fashion; and in the third, the men act according to our stereotype for women — are catty, wear curls and go shopping, while the women are energetic, managerial, unadorned partners.[16]

The astonishing thing is that these three groups were living within a hundred miles of one another. Also, it's worth pointing out that they weren't specially chosen to demonstrate the above gender roles.

Mead's purpose, in undertaking her field study, is very much to the point here. It was:

> to discover to what degree temperamental differences between the sexes were innate and to what extent they were culturally determined, and furthermore to inquire minutely into the educational mechanisms connected with these differences.[17]

Although the author doesn't go into detail about games, she makes the interesting observation that the first group, the Arapesh, 'play none that encourage aggressiveness or competition' and adds that 'there are no races, no games with two sides'.

The norm, for the men of this culture, is 'to be gentle, unacquisitive, and co-operative' but, of course, neither the Arapesh nor the Mundugumor take any

278

account of sex difference as a basis for differences in personality. As Mead puts it: 'the Arapesh ideal is the mild, responsive man married to the mild, responsive woman; the Mundugumor ideal is the violent, aggressive man married to the violent, aggressive woman'.[18] Thus, the Arapesh have a feminine society while the Mundugumor have a masculine society and this is all the more remarkable as both groups share a very similar economic, social and cultural background. Amongst the Tchambuli, the woman is the 'dominant, impersonal, managing partner' while the man is 'less responsible' and 'emotionally dependent'; in other words, the reverse of the gender roles (or the presumed sex roles) in our society.

In view of her findings in these three cultures, Mead concludes that 'we no longer have any basis for regarding such aspects of behaviour as sex-linked' and adds, 'the evidence is overwhelmingly in favour of the strength of social conditioning'. She sums up as follows:

> We are forced to conclude that human nature is almost unbelievably malleable, responding accurately and contrastingly to contrasting cultural conditions. The differences between individuals who are members of different cultures, like the differences between individuals within a culture, are almost entirely to be laid to differences in conditioning, especially during early childhood, and the form of this conditioning is culturally determined.[19]

More specifically, Mead states that, 'To consider such traits as aggressiveness or passivity to be sex-linked is not possible in the light of the facts'.[20]

Nor are the societies described in this book isolated examples of variations between cultures. For instance, in *Cooperation and Competition Among Primitive Peoples*, edited by Mead, there are accounts of 12 other cultures, again showing great diversity. (The general approach in these two anthropological books, as shown by the use of the word 'primitive', isn't one I go along with, though the information recorded in them is valid and useful. Many technologically developed societies are extremely primitive, if not backward, in a moral sense.) Those wanting to look at differences in more industrialized societies should read *Two Worlds of Childhood* by Urie Bronfenbrenner (with the assistance of John C Condry, Jr) in which a comparison is made between children's upbringing in the USA and the USSR.

This has been, necessarily, a very brief look at a very large subject but I hope I've said enough here on aggression to show that something can be done about it.

What is to be done? If the human race is to survive, the masculine role of aggressor has to be dealt with. While confronting this problem in every way possible, it's obviously best to deal with it in its early stages, before boys have been completely strait-jacketed into the role and while they are moving through the education system, and before then if at all possible.

Children's playthings, as a whole, probably make up the most powerful of the cultural influences brought to bear on children by the adults of their society. This is because playthings can convey ideas, attitudes and values at a very early age when children are most impressionable and most open to influences. After all, children play with toys and simple games before they can read and long before they are able to question what the toys and games say to them. Also, the messages bound up in toys and games are largely at a subconscious level and in symbolic form, and are all the more powerful for that.

The question of banning playthings should not be undertaken lightly (and neither should the introduction of new ones, come to that). However, several countries have accepted the principle, and acted upon it, that children should be given some protection, as far as aggressive toys are concerned. (I haven't heard of any action being taken over games.) Usually, it's only toy weapons that are thought of in this connection but it seems to me that figures, of the Action Man and Action Force kind, which present adult roles to children, are more harmful. However, legislation along the lines of that adopted in Sweden — the banning of toy replicas of any weapons and armaments in use since 1914 — would effectively disarm the likes of Action Man, and this would be a step in the right direction.

It has to be understood, though, that banning war toys, and perhaps war games as well, without doing anything else, would be treating the symptoms and not the disease. We need to recognize that such things exist within a war culture. People have often told me of how children who are forbidden to have toy weapons simply proceed to improvise them. Of course they do. What could anybody expect? This just goes to show that the problem is wider than the toys and games themselves — but it certainly doesn't mean that we can neglect the matter of playthings and their manufacture until wider changes are made. War culture takes many different forms and we have to confront them all.

Also, it's important to note that the situation doesn't stand still. In autumn, 1986, I saw two estimates about the sale of war toys in the USA. One said that sales had risen about 500 per cent since 1982 and the other that they rose 600 per cent from 1982-5.

The remaining problems that playthings give rise to can only be dealt with, in the end, by bringing the toys and games industry under public control so that it's answerable to its clients. Responsibility for all playthings, on behalf of the public, could go to the local education authorities which could form a council to approve toys and games. These authorities could, in fact, take on more of the actual manufacture. Here, the Cambridgeshire authority and, most notably, the Inner London Education Authority have shown the way. Toys and games for children under five could also come within such a scheme (and better still, of course, in the context of a national system of crèches and nursery schools).

This is only the sketch of a solution. As I see it, my task in this book has been to outline the problems and alert people to them. That has to be the first task, in any case.

Nor can the suggestions I've made be seen in isolation. Bigger problems have to be tackled, of which playthings are only a part, however important. The role of fighter is only one of the gender roles into which children are manacled, even though it is the one most needing urgent attention. We have to ask what kind of society it is which needs these gender roles and why it needs them. And we have to ask, who benefits?

References

1   Greta Sykes, Helen Mercer and Jan Woolf, *Deadly Persuasion:* Teaching the Cold War; a Study of School History Textbooks, London, 'Teaching the Cold War' Study Group 1985, p.9.

2   See *Catching Them Young,* vol. 2, pp.44-50 and p.18.

3   Carol R Andreas, 'War Toys and the Peace Movement', *Journal of Social Issues,* New York, vol. 25 no. 1, 1969, p.89.

4   *ibid.*

5   *ibid.*

6   Antonia Fraser, *A History of Toys,* London, Weidenfeld and Nicolson 1966, p.230.

7   Described in Albert Bandura, *Aggression:* A Social Learning Analysis, New Jersey, Prentice-Hall 1973, pp.17-18.

8   This and the experiment with chaffinches are referred to in Roger Lewin (ed.) *Child Alive,* London, Temple Smith 1975, pp.173 and 176.

9   Lionel Tiger and Robin Fox, *The Imperial Animal,* London, Secker and Warburg 1972, p.148.

10 *ibid.* p.212.

11 Albert Bandura, *op.cit.* p.113.

12 *ibid.* pp.29-30.

13 Steven Rose, Leon J Kamin and R C Lewontin, *Not in Our Genes:* Biology, Ideology and Human Nature, Harmondsworth, Penguin 1984, p.257.

14 *ibid.* p.251.

15 *ibid.*

16 Margaret Mead, *Sex and Temperament in Three Primitive Societies,* 2nd ed. London, Routledge and Kegan Paul 1977, p.ix.

17 *ibid.* p.164.

18 *ibid.* p.219.

19 *ibid.* p.280.

20 *ibid.* p.282.

SELECT BIBLIOGRAPHY

Most of the research for this book has been directly based on the actual playthings studied or on the packaging and promotion associated with them, and not on other books or articles. In any case, there's been very little work done on the subject up to now. This list, therefore, is to do with background and history but, even so, I should add that there don't seem to be any good, overall histories — in English, at least — of either toys or games. The place of publication of the following books is London, unless otherwise stated.

Part One
Kenneth and Marguerite Fawdry, *Pollock's History of English Dolls and Toys*, Benn 1979.

Pauline Flick, *Discovering Toys and Toy Museums*, 2nd ed. Aylesbury, Shire Publications 1977.

Antonia Fraser, *A History of Toys*, Weidenfeld and Nicolson 1966.

Emanuel Hercík, *Folk Toys*, Prague, Orbis 1951.

Part Two
R C Bell, *Board and Table Games from Many Civilizations*, one-volume ed. New York, Dover Publications 1979.

John Butterfield, Philip Parker and David Honigman, *What is Dungeons and Dragons?* Harmondsworth, Penguin 1982.

Donald F Featherstone, *War Games*, Stanley Paul 1962.

Bruce Galloway (compiler and ed.) *Fantasy Wargaming*, Cambridge, Patrick Stephens 1981.

Frederic V Grunfeld, *Games of the World:* How to Make Them, How to Play Them, How They Came to Be, New York, Holt, Rinehart and Winston © 1975.

George Gush with Andrew Finch, *A Guide to Wargaming*, Croom Helm and, New York, Hippocrene 1980.

Linda Hannas, *The English Jigsaw Puzzle 1760-1890*, Wayland 1972.

Ian Livingstone, *Dicing with Dragons*, Routledge and Kegan Paul 1982.

Brian Love (compiler) *Great Board Games*, Ebury Press and Michael Joseph 1979.

Brian Love (compiler) *Play the Game*, Michael Joseph and Ebury Press 1978.

Bertell Ollman, *Class Struggle is the Name of the Game:* True Confessions of a Marxist Business Man, New York, William Morrow 1983.

David Pritchard, *Brain Games*, Harmondsworth, Penguin 1982.

David Pritchard (ed.) *Modern Board Games*, William Luscombe 1975.

H G Wells, *Little Wars*, Arms and Armour Press 1970.

F R B Whitehouse, *Table Games of Georgian and Victorian Days*, 2nd ed. Royston, Priory Press and Birmingham, Chad Valley 1971.

Part Three
Albert Bandura, *Aggression:* A Social Learning Analysis, New Jersey, Prentice-Hall 1973.

Brian Easlea, *Fathering the Unthinkable:* Masculinity, Scientists and the Nuclear Arms Race, Pluto 1983.

Margaret Mead (ed.) *Cooperation and Competition Among Primitive Peoples*, Boston (USA), Beacon Press 1961.

Margaret Mead, *Sex and Temperament in Three Primitive Societies*, 2nd ed. Routledge and Kegan Paul 1977.

M F Ashley Montagu (ed.) *Man and Aggression*, New York, Oxford University Press 1968.

Steven Rose, Leon J Kamin and R C Lewontin, *Not in Our Genes:* Biology, Ideology and Human Nature, Harmondsworth, Penguin 1984.

Greta Sykes, Helen Mercer and Jan Woolf, *Deadly Persuasion:* Teaching the Cold War; a Study of School History Textbooks, 'Teaching the Cold War' Study Group 1985.

Index

Page numbers in italics refer to illustrations